PERSONAL FINANCIAL LITERACY

⟨RYAN⟩

Joan S. Ryan

•

Business Department Chair
Clackamas Community College

SOUTH-WESTERN
CENGAGE Learning

Australia • Brazil • Japan • Korea • Mexico • Singapore • Spain • United Kingdom • United States

Personal Financial Literacy
Joan S. Ryan

VP/Editorial Director:
Jack W. Calhoun

VP/Editor-in-Chief:
Karen Schmohe

VP/Marketing:
Bill Hendee

Acquisitions Editor:
Dan Jones

Senior Developmental Editor:
Dr. Inell Bolls

Consulting Editor:
Dianne Rankin

Senior Marketing Manager:
Nancy Long

Marketing Coordinator:
Angela A. Glassmeyer

Senior Marketing Communications Manager:
Terron Sanders

Production Manager:
Tricia Matthews Boies

Senior Content Project Manager:
Kim Kusnerak

Technology Project Editor:
Chris Wittmer

Manufacturing Coordinator:
Kevin Kluck

Production House:
ICC Macmillan Inc.

Printer:
Quebecor World
Dubuque, IA

Art Director:
Bethany Casey

Cover Illustration/Internal Design:
Grannan Graphic Design, LTD

Photo and Permissions Editor:
Darren Wright

For more information about our products, contact us at:

South-Western Cengage Learning
5191 Natorp Boulevard
Mason, Ohio 45040
USA

- Adobe and Reader are either registered trademarks or trademarks of Adobe Systems Incorporated in the United States and/or other countries.
- AltaVista is a registered trademark of AltaVista, Overture Services, Inc.
- American Express is a registered trademark of American Express Company.
- Bloomberg and Bloomberg.com are trademarks and service marks of Bloomberg L.P. All rights reserved.
- Career Cluster icons are being used with permission of the:

 States' Career Clusters Initiative, 2006, www.careerclusters.org.

- Diners Club is a registered trademark of Diners Club International Ltd.
- ExamView is a registered trademark of FSCreations, Inc.
- Google™ is a trademark of Google Inc.
- iPod is a registered trademark of Apple Computer, Inc.
- MASTERCARD is a registered trademark of Mastercard Worldwide.
- Microsoft, Excel, OneNote, Windows, and PowerPoint are either registered trademarks or trademarks of Microsoft Corporation in the United States and/or other countries. Microsoft product screen shot(s) reprinted with permission from Microsoft Corporation.
- Morningstar is a registered trademark of Morningstar, Inc.
- *Quicken* is a trademark of Intuit Inc., registered in the United States and other countries.
- Reuters is a registered trademark of the Reuters group of companies around the world.
- Seeking Alpha™ is a trademark and/or service mark of Seeking Alpha or an affiliate.
- VISA is a registered trademark of Visa.
- Yahoo! and the Yahoo! logos are trademarks and/or registered trademarks of Yahoo! Inc.

Contents

iv

Reviewers

ABOUT THE AUTHOR

Joan Ryan, Ph.D.
Clackamas Community College

Dr. Joan Ryan has taught personal finance for over 20 years. She began at Willamette High School in Eugene, Oregon, where she developed original materials for publication in 1981. She also taught business classes at Lane Community College (Eugene, Oregon) and is currently business department chair at Clackamas Community College (Portland, Oregon). She also teaches accounting at Portland State University as an adjunct faculty and is a CMA (certified management accountant).

TO THE STUDENT

Welcome to the study of personal finance! The knowledge and skills you learn as you study this book will help you make good financial decisions—now and in the future. Decisions you make now can affect the income you will earn for the rest of your life.

In Part 1, Understanding Income, you will discover how career choices affect future income. You will learn about options for continuing your education and how you might pay for your education. You will study topics related to work, such as employee benefits and taxes. You will also learn about inflation and how it affects your decisions.

In Part 2, Money Management, you will learn to manage your money, use a checking account, and keep good records. You will learn to create a financial plan and follow it to accomplish your goals. You will also learn how using insurance and other options to manage risk can help you protect your income and property.

Part 3, Spending and Credit, focuses on buying wisely. In this part, you will learn the steps of an effective buying plan. You will study sources and costs of using credit. Some sources are more expensive than others. Unwise use of credit can lead to overspending and other problems. So that you can avoid credit problems, you will learn about pitfalls related to using credit. You will also learn about credit laws that help protect consumers.

As you study Part 4, Saving and Investing, you will think about reasons for saving and investing. You will learn about options and strategies you can use to help you achieve your financial goals. You will learn how to research, buy, and sell investments. You will also learn about agencies that protect and assist consumers and investors.

Features of the Textbook

To help you learn about personal finance, this textbook has a number of special features. These features are described in the following paragraphs.

Online Resources are listed on the first page of each chapter. They include materials, such as games and activities, that are available on the Web site for this textbook. Search terms are also included. You can use these terms to search the Internet and learn more about topics related to the chapter.

Outcomes appear at the beginning of each part and within the chapters. These statements are your learning goals. They tell you what you should know or be able to do when you complete a chapter.

Activities appear within each chapter and at the end of each chapter. These activities will help you review and apply concepts and skills

vi

learned in the chapters. Icons appear by some of the activities to alert you to the following:

academic.cengage.com/school/pfl
You will use the Internet as you complete the activity.

You will use a data file to complete the activity.

You will use critical thinking skills as you complete the activity.

You will work in a team to complete the activity.

Summary pages provide a quick review of the main points covered in the chapters.

Key Terms are vocabulary words that are highlighted in yellow and defined in the chapters. They are also listed at the end of each chapter and in the Glossary. These terms will help you understand the concepts presented.

Feature articles appear in each chapter. They provide valuable information related to the chapter topics. You will see the following types of articles:

○ **Building Communications Skills** articles will help you improve your listening, reading, speaking, and writing skills. Related activities appear in the *Personal Financial Literacy Student Workbook.*

○ **Technology Corner** articles present information about how technology relates to the topics studied in the chapter. You will learn about topics such as job scouts, online banking, and shopping on the Internet.

○ **Ethics** articles discuss issues related to moral and acceptable behavior. Being honest when applying for jobs, guarding your personal information to protect against identity theft, and price gouging are some of the topics you will learn about in these articles.

○ **Success Skills** articles discuss a variety of topics that can help you be more successful in school, at work, and in personal activities. Teamwork, leadership, and dealing with change are some of the topics covered in these articles.

○ **Focus on . . .** articles highlight topics related to chapter content such as check cashing services, Internet scams, and investment strategies. You will find one or more of these articles in each chapter.

○ **Exploring Careers** articles present information about jobs in one of the broad career areas identified by the U.S. Department of Education. You will explore various careers and answer questions about one or more jobs in that career. The answers can help you decide whether the career is one you might want to consider pursuing.

○ **Winning Edge** articles highlight some of the competitive events offered by student organizations such as Future Business Leaders of America (FBLA) or Business Professionals of America (BPA). Being a member of a student organization provides opportunities for students to explore careers of interest and learn skills, such as teamwork and leadership, that will help students succeed in any career.

Student Workbook

A *Personal Financial Literacy Student Workbook* is available for use with the textbook. The workbook contains the following exercises for each chapter:

○ **Review of Chapter Terms.** These are matching exercises in which you will review the meaning of key terms used in the chapter.
○ **Building Communications Skills.** Listening, reading, writing, and speaking exercises will help you build skills in these areas. For example, in writing activities, you will practice writing good news messages and bad news messages.
○ **Building Math Skills.** You will build basic math skills by completing problems related to the chapter content.
○ **Careers.** These exercises will introduce you to helpful information about careers, career searches, job opportunities, and the job market.
○ **Activities Related to Content.** One or more activities will allow you to apply content from the chapter or extend learning beyond what is covered in the chapter.

Web Site

The publisher of this textbook provides a Web site with information related to the textbook. The *Personal Financial Literacy* Web site contains data files for use in activities, games related to the content of the chapters, links to other sites, and other information that you can use as you complete the activities in this textbook.

Engage Student Interest with Features That Enhance Learning

Building Communications Skills
Provides tips on using the four basic communications skills of listening, reading, speaking, and writing

Building Communications Skills

LISTENING

Listening is one of the four basic communications skills (listening, reading, speaking, and writing). While hearing is easy, most people have to work at being good listeners. Listening is not the same thing as hearing. Hearing is the ability to process sounds. Anyone who is not hearing-impaired is able to hear. Listening means that information is heard and understood or thought about. According to the International Listening Association, 85 percent of what we know we have learned by listening.[1]

You have learned that your education and job choice affect the amount of money you are likely to earn. Listening is an important skill that will help you succeed at school and at work. Practice these tips to help you improve your listening skills:

- Face and look directly at the person who is talking to you.
- Focus on what the speaker is saying. Do not let your mind wander to other topics.

- Ignore distractions such as noises made by other people in the room or someone passing by a window.
- Turn off (or unplug) the phone, and eliminate other noises such as music if possible.
- When you are part of a group that the speaker is addressing, take notes about what the speaker is saying, but do not doodle. Write only key phrases or main ideas. Do not try to write every word the speaker says.
- In conversations with one or two people, give small feedback cues, such as "I see" or "Then what?" to let the speaker know you are listening. Nod frequently and wait quietly during pauses.
- Mentally summarize the main points of what you have heard. Ask the speaker questions to clarify points you do not understand.
- If you are listening to someone give you instructions for a task, repeat key phrases to review the important points.

Success Skills
Teaches skills needed to be successful in all areas of life, including handling conflict, time management, and teamwork

Success Skills

NETWORKING

Networking is the process of making contacts and building relationships with other people. Everyone you know is in your "network." All your contacts are important to you. They will help keep you informed about issues that affect your financial success. For example, you may learn about scholarships or grants from teachers or counselors in your network. Later in life, you may learn about a job opening from a friend at another company.

Your network may include many contacts. Record the name, address, phone number, and e-mail address of each one so

you can reach that person when you want to share information. Make a note of how you are related to or were introduced to each person. For example, you should include your school teachers, counselors, and principals. You should also include the leaders or members of community groups or other groups to which you belong. If you have a summer or part-time job, include the others with whom you work and your manager. Keep in touch with your contacts regularly. Let them know when you are looking for particular information, such as scholarships for which you can apply.

Ethics
Describes ethical situations that may arise in daily life, including filling out forms and using sick leave

Ethics

FINANCIAL PLANNERS AND COMMISSION EARNINGS

A **financial planner** is a person who provides financial advice to individuals. Financial planners help people develop financial plans in a very formal setting. If you work with a financial planner, you will share your personal information. Data about your assets, liabilities, and net worth are examples of the information you will share. The financial planner should guard your information and should not share it with others or use it for personal benefit. To do otherwise would be unethical. You must be able to trust the planner with your most sensitive personal data.

Some financial planners work for commission income. That means they make money when they sell financial products to their customers. When planners sell

products that earn higher commissions, rather than products that customers really need, they are being unethical. For consumers, it can be hard to tell whether or not they are buying the best product at the lowest price. To avoid this kind of dilemma, hire a financial planner who does not work on commission. Instead, pay for the advice separately from buying any financial products, such as insurance.

Every year, people are cheated out of their money by dishonest advisors. Be sure you can trust your financial planner. Find out if he or she has been in business long, whether complaints have been filed against her or him, and if he or she has a criminal background. Ask what measures the planner will take to keep your data secure.

Engage Student Interest with Features That Enhance Learning

Focus on . . .

THE FED

When inflation is rising too fast, it hurts consumers. Two tools are used in the United States to manage the effects of rising prices. These tools are called monetary policy and fiscal policy.

Monetary policy refers to actions by the Federal Reserve System. The Federal Reserve System is commonly called the Fed. The Fed is the central bank in the United States. The Fed was created by Congress in 1913. It has many roles, including controlling the money supply. One thing the Fed does is watch the economy. When the Fed sees that prices are rising too fast, it tries to slow them down. One way to slow rising prices is by raising interest rates. When interest rates increase, both individuals and businesses find it more expensive to borrow money to buy goods and services. This slows down spending. As you learned earlier, demand-pull inflation is caused by spending in the economy.

There are several types of interest rates that are controlled by the Fed. The discount rate is the rate that banks have to pay to borrow money from the Fed. Banks borrow money when they have the opportunity to make loans but do not have enough cash on hand. Banks are required to have a certain amount of cash on hand, called reserves. If these reserves go below the required amount, banks must borrow money.

The federal funds rate is the rate at which banks can borrow from the excess reserves of other banks. For example, if one bank has more money than it needs, it can loan that extra money to other banks.

The prime rate is the rate that banks charge to their most creditworthy business customers. When the discount rate increases, the prime rate also goes up. The prime rate is usually 3 percent (or more) higher than the discount rate or the federal funds rate.

Fiscal policy refers to actions taken by the federal government to manage the economy. To help curb inflation, one thing the government can do is raise taxes. When taxes go up, people have less money to spend. This slows down inflation (demand-pull). On the other hand, the economy may be sluggish because people are not buying. The government can increase spending by lowering tax rates. This gives consumers more money to spend. These actions, taken together, either speed up or slow down spending. Spending can affect inflation because it can cause prices to rise.

Focus on . . .
Presents interesting topics to spark discussion, such as phishing, social security benefits, and student organizations

Technology Corner
Examines different uses of technology that relate to personal finance, such as buying goods online and e-filing taxes

---

Technology Corner

JOB SCOUTS

Technology is changing the way people find and use information. The **Internet** is a worldwide network of computers that can share information. The Internet allows users to find and share information about many topics, including jobs. When you are ready to begin working full-time, you may want to use a **job scout** to help you find job openings. A job scout is a type of computer program that is called an *intelligent agent*. Such a program does tasks using rules or options you set. In the case of a job scout, the task is searching the Internet to find job listings and returning those listings to you. The rules you set might state the type of job and the location of the job (city or state). You may choose to have the job listings sent to you daily or weekly. Job scouts are also called *job agents*.

Using a job scout can help you find a job that will allow you to build financial security. To see an example of a site that offers a job agent, visit the USAJobs Web site as shown in Figure 1-2.1. A link to this site is provided on the Web site for this textbook (academic.cengage.com/school/pfl).

Other Special Features

EXPLORING CAREERS IN EDUCATION AND TRAINING

Career Clusters
Links the content from the text with job opportunities in the field of study to spark student interest

Do you like to work with people? Are you good at explaining concepts and tasks? If the answer is yes, a career in education and training might be right for you. Jobs in education involve teaching children and adults. Some workers in this field, such as a school principal, handle administrative tasks. Others, such as counselors, provide support services related to education. Child care workers provide care for children who have not yet entered school and also work with older children before and after school hours.

Jobs in education are found in public and private schools. Training jobs are also found in government and businesses. Some trainers are entrepreneurs and have their own small businesses. The need for jobs in the education and training area is expected to grow over the next few years. The outlook varies somewhat by job.

Skills Needed

Some of the skills and traits needed for a career in education and training include the following:

- Ability to work well with others
- Content area knowledge
- Communications skills
- Computer/technology skills
- Decision-making skills
- Problem-solving skills
- Leadership skills

Job Titles

Many jobs are available in the education and training field. Some job titles for this career area include the following:

- Child care worker
- Coach
- College professor
- Counselor
- Language pathologist
- Librarian

Explore a Job

1. Choose a job in education to explore further. Select a above, or choose another job in this career area.
2. Access the *Occupational Outlook Handbook* online. is provided on the Web site for this textbook.
3. Search for more information about the job you select these questions:
   - What is the nature of the work this job involves?
   - What is the job outlook for this job?
   - What training or qualifications are needed for this
   - What are the median annual earnings for this job?

WinningEdge
Prepares students for success in competitive events

JOB INTERVIEW EVENT

Future Business Leaders of America (FBLA) and Business Professionals of America (BPA) are organizations that conduct competitive events for students. The FBLA Job Interview Event and BPA Interview Skills Event allow students to demonstrate their ability to apply for jobs. Both events require preparing a resume and a letter of application. Students must also fill out a job application form and take part in a mock job interview. Applicants should bring several ink pens and their resume to use when filling out the job application form.

Evaluation

Students who take part in these events are judged on their ability to:

- Create an effective resume.
- Fill out a job application accurately, neatly, and completely.
- Write a letter of application appropriate for a particular job.
- Answer interview questions.
- Discuss their skills, education, and experience for a job.
- Dress professionally for an interview.
- Demonstrate a professional attitude.

Sample Scenario

You are applying for a desk clerk position at a hotel in Austin, Texas. The desk clerk must check guests in and out of the hotel. The clerk must also answer guests' questions about things to do in Austin. This position requires someone who has a friendly attitude and enjoys working with people.

Think Critically

1. How should you dress for an interview at a hotel? Why?
2. Why is the letter of application an important part of the job application process?
3. Why should you take names, addresses, and telephone numbers of personal references when you go to an interview?
4. Give two tips for successful interviews.

www.fbla.org   www.bpa.org

Assessment and Review Is Built-in to Every Lesson and Chapter

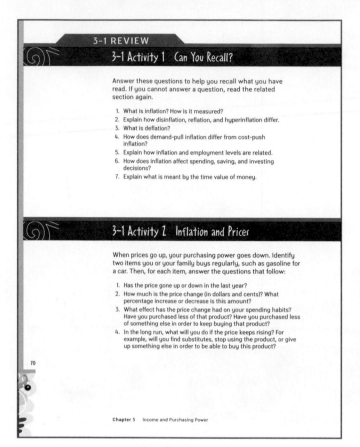

3-1 REVIEW

3-1 Activity 1 Can You Recall?

Answer these questions to help you recall what you have read. If you cannot answer a question, read the related section again.

1. What is inflation? How is it measured?
2. Explain how disinflation, reflation, and hyperinflation differ.
3. What is deflation?
4. How does demand-pull inflation differ from cost-push inflation?
5. Explain how inflation and employment levels are related.
6. How does inflation affect spending, saving, and investing decisions?
7. Explain what is meant by the time value of money.

3-1 Activity 2 Inflation and Prices

When prices go up, your purchasing power goes down. Identify two items you or your family buys regularly, such as gasoline for a car. Then, for each item, answer the questions that follow:

1. Has the price gone up or down in the last year?
2. How much is the price change (in dollars and cents)? What percentage increase or decrease is this amount?
3. What effect has the price change had on your spending habits? Have you purchased less of that product? Have you purchased less of something else in order to keep buying that product?
4. In the long run, what will you do if the price keeps rising? For example, will you find substitutes, stop using the product, or give up something else in order to be able to buy this product?

70

Chapter 5   Income and Purchasing Power

End-of-Lesson Review
Review lesson topics for comprehension before introducing new material

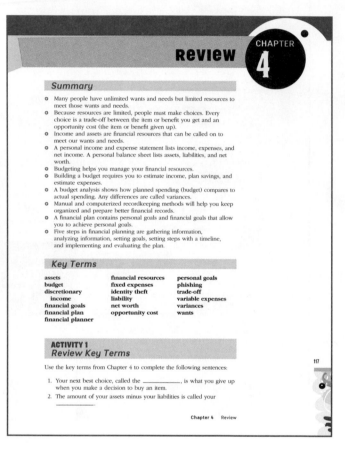

REVIEW   CHAPTER 4

Summary

- Many people have unlimited wants and needs but limited resources to meet those wants and needs.
- Because resources are limited, people must make choices. Every choice is a trade-off between the item or benefit you get and an opportunity cost (the item or benefit given up).
- Income and assets are financial resources that can be called on to meet our wants and needs.
- A personal income and expense statement lists income, expenses, and net income. A personal balance sheet lists assets, liabilities, and net worth.
- Budgeting helps you manage your financial resources.
- Building a budget requires you to estimate income, plan savings, and estimate expenses.
- A budget analysis shows how planned spending (budget) compares to actual spending. Any differences are called variances.
- Manual and computerized recordkeeping methods will help you keep organized and prepare better financial records.
- A financial plan contains personal goals and financial goals that allow you to achieve personal goals.
- Five steps in financial planning are gathering information, analyzing information, setting goals, setting steps with a timeline, and implementing and evaluating the plan.

Key Terms

assets	financial resources	personal goals
budget	fixed expenses	phishing
discretionary	identity theft	trade-off
income	liability	variable expenses
financial goals	net worth	variances
financial plan	opportunity cost	wants
financial planner		

ACTIVITY 1
Review Key Terms

Use the key terms from Chapter 4 to complete the following sentences:

1. Your next best choice, called the _____, is what you give up when you make a decision to buy an item.
2. The amount of your assets minus your liabilities is called your _____.

117

Chapter 4   Review

End-of-Chapter Review
End-of-Chapter Review includes a chapter summary, key terms, math activities, and other chapter-specific activities

Personal Financial Literacy

Text	0-538-44452-5
Adobe eBook	0-538-44465-7
Workbook	0-538-44460-6
Student Activity Binder with CD	0-538-44585-8
ExamView®	0-538-44462-2
Instructor's Resource CD	0-538-44463-0
Instructor's Manual	0-538-44466-5
Annotated Instructor's Edition	0-538-44461-4
Web site	academic.cengage.com/school/pfl

PART I

Understanding Income

OUTCOMES

After successfully completing this part, students should be able to:

* **Explain** how the job market and career choices affect the money a person may earn over a lifetime.
* **Describe** how the economy can affect income, career choices, and decisions.
* **List** sources of income and the types of taxes and deductions that reduce money available for spending.
* **Discuss** the value of workplace benefits as income incentives.
* **Define** inflation and explain how it affects prices.
* **Explain** how buying decisions are affected by internal and external sources.

PART 1, UNDERSTANDING INCOME, is the starting point for learning about financial literacy. Income is money you receive for work or from investments. Decisions you make now will affect the income you will earn for the rest of your life. In this part, you will learn how to make good personal financial decisions. You will discover how career choices affect future income. You will learn about types of income, deductions, and the value of benefits packages. You will also learn about inflation and how it will affect your shopping decisions.

© Getty Images/PhotoDisc

CHAPTER 1

CHOICES THAT Affect Income

© Digital Vision

he choices you make now when you are in school may affect your income in later life. Your personal values and the goals you set for yourself will influence the education and training you pursue. Your career and education choices can help pave the way for financial security. You should consider the economy and how it will affect your choices. You should also think about how to pay for the preparation you need to enter the job market in the career of your choice.

ONLINE RESOURCES

Personal Financial Literacy Web site:

Data Files

Vocabulary Flashcards

Sort It Out: The Job Market

Chapter 1 Supplemental Activity

Search terms:
- job skills
- job goals
- demand and supply
- tuition
- financial aid

Personal Financial Decisions

OUTCOMES

- Discuss how the job market changes over time.
- Explain how career choices affect earning potential.
- Explain how goals, values, and education are related to career choices.
- Describe how a person's education may affect the amount of money that person earns.

THE CHANGING JOB MARKET

Change is a vital part of all aspects of life, and the job market is no exception. The **job market** refers to the wide variety of job and career choices that will be available to you when you are prepared to go to work. The local job market may be different from the statewide or national job market in the short run. Over time, however, they tend to be very similar.

The job market changes as needs for different types of workers evolve. Jobs and careers that once were popular and paid good wages have disappeared as technology and needs of employers have changed. For example, *telephone installer* and *typist* are jobs that were common 20 years ago but are not popular today. Different types of careers, with new and unique job skills, have emerged. For example, the job *Web site designer* requires knowledge of current Web design programs. The job *physician assistant* requires knowledge of current medical procedures. **Job skills** are specific things you can do, such as prepare a spreadsheet or operate a machine, that are needed to be successful on the job. Other less technical job skills, such as being able to work well with others, are also important. Job skills are dynamic. That means they are changing. As new goods and services are developed, job skills needed to create or provide them will change also.

As you think about the type of work you would like to do later in life, consider the jobs that may exist in the future. Will the type of work you want to do be in demand? Will this type of work pay well? Begin asking questions and reading about jobs that sound interesting to you. You can do online or library research about careers that you might like to pursue in the future.

The U.S. Department of Labor publishes and places online *The Occupational Outlook Handbook*. The *Handbook* has data about the major job areas in the United States. From this book, you can learn about jobs in a wide range of fields. The 2006–07 edition has projections to 2014. Figure 1-1.1 on page 4 shows several job areas that are expected to grow in number of jobs from 2004 to 2014.

FIGURE 1-1.1   PROJECTED JOB GROWTH

PROJECTED JOB GROWTH FOR SELECTED OCCUPATIONS
(2004 and Projected 2014)

Occupation	Employment 2004	Employment 2014	% Change 2004–2014
Network systems and data communications analysts	231,000	357,000	54.6
Medical assistants	387,000	589,000	52.1
Physician assistants	62,000	93,000	49.6
Computer software engineers	800,000	1,169,000	46.1
Dental hygienists	158,000	226,000	43.3
Database administrators	104,000	144,000	38.2
Physical therapists	155,000	211,000	36.7
Medical scientists	77,000	103,000	33.6
Postsecondary teachers	1,628,000	2,153,000	32.2
Employment, recruitment, and placement specialists	182,000	237,000	30.5
Preschool and kindergarten teachers	601,000	782,000	30.1
Paralegals and legal assistants	224,000	291,000	29.7
Social and human services assistants	352,000	456,000	29.7
Registered nurses	2,394,000	3,096,000	29.4
Medical records and health information technicians	159,000	205,000	28.9
Emergency medical technicians and paramedics	192,000	244,000	27.3
Mental health counselors	96,000	122,000	27.2
Fitness trainers and aerobics instructors	205,000	260,000	27.1
Computer and information systems managers	280,000	353,000	25.9
Personal financial advisors	158,000	199,000	25.9
Medical and public health social workers	110,000	139,000	25.9
Pharmacists	230,000	287,000	24.6
Highway maintenance workers	143,000	177,000	23.3
Public relations specialists	188,000	231,000	22.9
Customer service representatives	2,063,000	2,534,000	22.8
Receptionists and information clerks	1,133,000	1,379,000	21.7
Bill and account collectors	456,000	554,000	21.4
Sales managers	337,000	403,000	19.7
Heating, air conditioning, and refrigeration mechanics and installers	270,000	321,000	19.0
Automotive service technicians and mechanics	803,000	929,000	15.7

Source: U.S. Department of Labor, Bureau of Labor Statistics, Employment by Occupation, 2004 and Projected 2014, http://stats.bls.gov/emp/emptabapp.htm (accessed February 9, 2006).

CAREER CHOICES AND INCOME

Some jobs pay a lot more than others and are in greater demand than others. Generally, the more skill, training, or education that you are required to have for a job, the more you can expect to earn. For example, a doctor must complete several years of education and training to prepare for his or her job. Typically, doctors are well paid. A salesclerk in a store may need only a high school education and some on-the-job training to prepare for his or her job. A salesclerk typically earns a much lower salary

FIGURE 1-1.2

JOBS AND MEAN
HOURLY EARNINGS

HOURLY EARNINGS FOR SELECTED OCCUPATIONS
(2004 National Compensation Survey)

Occupation	Mean Hourly Earnings
Accountants and auditors	$24.49
Architects	$32.54
Automotive mechanics	$18.58
Bakers	$11.69
Bill and account collectors	$14.23
Brickmasons and stonemasons	$27.44
Carpenters	$19.27
Cashiers	$9.49
Computer programmers	$29.05
Construction laborers	$14.17
Dental hygienists	$32.10
Dentists	$38.48
Groundskeepers and gardeners	$12.08
Heating, air conditioning, and refrigeration mechanics	$17.37
Lawyers	$48.63
Legal assistants	$20.38
Librarians	$28.47
Pharmacists	$42.69
Photographers	$16.60
Physician assistants	$34.22
Physicians	$57.38
Police and detectives, public service	$24.15
Receptionists	$11.52
Registered nurses	$26.61
Sales counter clerks	$10.46
Sales supervisors	$19.67
Social workers	$18.48
Teachers, secondary school	$32.52
Teachers' aides	$11.11
Textile sewing machine operators	$9.03
Tool and die makers	$23.21
Truck drivers	$14.99
Waiters, waitresses, and bartenders	$5.29
Welders and cutters	$16.33

Source: U.S. Department of Labor, Bureau of Labor Statistics, "National Compensation Survey: Occupational Wages in the United States, July 2004" http://www.bls.gov/ncs/ocs/sp/ncbl0727.pdf (accessed February 13, 2006).

than a doctor. Some examples of jobs and mean (average) hourly earnings are shown in Figure 1-1.2. Note that these are average earnings. Earnings for some workers in these jobs may be lower or higher. Earnings for the same job may vary by the job location. For example, the starting salary for a teacher may vary by state by $5,000 or more.

The number of jobs in a career area can also affect the income workers in that job are likely to make. When many workers compete for a few jobs, some of the workers will likely not find jobs in their chosen career area.

In some jobs, earnings may not be related to formal education. For example, some entertainers, supermodels, and professional athletes make a lot of money. However, these types of careers often last just a few years.

They may require natural talent, beauty, or athletic ability that few people have. They can also be very hard on the mind or body. For every person who succeeds in such a career, many others do not.

Job Titles and Descriptions

As you look for information about careers, you may see jobs listed by job titles. A **job title** is a name given to a particular job. It may be a word or phrase that describes the main duties or tasks of the job. For example, the job title *Long-haul Truck Driver* indicates clearly what the job involves. A person with this job drives a truck for long distances.

Being an athlete takes talent, hard work, and dedication.

Sometimes a job title alone is not enough to tell you what a person in this job does for a living. For example, reading the job title *Systems Analyst* might leave you wondering what a person would do for that job. A **job description** gives details about a job. It lists the job tasks and duties, the skills needed, and the education and experience required. It may contain other information such as the hours worked or details about the work site or location. A sample job description is shown in Figure 1-1.3 on page 7.

The skills and education required for jobs vary greatly.

FIGURE 1-1.3   SAMPLE JOB DESCRIPTION

JOB DESCRIPTION

Job Title
Sales Associate

Job Summary
A sales associate sells merchandise and serves as a retail cashier. This worker assists in restocking, display, and price marking of merchandise. A positive, friendly attitude is a must for this position.

Salary
$8.00 per hour starting salary

Principal Duties
- Provide friendly, courteous, and efficient service to customers
- Answer customers' questions about merchandise and advise customers on merchandise selection
- Record all sales in cash register, receive payment for sales, and issue correct change
- Assist in coding and price marking of merchandise
- Stock shelves, racks, and tables and arrange merchandise displays to attract customers
- Take special orders and handle returns
- Help monitor inventory levels and receive and unpack products
- Keep the store and the stockroom neat and well organized
- Open or close the store and work alone at times
- Attend weekly staff meetings and other meetings as needed
- Perform other related duties as required

Qualifications
- High school diploma required
- Must have worked for at least 6 months in a sales position
- Must have a courteous and cooperative attitude
- Must have good reading, math, and communications skills
- Must be able to operate a cash register
- Must be able to understand and carry out directions
- Must be honest, dependable, and punctual
- Must be willing to work any day of the week and both day and evening hours
- Must present a clean, neat, and well-groomed appearance
- Must dress in business or business casual attire
- Must be able to lift 40 pounds

Lifelong Learning

Learning new skills and information to help you become or stay qualified for a job is important for your financial security. When you are hired for a job, you will probably have the education and skills you need to do that job. As time goes by, however, the skills or education needed for the job may change. You may need to update your job skills. Workers and consumers need to continue learning throughout life. This lifelong learning will help prepare you to be a skilled worker and an informed consumer. As an informed consumer, you can make better choices regarding your personal finances.

CHOICES DEPEND ON VALUES AND GOALS

As you think about a career that you might pursue, consider the values and goals that are important to you. A **value** is a principle that reflects the worth you place on an idea or action. For example, if you think being honest is important, *honesty* would be one of your values.

Values are important. They influence the choices and decisions people make. Think about what you want to accomplish now and in later life. For example, if you think making a difference in other people's lives is important, then that value could be a reason for choosing one job over another. You might choose to be a teacher or a counselor rather than a construction worker.

Many people set goals that they want to accomplish. A **goal** is a plan that is based on values or desired outcomes. A person's goals affect his or her behavior. If you value good health, your goals may include eating

© CORBIS

This teacher has chosen a career that allows her to help others.

8

properly and exercising regularly. If you want to buy a digital camera, your goal may be to save enough money for the purchase. What goals do you want to accomplish?

EDUCATION CHOICES

Some jobs require little education. Other jobs require training that takes several years to complete. Education helps prepare you to do a job well. Education can be formal or informal. Formal education involves attending classes. Students must show that they have learned certain skills and concepts. The class in which you use this textbook is probably part of your formal education. Informal education may involve on-the-job training or learning as you go. You may learn new skills from reading and practicing on your own. For example, learning to use a digital camera by reading the instructions provided is a type of informal education.

The amount and type of education you complete can affect the amount of money you earn. Generally, people with more education earn more than people with less education. If the pay for a job is high compared to the education required, there is often a reason. The job might require high personal risks, a short career span, or completing tasks that others are not willing to do. For example, the employee might have to handle dangerous materials or work in a country where a war is going on.

Think about the type of education you want to complete and how well it will prepare you for the career or job you want later in life. Making choices about education is a serious responsibility. Your choices will affect the jobs you may be able to do. Your jobs will affect the amount of money you are able to earn.

© Getty Images/PhotoDisc

Formal education takes time and commitment to learning.

Listening is one of the four basic communications skills (listening, reading, speaking, and writing). While hearing is easy, most people have to work at being good listeners. Listening is not the same thing as hearing. Hearing is the ability to process sounds. Anyone who is not hearing-impaired is able to hear. Listening means that information is heard and understood or thought about. According to the International Listening Association, 85 percent of what we know we have learned by listening.[1]

You have learned that your education and job choice affect the amount of money you are likely to earn. Listening is an important skill that will help you succeed at school and at work. Practice these tips to help you improve your listening skills:

- Face and look directly at the person who is talking to you.

- Focus on what the speaker is saying. Do not let your mind wander to other topics.

- Ignore distractions such as noises made by other people in the room or someone passing by a window.

- Turn off (or unplug) the phone, and eliminate other noises such as music if possible.

- When you are part of a group that the speaker is addressing, take notes about what the speaker is saying, but do not doodle. Write only key phrases or main ideas. Do not try to write every word the speaker says.

- In conversations with one or two people, give small feedback cues, such as "I see" or "Then what?" to let the speaker know you are listening. Nod frequently and wait quietly during pauses.

- Mentally summarize the main points of what you have heard. Ask the speaker questions to clarify points you do not understand.

- If you are listening to someone give you instructions for a task, repeat key phrases to review the important points.

---

[1] International Listening Association (Shorpe), "Listening Factoids," http://www.listen.org/pages/factoids.html (accessed February 8, 2006).

1-1 Activity 1   Can You Recall?

Answer these questions to help you recall what you have read. If you cannot answer a question, read the related section again.

1. Why does the job market change over time? Give two examples of jobs that were popular 15 or 20 years ago but are not popular today.
2. What are job skills? List three job skills you have or plan to learn.
3. Explain how career choices may affect the amount of money a person will earn.
4. How is a job title different from a job description?
5. How are goals different from values? List one goal you have that is related to a job or career. What values are related to this goal?
6. Give one example of how a person's goals and values may affect his or her career choices.
7. What is formal education? What is informal education?

[handwritten notes: what job will grow in the next 5 years — what kind of job will you want to be in out of college? will they be hiring? why?]

1-1 Activity 2   Access the Web Site for This Textbook

 academic.cengage.com/school/pfl

The publisher of this textbook posts a Web site with information related to the textbook. The *Personal Financial Literacy* Web site contains data files, games, links to other sites, and other information that you will use as you complete the activities in this textbook. You will probably visit the site often. In this activity, you will explore the site. You will also create a link to make visiting the site quick and easy.

1. Access the Internet. Start your Web browser such as *Internet Explorer*. In the Address box, enter **academic.cengage.com/school/pfl.**
2. A Web site that contains Web pages related to your textbook should appear. Click a hyperlink, such as **Student Resources**. Quickly scan the new page to see the information that it provides. Click the **Back** button to return to the welcome page.
3. Find and click the **Links** page on the Web site. This page contains links to other sites that you can use as you complete activities.
4. Return to the welcome page for the site. Add the Web site to your Favorites or Bookmarks list. Use this Favorites or Bookmarks link whenever you need to visit the site for later activities.

11

Career Planning

OUTCOMES

- Describe how economic conditions can affect prices and income.
- Discuss training and skills that workers need for job success.
- Explore tuition costs for colleges and other educational programs.
- Explore the options available to pay for education and training.

ECONOMIC CONDITIONS AFFECT INCOME

Regardless of where you live, you are affected by the economy. The word **economy** means all the activities related to making and distributing goods and services in an area. An **economist** is a person who studies the economy. Economists try to predict what will happen, using current and projected data.

As an individual, you are faced with many decisions. For example, you must decide what to purchase for a friend's birthday or how much to save for the future. As you consider what to do and how to prepare for your future, you must also consider the economy. The economy will affect your income, and your income will affect the choices you make.

The Economy Affects Prices

The United States has a market economy. In a market economy, the price for an item is set at a point that consumers are willing to pay and sellers are willing to accept. In other words, sellers charge what the market will bear. Producers wish to increase their profits. Consumers wish to get high value for each dollar spent. The willingness and ability of consumers to buy products and services is called **demand**. The quantity of goods and services that producers are willing and able to provide is called **supply**.

Products and services that are very popular among consumers are said to have high demand. When demand exceeds supply, businesses may charge higher prices for the products. These prices affect your decisions on which items to buy as you spend your income. The study of economics is often said to be the study of scarcity. Although consumers' incomes are often limited, their needs and wants may be unlimited and growing. Consumers must make good decisions to save and spend wisely and get the most value from the dollars spent.

The Economy Affects Income

For many people, their main source of income is wages (hourly pay) or monthly salary. If you choose to work in a career field that is growing and in a job that is in demand, you will likely be able to earn a good income. Income is not the only reason people work. However, the money earned allows workers to meet basic needs and other goals.

When the economy is growing, people are buying goods and services. Jobs are being created, and businesses are hiring workers. Finding and keeping a job that will provide financial security is easier in a growing economy.

On the other hand, when the economy is slowing, people often buy fewer goods and services. The lower demand for goods and services may mean that businesses are not growing. Workers may be laid off or dismissed from their jobs. Fewer new workers are hired. Finding and keeping a job that will provide financial security can be harder in a slowing economy.

When the demand for products or services that are produced by your employer is very low, your job may be in danger. When faced with this situation, some people decide to prepare for a new career field. This process is called retraining. Others will spend weeks or months pursuing job openings for which their skills and education may not be good matches. They may or may not find a new job without getting new training. Understanding how the economy affects prices of products, the job market, and your income can help you make better financial decisions.

You will likely change jobs several times during your lifetime.

13

Technology Corner

JOB SCOUTS

Technology is changing the way people find and use information. The **Internet** is a worldwide network of computers that can share information. The Internet allows users to find and share information about many topics, including jobs. When you are ready to begin working full-time, you may want to use a **job scout** to help you find job openings. A job scout is a type of computer program that is called an *intelligent agent*. Such a program does tasks using rules or options you set. In the case of a job scout, the task is searching the Internet to find job listings and returning those listings to

you. The rules you set might state the type of job and the location of the job (city or state). You may choose to have the job listings sent to you daily or weekly. Job scouts are also called *job agents*.

Using a job scout can help you find a job that will allow you to build financial security. To see an example of a site that offers a job agent, visit the USAJobs Web site as shown in Figure 1-2.1. A link to this site is provided on the Web site for this textbook (academic.cengage.com/school/pfl).

FIGURE 1-2.1

Job scouts or agents can be helpful in locating job openings.

Source: United States Office of Personnel Management, USAJOBS, https://my.usajobs.opm.gov/modifyagents.asp?action=save (accessed February 14, 2006).

TRAINING AND SKILLS FOR JOB SUCCESS

Many jobs require very specific skills. To get those skills, you will need education and training. The skills needed may include both hard skills and soft skills. **Hard skills** are the ability to perform tasks or complete procedures. Examples of hard skills include the ability to safely run medical

14

Chapter 1   Choices That Affect Income

equipment or to give first aid to an accident victim. The ability to install plumbing in a house is another example of a hard skill. Several months or years of training may be needed to learn hard skills. As you consider which career field to pursue, consider the hard skills required for jobs in that career area.

In addition to hard skills, employers want workers who have certain soft skills. **Soft skills** are nontechnical skills needed by most workers. Examples of soft skills are listed below.

- Leadership skills
- Teamwork skills
- Effective communication skills
- The ability to deal with difficult people and situations
- Problem-solving skills
- Time management skills
- The ability to prioritize tasks

Some soft skills come naturally to some people, but not to others. For example, some people have natural leadership skills, while others do not. Soft skills can be learned through education and practice. As you get education and training to learn hard skills, you also need to develop soft skills that will help you be successful on the job and in other areas of your life. Having both good hard skills and good soft skills will improve your earnings potential.

Success Skills

TEAMWORK

During your lifetime, you will be on many teams. Whether you are taking part in a family event, a competitive sport, a work group, or a fun activity, teamwork skills will come in handy. Combining the efforts of many people makes the work go faster, and the result is often more creative. When you work with others, you can often achieve better results than when you work alone.

At least one activity in each chapter of this textbook offers the option of working in a team. Follow these guidelines to improve your teamwork skills:

- Set clear goals for the team. Create an action plan for achieving the goals.
- Define the duties of each team member.
- Identify how success will be measured. How will the team know its goals have been achieved?

- Identify problems or issues the team may face in meeting its goals. Discuss ways to overcome the obstacles.
- Talk with all team members, and be open to ideas from everyone. Have regular meetings to track the team's progress.
- Build on the strengths of team members. Encourage all members to take part in making decisions and sharing ideas. Each team member has different skills and ideas that can be valuable to the team.
- Recognize accomplishments of team members and the team as a whole.
- As an individual team member, develop trust by completing your duties. Show a positive attitude when discussing team activities.

Being successful requires a combination of hard and soft skills.

COSTS OF EDUCATION AND TRAINING

You will need to invest both time and money in your education. **Tuition** is the charge for instruction at a school. Students must pay for textbooks, pay fees, and meet other expenses that are not covered in tuition. Money is also needed for living expenses such as rent, food, clothing, and travel. Some schools have housing for students. At other schools, students must find housing on their own. Typically, students want to live close by the school. Rent and other costs may be higher in those areas.

When choosing a career, think about the cost and the rewards of each career you are considering. Will it pay well and offer job security? The cost of a college education may be high. However, you will likely be rewarded for the money you spend on education. According to U.S. Census Bureau estimates, people who have a bachelor's degree (or higher) can earn nearly twice as much as workers with only a high school diploma. This difference can amount to more than $1 million over a lifetime.[2]

---

[2] U.S. Census Bureau, "The Big Payoff: Educational Attainment and Synthetic Estimates of Work-Life Earnings," http://www.census.gov/prod/2002pubs/p23-210.pdf (accessed February 15, 2006).

College Education: Public or Private?

The cost of attending a public college or university is often less than the cost of private schools. A bachelor's degree is earned in a four-year college or university program. At a public school, earning this degree could cost $25,000 or more in tuition. At a private college or university, the tuition may be $100,000 or more for a bachelor's degree.

A formal education will give you many advantages over your lifetime.

Focus on . . .

STUDENT ORGANIZATIONS

Students in high school and college may join career-related organizations. One such organization for business students in junior high and high school is FBLA (Future Business Leaders of America). The college level of this organization is Phi Beta Lambda. Another group, the Future Educators Association, provides opportunities for high school students to explore careers in education. The National FFA Organization is for students interested in careers in agriculture. These are just a few of many student organizations that may be available to you.

Being a member of a student organization provides opportunities for students to:

- Explore careers of interest.
- Ask questions of people who are working in the career area.
- Take part in conferences to learn more about careers in those areas.

- Compete with other students to demonstrate skills learned.
- Apply for scholarships, grants, and other forms of financial aid.
- Learn about continuing education in the field.
- Take part in community service activities.
- Network and form friendships with others who have similar interests.

Student organizations usually have bylaws (rules). These bylaws outline the club's purpose and structure. The costs and requirements for belonging to the group are also given. Generally, the cost of joining is small. Many student organizations provide information about their goals and activities on a Web site. Search the Internet using the term *student organization* and a career area (such as *nursing*) to find groups that interest you.

Student organizations, such as FBLA, have many benefits to offer.

Career and Technical Schools

Career and technical schools teach specific skills. These schools may be public or private schools. The tuition for public schools is often less than for private schools. Public school programs often cost $5,000 or less in tuition. Private programs usually cost two or three times as much as public programs do. The completion time for career and technical school programs is often less than for college programs. Typical career and technical school programs last a few months to a year or more. Books must be paid for, along with living expenses. Students are also responsible for fees and other charges.

Graduate and Advanced Programs

Some jobs require advanced training before the worker can start work. For example, a medical doctor needs advanced training beyond a four-year college degree. Others jobs require that you update skills as you continue working. If advanced degrees are needed in the job you choose, you should consider their cost.

A master's degree is a graduate degree (beyond a bachelor's degree). It usually requires one to three years of study. The time needed depends on your background and the type of degree. A doctorate degree requires three to seven years of study beyond a master's degree in the same field. The course of study often requires doing research. Some programs require internships or have residency requirements. Residency means that classes must be taken in person on campus. Tuition is higher at the graduate level. A graduate degree may cost $15,000 or more at a public school and $45,000 or more at a private school.

18

PAYING FOR EDUCATION AND TRAINING

When you choose to pursue formal education and training, you must consider ways to pay for them. Do you or your parents have the money needed? Will you be able to get grants or scholarships? Do you qualify for financial aid? Will you work part-time to earn money as you attend classes? These options and others may be available to you.

Loans and Grants

Financial aid is money you receive from some outside source to help pay for education. Loans and grants are available from a variety of sources, including the federal government, local banks, and other lenders. A loan is money that you borrow and must repay. A grant is money that you are given to pay for educational expenses and do not repay.

FEDERAL FINANCIAL AID

The federal government offers financial aid to students who qualify. For those under 23 years of age, parents (or a custodial parent) must fill out papers showing their income and assets. Assets are money or things of value that are owned, such as a house or car. The student's income must also be reported. If you are able to show that you need financial aid, then you may receive loans or grants.

Interest is money paid for the use of money. In the case of a student loan, interest is the money the student pays the lender in addition to the amount borrowed. Interest may be considered the cost of borrowing money. Interest charged on student loans is much lower than for other types of loans. A **subsidized student loan** is a loan on which interest is not charged until after you graduate. With an unsubsidized loan, interest is charged from the time the loan is made. With both types of loans, you do not have to begin repaying the loan until after you graduate from college. Federal financial aid can be applied for online at the FAFSA Web site. A screen from this site is shown in Figure 1-2.2 on page 20. A link to the site is provided on the Web site for this textbook.

PRIVATE STUDENT LOANS

Some private lenders, such as banks and credit unions, make loans to students. These loans typically have higher interest rates than loans from the government. The loans are usually unsubsidized. This means that interest is charged from the time that you take out the loan. These sources of loans require that you have income and a good credit history. If your income is too high to qualify for federal financial aid, a private student loan may be a good option for you. You will need to fill out an application for the loan. You may need to show tax returns and proof of income.

19

FIGURE 1-2.2

Students can apply for financial aid online at the FAFSA Web site.

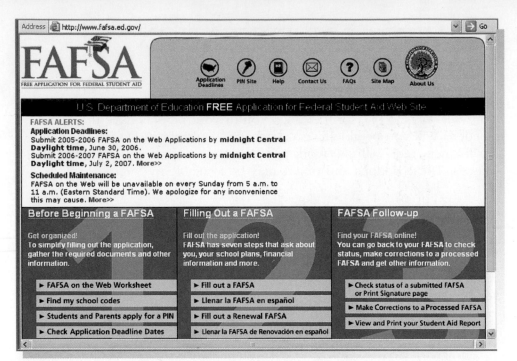

Source: U.S. Department of Education, Free Application for Federal Student Aid, http://www.fafsa.ed.gov/ (accessed February 14, 2006).

Scholarships

A **scholarship** is a gift of money or other aid (free tuition or books) made to a student to help pay for education. Scholarships may be available to students with high grades, strong athletic skills, or high test scores. Some scholarships are given based on need. Scholarships are available from local, state, and national organizations, including the federal government. Money from scholarships generally is not taxable.

Scholarships vary in amounts. A partial scholarship may be given to pay for some educational costs. A full, four-year scholarship may cover the entire tuition for a bachelor's degree. To learn about scholarships for which you can apply, talk to a teacher or counselor. The college you wish to attend can also provide information on scholarships that may be available. Search the Internet using the term *scholarships* to find other sources.

Work and Save

Some students decide to work and save money, starting college or a training program a few years after high school. As they complete their education, some students continue to work part-time. Others work full-time and complete their education part-time. This often means taking night classes or online classes. Such students may attend community or junior colleges where the tuition is low. Although these plans take a longer period of time, students can complete the educational program they choose. A benefit to this path may be the job experience students will gain as they work to pay for their education.

Many students work part-time to earn money for college.

Ethics

Whether filling out a job application or a financial aid form, many people are less than truthful on applications. Do not exaggerate or give information that will create false impressions when completing forms. Doing so is not ethical. **Ethics** are a system of moral values that people consider acceptable. Being fair and honest in your dealings with others is considered ethical behavior.

FILLING OUT FORMS

Always be truthful when completing forms. Fill in all the blanks and boxes on the form. Use *N/A* if the information is *not available* or *not applicable*. Print data clearly. When possible, download the document to your computer, and key the information into the form. Check the data you have entered. Make sure the information is clear, complete, and correct.

21

1-2 Activity 1   Can You Recall?

Answer these questions to help you recall what you have read. If you cannot answer a question, read the related section again.

1. Define *economy*. What does an economist do?
2. What is the definition of *demand*? Of *supply*?
3. Explain why economics is often called the study of scarcity.
4. How may a growing economy affect your job and income?
5. What is a job scout?
6. What are hard skills? What are soft skills? Give an example of each type of skill.
7. List several ways that students can pay for their formal education after high school.
8. What does *residency* mean when referring to completing a college degree?

1-2 Activity 2
Explore a Federal Financial Aid Form

You may want to apply for financial aid to continue your education when you finish high school. To learn about the information you will need to apply, you will explore the federal financial aid form in this activity.

1. Open the file *CH01 Aid Form* from the data files. This data file is provided as a PDF (portable document format) file. You will need a program such as *Adobe® Reader®* to view or print the file. Your teacher may provide this program for your use at school. A link is provided on the Web site for this textbook that will take you to a site where you can download *Adobe Reader* if you want to have the program on your computer at home. The program is free. This file contains the FAFSA worksheet for 2006–2007. Your teacher may provide you with a form for the current year to use instead of this form.
2. Review the FAFSA worksheet. This is a form you can complete to prepare information you will need to apply for aid online. How many pages long is the worksheet?
3. What types of questions are asked on the worksheet?
4. Who should complete this worksheet?
5. What is the earliest date the FAFSA form may be completed online according to this worksheet?

EXPLORING CAREERS

Artist, musician, engineer, police,
Doctor, lawyer, firehouse chief.

This variation of a children's rhyme mentions just a few of the many career areas a young person like you may choose to pursue. Your teen years can be an exciting time as you think about careers and other plans for the future. This time can also be challenging. With so many career paths available, how do you know which career is the right one for you?

Career exploration can help you learn how your interests and talents could be used in various careers. The remaining chapters in this textbook each contain an Exploring Careers page. These pages present information about jobs in one of the broad career areas identified by the U.S. Department of Education. As you explore various careers, think about the questions below. The answers can help you decide whether the career is one you should seriously consider.

- What does work in this career involve?
- Will I enjoy working in this career area?
- Will my interests, skills, or talents help me be successful in this career?
- What education, skills, or experience are needed for this career?
- Am I willing and able to acquire this education and experience?
- Will there be a continuing need for jobs in this career area?
- Will this job pay enough money to allow me to become financially secure?

A typical worker in the United States is employed for 30 to 40 years or more. Because you may spend many years working, you will want to choose a career that you find interesting and meaningful. You may have several different jobs during your working years. The jobs may be in the same field or in very different career areas. You may decide to pursue education that will prepare you for several jobs. Continuing your education, both formally and informally, will also be important in preparing for career changes.

Summary

○ The job market is continually changing. Job skills needed are evolving as well.

○ The career you choose will affect your income over your lifetime.

○ Decisions and choices you make, both personal and career, are based on values and goals.

○ The more and higher formal education you gain, the more you will probably earn over your lifetime.

○ The economy, or business activity as a whole, will affect your job and your career in terms of earnings and job security.

○ The state of the economy (growing or slowing down) will affect the prices you pay for goods and services.

○ Both hard skills and soft skills are necessary for career success.

○ Formal education and training programs require time and cost money. Many options for paying for educational programs are available.

○ Financial aid is money received from some outside source to help pay for education. A loan is money that is borrowed and must be repaid. A grant is money that is given to a student to pay for educational expenses and is not repaid.

○ Some students work to earn money to pay for education while attending college or a training program.

Key Terms

demand	interest	scholarship
economist	Internet	soft skills
economy	job description	subsidized student
ethics	job market	loan
financial aid	job scout or agent	supply
goal	job skills	tuition
hard skills	job title	value

24

Use the key terms from Chapter 1 to complete the following sentences:

1. The _____ is the sum total of business activity in an area.

2. Consumer willingness and ability to buy a product or service is called _____.

3. The charge for instruction at a school is called _____.

4. A principle that reflects the worth you place on an idea or action is called a(n) _____.

5. A(n) _____ lists the name or primary characteristic of a job.

6. The quantity of goods and services that producers are willing and able to provide is called _____.

7. The _____ refers to the wide variety of jobs and careers that exist at one point in time.

8. A(n) _____ may be short-term or long-term and is based on values or desired outcomes.

9. Skills other than technical skills, called _____, are important for job and career success.

10. Money obtained from an outside source to help pay for education is called _____.

11. Activities and duties you will be required to do on a job are called _____.

12. A(n) _____ is a loan on which interest is not charged until after graduation.

13. A(n) _____ is a detailed explanation of job duties.

14. Skills needed to perform technical tasks on a job are called _____.

15. A(n) _____ studies the economy and tries to predict what will happen, using current and projected data.

16. Money paid for the use of money, as in the cost of a loan, is called _____.

17. A(n) _____ is a computer program that searches the Internet to find job listings that meet certain criteria and returns those listings to the user.

18. _____ are a system of moral values that people consider acceptable.

19. A(n) _____ is a gift of money or other aid made to a student to help pay for education.

20. The _____ is a worldwide network of computers that can share information.

ACTIVITY 2
Math Minute

Complete these problems to build your math skills. You may use spreadsheet software or complete the problems manually.

1. The average tuition for four-year private colleges increased by 5.9 percent from last year. The cost last year was $20,051. What is the cost this year?

2. Use this year's tuition cost answer from step 1. If the tuition increases by 6 percent for each of the next three years, what will be the total tuition cost for the four years?

ACTIVITY 3
Values and Goals

Critical Thinking

Have you thought about what you want to do, to be, and to have as you become an adult? Complete the following steps to help you think about your values and goals.

1. List three goals that you would like to achieve by the time you graduate from high school.

2. After each goal, explain why that goal is important to you. Discuss the values on which you are basing that goal.

3. Consider how your goals have changed over time. A year ago, how were your goals different? How are they the same?

4. Which goals do you think are lifetime goals—based on values that you will firmly hold onto for a lifetime?

5. Do these values reflect your daily choices and decisions? List things you do (or don't do) that show you are consistent in applying your values to your choices.

6. Based on your values and goals, write a statement about your future life plans—career, family, travel, lifestyle—that you think will reflect your future choices and will shape your plans and goals.

7. Open the *Word* file *CH01 Goals* from the data files. Follow the directions in the file to complete a chart about your values and goals.

ACTIVITY 4
Research Colleges or Other Schools

  academic.cengage.com/school/pfl

Work with a classmate to explore programs offered and tuition costs of college or other postsecondary schools.

1. Working with your teammate, select a career area that interests you both.

2. Identify two or more colleges or other schools (such as career or technical schools offering a chef program or a cosmetology program) that provide training in this career area.

3. Visit the Web sites for at least two of the schools you listed in step 2. To find the address for a school Web site, enter the school name in a search engine such as Yahoo!® or Google™.

4. Compare the programs offered in this career area in terms of length. How many terms or years are required to complete the program at each school?

5. Compare tuition costs for the schools. Which school has the highest tuition?

CHAPTER 2

Income Sources

© Getty Images/PhotoDisc

People receive income from working and from other sources, such as investments. Another source of income for some people is government transfer payments. These payments help people who do not have other sources of income pay for their needs. Many workers receive benefits such as paid vacation or sick leave. You need to understand how benefits are a part of the total payments for a job. Various taxes must be paid on earnings. Taxes help cover the cost of government services and transfer payments. In this chapter, you will learn about income sources and benefits and about how taxes affect disposable income.

ONLINE RESOURCES

Personal Financial Literacy Web site:

Data Files

Vocabulary Flashcards

Beat the Clock:
    Income Sources

Chapter 2 Supplemental
    Activity

Search terms:
- minimum wage
- government transfer payments
- unearned income
- disposable income
- entrepreneur

2-1

Earned Income and Benefits

OUTCOMES

- List and discuss types of earned income, such as wages, salaries, tips, and commissions.
- Discuss the advantages and disadvantages of self-employment.
- Describe employee benefits.

TYPES OF EARNED INCOME

Many people work for hourly wages; others work for an annual salary. Some people have additional income through tips or commissions. Some people work for themselves, which is called self-employment. All these types of income are earned income and are subject to income taxes and other taxes. A **tax** is a required payment for the support of a government. The tax may be based on items such as earnings, property values, or the sale price of an item. More information about taxes is provided later in this chapter.

Wages

Employees who work for wages are paid for each hour worked. **Minimum wage** is the lowest pay rate allowed by law for each hour of work. The federal minimum wage is set by the U.S. Congress. In 2006, that rate was $5.15 per hour. Many states have minimum wage laws that set a rate higher than the federal rate. The state minimum wage rates can be found on the U.S. Department of Labor Web site as shown in Figure 2-1.1 on page 30. In many jobs, new workers will begin at minimum wage. This is because they do not have the education or experience that would allow them to earn a higher wage rate.

Employees who are paid by the hour must sometimes work more than the set regular number of hours. When this happens, they are entitled to extra pay called **overtime pay**. By law, overtime pay of at least $1\frac{1}{2}$ times regular pay must be paid for hours worked above 40 work hours in a week. For example, a worker who earns $8 per hour for regular pay might earn $12 per hour for overtime pay. People who work on holidays may be entitled to even higher pay rates for those hours. Both federal and state laws control when extra pay is required for more time worked.

Salaries

Some people work for a set salary, such as $3,000 a month or $36,000 a year. Salaried workers usually do not keep time cards or count hours worked. They may have more flexibility in the times they work than do

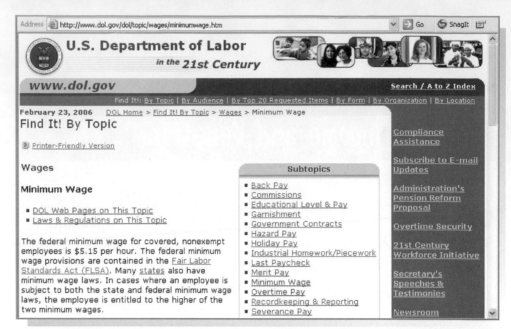

Address http://www.dol.gov/dol/topic/wages/minimumwage.htm

U.S. Department of Labor
in the **21st Century**

www.dol.gov   Search / A to Z Index

Find It!: By Topic | By Audience | By Top 20 Requested Items | By Form | By Organization | By Location

February 23, 2006   DOL Home > Find It! By Topic > Wages > Minimum Wage

Find It! By Topic

Printer-Friendly Version

Wages

Minimum Wage

- DOL Web Pages on This Topic
- Laws & Regulations on This Topic

The federal minimum wage for covered, nonexempt employees is $5.15 per hour. The federal minimum wage provisions are contained in the Fair Labor Standards Act (FLSA). Many states also have minimum wage laws. In cases where an employee is subject to both the state and federal minimum wage laws, the employee is entitled to the higher of the two minimum wages.

Subtopics
- Back Pay
- Commissions
- Educational Level & Pay
- Garnishment
- Government Contracts
- Hazard Pay
- Holiday Pay
- Industrial Homework/Piecework
- Last Paycheck
- Merit Pay
- Minimum Wage
- Overtime Pay
- Recordkeeping & Reporting
- Severance Pay

Compliance Assistance

Subscribe to E-mail Updates

Administration's Pension Reform Proposal

Overtime Security

21st Century Workforce Initiative

Secretary's Speeches & Testimonies

Newsroom

Source: U.S. Department of Labor, http://www.dol.gov/dol/topic/wages/minimumwage.htm (accessed March 8, 2006).

Some workers make most of their earnings from tips rather than wages.

hourly workers. They often work more than 40 hours a week but do not receive overtime pay.

People who work for a salary must often be self-directed. They must complete their work in a timely manner with little supervision. Managers and supervisors are typically paid a salary.

Tips and Commissions

Some workers receive tips in addition to wages. A **tip** is money, often a percentage of the total bill, or a gift given to a person for performing a service. The amount of the tip may be based on the quality of service provided. For example, a waiter may receive tips in the form of money from customers. A caddy at a golf course might receive free tickets to a show as a tip. Some workers make most of their earnings from tips rather than hourly pay.

Tips are subject to federal taxes. Tips may be subject to state taxes as well. The law requires some employers (such as restaurants and hair salons) to withhold taxes based on tips, even though tips may have been received in cash directly from customers.[1]

Some workers are paid a commission. A **commission** is a set fee or a percentage of a sale paid to a salesperson instead of or in addition to salary or wages. Sales commissions are earned only when a sale is made. If no sale is made, no

---

[1] Internal Revenue Service, "Tips Are Subject to Taxes," http://www.irs.gov/newsroom/article/0,,id=106783,00.html (accessed February 23, 2006).

NETWORKING

Networking is the process of making contacts and building relationships with other people. Everyone you know is in your "network." All your contacts are important to you. They will help keep you informed about issues that affect your financial success. For example, you may learn about scholarships or grants from teachers or counselors in your network. Later in life, you may learn about a job opening from a friend at another company.

Your network may include many contacts. Record the name, address, phone number, and e-mail address of each one so you can reach that person when you want to share information. Make a note of how you are related to or were introduced to each person. For example, you should include your school teachers, counselors, and principals. You should also include the leaders or members of community groups or other groups to which you belong. If you have a summer or part-time job, include the others with whom you work and your manager. Keep in touch with your contacts regularly. Let them know when you are looking for particular information, such as scholarships for which you can apply.

commission is received. In some types of jobs, such as real estate sales, the worker's entire earnings may be based on commission. For example, a real estate agent who arranges the sale of a home for $200,000 might receive a $12,000 commission. In other types of jobs, workers may be paid a base salary plus commissions. For example, a person who sells cars might receive a salary of $10,500 a year plus 25 percent of the profit on each car sold.

SELF-EMPLOYMENT

Working for yourself is called self-employment. A person who takes the risks of being self-employed and owning a business is called an **entrepreneur**. Owning a business can be challenging, but it can have rewards as well. If the business fails, the money invested in the business may be lost. The owner may have to work long hours and do many different tasks to keep the business running. These can be disadvantages of owning a business. An advantage of owning a business is that the owner can make decisions about how the business will be run. She or he also keeps all the earnings or profits from the business. **Profit** is the amount left after all costs are deducted from the income of a business. This is another advantage of being an entrepreneur.

Some entrepreneurs want to keep their businesses small. They want to be able to oversee all the daily operations of the business. Others want their businesses to grow into large companies with many workers. In a large company, the owner cannot oversee all the daily operations.

Some people start a business at an early age. Some people work for other businesses first to gain knowledge and experience. Some people

31

seek education about how to run a business before they start a company. Owning a business involves much risk for the entrepreneur. He or she may need to borrow money to start the business. Repaying the money and paying other debts of the business are responsibilities of the owner. The owner may need to reinvest part of the income from the business to help the business grow. The owner will typically have to work hard to make the company successful.

EMPLOYEE BENEFITS

Full-time workers usually have benefits provided by the employer. **Benefits** are forms of pay other than salary or wages. Paid vacation and holidays are examples of benefits. Some benefits are paid for by the company. For other benefits, such as health insurance, the worker may need to pay part or all of the cost.

A **cafeteria plan** is a benefit plan that allows workers to choose from a number of options. Workers may be able to save money by selecting only the options they need. Most plans include basic choices for health, life, and other insurance. Other options, such as a savings plan, may also be available.

Benefits increase the overall value a worker receives for a job. **Disposable income** refers to the money a person has available to spend or save after taxes have been paid. Money received from some benefits, such as a profit-sharing plan, can directly increase a worker's disposable income. Other benefits have the effect of increasing disposable income. For example, health insurance bought through a company plan may be cheaper than an individual policy. The money saved by buying the company plan is available to save or spend on other items.

Benefits are also important to workers for several other reasons:

o Workers are not taxed on most benefits. This means that workers receive something of value without paying tax as part of the cost.

o Some benefits allow workers to buy services at a cheaper price than they could otherwise. For example, group insurance costs a lot less than individual policies. Paying a lower cost for insurance increases the worker's disposable income.

o Some benefits that are offered to workers may not be available to individuals. Company retirement plans and stock options are examples of these benefits.

o Some benefits that are offered to workers may not be affordable at individual prices. For example, workers who have health problems might not be able to afford insurance at individual rates.

o Some benefits help workers reach financial goals. For example, some people find it hard to save money. With company-sponsored savings plans, saving becomes easier because the money is deducted from the worker's paycheck.

Pay Without Work

Pay without work refers to times when an employee who is not working will be paid. Vacation, holidays, and sick leave are examples of pay without work. Full-time and salaried employees usually get annual paid vacations.

32

Ethics

Many employers provide sick leave for employees. Sick leave is a valuable benefit. Employers usually have rules about what situations qualify for use of sick leave. In some cases, the employee must be ill to use sick leave time. In other cases, the company may allow employees to use sick leave time to care for a sick child or other relative. An employee may be able to use sick leave time to visit a doctor or hospital for tests or checkups.

Employers expect workers to be honest in their dealings with the company. Employees should know and follow the rules that apply to using sick leave. Pretending to be sick or to have another situation that qualifies for sick leave use is not ethical.

Typically, after the first year, an employee gets 1 or 2 weeks of vacation per year.

Most employers provide certain **paid holidays**. Examples of paid holidays are Thanksgiving, Christmas Day, Easter, Labor Day, Memorial Day, Veterans Day, and Presidents' Day. On those days, employees will be paid but will not have to work. Employees who do work on holidays may receive extra pay. Typically, working on holidays pays two times the regular rate of pay.

Many companies allow workers to take a certain number of sick leave days per year. **Sick leave** covers days the worker is paid even though she or he is not at work due to illness. Some companies allow the use of sick leave to care for a sick child or other family member. Typically, sick leave is 10 days a year. Some companies allow unused sick leave to accumulate. That means that workers can save sick leave and use it later. Workers might also get paid for unused sick leave at some time in the future.

Some companies also offer personal leave. **Personal leave** is time away from work for personal reasons. The worker usually does not have to give a reason. Typically, personal leave is 2 or 3 days a year. Unused personal leave usually is not carried forward to another year.

These and other pay-without-work benefits allow employees to rest and get away from work pressure and stress. They also allow workers to plan family vacations and special events and to enjoy a balanced and healthy life.

Educational Reimbursement

Some employers provide plans that reimburse (pay back) money spent on education. For example, some companies will pay for the cost of classes or training related to the worker's job. This training can benefit the company because the worker may be able to do a better job using the skills learned. The training benefits the worker on the present job. It may also improve the chances of getting a promotion or a better job with the same or a different company. Some employer plans will pay for classes

33

A perk that many people value is a preferred parking spot.

toward a degree. Getting a college degree paid for by an employer is a benefit of great value, not just for this job, but for all future jobs as well.

In a typical education plan, the worker might be paid 100 percent of the cost of tuition and books if an A grade is received in the class. If the worker earns a B grade, 90 percent of the costs will be paid. If the worker earns a C grade, 80 percent of the costs will be paid. If the worker's grade is below a C, no costs will be paid.

Perks

Providing high wages and good benefits like pay without work and education plans is one way that companies motivate workers. Other types of benefits, called perks, have a different value. They provide emotional satisfaction or social status rather than money. Examples of perks are a prime parking space, an office with a view, an expense account, and a company car. Some of these benefits are not taxable.

Insurance

Health insurance is an important benefit for many workers. The price paid for health insurance is called a premium. Premiums are typically paid by employers and employees. In the past, many employers paid the full price of insurance for employees. However, the costs of health care have risen steadily over the past several years. The costs are expected to continue increasing. Today, employees typically pay a portion or all of insurance premiums.

The premiums employees pay vary depending on the coverage provided. For example, an employee with a spouse and children would pay more for health insurance than a single employee. Group health insurance premiums are lower than those for individual policies.

Group life insurance is often available at work. The premium may be paid by the employer or the employee. In some companies, the employer pays for a certain amount of life insurance. For example, this amount may be twice the employee's annual salary. The employee may be able to purchase additional coverage at the group rate. The premium is often lower than for an individual policy. Life insurance paid for by the employee may be portable. A portable policy goes with the employee when he or she leaves the employer.

Disability insurance provides payments to replace income lost when illness or injury prevents the employee from working. This type of insurance is an option for many employees. Coverage for short-term disability (up to two years) is often paid for by the employer. The employee may be able to purchase long-term disability coverage. Long-term disability insurance typically covers periods longer than two years and up to retirement. The premiums are deducted from the employee's paycheck.

34

Workers' compensation is an insurance plan that employers are required to provide for employees. It pays medical and disability benefits to workers who are injured or contract diseases on the job. Benefits may be paid to the worker's family if the worker is killed on the job.

Other types of group insurance coverage may also be available. For example, the employer may offer dental, vision, or long-term care.

Retirement Plans

Some companies offer 401(k) retirement plans. This type of plan allows employees to put aside money for retirement that is not subject to federal income tax at the time it is earned. Some states also do not require that state income tax be paid on money placed in a 401(k). The employer may match the contribution to some extent, such as 25 percent or more. The money put into the plan will be taxed later when it is taken from the account. Deductions for the plan are made from the worker's pay.

Some companies offer retirement accounts that are paid for entirely by the employer. These accounts are also called pension plans. Pension plans provide payments to retired workers. Typically, employees must work for the company for a certain number of years to qualify. The payment amounts vary depending on the number of years worked, the worker's salary, and other factors. This type of fringe benefit is being offered by fewer companies now than in the past.

Profit-Sharing Plans

A profit-sharing plan means that when the company does well, employees are paid a share of the profits. This money can be paid in cash, or it can be added to a retirement account. When the money is paid in cash, it is taxable in the year received. When the money is added to a retirement account, it is taxed when withdrawn by the employee.

Stock Option Plans

Some companies allow employees to buy stock in the company at a reduced price. The purchase price of the stock may be deducted from the employee's pay. This is a convenient way to acquire stock, and it does not involve brokerage or trading fees. Other companies may give shares of stock in the company to employees as a benefit.

Health Flexible Spending Arrangements

A health flexible spending arrangement (FSA) allows employees to set aside money to pay for qualified medical expenses. The money set aside is not included in the amount on which employment or federal income taxes are paid. The plans are often set up by employers as an employee benefit. Deductions are made from the employee's pay to fund the account. The employer may also contribute. The employee files claims to be paid from the account for qualified expenses.

35

2-1 Activity 1   Can You Recall?

Answer these questions to help you recall what you have read. If you cannot answer a question, read the related section again.

1. What does the term *minimum wage* mean? Why do people often have to start a new job for minimum wage?
2. What is overtime pay? How much is overtime pay compared to regular pay?
3. How is being paid a salary different from being paid hourly wages?
4. Give an example of a worker whose pay may include tips.
5. What are some advantages of self-employment? What are some disadvantages?
6. What are employee benefits? Give two examples. Why are employee benefits important to employees?
7. Give three examples of pay without work.
8. Why is educational reimbursement a valuable benefit for employees?
9. Give two examples of perks that employees might want.
10. Why are employees at many companies expected to help pay for the cost of health insurance?
11. Describe two types of retirement plans offered by companies as a benefit.
12. How does a health flexible spending arrangement (FSA) benefit employees?

2-1 Activity 2   Compute Gross Pay

Gross pay is the amount of salary or wages a worker receives before deductions are made. Deductions may be taken for taxes and some benefits, such as health insurance premiums. Tips and commissions are included in gross pay.

To calculate gross pay, multiply the hourly rate times the number of hours worked. If tips or commissions are included, add them to the total salary or hourly wages earned.

1. Kim Chin works for an hourly rate of $6.50. This week Kim worked 39 hours. What is Kim's gross pay for this week?

2. Juan Perez is paid a monthly salary of $500. He is also paid a 10 percent commission on sales he makes. This month, Juan made $7,575 in sales. What is Juan's gross salary for this month?

3. Alice Jones worked 32 hours this week. She is paid $4.00 per hour. She also earned $250 in tips. What is Alice's gross pay for this week?

4. John O'Malley worked 40 regular hours and 10 overtime hours this week. His regular rate of pay is $8.50. For overtime pay, he earns 1.5 times his regular pay. What is John's gross pay for this week?

5. Gloria Adams is starting a new job. She will be paid $10.50 per hour. She plans to work 40 hours per week for 50 weeks a year. What will her gross yearly pay be? The value of the benefits Gloria will receive amounts to 30 percent of her gross pay. What will the value of her benefits be? What is the total value of the pay and benefits Gloria will receive?

Unearned Income

OUTCOMES

- List private sources of unearned income.
- List several types of government transfer payments.
- Explain the difference between in-kind and in-cash transfer payments.
- Discuss the costs and benefits of paying taxes.

PRIVATE SOURCES

Unearned income is money received from sources other than working in a job, either for yourself or for someone else. There are several private sources of unearned income. For example, interest earnings on a savings account is money received that the owner does not work to get. People who buy stocks in a corporation may receive dividend payments.

All sources of income offer financial security to retired people.

© Getty Images/PhotoDisc

FIGURE 2-2.1

TYPES OF INCOME

CLASSIFICATION OF TYPES OF INCOME		
Earned Income	**Unearned Income**	**Variable Income**
Salaries and wages	Dividends	Business profits
Commissions	Interest	Royalties
Bonuses	Capital gains	Rents
Professional fees	Gambling winnings	
Tips	Alimony	
	Social Security benefits	
	Pensions	
	Annuities	

Source: Internal Revenue Service, http://www.irs.gov/businesses/small/international/article/ 0,,id=96811,00.html (accessed March 6, 2006).

A **dividend** is money shared with stockholders when a corporation makes profits. Retired people may receive pension payments. These are examples of unearned income.

The Internal Revenue Service (IRS) lists some types of income as variable income. The income may be earned or unearned, depending on the situation in which it is received. Royalties and rent are examples of variable income. Figure 2-2.1 shows different types of income as listed by the IRS.

Unearned income is taxable. However, the tax rates may be lower than income tax rates on earned income. For example, qualified dividend income is subject to a maximum 15 percent tax rate. Because this income is not earned, it also is not subject to employment taxes.

Building Communications Skills

CRITICAL LISTENING

Critical listening involves evaluating the information you hear. The goal is to consider only the important or relevant information. Unneeded, untrue, or conflicting information can be ignored. When you listen critically, you are able to make good decisions based on what is accurate and useful.

For example, pretend you are buying a used car. The seller is telling you about the car and its features. He tells you that the car runs great and will run for years to come. It is the best car he ever had. These statements are not useful for making a decision about whether to buy the car. Next, the seller tells you that the car was serviced regularly (and he can prove it), has traveled 34,000 miles, and was kept in a garage every night. Using this information can help you make a good decision.

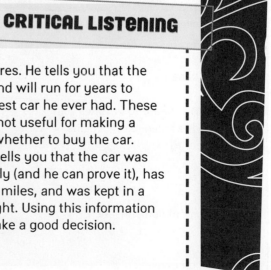

GOVERNMENT TRANSFER PAYMENTS

Money and benefits received from local, state, or federal governments are called **transfer payments**. Transfer payments are made from many different programs. Transfer payments increase the disposable income of those who receive them.

Some transfer payments provide income to retired people. When people get older, they stop working. However, their needs continue. In fact, some needs increase, such as the need for medical care. For some people, medical care and prescriptions are their largest expenses. Retired people also need health insurance. Social Security and Medicare programs provide benefits for these retired workers.

Other programs provide benefits to help low-income families with medical needs or living expenses. For example, Medicaid is a program of medical aid designed for those unable to afford medical service. It is financed by the state and federal governments in the United States.

Examples of transfer payments provided from state and federal governments are shown in Figure 2-2.2. Transfer payments may be in-cash or in-kind payments. Examples of each are discussed in the following sections.

In-Kind Transfer Payments

In-kind transfer payments include food stamps, rent subsidies, and vouchers that can be exchanged for goods and services. People do not receive money directly. Instead, they are provided with the means to get goods and services. In-kind payments are made available to those in need.

The federal government and state governments make in-kind transfer payments. For example, Medicaid is a program of medical aid designed for those unable to afford medical service. It is financed by the state and

FIGURE 2-2.2   *Transfer payments are made possible by taxes collected from taxpayers.*

TRANSFER PAYMENT EXAMPLES

Aid to Families with Dependent Children	Payments to needy families with children. Programs vary by state.
Medicaid	Benefits that provide health care and related services for low-income individuals
Veterans' benefits	Benefits for veterans (those who have completed active military service), their families, and their survivors
Supplemental Security Income (SSI)	Benefits for low-income elderly and disabled persons
State-provided medical care plans	Benefits for people who cannot afford health insurance
Social Security	Benefits for retired people, disabled workers, and their dependents
Medicare	Health insurance for retired people and those who receive Social Security benefits
Unemployment compensation	Benefits for workers who are laid off or dismissed from jobs. To qualify, individuals must have worked for a required time. Program rules vary by state.
Workers' compensation	Benefits for workers who become injured or ill on the job

40

Transfer payments help people who are in need.

federal governments in the United States. Many people age 65 or older qualify for Medicare hospital insurance (Part A) based on their own or their spouse's work record. Some people under age 65 who are disabled may also qualify for Medicare hospital insurance. This is another type of in-kind transfer payment.

In-Cash Transfer Payments

In-cash transfer payments are money in the form of a check, debit card, or other direct payment. For example, after Hurricane Katrina, flood victims were given debit cards worth $1,000. They used the cards to buy food,

Focus on . . .

SOCIAL SECURITY BENEFITS

Most workers in the United States pay into the Social Security fund. A Social Security number is assigned to each person's account. Payments are made into the account by employees. The payments are matched by employers. Based on the amount paid into the account and other factors, the worker will receive monthly benefit checks when retired.

Each year while paying into the fund, workers should receive a Social Security Statement. The statement allows workers to see that earnings are being posted properly to the account. If you are a worker and do not receive a statement, you should request one. A statement can be requested at a local Social Security office or on the Social Security Web site. A link to this site is provided on the Web site for this textbook.

clothing, and other items. Social Security payments, unemployment benefits, and workers' compensation payments are examples of in-cash payments. People receive checks or have direct deposits made to their checking accounts.

COSTS AND BENEFITS OF PAYING TAXES

Taxes are collected from many sources. Income taxes, use taxes, and excise taxes are examples. Income taxes are paid on earned and unearned income. You will learn more about income taxes later in this chapter.

Use taxes are paid by people who use certain goods or services provided by the government. For example, people who visit a state or national park may be charged a use tax. This money is used to help pay for operation of the park. Drivers may have to pay a toll to be able to cross a bridge. This use tax helps to pay for the bridge maintenance and operation.

Another form of tax is called the **excise tax**. Excise taxes are charged on the purchase of specific goods, such as motor fuel, cigarettes, and alcohol. They are also charged on services such as phone service, utilities, and garbage collection. Excise taxes are usually included in the price of the product or service. They help pay for the cost of government goods and services. When the excise tax is on a product that is not considered essential for a normal standard of living, such as an expensive car, it is often called a luxury tax.

Costs of Paying Taxes

Paying taxes reduces the disposable income of an individual. The person has less money available to save or spend than if taxes were not paid. This is the main cost of paying taxes for an individual. When people have

Gasoline excise taxes help pay for roads and highways.

less money to spend, the economy of the area may be affected. When people spend less on goods and services, businesses have lower sales. Lower sales may lead to lower profits. Workers may have to be laid off or dismissed from their jobs. Charitable groups may receive less money from donations. Having less money means the groups are able to help fewer people in need. In fact, cutting taxes is a method governments can use to stimulate the economy.

Benefits of Paying Taxes

Paying taxes can benefit the person making the payments and others who do not make payments. For example, Social Security tax provides a system of old-age, survivors, and disability insurance. Workers pay Social Security tax during their working years. When they retire, workers receive payments from the fund. This is an example of a direct benefit from paying taxes.

Money collected from various taxes is used by governments to provide goods and services for citizens. For example, roads and highways are paid for with government money—either federal or state. Everyone (whether or not they paid taxes) is able to use them. Government transfer payments, in-kind and in-cash, are funded with taxes.

Everyone benefits from government goods and services that are paid for with tax dollars. Examples include public education, national defense, police protection, and parks. Most individuals could not afford to pay for these items. Not everyone benefits directly from every type of tax. For example, some people may never visit a state or national park. However, everyone benefits from some government services.

© Getty Images/PhotoDisc

Taxes help provide parks for everyone to enjoy.

2-2 Activity 1   Can You Recall?

Answer these questions to help you recall what you have read. If you cannot answer a question, read the related section again.

1. How is unearned income different from earned income?
2. List three sources of private unearned income.
3. What are government transfer payments? How are in-kind payments different from in-cash payments?
4. From Figure 2-2.2, explain how Medicaid is different from Medicare.
5. What is an excise tax? Give one example of a product that has an excise tax.
6. What is the main direct cost of paying taxes for an individual?
7. How can having citizens pay high taxes affect the economy?
8. Give one example of how paying taxes can directly benefit a person.
9. How are government transfer payments funded?
10. Give one example of goods or services funded by taxes that benefit everyone.

2-2 Activity 2   Taxes, Taxes, Taxes

  academic.cengage.com/school/pfl

Many different types of taxes are paid by people in your area. Work in a group with two or three classmates to learn about the kind of taxes being paid.

1. To learn about the taxes paid by people in your area, interview people. Ask adult relatives or friends who work to tell you what types of taxes are deducted from their pay. Call or visit officials in local government or search the Internet to learn about other taxes.
2. List all types of taxes paid by people who live and work in your city, county, or state. Include sales taxes, use taxes, excise taxes, income taxes, property taxes, and so on. You may find taxes listed on bills for phone, utilities, water, sewer, and garbage services. You will also find taxes on gasoline, cigarettes, and other luxuries.
3. To your list of local and state taxes, add federal income taxes, Social Security and Medicare taxes, workers' compensation taxes (if paid by employees in your state), and other taxes of any kind.

44

Taxes and Other Deductions

OUTCOMES

- Explain how taxes affect disposable income.
- List types of deductions required for taxes.
- Compute net pay.
- List examples of optional deductions from pay.
- Complete a Form I-9 and a Form W-4.
- Complete a federal income tax return.

TAXES AND DISPOSABLE INCOME

Wages, salaries, and profits from owning a business are taxable. Unearned income, such as interest from a savings account, is also taxable. As you learned earlier, *disposable income* refers to the money left to save or spend after taxes are paid. Lower taxes result in higher disposable income. Higher taxes result in lower disposable income.

REQUIRED DEDUCTIONS

Workers are required to have money withheld from their paychecks for income tax, Social Security tax, and Medicare tax. Other taxes and deductions may also be withheld. Many states have a state income tax. Some counties and cities have an income tax.

Taxes and payments for other items are subtracted from the worker's gross pay to calculate net pay. The paycheck stub in Figure 2-3.1 on page 46 shows a worker's gross earnings, deductions, and net pay.

Income Tax Withholding

Federal and state income taxes are withheld according to income amount and the number of exemptions claimed on Form W-4. A sample form is shown in Figure 2-3.2 on page 46. Exemptions are persons you claim on your tax return as dependents. The Internal Revenue Service provides details of how a person qualifies as a dependent. For example, your child who lives with you and for whom you provide more than 50 percent of living expenses would be a dependent. The more exemptions you claim, the less tax is withheld. Everyone is allowed to claim one exemption (unless that person is claimed as an exemption by someone else). People who are married or have children can claim more exemptions. Federal

EMPLOYEE NAME	EMPLOYEE ID	PAY PERIOD	CHECK DATE	CHECK NO.
Gloria M. Perez	482975	2/1/20-- thru 2/14/20--	2/21/20--	A001161
EARNINGS	HOURS	RATE	THIS PERIOD	YEAR-TO-DATE
Regular	80	$13.00	$1,040.00	$3,120.00
Overtime				
		TAXES		
		Federal Income Tax	$82.19	$246.57
		Social Security Tax	64.48	193.44
		Medicare Tax	15.08	45.24
		State Income Tax	34.27	102.81
		City Income Tax	3.14	9.42
		SUBTOTAL	$199.16	$597.48
		DEDUCTIONS		
		Health Insurance	$150.00	$450.00
		Life Insurance	12.00	36.00
		401(k) Plan	52.00	156.00
		Dental Insurance	10.00	30.00
		SUBTOTAL	$224.00	$672.00
NET PAY			$616.84	$1,850.52

income tax withholding rates can be viewed at the Internal Revenue Service Web site. A link to this site is provided on the Web site for this textbook.

Social Security Tax

Social Security tax is withheld by the federal government. The purpose of this tax is to provide a system of old-age, survivors, and disability insurance. The rate of the tax and the amount of income that is taxable change each year. In 2006, the rate was 6.2 percent on earnings up to $94,200. Money withheld for this tax is paid into an account under your name and

FIGURE 2-3.2   *Form W-4 shows the number of exemptions claimed.*

Form **W-4**	**Employee's Withholding Allowance Certificate**	OMB No. 1545-0074
Department of the Treasury Internal Revenue Service	▶ Whether you are entitled to claim a certain number of allowances or exemption from withholding is subject to review by the IRS. Your employer may be required to send a copy of this form to the IRS.	20**06**

1 Type or print your first name and middle initial. **Gloria M.**	Last name **Perez**	2 Your social security number **000 22 2105**
Home address (number and street or rural route) **123 Maple Street**	3 ☑ Single ☐ Married ☐ Married, but withhold at higher Single rate. Note. If married, but legally separated, or spouse is a nonresident alien, check the "Single" box.	
City or town, state, and ZIP code **Monticello, KY 42633-0123**	4 If your last name differs from that shown on your social security card, check here. You must call 1-800-772-1213 for a new card. ▶ ☐	

5	Total number of allowances you are claiming (from line **H** above **or** from the applicable worksheet on page 2)	**5**	**1**
6	Additional amount, if any, you want withheld from each paycheck	**6** $	
7	I claim exemption from withholding for 2006, and I certify that I meet **both** of the following conditions for exemption.		
	● Last year I had a right to a refund of **all** federal income tax withheld because I had **no** tax liability **and**		
	● This year I expect a refund of **all** federal income tax withheld because I expect to have **no** tax liability.		
	If you meet both conditions, write "Exempt" here . . . . ▶	**7**	

Under penalties of perjury, I declare that I have examined this certificate and to the best of my knowledge and belief, it is true, correct, and complete.

Employee's signature
(Form is not valid
unless you sign it.) ▶ *Gloria M. Perez*   Date ▶ *May 20, 20--*

8 Employer's name and address (Employer: Complete lines 8 and 10 only if sending to the IRS.)	9 Office code (optional)	10 Employer identification number (EIN)

For Privacy Act and Paperwork Reduction Act Notice, see page 2.   Cat. No. 10220Q   Form **W-4** (2006)

Department of Homeland Security
U.S. Citizenship and Immigration Services

OMB No. 1615-0047; Expires 03/31/07
Employment Eligibility Verification

Please read instructions carefully before completing this form. The instructions must be available during completion of this form. ANTI-DISCRIMINATION NOTICE: It is illegal to discriminate against work eligible individuals. Employers CANNOT specify which document(s) they will accept from an employee. The refusal to hire an individual because of a future expiration date may also constitute illegal discrimination.

Section 1. Employee Information and Verification. To be completed and signed by employee at the time employment begins.

Print Name: Last	First	Middle Initial	Maiden Name
Perez	Gloria	M.	Valdez

Address *(Street Name and Number)*	Apt. #	Date of Birth *(month/day/year)*
123 Maple Street		3/20/1979

City	State	Zip Code	Social Security #
Monticello	KY	42633-0123	000222105

I am aware that federal law provides for imprisonment and/or fines for false statements or use of false documents in connection with the completion of this form.

I attest, under penalty of perjury, that I am (check one of the following):

[X] A citizen or national of the United States
[ ] A Lawful Permanent Resident (Alien #) A _____
[ ] An alien authorized to work until _____
 (Alien # or Admission #) _____

Employee's Signature *Gloria M. Perez*

Date *(month/day/year)* *May 20, 20--*

Social Security number. The employer pays the same amount into your account. People who are self-employed must pay 12.4 percent on earnings up to $94,200. Amounts may be different for the current year. Your account continues to grow as you are working and paying the tax. Social Security tax is also known as FICA because it was created by the Federal Insurance Contribution Act.[2]

Employers are required to verify that workers are eligible for employment. When a worker begins a job, the worker is required to complete Section 1 of Form I-9, Employment Eligibility Verification. Section 1 of the form is shown in Figure 2-3.3. The employee must enter a name, an address, and a Social Security number. The Social Security number recorded on this form is used to report Social Security taxes for the employee. The form also shows whether the employee is a citizen of the United States, a lawful permanent resident, or an alien who is authorized to work. The employer must verify the information by looking at certain documents. A U.S. passport, a driver's license, and a U.S. Social Security card are examples of these documents.

Medicare Tax

Medicare tax is withheld by the federal government. This tax pays for medical care for retired persons and those who receive Social Security benefits. In 2006, workers paid 1.45 percent on all earnings for this tax. The employer also pays the same amount into your account. In 2006, people who were self-employed paid 2.9 percent on all earnings.[3] Amounts may be different for the current year.

---

[2] Social Security Online, "Electronic Fact Sheet," http://www.ssa.gov/pubs/10003.html (accessed February 23, 2006).

[3] Ibid.

47

Focus on . . .

All workers are entitled, by law, to a safe place to work. This includes safe working methods and safety training. Workers' compensation costs are based, in part, on the safety record of the company. Having a safe workplace and reducing the number of accidents or injuries benefits both workers and the company.

Safety begins with good work attitudes. Safety is part of everyone's job. All workers must understand safety needs and make safety a priority. Major work-related accidents, injuries, and illnesses are related to the following factors:

• Carelessness of workers

• Failure to use safety equipment

• Lack of awareness of dangers

• Not knowing how to avoid and reduce risks

• Lack of a practiced and workable emergency plan

An emergency plan is a vital part of safety. An effective emergency plan provides for the safety of workers, employees, visitors, and others. A good emergency plan has the following parts:

• Detailed steps to follow in an emergency

• A list of who is responsible for each activity

• A list of who has back-up roles

• A second plan in case one course of action fails

• A data back-up system

• A process to communicate status

• Practice drills so that everyone will know what to do in a real emergency

Emergency plans should be in writing and shared with everyone. If special training is required, it should be completed and practiced regularly.

© Getty Images/PhotoDisc

Following an emergency plan helps prevent injuries in times of danger.

Workers' Compensation Insurance

Workers' compensation is an insurance plan that pays medical and disability benefits to workers who are injured or contract diseases on the job. Benefits may be paid to the worker's family if the worker is killed on the job. The laws that cover workers' compensation vary by state. In some states, the entire cost of the insurance is paid by the employer. In other states, such as Oregon, the worker must also pay some fees related to workers' compensation. In those states, workers may have the fees deducted from their paychecks.

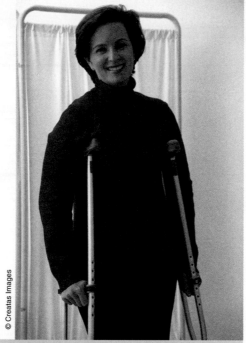

© Creatas Images

Workers' compensation provides benefits for people who are injured on the job.

OPTIONAL DEDUCTIONS

Employees may have optional deductions made from their pay. Full-time workers usually have benefits provided by the employer. Employees may share in the cost of some benefits, such as health insurance. Workers may also have money deducted from their pay for items such as the following:

- Health insurance
- Life insurance
- Disability insurance
- Dental insurance
- Vision insurance
- Long-term care insurance
- Savings plan
- Retirement plan
- Health flexible spending plan
- Stock purchase plan

FEDERAL TAX FILING

If you are a U.S. citizen or resident, whether you must file a federal income tax return depends upon your gross income, your filing status, your age, and whether you are a dependent. After taxes are filed the first time, the IRS may send paper forms to use in filing. Forms can be accessed online at the IRS Web site. A link to the site is found on the Web site for this textbook. Users can download, save, and print tax forms needed for filing federal tax returns.

49

FIGURE 2-3.4 *A Form W-2 reports taxable income.*

a Control number			OMB No. 1545-0008	Safe, accurate, FAST! Use **IRS e-file**	Visit the IRS website at *www.irs.gov/efile.*

b Employer identification number (EIN) 00-000000	**1** Wages, tips, other compensation $25,688.00	**2** Federal income tax withheld $2,136.94
c Employer's name, address, and ZIP code ABC Company 781 Weston Street Monticello, KY 42633-0781	**3** Social security wages $27,040.00	**4** Social security tax withheld $1,676.48
	5 Medicare wages and tips $27,040.00	**6** Medicare tax withheld $392.08
	7 Social security tips	**8** Allocated tips
d Employee's social security number 000 22 2105	**9** Advance EIC payment	**10** Dependent care benefits
e Employee's first name and initial Last name Suff.	**11** Nonqualified plans	**12a** See instructions for box 12 D $1,352.00
Gloria M. Perez 123 Maple Street Monticello, KY 42633-0123	**13** Statutory employee ☐ Retirement plan ☒ Third-party sick pay ☐	**12b**
	14 Other	**12c**
		12d
f Employee's address and ZIP code		

15 State Employer's state ID number	**16** State wages, tips, etc.	**17** State income tax	**18** Local wages, tips, etc.	**19** Local income tax	**20** Locality name
KY 00000	$25,688.00	$891.02	$27,040.00	$81.64	Mont.

Form **W-2** Wage and Tax Statement   **2006**   Department of the Treasury—Internal Revenue Service

Copy B—To Be Filed With Employee's FEDERAL Tax Return.
This information is being furnished to the Internal Revenue Service.

Form W-2

Form W-2 is used to report the taxable income a worker received during the calendar year. This form is required to prepare an income tax return. Employers are required to send workers a W-2 for the calendar year (January 1 through December 31) by the following January 31. A sample Form W-2 is shown in Figure 2-3.4. The information on the form is sent to the federal, state, and local governments as well as to the worker. Multiple copies are provided for the worker to attach to tax forms and to keep on file. If the worker's tax returns are filed in paper form, the appropriate copy should be attached to each return.

Note that the amount shown in box 1, *Wages, tips, other compensation,* and in box 16, *State wages, tips, etc.,* is $25,688.00. This figure is the amount of gross pay less the money paid into a 401(k) plan. Money paid into a 401(k) plan is not subject to federal income taxes until it is withdrawn, usually during retirement. Some states also defer taxes on money paid into a 401(k) plan.

Form 1040EZ

Several different forms can be used to file a federal tax return. The form that should be used depends on the type of income and deductions claimed. Form 1040EZ, shown in Figure 2-3.5 on page 51, is designed for use by single and joint filers with no dependents. This is a simple, one-page form that can be completed using information found on the filer's Form W-2 and tax tables provided by the IRS. Refer to Figure 2-3.5 as you read the following points about Form 1040EZ. Note that this form

FIGURE 2-3.5   1040EZ TAX FORM

Department of the Treasury—Internal Revenue Service

Form **1040EZ**

Income Tax Return for Single and Joint Filers With No Dependents (99) **2005**

OMB No. 1545-0074

Label

(See page 11.)

Use the IRS label. Otherwise, please print or type.

Your first name and initial	Last name
Gloria M.	Perez

If a joint return, spouse's first name and initial	Last name

Home address (number and street). If you have a P.O. box, see page 11. | Apt. no.

123 Maple Street

City, town or post office, state, and ZIP code. If you have a foreign address, see page 11.

Monticello, KY 42633-0123

Your social security number

000 : 22 : 2105

Spouse's social security number

▲ You **must** enter your SSN(s) above. ▲

Checking a box below will not change your tax or refund.

Presidential Election Campaign (page 12) ▶

Check here if you, or your spouse if a joint return, want $3 to go to this fund? . . . ▶ ☐ **You**   ☐ **Spouse**

Income

Attach Form(s) W-2 here. Enclose, but do not attach, any payment.

1	Wages, salaries, and tips. This should be shown in box 1 of your Form(s) W-2. Attach your Form(s) W-2.	1	25,688	00
2	Taxable interest. If the total is over $1,500, you cannot use Form 1040EZ.	2		
3	Unemployment compensation and Alaska Permanent Fund dividends (see page 13).	3		
4	Add lines 1, 2, and 3. This is your **adjusted gross income.**	4	25,688	00
5	If someone can claim you (or your spouse if a joint return) as a dependent, check the applicable box(es) below and enter the amount from the worksheet on back. ☐ **You** ☐ **Spouse** If someone cannot claim you (or your spouse if a joint return), enter $8,200 if **single;** $16,400 if **married filing jointly.** See back for explanation.	5	8,200	00
6	Subtract line 5 from line 4. If line 5 is larger than line 4, enter -0-. This is your **taxable income.** ▶	6	17,488	00

Payments and tax

7	Federal income tax withheld from box 2 of your Form(s) W-2.	7	2,136	94
8a	**Earned income credit (EIC).**	8a		
b	Nontaxable combat pay election. 8b			
9	Add lines 7 and 8a. These are your **total payments.** ▶	9	2,136	94
10	**Tax.** Use the amount on **line 6 above** to find your tax in the tax table on pages 24–32 of the booklet. Then, enter the tax from the table on this line.	10	2,256	00

Refund

Have it directly deposited! See page 18 and fill in 11b, 11c, and 11d.

| 11a | If line 9 is larger than line 10, subtract line 10 from line 9. This is your **refund.** ▶ | 11a | | |

▶ b Routing number [ ][ ][ ][ ][ ][ ][ ][ ][ ]   ▶ c Type: ☐ Checking ☐ Savings

▶ d Account number [ ][ ][ ][ ][ ][ ][ ][ ][ ][ ][ ][ ][ ][ ][ ][ ][ ]

Amount you owe

| 12 | If line 10 is larger than line 9, subtract line 9 from line 10. This is the **amount you owe.** For details on how to pay, see page 19. ▶ | 12 | 119 | 06 |

Third party designee

Do you want to allow another person to discuss this return with the IRS (see page 19)? ☐ **Yes.** Complete the following. ☑ **No**

Designee's name ▶   Phone no. ▶ (   )   Personal identification number (PIN) ▶ [ ][ ][ ][ ][ ]

Sign here

Under penalties of perjury, I declare that I have examined this return, and to the best of my knowledge and belief, it is true, correct, and accurately lists all amounts and sources of income I received during the tax year. Declaration of preparer (other than the taxpayer) is based on all information of which the preparer has any knowledge.

Joint return? See page 11. Keep a copy for your records.

Your signature	Date	Your occupation	Daytime phone number
Gloria M. Perez	2/5/20–	Product assembler	(606) 555-0134
Spouse's signature. If a joint return, **both** must sign.	Date	Spouse's occupation	

Paid preparer's use only

Preparer's signature ▶		Date	Check if self-employed ☐	Preparer's SSN or PTIN
Firm's name (or yours if self-employed), address, and ZIP code ▶			EIN :	
			Phone no. ( )	

For Disclosure, Privacy Act, and Paperwork Reduction Act Notice, see page 23.

Cat. No. 11329W

Form **1040EZ** (2005)

51

is for 2005. The form for the current year may differ somewhat but will contain similar information.

- The filer's name, address, and Social Security number are entered in the boxes in the *Label* section near the top of the form. For a joint return, the spouse's name and Social Security number would also be included.
- In the *Income* section (lines 1 through 6), line 1 provides space to enter wages, salaries, and tips. Taxable interest of $1,500 or less can be entered on line 2.
- Line 3 is for unemployment payments received and Alaska Permanent Fund dividends.
- Line 4 is for adjusted gross income. This amount is the total of lines 1, 2, and 3.
- Line 5 shows the amount that can be deducted from adjusted gross income. For a single filer, as shown in the figure, the amount is $8,200. For a married couple filing jointly, the amount would be $16,400. This amount is not counted as part of the income on which tax must be paid.
- Line 6 should have a 0 (zero) if line 5 (the deduction) is larger than line 4. This means you have no taxable income. Line 6 should show the amount of adjusted gross income (line 4) minus the standard deduction (line 5) if the line 4 amount is larger than line 5. This amount is the taxable income.
- Line 7 in the *Payments and tax* section should show the amount of federal income tax withheld. This number comes from a Form W-2.
- Line 8a is for an earned income credit (EIC). This is a credit for certain people who work. The credit may give the filer a refund, even if the filer does not owe tax. A separate worksheet can be completed by those who think they may qualify for an EIC. Line 8b is for nontaxable combat pay.
- Line 9 is for total payments (lines 7 and 8a).
- Line 10 is for the tax on the taxable income amount. The tax is found by looking at tax tables provided by the IRS. If filing using a paper form, you can find the tax tables in the paper booklet. Tax tables can also be found on the IRS Web site.
- Line 11a in the *Refund* section is where a refund amount, if any, appears. This amount is found by subtracting tax (line 10) from total payments (line 9).
- Line 12 in the *Amount you owe* section is where the amount of tax the filer has to pay, if any, appears. This amount is found by subtracting total payments (line 9) from the tax amount (line 10).
- The *Third party designee* section is where the filer can allow another person to discuss the tax return with the IRS.
- The *Sign here* section is where the filer signs and dates the form.
- If another party fills out the tax return, that person's information should be recorded in the *Paid preparer's use only* section.

Other Forms

Form 1040A is a two-page form that allows more options for income and deductions to be entered. Some sections require the filer to attach additional forms, often called schedules. Taxpayers might use Form 1040A instead of Form 1040EZ if they have more than $1,500 in interest income. Form 1099-INT shows the interest income earned during the year. Form 1099-INT is shown in Figure 2-3.6 on page 53. This form is sent to individuals by the bank or other institution that pays the interest. If tax returns are filed in paper form, the appropriate copy of the form should be attached to the return.

FIGURE 2-3.6   *Form 1099-INT shows interest income earned.*

☐ VOID   ☐ CORRECTED

PAYER'S name, street address, city, state, ZIP code, and telephone no.	Payer's RTN (optional)	OMB No. 1545-0112	
First Bank 201 Main Street Monticello, KY 42633-0201		20**05** Form **1099-INT**	**Interest Income**

PAYER'S Federal identification number 00-0827701	RECIPIENT'S identification number 000-22-0011	**1** Interest income not included in box 3 $ 2,500.00		
RECIPIENT'S name Mr. William Patel		**2** Early withdrawal penalty $	**3** Interest on U.S. Savings Bonds and Treas. obligations $	**Copy C** **For Payer**
Street address (including apt. no.) 206 Brookhaven Drive		**4** Federal income tax withheld $	**5** Investment expenses $	For Privacy Act and Paperwork Reduction Act Notice, see the **2005 General Instructions for Forms 1099, 1098, 5498, and W-2G.**
City, state, and ZIP code Somerset, KY 42502-0206		**6** Foreign tax paid 	**7** Foreign country or U.S. possession	
Account number (see instructions) 4000326	2nd TIN not. ☐	$		

Form **1099-INT**   Department of the Treasury - Internal Revenue Service

Technology Corner

E-FILING

E-filing is a fast, safe way to file a federal tax return electronically. In 2005, more than 68 million Americans filed their tax returns electronically. Several options are available for using e-file. The filer can hire an *Authorized IRS e-file Provider*. This is a tax preparer who is approved by the IRS and can e-file the tax return for you. Another option is to purchase or get free tax preparation software that supports e-filing. Users prepare the return and e-file using a computer with a modem.[4]

Some people can prepare and file a tax return online. This option is called Free File. It is available to filers who have $50,000 or less of adjusted gross income. A link on the IRS Web site takes users to a list of companies that provide free filing services. Each company may also have a list of requirements, so a company must be chosen carefully. Once a company is selected, the user answers questions and provides the information needed to complete the return. The filing company sends the return to the IRS electronically.

Using e-file provides fast results for those entitled to a refund. Refunds are often received much more quickly than when a paper return is filed. Having the refund deposited directly into a checking account makes receiving refunds fast and safe.

---

[4] Internal Revenue Service, "Individual E-file Program Overview," http://www.irs.gov/efile/article/0,,id=118451,00.html (accessed March 9, 2006).

2-3 Activity 1   Can You Recall?

Answer these questions to help you recall what you have read. If you cannot answer a question, read the related section again.

1. How does the amount of tax a person pays affect the person's disposable income?
2. List three types of required deductions for taxes.
3. How is net pay calculated?
4. What is an exemption as it relates to a Form W-4?
5. Give an example of a person who may qualify as a dependent and can be claimed as an exemption on your Form W-4.
6. What form must a new employee complete to provide a Social Security number and claim status as a citizen of the United States, a lawful permanent resident, or an alien who is authorized to work?
7. Medicare taxes pay for what services?
8. To whom does workers' compensation pay benefits?
9. List four factors related to workplace accidents and injuries.
10. List the parts of a good emergency plan.
11. List three optional deductions that might be taken from a worker's pay.

2-3 Activity 2   Complete Employment Forms

When you begin a new job, you will be asked to complete a Form I-9 and a Form W-4. Practice completing these forms in this activity.

1. Open and print the PDF file *CH02 Form I-9* from the data files.
2. Complete the employee portion of the form at the top of page 2 using your information. If you do not have a Social Security number or want to keep your number private, use 000-22-1111 as the number. Refer to Figure 2-3.3 on page 47 for an example form.
3. Open and print the PDF file *CH02 Form W-4* from the data files.
4. Complete the Employee's Withholding Allowance Certificate portion of the form using your information. If you do not have a Social Security number or want to keep your number private, use 000-22-1111. For this activity, indicate that you are single, and claim one exemption. Refer to Figure 2-3.2 on page 46 for an example form.

EXPLORING CAREERS IN FINANCE

Do you like to work with numbers? Would you enjoy creating long-term plans to reach goals? If the answer is yes, a career in finance might be right for you. Jobs in finance involve managing money and other assets. Banking, investments, and insurance are part of this career area. Retirement planning and financial counseling are also part of the finance career cluster.

Jobs in finance are found in government and in private companies. This job area also presents good opportunities for entrepreneurs. For example, accountants and financial advisors may form their own small businesses. The need for jobs in the finance area is expected to grow in the next few years. The outlook will vary somewhat by job.

Skills Needed

Some of the skills and traits needed for a career in finance include the following:

- Math skills
- Analytical skills
- Communications skills
- Computer skills
- Decision-making skills
- Problem-solving skills
- Honesty
- Leadership

Job Titles

Many jobs are available in the finance area. Some job titles for this career area include the following:

- Accountant
- Auditor
- Bank teller
- Budget analyst
- Claims adjuster
- Financial manager
- Insurance underwriter
- Loan officer
- Personal financial advisor
- Stockbroker (securities sales agent)
- Tax examiner

Explore a Job

1. Choose a job in finance to explore further. Select a job from the list above, or choose another job in this career area.

2. Access the *Occupational Outlook Handbook* online. A link to the site is provided on the Web site for this textbook.

3. Search for more information about the job you selected to answer these questions:
   - What is the nature of the work this job involves?
   - What is the job outlook for this job?
   - What training or qualifications are needed for this job?
   - What are the median annual earnings for this job (given in the Earnings section of the Web page)?

55

Review

Summary

- Sources of earned income include wages, salaries, tips, commissions, and self-employment. Earned income is subject to income taxes and other taxes.
- Minimum wage is the lowest hourly pay rate allowed by law. Many states have minimum wage laws that set a rate higher than the federal rate.
- By law, overtime pay of at least $1\frac{1}{2}$ times the regular rate must be paid for hours worked above 40 work hours in a week.
- Networking is the process of making contacts and building relationships with other people.
- Disposable income refers to the money a person has available to spend or save after taxes have been paid.
- Benefits are forms of pay other than salary or wages. Benefits can directly increase disposable income or can have the effect of increasing disposable income.
- Benefits such as profit sharing and retirement accounts provide valuable resources for workers later in their lives.
- Unearned income is money or benefits received without working directly to earn them. Examples of unearned income are interest and dividends.
- Paying taxes reduces the disposable income of an individual. This is the main cost of paying taxes for an individual.
- Government transfer payments are funded by taxes collected by the government. This is a benefit of paying taxes.
- Government goods and services are available to all people who qualify, regardless of taxes paid. This is a benefit or paying taxes.
- Required deductions for taxes reduce disposable income.
- Workplace safety is required by law; it is everyone's responsibility.
- If you are a U.S. citizen or resident, whether you must file a federal income tax return depends upon your gross income, your filing status, your age, and whether you are a dependent.
- E-filing is a fast, safe way to file a federal tax return electronically.

Key Terms

benefits	excise tax	sick leave
cafeteria plan	minimum wage	tax
commission	overtime pay	tip
disposable income	paid holidays	transfer payments
dividend	personal leave	unearned income
entrepreneur	profit	

ACTIVITY 1
Review Key Terms

Use the key terms from Chapter 2 to complete the following sentences:

1. A(n) _____, or business owner, takes the risks of owning and operating a business.

2. Money received from sources other than working in a job is called _____.

3. Money left over to spend or save after taxes are paid is called _____.

4. Most companies have _____, such as Christmas, Veterans Day, or Memorial Day.

5. _____ is time away from work for personal reasons.

6. The lowest pay rate allowed by law for each hour of work is called _____.

7. Money received from customers, called a(n) _____, is based on quality of service.

8. _____ are forms of pay other than salary or wages, such as paid vacations or holidays.

9. Days you are paid for even though you are not at work due to illness are called _____.

10. Earnings that are paid only when efforts result in a sale are called a(n) _____.

11. Earnings paid when an employee works more than 40 hours in a 1-week period are called _____.

12. Money or benefits received from government without working for them when they are received are called _____.

13. A(n) _____ is cash paid to stockholders of a corporation.

14. A benefits package, called a(n) _____, is where employees can pick and choose the benefit options they want to have.

15. _____ are taxes charged on the purchase of specific goods, such as motor fuel, cigarettes, and alcohol.

16. A(n) _____ is a required payment for the support of a government.

17. _____ is the amount left after all costs are deducted from the income of a business.

57

ACTIVITY 2
Math Minute

Complete these problems to build your math skills. You may use spreadsheet software or complete the problems manually.

Gross pay includes regular hours times regular pay, plus overtime hours times overtime pay. The overtime pay rate is 1½ times the regular rate of pay.

1. Max worked 44 hours last week. His hourly rate is $6.00. What was his gross pay (regular pay plus overtime pay)?

2. Elaine worked 48 hours last week. Her hourly rate is $7.50. What was her gross pay?

3. Jackson worked 44 hours last week. His hourly rate is $8.60. He has the following deductions taken from his gross earnings. What was his net pay?
   - Federal income tax withheld at the rate of 10%
   - Social Security tax withheld at the rate of 6.2%
   - Medicare tax withheld at the rate of 1.45%
   - Health insurance premiums of $12.80
   - Union dues of $8.50

4. Rachelle worked 46 hours last week; her hourly rate is $7.90. She has the following deductions taken from her gross earnings. What was her net pay?
   - Federal income tax withheld at the rate of 10%
   - Social Security tax withheld at the rate of 6.2%
   - Medicare tax withheld at the rate of 1.45%
   - Health insurance premiums of $11.20

ACTIVITY 3
Professional Careers

   academic.cengage.com/school/pfl

Work with a classmate to complete this activity. Pick a career in which the worker earns a salary, such as teacher, manager, or accountant. Do some online and library research or interview a worker in this profession to answer the following questions:

1. How many hours a week does a beginning-level employee work?
2. What is the beginning pay level?
3. What kinds of benefits currently are being offered to people in this profession?
4. Would you like to do this kind of work? Why or why not?

58

ACTIVITY 4
Unemployment Compensation

 academic.cengage.com/school/pfl

When workers are laid off from their jobs, they may be entitled to unemployment compensation benefits. These benefits are taxable income. Each state has unemployment compensation rules; the federal government also has a program.

Visit your state Web site to find out how unemployment compensation laws and insurance work in your state. Find answers to the following questions:

1. What are the requirements for drawing unemployment benefits?
2. How is the amount of the benefit determined?
3. For how long can a person draw benefits?

ACTIVITY 5
Evaluate and Select Benefits

1. Open and print the *Word* file *CH02 Benefits* found in the data files. A cafeteria plan of benefit choices, along with their dollar value, is shown in the document.
2. Assume that your salary is $1,600 per month and that your total benefits package (including salary) can total up to $2,000.
3. Review and evaluate the list of benefits offered. Decide which ones would be of the most value to you. You can go over $2,000 in total pay and benefits costs only if you wish to have any payments over $2,000 deducted from your paycheck.
4. Indicate your choices on the form.

ACTIVITY 6
Complete Tax Form 1040EZ

1. Open and print the PDF file *CH02 Form 1040EZ* found in the data files.
2. Enter your name, address, and Social Security number in the boxes in the *Label* section of the form. If you do not have a Social Security number or want to keep your number private, use 000-22-1111 as the number. You are filing a single return.
3. Your Form W-2 shows that you have $29,521.00 of taxable income. Enter this amount on line 1.
4. Your 1099-INT shows that you have $421.00 in taxable interest. Enter this amount on line 2.

59

5. Find the total of lines 1, 2, and 3. Enter the total on line 4 for adjusted gross income.

6. On line 5, enter **$8,200.00**, the amount for a single filer. This amount is not counted as part of the income on which tax must be paid.

7. Subtract the amount on line 5 from the amount on line 4 to find your taxable income. Enter this amount on line 6.

8. Your Form W-2 shows federal income tax withheld as $2,850.00. Enter this amount on line 7.

9. Enter the amount shown on line 7 on line 9 for total payments.

10. Open the PDF file *2005 Partial Tax Tables* from the data files. Find the amount of tax that applies to the amount shown on line 6. Enter this amount on line 10.

11. Subtract the amount on line 9 from the amount on line 10. This is the amount of tax you owe. Enter the amount on line 12.

12. Sign and date the form in the *Sign here* section. Enter **Sales Associate** for your occupation. Enter your phone number.

ACTIVITY 7
Complete Tax Form 1040A

1. Open and print the PDF file *CH02 Form 1040A* found in the data files.

2. Enter your name, address, and Social Security number in the boxes in the *Label* section of the form. If you do not have a Social Security number or want to keep your number private, use 000-22-1111 as the number. You are filing a single return.

3. In the *Filing status* section, place an **x** in box 1 for Single.

4. In the *Exemptions* section, place an **x** in box 6a for Yourself. Enter **1** in the blank at the right (*Boxes checked on 6a and 6b*). Enter **1** in the box at the right on line 6d.

5. Your Form W-2 shows that you have $28,429.00 of taxable income. Enter this amount on line 7.

6. Your 1099-INT shows that you have $1,825.00 in taxable interest. Enter this amount on line 8a.

7. Find the total of lines 7 and 8a. Enter the total on line 15 for total income. Enter the same amount on lines 21 and 22 for adjusted gross income.

8. On line 24, enter **$5,000.00** for the standard deduction for a single filer.

9. Subtract the amount on line 24 from the amount on line 22. Enter this amount on line 25.

10. On line 26, enter **$3,200.00**, the amount for one exemption.

11. Subtract the amount on line 26 from the amount on line 25 to find your taxable income. Enter this amount on line 27.

12. Open the PDF file *2005 Partial Tax Tables* from the data files. Find the amount of tax that applies to the amount shown on line 27. Enter this amount on line 28. Enter the same amount on lines 36 and 38.

13. Your Form W-2 shows federal income tax withheld as $2,726.00. Enter this amount on line 39. Enter the same amount on line 43 for total payments.

14. Subtract the amount on line 43 from the amount on line 38. This is the amount of tax you owe. Enter this amount on line 47.

15. Sign and date the form in the *Sign here* section. Enter **Sales Associate** for your occupation. Enter your phone number.

ACTIVITY 8
Emergency Plans

 Work in a group with three or four other students to complete this activity.

1. You have learned that safety procedures and emergency plans are important in the workplace. Such plans are also important in schools. Consult your school handbook, the school Web site, or other materials available to learn about the emergency plans for your school. You may need to talk with a principal, counselor, or school safety or security officer.

2. Choose one of the following situations and find the plan that should be followed in that situation. Be prepared to share the main points of the plan with the class.
   o Fire in the building
   o Severe weather (tornado, hurricane, blizzard)
   o Bomb threat
   o Hostage situation
   o Chemical spill or other dangerous substance release
   o Bus accident
   o Other emergency

61

Income and Purchasing Power

© Digital Vision

hapter 3 is about prices and how inflation affects what consumers can buy. Inflation is an increase in general price levels. Inflation erodes the value of money and takes away purchasing power. There are different types of inflation. Each type works in a different way to cause prices to rise. Inflation also affects the value of money, whether it is money you will receive in the future or money you have now. Selling strategies are used to convince consumers to buy goods and services. Buying strategies of consumers help them prepare for and make wise buying choices.

ONLINE RESOURCES

Personal Financial Literacy Web site:

Vocabulary Flashcards

Sort It Out: Income and Purchasing Power

Chapter 3 Supplemental Activity

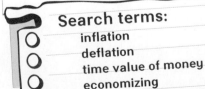

Search terms:
- inflation
- deflation
- time value of money
- economizing

Inflation and Prices

OUTCOMES

- Define inflation and explain how it is measured.
- Describe types of inflation.
- Describe the causes of inflation.
- Explain how inflation and employment levels are related.
- Explain how inflation affects spending, saving, and investing decisions.

WHAT IS INFLATION?

Price is the amount a buyer pays for a product or service. **Inflation** is an increase in the general level of prices for goods and services. Inflation reflects how much prices are rising. When prices are rising faster than income, buyers lose purchasing power. In other words, the money workers earn will buy less as prices rise.

Changing prices affect the spending power of both producers and consumers. The economy changes over time based on events and on habits and attitudes of producers and consumers. For example, an event such as a flood or hurricane that wipes out crops may affect prices. Habits explain how people react to changes in the supply of goods, world events, and their individual situations. For example, when consumers think they may soon lose their jobs, they tend to buy less and to buy different goods. Attitudes reflect how people think about their future and about the product being sold. Will the product help me stay healthy? Is it worth the price? These are questions a consumer might ask that reflect attitudes. All these factors affect prices and inflation.

Measuring Inflation

Inflation is measured by the U.S. government. The measurement tool used is called the Consumer Price Index (CPI). The CPI uses a list of goods and services that are commonly bought by consumers. The index measures changes in price from a base or starting point in time to the current time. For example, if the price of an item was $1.00 in the base year and it is now $1.12, that is a 12 percent increase in the price. If the increase happened in just one year and it happened to all the goods on the list, the inflation rate for that year would also be 12 percent. You can learn more about the CPI at the Bureau of Labor Statistics Web site as shown in Figure 3-1.1 on page 64.

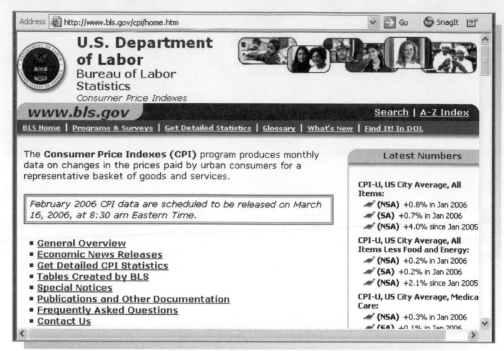

Source: U.S. Department of Labor, Bureau of Labor Statistics, http://www.bls.gov/cpi/home.htm (accessed March 14, 2006).

The government also gathers information about consumer spending. Its surveys measure spending habits of consumers and track data such as income.

Types of Inflation

Businesses base price decisions in part on what consumers are buying and not buying. Several price change patterns may happen over time. These patterns result in varying types of inflation.

Consumer buying habits change over time.

DISINFLATION

Disinflation occurs when prices are rising, but at a slow rate. In other words, prices are rising, but at a decreasing rate. Some products and services do not increase in price as fast as others. Often, this happens when demand for a product is not the same throughout the year. For example, in spring and summer, the price of swimsuits may be high and rising. In fall and winter, however, if the price is rising, it is doing so at a much slower rate.

REFLATION

Reflation occurs when prices are high but then drop due to lower demand; then they are restored to the previous high level. Perhaps you have heard a news reporter use this term to describe crude oil prices. Reflation can happen when the available supply of a product, such as oil, goes up and down. Reflation can also happen when consumers temporarily stop buying a product or service. Then, for some reason, they start buying it again. For example, when gas prices surge, people may not buy as many big cars and trucks that use a lot of gas. They wait to see what will happen with gas prices. When gas prices fall, they begin buying large vehicles again.

HYPERINFLATION

When prices are rising so rapidly they are out of control, this is called **hyperinflation**. In the United States, there have been periods of double-digit inflation (10 percent or higher in a year). However, hyperinflation rates are much higher. Although there is no set rule, many economists consider inflation rates of 50 percent or higher to be hyperinflation. Some countries have had rates of several hundred percent per month. For example, in Germany after World War I in 1923, the monthly inflation rate reached over 300 percent.[1]

© Getty Images/PhotoDisc

When gas prices surge, car buyers pay more attention to gas mileage.

65

---

[1] Michael K. Salemi, "Hyperinflation," *The Concise Encyclopedia of Economics*, http://www.econlib.org/library/enc/Hyperinflation.html (accessed March 14, 2006).

The effects of very high inflation rates can be devastating. With hyperinflation, prices are rising so rapidly that consumers spend their money as fast as they can. They do this because they fear that prices will be even higher if they wait. This spending leads to even more inflation. Then people are unable to buy the goods they need to live comfortably.

DEFLATION

Deflation is the lowering of overall price levels. It is the opposite of inflation. In other words, prices are going down. This happens in periods when events cause consumers to buy less and when producers are able and willing to provide goods at lower prices.

Some products go down in price over time even when the country is not in a time of deflation. For example, a computer that uses a new, faster processor may sell at a high price when it first comes on the market. A year later, the same computer may sell for hundreds of dollars less. The price is lower because it is no longer the newest, fastest computer available. Other, newer models have been released.

CAUSES OF INFLATION

Inflation can be caused by different factors in the economy. Consumers may want to buy more goods or services than are available, driving up prices. Producers may have to pay more to produce products and may need to raise prices. Both situations can lead to inflation.

Demand-Pull Inflation

The most common type of inflation is called demand pull. **Demand-pull inflation** occurs when consumers want to buy more goods and services than producers supply. Consumers may spend their income as soon as it is received, and they are willing to spend future income (credit) as well. This spending causes businesses to scramble to meet the demand for goods. Because products are selling so quickly, businesses are able to raise prices to balance supply with demand and to make bigger profits. This type of inflation is often described as "too many dollars chasing too few goods."

Cost-Push Inflation

Cost-push inflation occurs when producers raise prices because their costs to create products are rising. For example, when wages go up, the cost of producing a product goes up. Producers may then raise prices. If producers did not raise prices, profits would shrink. Cost-push inflation occurs when cost increases are not offset with greater output that lowers the cost of each unit made.

Productivity is a measure of the efficiency with which goods and services are made. When productivity rises, the cost of a wage or other increase is offset by producing more and better products. In this case, inflation (price increases) does not occur. Instead, more and better products and services are made at the same price level.

66

Real-Cost Inflation

As resources diminish or become harder to get, prices rise in the form of **real-cost inflation**. For example, when there is less natural gas, or companies have to dig deeper to get it, this causes the cost of providing natural gas to rise. Over time, resources that are in high demand may shrink in supply. With a growing population's ever-increasing demands, this may happen with many products. To avoid this type of inflation, people must find other resources to use instead of the one that is scarce.

© Getty Images/PhotoDisc

Finding alternate sources of energy, such as wind power, will help control energy prices.

INFLATION AND EMPLOYMENT

Economists think there is a relationship between inflation and employment. In times when prices are high, producers often make more money. They are able to hire more people. Thus, higher inflation also means higher employment. When inflation is reduced, people may be laid off. This is because prices are not increasing, and therefore profits are not increasing. With lower profits, producers may start laying off workers.

In times of zero inflation, price levels are flat (not increasing or decreasing). Businesses may not be able to afford to hire workers. Thus, mild inflation of 2 or 3 percent can be good for the economy.

INFLATION AFFECTS SPENDING, SAVING, AND INVESTING

Inflation has a negative effect on the value of money. As general price levels rise, the value of money falls. Thus, employees who work for a set rate of pay are able to buy less in times of inflation when prices rise. This is because some jobs provide pay raises only annually or less often. While prices are rising on the goods and services employees buy, their pay is not rising at the same rate. Thus, consumers have two choices: they can buy less, or they can borrow money to continue the same level of spending. Either way, it takes more money to keep getting the same amount of goods and services.

Inflation also affects the amount of money consumers may be able to save. In times of rising prices, consumers may have to use more of their disposable income to buy needed goods and services. Less money may be available for saving.

The **time value of money** is a concept that says a dollar you will receive in the future is worth less than a dollar you receive today. This assumes that prices are rising. For example, suppose you loan a friend $20 today. Your friend promises to pay back the $20 one year from today. The money you receive one year from today will not have the same value as the money you loaned your friend today. This is because prices will be higher one year from today, and the money will not buy as many goods one year from now as it will today.

Consumers consider the expected rate of inflation when choosing investments. They want to invest their money in a way that will provide a return that is greater than the rate of inflation. For example, suppose the inflation rate over 5 years is 5 percent. Investments such as savings accounts, stocks, or bonds must have a growth rate of at least 5 percent for the money invested to keep its purchasing power.

68

When inflation is rising too fast, it hurts consumers. Two tools are used in the United States to manage the effects of rising prices. These tools are called monetary policy and fiscal policy.

Monetary policy refers to actions by the Federal Reserve System. The Federal Reserve System is commonly called the Fed. The Fed is the central bank in the United States. The Fed was created by Congress in 1913. It has many roles, including controlling the money supply. One thing the Fed does is watch the economy. When the Fed sees that prices are rising too fast, it tries to slow them down. One way to slow rising prices is by raising interest rates. When interest rates increase, both individuals and businesses find it more expensive to borrow money to buy goods and services. This slows down spending. As you learned earlier, demand-pull inflation is caused by spending in the economy.

There are several types of interest rates that are controlled by the Fed. The discount rate is the rate that banks have to pay to borrow money from the Fed. Banks borrow money when they have the opportunity to make loans but do not have enough cash on hand. Banks are required to have a certain amount of cash on hand, called reserves. If these reserves go below the required amount, banks must borrow money.

The federal funds rate is the rate at which banks can borrow from the excess reserves of other banks. For example, if one bank has more money than it needs, it can loan that extra money to other banks.

The prime rate is the rate that banks charge to their most creditworthy business customers. When the discount rate increases, the prime rate also goes up. The prime rate is usually 3 percent (or more) higher than the discount rate or the federal funds rate.

Fiscal policy refers to actions taken by the federal government to manage the economy. To help curb inflation, one thing the government can do is raise taxes. When taxes go up, people have less money to spend. This slows down inflation (demand-pull). On the other hand, the economy may be sluggish because people are not buying. The government can increase spending by lowering tax rates. This gives consumers more money to spend. These actions, taken together, either speed up or slow down spending. Spending can affect inflation because it can cause prices to rise.

3-1 REVIEW

3-1 Activity 1 Can You Recall?

Answer these questions to help you recall what you have read. If you cannot answer a question, read the related section again.

1. What is inflation? How is it measured?
2. Explain how disinflation, reflation, and hyperinflation differ.
3. What is deflation?
4. How does demand-pull inflation differ from cost-push inflation?
5. Explain how inflation and employment levels are related.
6. How does inflation affect spending, saving, and investing decisions?
7. Explain what is meant by the time value of money.

3-1 Activity 2 Inflation and Prices

When prices go up, your purchasing power goes down. Identify two items you or your family buys regularly, such as gasoline for a car. Then, for each item, answer the questions that follow:

1. Has the price gone up or down in the last year?
2. How much is the price change (in dollars and cents)? What percentage increase or decrease is this amount?
3. What effect has the price change had on your spending habits? Have you purchased less of that product? Have you purchased less of something else in order to keep buying that product?
4. In the long run, what will you do if the price keeps rising? For example, will you find substitutes, stop using the product, or give up something else in order to be able to buy this product?

70

Price and Demand

OUTCOMES

- Describe three methods of setting prices in a market economy.
- Explain how consumers' buying strategies affect demand and prices in a market economy.

SETTING PRICES IN A MARKET ECONOMY

In a market economy, prices are affected by a number of factors. Some factors are controlled by producers. Consumers' actions also affect prices in the marketplace. In Chapter 1, you learned that demand is the willingness and ability of consumers to buy products and services. If consumers' demand for a product is low, prices may fall or the product may no longer be produced.

Sellers offer products to consumers at certain prices. Sellers must be careful, however, in setting a price. If the price is too high, consumers may not buy the product. They may not be able to afford the price, or they may simply think the price is too high for the value received. If the price is too low, the demand for the product may be low. Consumers may think the product has a low value and, again, may not buy the

Demand for products affects prices.

Item	Cost
Wood, 6 board feet at $3.96 per foot	$23.76
Labor, 2 hours at $10.00 per hour	20.00
Paint, varnish, nails, and glue	1.24
Indirect costs (benefits of workers, rent, insurance, and general overhead)	12.00
Total cost	$57.00
Markup (40%)	22.80
Price	$79.80

product. Also, if the price is too low, the company may not make any profit on the sale of the product. Setting the right price for a product can be tricky. Having products available at the right price is critical to business success.

Companies use different methods to set prices. Sometimes more than one method is considered when setting a price. Sellers want to set a price that will support the greatest demand and will be profitable. Some methods of setting prices are discussed in the following sections.

Cost-Plus Pricing

One way that sellers set prices is called cost-plus pricing. **Cost-plus pricing** computes the total cost of making and delivering a product. Then a percentage of that amount, called markup, is added to the cost. The markup is also called the profit margin or gross profit. Using this method ensures that the company will make a certain profit if the product is successful. An example of cost-plus pricing is shown in Figure 3-2.1.

A mall provides many places to buy goods and services.

© Getty Images/PhotoDisc

Value-Based Pricing

Using **value-based pricing**, the seller tries to determine how much consumers will be willing to pay for the product. In other words, it will be sold for the highest price that the market (consumers) will bear. If consumers value the product or service, they will pay whatever price is set, within reasonable limits. This is especially true of new, high-tech, and fad items. Consumers are willing to pay high prices because there are no less expensive choices.

Companies may do market research to determine what the demand for a product will be. They also want to learn how much consumers will be willing to pay for the product. Perhaps you have been asked to complete a market survey while shopping at a mall. Telephone and Internet surveys are other popular ways that companies learn about consumers' wants and needs.

Market-Based Pricing

With **market-based pricing**, the price is set to be competitive with prices of similar products currently being sold. If one business charges a lot more than others do for a similar

Many successful businesses have a Web site. Retail Web sites provide an alternate location for consumers to buy goods and services. The total amount paid for goods may be slightly higher because of shipping costs. Some companies may not keep all types or models of their products in their stores. They may offer additional products or more sizes or colors online. Some companies sell only online. They do not have a store that consumers can visit. With online buying, consumers have the convenience of buying products without leaving home.

Retail Web sites typically provide full descriptions of products, including pictures. Shoppers need a computer with enough speed and memory to open Web pages for viewing products. Shoppers can save items to a virtual shopping cart. The items can usually be purchased at the time of selection or saved for later access. This allows buyers to shop online at their convenience.

When shoppers visit retail Web sites, they can often set up an account. The account usually has a user name and a password. When the site is visited again, the shopper enters the user name and password. This prevents having to enter a name and shipping address each time an item is bought from the site. Cookies may also be placed on the shopper's computer. Cookies are small text files that contain information about the user. Cookies often track the Web pages or sites that a user visits. Retailers can use this information to suggest products or to target advertising. For example, suppose the shopper looked at several mystery novels on the Web site for a bookseller. The next time the shopper logs in at that site, a suggested list of mystery novels may appear.

Shoppers who buy products online need a debit card, a credit card, or a bank account. The purchase is billed to the card or deducted from the bank account. Merchandise is shipped to the buyer's address. The goods take a few days to arrive and are delivered by the U.S. Postal Service or a private delivery company.

Many people use the Internet for comparison shopping. They learn about product prices and features without feeling pressured to buy. A major advantage of the Internet is that it is open 24 hours a day. Consumers can shop at their convenience.

product, consumers are likely to buy from the other companies that offer a lower price. The manufacturer or retailer simply decides whether or not it can provide the product or service at that existing price and still make a profit. This is the easiest form of setting a price. It helps producers or sellers decide what products to include in their marketing mix. The marketing mix is the group of products or services offered for sale by a business at any point in time.

A seller may introduce a new product at a higher price than similar products on the market. In this case, the seller tries to show how the new product is different from or better than other products. For example, many models of digital phones are available. A seller offering a new phone might cite the phone's small size or new features. The phone might take digital pictures or send text messages. These features are advertised to

73

make the new phone seem more desirable. The seller may use these new or added features to justify a somewhat higher price. This strategy is not always successful. Consumers may not think the new features are useful or worth the higher price.

BUYING STRATEGIES AFFECT DEMAND

Consumers play a vital role in setting prices in a market economy. Consumers use two basic strategies when buying goods and services. They try to spend as little as possible, or they try to get as much value as they can for the money they spend. These two approaches are not mutually exclusive; that is, buyers do not use just one plan or the other for all purchases. Consumers can use the plan that best fits their needs for different goods and services.

Economizing

Consumers are **economizing** when they are saving as much as possible and spending money only when necessary. Using this approach, consumers wait until it is necessary to buy a product. Then they buy as little as possible and at the lowest price. They do not buy large quantities or more than is needed at the present time. They simply try to spend as little money as they can for the needed product.

Most people go through periods of time when they economize. Others follow this spending pattern all the time. Economizing has its advantages. For example, holding back on spending often results in not buying some items at all. Economizing can lead to savings and better buying habits.

For some people, economizing is the only plan that allows them to meet their basic needs. For other people, economizing is a strategy used during certain times as a way to save money for later spending or investment. When economizing, people may spend little or no money on luxuries. This can lower the demand for luxury items. People may also spend less on items for basic needs, such as food or clothing. Lower demand for products may lead to lower prices.

Optimizing

Another spending strategy is called optimizing. **Optimizing** means getting the highest value for the money spent. High value may come in the form of a large number of products or services or in the form of high-quality products or services. For example, if a product is on sale, is used a lot, and stores well, a large quantity can be purchased. The cost per item will be lower when the item is

Economizing means spending as little as possible.

bought in quantity. When customers are optimizing, demand is higher when prices are lower. Consumers will buy more products to take advantage of lower prices.

Consumers should be careful not to let optimizing lead to overspending. Spending too freely can lead to poor buying habits. Shoppers may buy items they do not need simply because the items are a bargain. Items that have been stockpiled may be used more freely than usual because the consumer has a large quantity of the item. Overspending can also lead to credit problems. Using both economizing and optimizing strategies at the proper times may be the best solution for many people.

© Digital Vision

Optimizing means getting the highest value for the money spent.

Success Skills

TIME MANAGEMENT

Consumers often buy things when they are in a hurry. Those purchase decisions are sometimes not the best decisions. Through time management, a person can make better decisions because she or he has planned the purchase and has had sufficient time to make a good choice. Using time management strategies can help a person be more productive in school, work, and personal activities.

Time management involves several key points:

- Be aware of how you are using your time. This is the first step toward managing your activities to use time wisely.
- Identify *peak* performance times, when you are most productive, and *weak* performance times. Schedule important activities at peak times.
- Use a daily or weekly planner to keep track of important dates and times.
- Keep a to-do list; mark off items as they are completed.
- Prioritize your activities so you get the important ones done first.
- Break large projects or tasks into smaller parts, and plan time for completing each part.
- Save some time for doing things you enjoy.
- Schedule times for shopping and making purchases.
- Do not rush or be pressured for time while shopping.

3-2 Activity 1 Can You Recall?

Answer these questions to help you recall what you have read.
If you cannot answer a question, read the related section again.

1. How are prices set when using the cost-plus pricing strategy?
2. How is a market-based pricing strategy different from a value-based pricing strategy?
3. Why might shoppers want to set up an account on a retail Web site they use often?
4. What is economizing? How does using this buying strategy affect demand and prices in a market economy?
5. What is optimizing? How does using this buying strategy affect demand and prices in a market economy?
6. How can using effective time management strategies lead to better buying decisions?

3-2 Activity 2 Prices and Spending

List three items your family has purchased in the last year—
something with a high price ($100 or more), something that cost
between $5 and $50, and something with a low price (under $5).
Answer the questions that follow for each item.

1. How do you think the price was set for this product—using cost-plus, value-based, or market-based pricing? Why?
2. Was this item purchased as a result of economizing or optimizing?
3. If you had to make this purchase decision again, would you choose the same item? Why or why not?

76

Selling and Buying Strategies

OUTCOMES

- Describe strategies used by businesses to sell goods and services.
- Explain how businesses are able to create demand for a product.
- Discuss strategies buyers can use before, during, and after a purchase.

SELLING GOODS AND SERVICES

Business owners take the risk of bringing products and services to the market. To stay in business, they must sell those products or services to customers and make a profit. Sellers use other strategies, in addition to price, to promote the sale of goods and services to customers.

Convenience

One strategy companies use to promote sales is to make shopping convenient and pleasant for customers. A store location that is easy for customers to visit makes shopping more convenient. A clean, comfortable, and safe place to buy goods and services makes the shopping experience more pleasant for customers. Friendly and helpful salesclerks also help promote sales.

An important part of convenience is the payment method. Most businesses allow for cash and credit purchases. This includes the use of debit and national credit cards, as well as writing checks or having store credit.

Customer Service

Businesses depend on good customer service to promote sales. Good customer service includes a lot of things. A warm, friendly greeting and prompt and courteous help when it is needed are examples of good customer service.

Good customer service increases the chances that shoppers will return to the store to buy again. Satisfied customers also tell others about their experience. This word-of-mouth promotion is good for sales.

Poor customer service may keep shoppers from returning to buy again. Even if prices are low or the store is convenient for the shoppers, they may not return if they had a bad experience. Dissatisfied customers also tell people about their bad experience. This message can be very harmful to future sales.

Advertising stimulates interest in buying products that meet needs or wants.

Meeting Needs and Wants

Businesses try to make available to customers the types of products they need or want. Making the right products available increases the chances of business success.

Some products meet basic food, clothing, and shelter needs. Everyone needs to be able to eat and stay warm and safe. Examples of products that fill basic needs include groceries, clothing, shoes, and housing.

Products that save time are valuable to consumers. Often, these same products also save energy. Examples of products that save time and energy include washing machines, power tools, and food processors.

Products that make users feel or look younger or more attractive are appealing to consumers. These products have emotional appeal. Although the products may fill wants rather than needs, they represent great profits to sellers. Examples of these products include makeup and hair dye. Products that support good health and help users feel better also appeal to consumers. These products tend to be more expensive and specialized. Examples are vitamins and organic foods.

Creating Demand

To sell goods, businesses may need to create or stimulate demand. **Advertising** is a method of informing consumers and promoting and selling products. Advertising, also called ads, comes in many different forms. They all have the same purpose—to get people to buy.

NEWSPAPERS AND MAGAZINES

Placing ads in newspapers and magazines is a popular way to reach large numbers of people. The ad may promote a product or a company. It may be a short one-item ad or a full-page color ad showing many products. Typically, ads include special prices, coupons, or other incentives to bring customers into the store.

78

TELEVISION AND RADIO

Television ads are very expensive. However, they reach large numbers of people. Television ads are written to appeal to a target audience. A **target audience** is a specific group of people who are likely to be watching and are likely to buy the product. For example, different people watch various TV programs or tend to watch TV at certain times. Some people watch news shows. Others watch on Saturday mornings or on Super Bowl Sunday. Companies design ads that will appeal to these target audiences. They run the ads on certain shows and at specific times.

Radio advertising attracts audiences with special interests. Radio programs range widely in content. News programs, talk shows, religious messages, and many types of music can be found on radio. Radio ads often involve appeals to emotions. They may use slogans or have catchy tunes. As with TV ads, radio ads target people who are thought likely to listen to a particular program.

THE INTERNET

The Internet is a popular place to shop. Many types of advertising can be found on the Internet. The ads help sell products by informing shoppers and encouraging them to buy. Banner ads span the top, bottom, or sides of a Web page or site users visit. They have bold statements or pictures that grab the user's attention. Pop-up ads appear while the user is visiting Web sites or browsing. They pop onto the screen. The user must click *No* or a similar command to close them. Some people buy special software to block pop-up ads.

Many online retailers customize ads to shoppers who have visited their site. The user logs in and does some shopping. The site tracks the products clicked and Web pages visited. The retailer may send the shopper an e-mail offering a product or service that he or she showed interest in previously. Such e-mails often offer specials, such as free shipping or a price reduction for online purchases.

Building Communications Skills

CREATIVE LISTENING

Creative listening is a skill used to solve problems. With creative listening, a person searches through information and forms questions to ask. The listener evaluates what has been heard and makes a decision or choice. Creative listening is a highly active process that involves logic as well as listening.

For example, suppose you are listening to a debate about a new law that has been proposed. One side is listing its positive features and all the reasons why you should vote in favor of it. The other side is explaining all the bad things that will happen if the law is enacted. In order for you to decide, you must listen carefully, make sure you have accurate information, and come to a decision that will be your vote. Creative listening requires that you understand who is proposing the law and what they have to gain. You also need to know who is opposing the law and what they have to lose. By practicing creative listening, you can reach an informed decision.

Good buying strategies help consumers spend money more wisely.

© Getty Images/PhotoDisc

Other Web sellers place cookies on the shopper's computer. Cookies enable the seller to recognize the shopper in the future. They may also contain information about products the user viewed or bought in the past. Some online sellers share this data with other retailers. Shoppers may get e-mails, pop-ups, or other forms of targeted ads from online sellers they have never visited.

Some sellers use electronic newsletters sent monthly or at other set times to encourage customers to buy. These ads feature pictures and prices of products. Users sign up to receive them and are usually able to cancel them if desired.

DIRECT ADVERTISING OR SALES

Direct advertising takes the product directly to consumers. It involves actions such as sending free samples in the mail and giving out samples in a store. This form of advertising allows the customer to try the product.

One form of direct advertising is direct sales. A salesperson goes door-to-door to give customers a catalog or to show them a product. Another method is holding a party to sell products to a group of friends. This approach takes the product directly to the consumer, using a person-to-person approach.

OTHER TYPES OF ADVERTISING

There are many other forms of advertising. Some are subtle and indirect, such as placing coupons in entertainment books. Others are up-front and bold, such as billboards. A brochure listing used cars or houses for sale is another method. Whatever the medium, ads catch the consumer's attention and stimulate interest in buying a product or service.

BUYING STRATEGIES

Sellers have strategies to encourage you to buy. You should have a plan to maximize your buying power. Some ideas to help you in your role as consumer are given in the following sections.

Before You Shop

Before going to the store, prepare a shopping list of the things you need. Base your list on well-thought-out ideas, such as a menu plan, so you can resist impulse buying. Decide ahead of time what you will buy and about how much you will spend. Also plan how you will pay for the items. Planning ahead will help you avoid overspending or buying items you do not need.

For major purchases, you may deal with a salesclerk who is paid on commission. The clerk may encourage you to spend more than you

80

intended. Plan your strategy ahead of time. Before you leave home, decide what you want or need and how much you are willing to pay. Prepare questions to ask. Do not allow a salesclerk to convince you to spend more than you planned.

While You Shop

While at the store, stick to your list. Compute unit prices, and make sure you are getting the best deal for the products you are buying. Do not go grocery shopping when you are hungry—being hungry will affect your choices. If you have made decisions about how much you will spend for an item, stick with them. Do not make on-the-spot decisions that you may regret later or allow yourself to be pressured into buying. If necessary, take someone with you to give you support. Do not select last-minute purchases at the checkout line. These items are often high-priced, low-value purchases.

After You Buy

Keep the receipts and warranties for all items purchased. Remove a product carefully from its packaging. If there is a box or bag, keep it until you are sure that you have all the pieces for the product and that it works properly. If you need to return an item, be sure all the pieces are back in the package.

Evaluate your purchase. Are you satisfied with the product? Is it what you had intended to buy? Are you satisfied with the service you were given? Answering these questions will help you make better decisions in the future.

3-3 Activity 1   Can You Recall?

Answer these questions to help you recall what you have read. If you cannot answer a question, read the related section again.

1. List strategies, other than having the right price, for selling goods to consumers.
2. List three types of media that sellers can use to help create demand for a product.
3. List three things you can do before you shop to improve your buying power.
4. List three things you can do while shopping to make better purchase decisions.
5. List three things you can do after your purchase to make better decisions in the future.

3-3 Activity 2   Ad Appeal

Shopping is something everyone has to do. Goods and services provide us with basic needs as well as luxury items. How many times have you thought that you were misled by an advertisement? Have you been convinced to buy something that you later thought was not worth the money? Choose one of the media in the following list. Then describe the target audience and the appeal for the ads it shows.

1. Watch television for one-half hour. During that period, write down every ad (commercial) you watch. For each ad, describe the people you think are in its target audience. Then tell whether the appeal is logical (to meet real needs) or emotional (to convince people they need a product). Tell whether or not you think the ad is effective, and explain why.
2. Listen to a local radio station for one-half hour. Write down every commercial you hear. For each ad, describe the people you think are in its target audience. Then tell whether the appeal is logical (to meet real needs) or emotional (to convince people they need a product). Tell whether or not you think the ad is effective, and explain why.
3. Look through a daily newspaper or magazine. Make a list of the types of advertisements you find. For each type of ad, describe the target audience. Then tell whether the appeal is logical (to meet real needs) or emotional (to convince people they need a product). Tell whether or not you think the ad is effective, and explain why.

82

EXPLORING CAREERS IN EDUCATION AND TRAINING

Do you like to work with people? Are you good at explaining concepts and tasks? If the answer is yes, a career in education and training might be right for you. Jobs in education involve teaching children and adults. Some workers in this field, such as a school principal, handle administrative tasks. Others, such as counselors, provide support services related to education. Child care workers provide care for children who have not yet entered school and also work with older children before and after school hours.

Jobs in education are found in public and private schools. Training jobs are also found in government and businesses. Some trainers are entrepreneurs and have their own small businesses. The need for jobs in the education and training area is expected to grow over the next few years. The outlook varies somewhat by job.

Skills Needed

Some of the skills and traits needed for a career in education and training include the following:

- Ability to work well with others
- Content area knowledge
- Communications skills
- Computer/technology skills
- Decision-making skills
- Problem-solving skills
- Leadership skills

Job Titles

Many jobs are available in the education and training field. Some job titles for this career area include the following:

- Child care worker
- Coach
- College professor
- Counselor
- Language pathologist
- Librarian
- Principal
- Social worker
- Teacher

Explore a Job

1. Choose a job in education to explore further. Select a job from the list above, or choose another job in this career area.

2. Access the *Occupational Outlook Handbook* online. A link to the site is provided on the Web site for this textbook.

3. Search for more information about the job you selected to answer these questions:
   - What is the nature of the work this job involves?
   - What is the job outlook for this job?
   - What training or qualifications are needed for this job?
   - What are the median annual earnings for this job?

Review

Summary

- Inflation is an increase in general price levels for goods and services. Inflation is measured by the U.S. government using the Consumer Price Index (CPI).
- Deflation is a decrease in general price levels. It is the opposite of inflation.
- Demand-pull inflation occurs when consumers want to buy more goods and services than producers supply. Cost-push inflation occurs when producers raise prices because their costs to create products are rising. Real-cost inflation is rising prices due to scarce resources that are diminishing or are harder to acquire.
- There is a connection between inflation and employment. Higher inflation usually means that more people are employed.
- Inflation reduces the value of money. As prices rise, money buys less.
- Inflation affects the amount of money consumers may be able to spend, save, or invest.
- In a market economy, prices are affected by producers, consumers, and other factors.
- Cost-plus pricing adds the total cost of making a product to a profit margin. Value-based pricing sets a price that is as high as consumers will pay. Market-based pricing sets a price based on prices of similar products in the marketplace.
- Consumers can economize (spend as little as possible) or optimize (spread dollars as far as they will go).
- To sell products, businesses make shopping convenient, provide customer service, meet needs and wants, and create demand.
- Advertising is an effective method for sellers to create and stimulate demand for products.
- Consumers can use good buying strategies to spend money wisely.

Key Terms

advertising
cost-plus pricing
cost-push inflation
deflation
demand-pull
    inflation
disinflation

economizing
hyperinflation
inflation
market-based
    pricing
optimizing
productivity

real-cost inflation
reflation
target audience
time value of money
value-based pricing

ACTIVITY 1
Review Key Terms

Use the key terms from Chapter 3 to complete the following sentences:

1. The spending habit called _____ is spending money only when you have to and then spending as little as possible.

2. _____ occurs when businesses raise prices due to rising costs for producing products.

3. _____ occurs when prices are high, drop, and then rise to their previous high level.

4. _____ is a method of informing consumers and promoting and selling products.

5. The _____ concept says that money received today is worth more than money received in the future.

6. Setting a price based on how much the consumer is willing to pay is called _____.

7. The lowering of overall price levels is called _____.

8. _____ is caused by scarce resources or an increase in the cost of getting those resources.

9. A consumer spending pattern called _____ occurs when people spread money to cover as many needs as possible or to get as much value as possible.

10. _____ is an overall increase in general price levels.

11. A specific group of people called a(n) _____ is the focus of a specific advertising strategy.

12. A type of inflation called _____ occurs when prices are rising, but at a slow rate.

13. A pricing strategy called _____ sets the price for a product based on existing prices in the marketplace.

14. Rapidly rising, out-of-control prices are called _____.

15. _____ is setting a price based on the cost to produce and deliver a product plus a profit margin.

16. A type of inflation that occurs when consumers want to buy more goods and services than producers supply is called _____.

17. _____ is a measure of the efficiency with which goods and services are made.

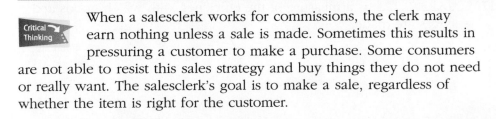

ACTIVITY 2
Math Minute

Complete these problems to build your math skills. You may use spreadsheet software or complete the problems manually.

Comparing unit prices can help a consumer determine which size or package of a product is the best value. To find the unit price of a product, divide the total price by the number of units. Example: A product contains four items and is priced at $1.00. The unit price is 25 cents.

1. Find the unit prices for the following items. Round to three decimal places.

Product A	$3.96 for 24 ounces
Product B	$2.99 for a 16-ounce box
Product C	$3.69 for 12 cookies
Product D	$4.99 for 6 muffins
Product E	$12.99 for a pack of 6
Product F	$25.00 for a case of 36

2. Determine which of these items has the lowest per-unit cost and, thus, is the best buy.

Product A $1.99 for a 6-ounce bag	or	$2.49 for an 8-ounce bag
Product B $24.00 for a box of 10	or	$36.00 for a box of 15
Product C $10.00 for a pack of 3	or	$15.00 for a pack of 5

3. The price of gasoline rose from $2.50 on March 1 to $2.89 on March 31. By what percent did the price increase?

4. The price of an air conditioner fell from $250.00 on August 1 to $200.00 on October 1. By what percent did the price decrease?

5. You plan to loan $1,000 to a neighbor for 6 months. You realize that the value of a dollar may be less 6 months from now than it is today. You want to charge enough interest so that the money you receive back from your neighbor will have the same purchasing power as the money you loan. The inflation rate for the next 6 months is predicted to be 5 percent. How much interest (in dollars) should you charge on the loan to maintain the purchasing power of your money?

ACTIVITY 3
Ethics in Sales

Critical Thinking When a salesclerk works for commissions, the clerk may earn nothing unless a sale is made. Sometimes this results in pressuring a customer to make a purchase. Some consumers are not able to resist this sales strategy and buy things they do not need or really want. The salesclerk's goal is to make a sale, regardless of whether the item is right for the customer.

1. Have you ever bought something that you later felt you had been pressured into buying? How satisfied were you with that purchase?

2. What will you do differently the next time you are faced with this situation?

3. Ethically speaking, what is wrong with pressuring someone into buying when she or he is not ready or does not really need or want the item?

ACTIVITY 4
Compare a Pay Increase to the Inflation Rate

According to government statistics, the inflation rate for the past year was 4 percent. You are worried that your pay is not keeping pace with your cost of living. Your average net pay this year is $1,625.00 per month. It was $1,576.00 last year.

1. By what dollar amount did your average net pay per month increase?

2. By what percent did your average net pay per month increase? Round your answer to one decimal place.

You have learned that the government calculates the rate of inflation based on the change in the Consumer Price Index (CPI). The CPI includes many types of goods and services. The CPI is designed to represent the economy as a whole. Most people buy only a portion of the goods and services used in the CPI in any one year. Because of this, the increase in the cost of living for each person may be more or less than the overall inflation rate.

Assume the following numbers are the average of what you pay each month for the goods and services you use.

Type of Expense	This Year	Last Year
Rent	$400.00	$400.00
Car payment	$299.00	$299.00
Telephone	$26.00	$26.00
Cell phone	$40.00	$40.00
Electricity	$65.00	$65.00
Water	$17.00	$15.00
Groceries	$157.00	$150.00
Internet access	$20.00	$20.00
Gasoline	$46.00	$38.00
Clothing	$30.00	$25.00
Lunches at work	$125.00	$120.00
Satellite TV	$35.00	$35.00
Movies in theaters	$32.00	$28.00
Other entertainment	$67.00	$60.00
Car maintenance	$25.00	$25.00
Health insurance	$20.00	$15.00
Auto and renter's insurance	$125.00	$125.00
Total	**$1,529.00**	**$1,486.00**

(For this exercise, the costs of medical care and prescriptions not covered by health insurance are not included. These costs can vary widely from year to year.)

87

3. What is the dollar amount of the change for each item and for the total?

4. By what percent did the price of each item and the total change? Round answers to one decimal place.

5. For which goods or services did the price change by more than 4 percent, the national inflation rate? For which goods or services did the price change by less than the national inflation rate?

6. How does the overall (total) rate of change compare to the national inflation rate? Is your pay increasing enough to cover the increase in your cost-of-living expenses?

ACTIVITY 5
Online Buying

  academic.cengage.com/school/pfl

Many companies that have traditional stores also have a retail Web site. The Web site typically has complete product descriptions, pictures, details, and prices. Ordering merchandise from the site is usually convenient and easy. As a result, consumer purchases on the Internet are rapidly growing.

Work with another student to complete this activity. Identify a large and well-known department store. Visit the store's Web site. To find the Web site, enter the store's name in an Internet search engine. Answer the following questions about the Web site:

1. Is the Web site easy to use? Can you move from screen to screen easily?

2. Are you able to find information about a particular product easily?

3. Is complete information about the product provided?

4. Are you able to proceed to checkout (if you wish) with ease?

5. Is the Web site colorful and well designed?

6. Overall, how would you rate your shopping experience at this site?

ACTIVITY 6
Shopping Strategies

1. Think of an item you would like to buy. Choose an item that costs more than $10 and that will require some planning, saving, and shopping. Perhaps it is a gift for someone's birthday or a special item that you have wanted for some time.

2. List the things you will consider before buying, such as places you will shop, features you are seeking, and price you are willing to pay.

3. Describe where you will go and what you will do as you are making the purchase. This includes the stores you will visit, questions to ask, and techniques to get the best deal.

4. Explain what you will do after the purchase, such as keep the receipt, mail a warranty card, or follow up on delivery.

JOB INTERVIEW EVENT

Future Business Leaders of America (FBLA) and Business Professionals of America (BPA) are organizations that conduct competitive events for students. The FBLA Job Interview Event and BPA Interview Skills Event allow students to demonstrate their ability to apply for jobs. Both events require preparing a resume and a letter of application. Students must also fill out a job application form and take part in a mock job interview. Applicants should bring several ink pens and their resume to use when filling out the job application form.

Evaluation

Students who take part in these events are judged on their ability to:

- Create an effective resume.
- Fill out a job application accurately, neatly, and completely.
- Write a letter of application appropriate for a particular job.
- Answer interview questions.
- Discuss their skills, education, and experience for a job.
- Dress professionally for an interview.
- Demonstrate a professional attitude.

Sample Scenario

You are applying for a desk clerk position at a hotel in Austin, Texas. The desk clerk must check guests in and out of the hotel. The clerk must also answer guests' questions about things to do in Austin. This position requires someone who has a friendly attitude and enjoys working with people.

Think Critically

1. How should you dress for an interview at a hotel? Why?
2. Why is the letter of application an important part of the job application process?
3. Why should you take names, addresses, and telephone numbers of personal references when you go to an interview?
4. Give two tips for successful interviews.

89

PART 2

Money Management

OUTCOMES

After successfully completing this part, students should be able to:

* **Explain** how resources can limit financial choices.
* **Prepare** a personal income and expense statement, personal balance sheet, and personal budget.
* **Create** a personal financial plan.
* **Prepare** a bank reconciliation and balance a checkbook.
* **List** banking services and fees.
* **Describe** the role of the Federal Reserve System.
* **Discuss** risk management strategies.
* **Explain** provisions of income protection insurance.
* **Explain** coverage for property insurance.

PART 2, MONEY MANAGEMENT, focuses on planning for your financial future. It includes assessing where you are now and looking forward. You will learn how to prepare a personal income and expense statement, balance sheet, budget, and financial plan. You will study banking services and their costs. You will learn how to use a checking account. Keeping good records is an important step in preparing for the future. Risk management will help you to learn to protect your financial resources, including income and property.

CHAPTER 4

Financial Decisions and Planning

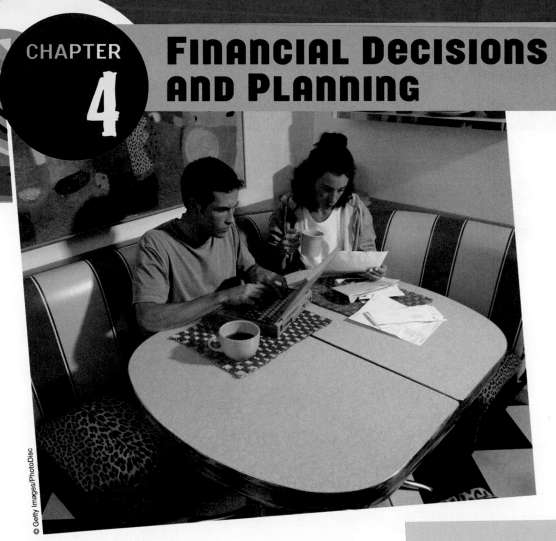

© Getty Images/PhotoDisc

C hapter 4 focuses on the starting point of good money management—assessing your needs and wants. In this chapter, you will learn how your financial resources impact your choices. You will look at where you are now (financially) and prepare a personal balance sheet. You will study strategies you can use to make better financial choices. You will then explore budgeting and create a simple budget. You will learn about budget variances and how to keep good financial records. Finally, you will examine a five-step financial planning process, which begins with setting your personal and financial goals.

ONLINE RESOURCES

Personal Financial Literacy Web site:

Vocabulary Flashcards

Beat the Clock: Financial Planning

Chapter 4 Supplemental Activity

Search terms:
- assets
- financial planning
- fixed expenses
- identity theft
- liabilities
- variable expenses

Resources and Choices

OUTCOMES

- Explain how basic needs, other needs, and wants differ.
- Describe how limited resources affect consumer choices.
- Prepare a personal income and expense statement.
- Prepare a personal balance sheet.
- Apply a decision-making process to personal financial choices.

MEETING NEEDS AND WANTS

Basic needs include food, clothing, shelter, and medical care. People need these items to survive. People who do not have their basic needs met are not able to provide for other needs or wants. Other needs include things such as more than one pair of shoes, clothing for different purposes,

A fast, expensive car is a luxury item.

education, or furniture to make life more comfortable. Items to fill some of these needs can be rented instead of purchased. For example, a person can go to a library to borrow books rather than buy them. Other items, such as a washer and dryer, save the owner both time and money as compared to renting their use. While these items are not basic to survival, they are needed to have a comfortable lifestyle.

The term **wants** refers to things people desire for reasons beyond survival and basic comfort. These items allow people to enjoy life more. Examples of wants are new cars, vacation trips, a large wardrobe, dozens of pairs of shoes, and so on. Luxury items, which are very costly, often fill emotional wants rather than physical needs.

Resources Limit Choices

The term **financial resources** refers to money or other items of value that people can use to acquire goods and services. Although their financial resources are limited, wants and needs for many people are unlimited and growing. Every day, new products and services appear to tempt consumers. Because most people do not have enough resources to meet all their needs and wants, people must make choices. For a person who has few resources, the choices available will also be few. This person may need to spend all resources to cover basic and other needs. For a person with more resources, more choices will be available. The amount of money a person has to spend after needs are met is called **discretionary income**. A person who has high discretionary income can consider buying a larger number or higher quality of goods.

Financial Resources

Income is the inflow of money you receive from working, investments, or other sources. You can spend this amount of money without using savings or other assets. **Assets** are money and items of value that you own. Their value is the price you could get if you sold them (for goods, such as a car) or the monetary value (for cash or savings).

Expenses are items for which you must spend money. An income and expense statement lists income received and money spent for expenses for a certain period of time, such as a month or a year. If you have more income than expenses, you have a net income for the period. If you have more expenses than income, you have a net loss for the period. Comparing monthly income and expense statements can help you see whether you are meeting your financial goals. The income and expense statement in Figure 4-1.1 on page 94 shows a net income of $50.00.

© PR NEWSWIRE APPLE COMPUTER, INC.

Having high discretionary income allows consumers to consider buying expensive products they want.

93

FIGURE 4-1.1   PERSONAL INCOME AND EXPENSE STATEMENT

ANDREA MCCALL
PERSONAL INCOME AND EXPENSE STATEMENT
April 1-30, 20--

Income

Work (part-time)	$150.00	
Allowance for doing household chores	40.00	
Lunch money allowance	60.00	
Total Income		$250.00

Expenses

Gifts	$20.00	
Clothes and shoes	60.00	
Spending money (miscellaneous)	20.00	
Lunches	60.00	
Entertainment	40.00	
Total Expenses		200.00
Net Income		$50.00

A personal balance sheet lists assets you own and their current value on a certain date. The balance sheet also lists debts you owe, called liabilities. A **liability** is any debt that you must repay. The difference between your assets (what you own) and your liabilities (what you owe) is called **net worth**. In the balance sheet shown in Figure 4-1.2, the net worth is $3,351.58.

FIGURE 4-1.2   PERSONAL BALANCE SHEET

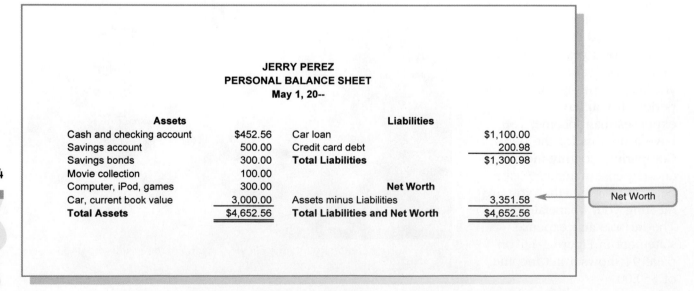

JERRY PEREZ
PERSONAL BALANCE SHEET
May 1, 20--

Assets		Liabilities	
Cash and checking account	$452.56	Car loan	$1,100.00
Savings account	500.00	Credit card debt	200.98
Savings bonds	300.00	**Total Liabilities**	$1,300.98
Movie collection	100.00		
Computer, iPod, games	300.00	**Net Worth**	
Car, current book value	3,000.00	Assets minus Liabilities	3,351.58
Total Assets	$4,652.56	**Total Liabilities and Net Worth**	$4,652.56

Net Worth

94

Houses may grow in value over time.

Assets that are growing in value are said to be appreciating. Savings bonds and other types of savings will grow over time and will increase in value. The value of land or a house may also increase over time. Other assets, such as cars and electronic items, may be depreciating, or going down in value. These items have temporary value that will be used up over time.

MAKING GOOD FINANCIAL CHOICES

Buying decisions play an important part in managing your money. When you give up a particular benefit or item to get another that you think is more desirable, you are making a **trade-off**. For example, you may choose to buy a music player such as an iPod®. To have enough money to buy the iPod, you must not buy something else that you want. The benefit or item you give up (do not buy) is called the **opportunity cost**. For example, instead of the iPod, you might have bought a bicycle. In this situation, the bicycle is the opportunity cost.

To help you make good financial decisions, use a step-by-step decision-making process.

1. Define the need or problem to be resolved by buying the item or service. For example, you might need access to a computer to use in doing homework and surfing the Internet. Think about all the ways in which the item or service could be used and features it should have to meet your needs.

2. List options for filling the need or solving the problem. For example, you could buy a new computer. You could rent a computer. You could use a computer at a local library. List the cost of each option. Research the features of any items you consider buying.

95

3. Compare the options you have identified. List the advantages and disadvantages of each one. For example, renting a computer may be more costly in the long term than buying one. Using a computer at the library will be less costly than buying a computer. However, you will have to travel to the library each time you want to use the computer. You can only use the computer during hours the library is open. Think about the opportunity cost of each option.

4. Make a decision based on your research and evaluation of the information you have gathered.

5. Take action based on your decision. For example, buy a computer or plan times to use one at the library.

6. Reevaluate your choices. After some time has passed, think about your decision again. Did the option you chose resolve the problem, or is it filling the need for which it was selected? If the answer is no, or if your needs have changed, follow the process again to make a new decision.

Financial choices you make today will affect your finances tomorrow. If you plan ahead, you will be better prepared to use your resources to fill your needs and wants. Making good financial choices will help prevent worry over financial matters. Follow these strategies to help you make good financial choices:

- Financial choices should be forward-looking. Ask yourself how a choice will affect your future.
- Consider the opportunity cost of each item or service you purchase. Doing so will help you decide whether the item or service selected is the best choice for you.
- When in doubt about whether to buy a particular item or service, do not make the purchase. If you are not sure of a choice, keep asking questions or doing research until you know enough to make a good decision.
- Do not make snap decisions about financial matters. Buyer's remorse occurs when you make a purchase and then later regret it.
- Spend less than your income each month. Set aside money for unexpected expenses.
- Be realistic when deciding which wants you can fill. Learn to enjoy items you have rather than always wanting more items.
- Take enough time to read all financial agreements. Ask lots of questions; be sure you understand what you are agreeing to before you sign a financial document.
- Learn from mistakes that others have made. Listen to the experiences of others to learn about possible financial problems. This will help you avoid the same situations.

READING VOCABULARY

Reading is a basic communications skill. Much of the information people need comes in written form. People read for many reasons. They read to learn new ideas related to school, work, or personal activities. They read directions for doing a task or following a particular route. Many people also read stories, novels, or poems for pleasure.

Your vocabulary is the words you know and understand how to use. Whatever your purpose in reading, improving your vocabulary will help you better understand the material you read. For example, key terms are listed in each chapter of this textbook. Learning these words will help you understand the concepts presented. Use the following strategies to add new words to your vocabulary:

- Try to learn the meaning of a word from the way it is used in a sentence. Then check a dictionary to see if that meaning is correct.

- Divide a long word into parts. If you know the meaning of one part, you may be able to guess the meaning of the entire word. Again, check a dictionary to see if that meaning is correct.

- When you are reading and see a word you do not know, find the meaning in a dictionary at that time, if possible. If you cannot check the dictionary right away, make a note of the word and find it in a dictionary later.

- If you find a word you do not know when reading a textbook, see if the word is defined in a glossary at the end of the book.

- Use new words that you learn in conversation or writing to help you remember the meanings.

97

4-1 Activity 1 Can You Recall?

Answer these questions to help you recall what you have read. If you cannot answer a question, read the related section again.

1. How are other needs different from basic needs? Besides food, clothing, shelter, and medical care, what are some other needs?
2. How are wants different from needs? What are some wants that you have?
3. How do financial resources limit a person's spending choices?
4. What are assets? What are liabilities?
5. How is a person's net worth calculated?
6. What is a trade-off? What is an opportunity cost?
7. Briefly list five steps to follow when making a financial decision.
8. You have given careful thought to buying either a new book bag or a music CD. You decide to buy the music CD. What is your opportunity cost?
9. List some strategies you can use to make good financial choices.

4-1 Activity 2 Personal Financial Statements

Identifying the income, expenses, assets, and liabilities you have now is a good place to begin planning for your financial future. In this activity, you will create a personal income and expense statement and find your net worth or net loss for one month. You will also create a personal balance sheet and determine your net worth.

1. Review the personal income and expense statement shown in Figure 4-1.1 on page 94. Create a similar document using your information. Use spreadsheet software, if available, to create the statement.
2. List all your income—money you receive from any source during one month.
3. List all your expenses—money you pay for goods and services during the same month.

4. Find the total of your income and the total of your expenses. Subtract the two total amounts to find your net income or net loss.

5. Review the personal balance sheet shown in Figure 4-1.2 on page 94. Create a similar document using your information. Use spreadsheet software, if available, to create the balance sheet.

6. List all your assets—money you have or things of value you own.

7. List all your liabilities—money you owe that must be repaid.

8. Subtract your liabilities from your assets to find your net worth. Note that if your liabilities are larger than your assets, you will have a negative net worth.

OUTCOMES

- Identify the purpose of a budget.
- Prepare a personal budget using the "pay-yourself-first" philosophy.
- Describe recordkeeping methods used in the budgeting process.

THE PURPOSE OF BUDGETING

Budgeting is a critical part of managing your money. The purpose of a budget is to plan how you will spend or save money. A **budget** is a spending and saving plan based on expected income and expenses. It lists expenses and the source of income to pay those expenses. Using a budget allows you to compare your financial resources with your financial needs.

You may need to adjust amounts in a budget several times. Your goal is to create a plan that meets your spending and saving needs with your expected income. Using spreadsheet software, such as *Microsoft® Excel®*, makes adjusting amounts and recalculating totals easy. Using *Excel*, you can record your financial goals and then prepare the budgets that will help you achieve them. A sample budget is shown in Figure 4-2.1 on page 101.

Spreadsheets allow you to insert numbers and then change them later. You can use formulas to compute the amounts of budget variances and the percentage of variances.

Excel also makes changing a budget or a financial plan easy. For example, what if your expenses go up by 8 percent? How will the budget be affected? What if the price of a car you are saving to buy goes up by 10 percent during the time you are saving for it? How much money will you need for the car? Allowing you to answer "what if" questions easily is one of the strengths of a spreadsheet program. When you change a number in *Excel* that is part of a calculation, the result is automatically updated. When you enter a new expense amount, for example, the total expense amount will be updated. Because amounts are calculated using formulas, math errors are eliminated.

BUILDING A BUDGET

A budget should be designed to help meet financial goals such as paying for current expenses and saving for the future. To create a budget, begin by looking at the amount you have available to spend or save. Then

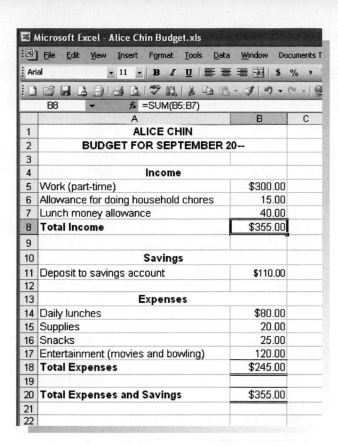

FIGURE 4-2.1

Using a spreadsheet will make creating a budget easier.

decide how much of that amount you will save and how much you will spend. You must also choose the items or services for which you plan to spend. Remember that a budget is a plan. Your actual income, saving, and spending may not be exactly as planned. You can compare your actual spending and saving to the budget to see how well you planned. This process will help you create better budgets in the future.

Figure 4-2.2 on page 102 shows a sample budget. Look at each part of the budget as you read the steps for creating a budget in the following sections.

Step 1 Estimate Income

You may have many different sources of income. Whether the money is earned or unearned, you should keep track of where it comes from and how often it is received. Because most budgets are prepared once a year, you should calculate income for an entire year. Locate the total estimated yearly income amount, $2,640.00, in the budget in Figure 4-2.2.

Money you will receive during the year is estimated in a budget. You may receive the money weekly, monthly, yearly, or on some other schedule. No matter when the money is received, it can be accounted for in terms of a monthly budget.

If you receive money weekly, multiply the weekly amount by 4 to see how much that is per month. For example, $10 received per week would be $40 a month. (Rounding is okay as long as your total yearly amount is accurate.) If you get money once a month, you can multiply by 12 to get yearly income. When you look at the big picture—how much money comes in and goes out during an entire year—it may change the way you think about money.

101

FIGURE 4-2.2   **PERSONAL BUDGET FOR ANDREA MCCALL**

ANDREA MCCALL
BUDGET FOR 20--

	Weekly	Monthly	Yearly
Income			
Work (part-time)	$30.00	$120.00	$1,440.00
Allowance for doing household chores	10.00	40.00	480.00
Lunch money allowance	15.00	60.00	720.00
Total Income	$55.00	$220.00	$2,640.00
Savings			
Deposit to savings account	$5.00	$20.00	$240.00
Expenses			
Gifts	$5.00	$20.00	$240.00
Clothes and shoes	15.00	60.00	720.00
Spending money (miscellaneous)	5.00	20.00	240.00
Lunches	15.00	60.00	720.00
Entertainment	10.00	40.00	480.00
Total Expenses	$50.00	$200.00	$2,400.00
Total Expenses and Savings	$55.00	$220.00	$2,640.00

Step 2 Plan Savings

Pay yourself first—put money into savings before you consider other expenses. If you plan what you want to spend first, you may have no money left for savings. Enter an amount that you would like to save. After entering expenses, you may need to adjust this amount. You might not be able to save as much as you want and still pay for all expenses. Plan to save some money, however, if at all possible. Savings allow you to plan for the future. You can identify items you would like to purchase at a future time with savings. Savings can also be used to pay for unexpected expenses that you may have in the future. Locate the yearly savings amount, $240.00, in the budget in Figure 4-2.2.

Step 3 Estimate Expenses

Expenses are items for which you spend money. Clothes, lunches at school, and bus fares are examples of expenses. You may make payments on an asset you purchase, such as a car. Other expenses are related to living costs and entertainment. Keeping track of what you spend will help you estimate expenses for the future. If you are trying to control

expenses, seeing exactly how much you spend for each expense can be helpful. Locate the expense amounts in the budget in Figure 4-2.2.

VARIABLE EXPENSES

Expenses that can go up and down each month are called **variable expenses**. Examples of variable expenses are food, entertainment, and clothing. These expenses go up or down as you need more or fewer items. For example, when the weather is cold, the heating expense may go up. Expenses can also vary due to changing prices. For example, as the price of gasoline rises, the transportation expense will also rise.

© Getty Images/PhotoDisc

Eating at a fancy restaurant is entertainment, a variable expense.

Some variable expenses can be decreased when you have less income or higher expenses than expected. For example, you could spend less than planned on entertainment. You can spend more on variable expenses, such as clothes, if you have more income or fewer expenses than expected. For example, if you receive a gift of cash for your birthday, you can use the money to make an unplanned purchase.

FIXED EXPENSES

Expenses that do not change each month are called **fixed expenses**. Examples of fixed costs are rent, insurance, and car payments. Renters typically have a contract that states a monthly rent amount. The rent does not change each month. Although rent and insurance expenses do go up periodically, these increases typically occur on a yearly basis. Monthly car payments are usually fixed for the term of the car loan. Fixed expenses remain constant each month and must be paid even when income is less than expected. If income continues to be less than planned, a fixed expense may have to be eliminated. For example, suppose Terry's income goes down because he loses his job. Terry may have to sell his car and pay off his car loan to eliminate this fixed expense that he can no longer afford.

Step: 4 Balance the Budget

Find the total of each category in the budget—income, savings, and expenses. Find the total of savings and expenses. This amount should be the same as the total income amount. When these amounts are the same, the budget is in balance. Locate the total income, total savings, and total expenses amounts in the budget in Figure 4-2.2.

PREPARING A BUDGET ANALYSIS

103

A budget is a plan for saving and spending. You should not expect income, savings, and expenses to be exactly as you planned in a budget. Looking at differences between planned income or spending and actual income or spending, called **variances**, can help you plan better when creating budgets in the future.

Sometimes you will earn or save more than you estimated. This is a favorable variance. If you earn or save less than you estimated, it's an unfavorable variance. The same is true with expenses. If you spend less money than you planned to spend, this is a favorable variance, but if you spend more than you planned to spend, it is an unfavorable variance. Figure 4-2.3 on page 105 shows budget variances—both in dollar amounts and in percents. To compute the percents for income and savings, subtract the budgeted amount from the actual amount; then divide the difference by the budgeted amount. To compute the percents for expenses, subtract the actual amount from the budgeted amount; then divide the difference by the budgeted amount.

By looking carefully at variances, you can see where you spent more or less than the estimated amounts. Any variance that is more or less than 10 percent of what you had planned should be looked at carefully. For example, Andrea had planned to spend $60 on clothes and shoes for the month, but she actually spent $70. That is $10 more than budgeted, or a 17 percent difference. Andrea should think about why this happened. She may decide that she needs to revise the budget or change her spending habits. Analyzing variances will help you understand and better estimate your income and expenses.

RECORDKEEPING METHODS

Keeping good records will help you prepare a better budget. Good information will also help you do a better job analyzing your budget. There are several methods you can use as you keep track of what you are earning, spending, saving, and investing.

FIGURE 4-2.3   **VARIANCES FOR A MONTHLY BUDGET**

ANDREA MCCALL
BUDGET VARIANCES FOR AUGUST

	Budgeted Amount	Actual Amount	Dollar Variance	Percent Variance
Income				
Work (part-time)	$120.00	$110.00	-$10.00	-8% U
Allowance for doing household chores	40.00	50.00	10.00	25% F
Lunch money allowance	60.00	60.00	0.00	0%
Total Income	$220.00	$220.00	$0.00	0%
Savings				
Deposit to savings account	$20.00	$20.00	$0.00	0%
Expenses				
Gifts	$20.00	$18.00	$2.00	10% F
Clothes and shoes	60.00	70.00	-10.00	-17% U
Spending money (miscellaneous)	20.00	22.00	-2.00	-10% U
Lunches	60.00	55.00	5.00	8% F
Entertainment	40.00	35.00	5.00	13% F
Total Expenses	$200.00	$200.00	$0.00	0%
Total Expenses and Savings	$220.00	$220.00	$0.00	0%

Percents are rounded to the nearest whole number.

Manual Records

You can keep logs or journals on paper that list types and amounts of income, savings, and expenses. You can manually compute your variances and make notations about what to change. You will want to keep these journals over time so you can compare them. For example, you can look at the previous year's budget and see how your income has grown. You can also see how your spending habits have changed.

Computerized Records

Software packages such as *Quicken*® or *Microsoft Money* allow you to keep financial records using a computer. The software will retain the data and will allow you to print reports, such as a personal balance sheet. It will also allow you to quickly reference expense information. Versions of programs such as *Microsoft Money*, shown in Figure 4-2.4 on page 106, are available for use on handheld computers. Using such a program on a handheld computer makes recording data quick and easy at any location.

105

FIGURE 4-2.4

Keeping good records is essential to good financial planning.

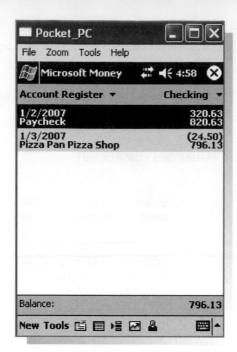

You can also use spreadsheet programs, such as *Microsoft Excel*, for data entry and budget analysis. The program will allow you to compute variances in dollar amounts as well as percentages. You can set up worksheets and link them together. This will allow you to make estimates and change amounts easily.

Success Skills

DEALING WITH CONFLICT

Conflicts are bound to happen sooner or later. People you know will not be able to get along with each other. Maybe you will have a hard time working out a problem with another person. The ability to deal with conflict is an important personal skill—it will help you both in your personal life and in your work life.

When faced with a conflict, stop and take a ten-second time out. For those ten seconds, ask yourself, "What is happening here?" Listen rather than talk. Think about who is speaking and why that person is upset. Repeat a short summary of the problem or complaint to acknowledge that you understand the issue and confirm what you have heard.

If the person is upset or angry and not speaking rationally, suggest that you continue your talk later. This will give you and the other person time to think about the issue. Resume talking when you are both calm and can speak in a courteous manner.

Focus on the problem, not on the person. Be objective. Do not let your personal feelings—whether you like or dislike the person—cloud your judgment. Look for positive ways to address the issue. Be willing to compromise, when appropriate, to reach a solution that will be acceptable to all parties.

The next time you must deal with conflict, practice these skills. Reflect on a past situation—how could you have handled it differently?

4-2 Activity 1   Can You Recall?

Answer these questions to help you recall what you have read.
If you cannot answer a question, read the related section again.

1. What is the purpose of a budget?
2. What three types of amounts are included in a "pay-yourself-first" budget?
3. How are variable expenses different from fixed expenses?
4. Why is it important that a budget be balanced? If your budget does not balance, what can you do to bring it into balance?
5. What is an unfavorable variance?
6. Describe ways to keep financial records manually.
7. Name three software programs that can be used to keep financial records.
8. List steps you can take to help resolve a conflict in a positive manner.

4-2 Activity 2   Personal Budget

In this activity, you will create a personal budget. You will keep track of your finances for one month and then compute budget variances. In 4-1 Activity 2, you created a personal income and expense statement. Refer to that document to see income and expense items you have already identified.

1. Review the personal budget shown in Figure 4-2.2 on page 102.
2. Create a similar budget for yourself for the coming month. Use spreadsheet software to prepare the document, if it is available.
   - Enter your expected income from all sources during the month.
   - Enter an amount you want to save for the month.
   - List all your estimated expenses for the month.
   - Total the sections of the budget to see if the budget is in balance. If it is not, change the savings or expense amounts to make the budget balance.
3. Keep track of the amount of money you receive, the amount you save, and the amount you spend during the coming month. Continue this exercise after one month has passed.
4. Review the personal budget variance examples shown in Figure 4-2.3 on page 105.
5. Create a similar monthly budget variance report for yourself. Use the budget you created for the month and the actual amounts of your income, savings, and expenses.

107

4-3

Personal Financial Planning

 **OUTCOMES**

- Explain the purpose of a financial plan.
- List the steps of the financial planning process.
- Describe how financial goals help make achieving personal goals possible.
- Prepare a personal financial plan.

FINANCIAL PLANNING

A **financial plan** contains personal goals you want to accomplish. It also contains a timeline for reaching these goals and methods you will use to finance them. Getting a college education, owning a car, and owning a home are examples of personal goals. For each personal goal, you will have a related financial goal. Paying for living expenses, tuition, books, and other related expenses while in college is a financial goal. Saving for a down payment and having a job that provides enough income to make monthly car payments are financial goals. Saving for a down payment and having a job that provides enough income to make monthly house payments are financial goals. A financial plan is more than a budget. Its purpose is to plan for earning, spending, saving, and investing that will allow you to achieve your personal goals in the present and the future.

A FIVE-STEP FINANCIAL PLANNING PROCESS

Financial planning is a formal process. It involves looking carefully at your current situation and thinking about your future. It also requires a long-term commitment. You must put your plan into action and monitor it periodically. At least once a year, you should review and update the plan. Your plan should contain details, but it should not be too complicated to review and follow.

Some people create a plan by themselves. They may think they do not need help, or they may want to keep their financial information and goals private. Other people hire a financial planner. A financial planner is trained to help people with advice about how to invest earnings, plan for retirement, and manage other financial matters. Whether you do planning by yourself or with help from others, you will need to complete five steps.

Financial planning begins with getting organized.

Step 1 Gather Information

The first step in financial planning is gathering information. Everything related to your finances should be considered. The purpose of gathering information is to look at the state of your finances now—your starting point. The following list shows examples of items you may need to gather. You may not have all the items listed at this time in your life. However, you can gather or prepare the first three items. Other items may become part of your plan in later life.

- Personal income and expense statement
- Personal balance sheet
- Personal budget
- Checkbooks
- Current bank account statements
- Investment account statements
- Insurance policies
- Current paycheck stub
- Tax returns
- Will
- Trusts
- Financial contracts for items purchased on credit
- Other legal documents related to your finances

At some point when you review your plan, you will need to think about how to finance your retirement. You may want to gather data about your medical history and the medical history of family members. This data may help you estimate your life span, which affects the amount of income you will need over your lifetime. For example, many people may live until age 85 or 90 and should plan how to meet financial needs through that age.

PHISHING

When providers of financial products contact you directly by e-mail or using Web sites, you should be careful. There are many scams on the Internet. Web pages that appear to be genuine may not be posted by the company indicated.

One common Internet scam is called **phishing**. In this scam, a person is sent an e-mail saying, for example, that there is a problem with his or her bank account. The individual is asked to confirm a Social Security number, account number, password, or other sensitive information. The From field of the e-mail may have the real name of your bank. The real company logo may be shown. However, the message is not from the real bank. Do not respond to such an attempt to get personal information. The message is most likely from a phisher. The phisher wants to use your information illegally. **Identity theft** occurs when someone uses your personal information without your permission to commit fraud or other crimes.

If you think that a message regarding your bank account or other financial matters may be real, contact the bank or other business by phone. Ask if there is a problem with your account. Do not reply to the e-mail message or go to the link provided.

Step 2 Analyze Information

Take a careful look at the documents and information you have gathered. Find out if any data are missing, and take steps to get the data. Carefully look at each document, and make notes about what you see. Review your income and expense statement to see what your current sources of income are. Look at your expenses. Do you have enough income to pay for your expenses and save for the future? If not, try to find ways to increase income and decrease expenses.

Review your personal balance sheet. What are your assets? What liabilities do you have? What is your net worth? Review a current monthly or yearly budget. Look at the items for which you spend money. Is there a way you can spend less and save more to meet long-term goals?

As you review your financial plan each year, consider the following questions. Some of them may apply now. Others may not apply to you for a few years or for many years.

- Is your income steadily growing over time? If so, by what amount and percentage? For example, you may have $2,000 more in income this year than last year. This is a favorable trend that will help you reach your goals.
- Is your net worth growing over time? When you compare the current balance sheet to previous ones, do you see growth? If so, by what amount and percentage?
- How are your spending habits changing? What types of things are you buying (needs versus wants), and what are your purchasing plans over time?
- Who else depends on your income? Do you have a spouse or children that will be affected by your financial plan? What will they contribute?

○ What new goals do you need to add and plan for? Do you need a plan to pay for a college education for your child? Is it time to plan for retirement? Does your will need to be updated to include a new grandchild?

Step 3 Set Goals

Two types of goals should be considered when creating a financial plan—personal goals and financial goals. **Personal goals** are the things you want to achieve. Living in your own apartment, owning a car, and taking a two-week vacation are personal goals. Personal goals should be set first because your financial goals will be based on them.

Financial goals describe how you will pay for your personal goals. Financial goals may be short-term, intermediate, or long-term. Short-term goals include what you will do this week, this month, and this year. A financial plan for the short term tells you on a week-to-week or month-to-month basis what you would like to achieve. Perhaps you would like to save $40 by the end of the month. Perhaps you want to add $200 to your savings account by the end of the year. Short-term financial goals are usually for between 1 week and 2 years. Using monthly and yearly budgets can help you achieve short-term goals and save for long-term goals.

Intermediate goals include what you want to achieve up to 3 or 4 years from now. You may wish to save money for college or for a future purchase or need. You may want to increase your yearly income by $100 a month within 3 years. Intermediate goals are usually for between 2 and 5 years.

Long-term goals typically include what you want to achieve more than 5 years from now. You may wish to save enough money to buy a car

Expensive vacations require planning and financial resources.

111

or go on an expensive vacation. You may want to repay loans for money you borrowed to complete college. When you begin working full-time, you may contribute to a 401(k) to save money for your retirement.

Achieving intermediate and long-term goals may require that you save money for a long time. Doing without an item you would like to buy now in order to save money for a long-term goal is an example of delayed gratification. For instance, you may have a goal of saving $30 per month to help pay for your college education. This month, you would like to buy a music CD. However, if you do so, you will not be able to make your savings goal. Doing without the CD now in order to be able to pay for college later is an example of delayed gratification.

Step 4 Develop a Timeline

Plan a time to put your goals into action. How soon do you need or want to achieve a certain goal? For each personal goal, there may be a financial goal you must first achieve. Financial goals can further be divided into parts or steps. For each step, consider how long it will take to complete. Then set a target date for completion. The record of what you intend to accomplish is your financial plan. Once you clearly understand your current finances and the goals you want to accomplish, you can then take steps to reach your goals. A sample timeline for one goal is shown in Figure 4-3.1.

FIGURE 4-3.1   **ONE GOAL IN A FINANCIAL PLAN**

BILL WONG FINANCIAL PLAN
Updated April 1, 20--

Net Worth on April 1, 20-- $525.56

Personal Goal	Financial Goal	Steps to Take	Timeline
Live in my own house in the country	Own a house in the country	1. Save money for a down payment ($12,000)	5 years
		• Set aside $200 per month	Once per month
		• Open a separate account for money saved	April 8 (next week)
		• Talk to a mortgage broker to get prepared	Make an appointment for April 15
		2. Have a job that provides enough income to make monthly payments	5 years

112

Step 5 Implement and Evaluate the Plan

Once you have decided on your personal and financial goals, begin working toward achieving them. Check off the items on your timeline as they are completed. Set new steps as you learn about other or better ways of meeting your goals. Most importantly, take a look at your financial plan often. At least once each year, you should evaluate the financial plan and update or revise it as needed.

Your financial plan represents your personal and financial goals at one point in time. Those goals are likely to change over time. For example, you may inherit money, or you may have children. You may have a job opportunity overseas, or you may wish to spend more time on a hobby or a side business. As your personal and family goals change, your financial plan should be updated to reflect new goals. The financial plan is a work in progress; it is never finished. As one goal is accomplished, another personal goal is defined.

Keep your financial plan and all the related documents in a safe place where you can work on them regularly.

Ethics

FINANCIAL PLANNERS AND COMMISSION EARNINGS

A **financial planner** is a person who provides financial advice to individuals. Financial planners help people develop financial plans in a very formal setting. If you work with a financial planner, you will share your personal information. Data about your assets, liabilities, and net worth are examples of the information you will share. The financial planner should guard your information and should not share it with others or use it for personal benefit. To do otherwise would be unethical. You must be able to trust the planner with your most sensitive personal data.

Some financial planners work for commission income. That means they make money when they sell financial products to their customers. When planners sell products that earn higher commissions, rather than products that customers really need, they are being unethical. For consumers, it can be hard to tell whether or not they are buying the best product at the lowest price. To avoid this kind of dilemma, hire a financial planner who does not work on commission. Instead, pay for the advice separately from buying any financial products, such as insurance.

Every year, people are cheated out of their money by dishonest advisors. Be sure you can trust your financial planner. Find out if he or she has been in business long, whether complaints have been filed against her or him, and if he or she has a criminal background. Ask what measures the planner will take to keep your data secure.

4-3 Activity 1   Can You Recall?

Answer these questions to help you recall what you have read.
If you cannot answer a question, read the related section again.

1. What is the purpose of a financial plan?
2. List the five steps in creating a financial plan.
3. What types of information or documents are needed to create a financial plan?
4. What information should you be able to learn from your personal balance sheet?
5. Why are personal goals set before financial goals? How do financial goals help make achieving personal goals possible?
6. How are short-term goals different from long-term goals?
7. What does the term *delayed gratification* mean?
8. How often should you review your financial plan at a minimum?
9. Why might you choose a financial planner who does not work on commission rather than one who does?

4-3 Activity 2   Personal Financial Plan

1. Review the example of one goal in a financial plan shown in Figure 4-3.1 on page 112.
2. Gather the personal income and expense statement, the personal balance sheet, and the personal budget you created earlier. Gather any other financial documents you have. See the list under Step 1 Gather Information on page 109 for examples.
3. Use spreadsheet or word processing software for this activity, if it is available. If not, complete the work using paper and pen. Center the following heading at the top of the document:

(YOUR NAME) FINANCIAL PLAN
Updated (current date)

4. Refer to your personal balance sheet created earlier to find your net worth amount. Enter this amount below the headings. For example:

Net Worth on (current date) $525.56

5. Below the net worth information, create a table with four columns as shown in Figure 4-3.1. Enter the following column headings:

Personal Goals
Financial Goals
Steps to Take
Timeline

6. Think of a personal goal you would like to accomplish within the coming year. List this short-term goal in the table under Personal Goals.

7. Think of the financial goal or goals you will need to meet in order to achieve the personal goal. List these goals in the table under Financial Goals.

8. Determine the steps you will need to take to achieve the financial goals. Refer to your budget and income and expense statement. Do you need to increase your income or savings to meet the goals? Do you need to decrease expenses? List the steps you will take to meet the goals in the table under Steps to Take.

9. Set a time for completing each step you listed. Enter the completion time for each step in the table under Timeline.

10. Repeat steps 6 through 9 to list other goals. List at least one more short-term goal to be achieved in 2 years or sooner. List at least two intermediate goals to be completed within 3 to 5 years. List at least two long-term goals to be completed in more than 5 years. You may list as many other goals as you wish. For the long-term goals, the steps to take may be more general than for the short-term or intermediate goals. Having long-term goals that you do not yet know exactly how to accomplish is fine.

11. Work toward achieving your goals by taking the steps you have listed. Refer to your timeline often to see if you are accomplishing the steps or goals when planned.

12. At least once a year, review and revise your financial plan. Check off goals that you have achieved. Add new goals as your needs and wants change over time. Refine the steps to take in achieving your long-term goals as the steps needed become clearer.

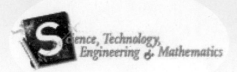
EXPLORING CAREERS IN SCIENCE, TECHNOLOGY, ENGINEERING, AND MATHEMATICS

Do you always want to understand how things work? Are you inventive and curious? Do you like to find new and better ways to build things? Are you fascinated by technology? If the answer is yes, a career in science, technology, engineering, and mathematics might be right for you. Jobs in this area are varied. Some workers in this field do scientific research or testing. Others are engineers who design products or buildings. Some workers in this area develop new technologies that are used in consumer and business products.

Jobs in this career area are found in government and businesses. Some inventors and engineers are entrepreneurs and have their own small businesses. The need for some jobs in science, technology, engineering, and mathematics is expected to grow. The need for other jobs will stay about the same or decrease. The outlook varies by job.

Skills Needed

Some of the skills and traits needed for a career in science, technology, engineering, and mathematics include the following:

- Math and science knowledge
- Analytical skills
- Communications skills
- Computer/technology skills
- Decision-making skills
- Problem-solving skills
- Leadership skills

Job Titles

Many jobs are available in science, technology, engineering, and mathematics. Some job titles for this career area include the following:

- Biological scientist
- Civil engineer
- Conservation scientist
- Drafter
- Economist
- Engineering technician
- Physicist
- Science technician
- Technical writer

Explore a Job

1. Choose a job in science, technology, engineering, and mathematics to explore further. Select a job from the list above, or choose another job in this career area.

2. Access the *Occupational Outlook Handbook* online. A link to the site is provided on the Web site for this textbook.

3. Search for more information about the job you selected to answer these questions:
   - What is the nature of the work this job involves?
   - What is the job outlook for this job?
   - What training or qualifications are needed for this job?
   - What are the median annual earnings for this job?

review

Summary

- Many people have unlimited wants and needs but limited resources to meet those wants and needs.
- Because resources are limited, people must make choices. Every choice is a trade-off between the item or benefit you get and an opportunity cost (the item or benefit given up).
- Income and assets are financial resources that can be called on to meet our wants and needs.
- A personal income and expense statement lists income, expenses, and net income. A personal balance sheet lists assets, liabilities, and net worth.
- Budgeting helps you manage your financial resources.
- Building a budget requires you to estimate income, plan savings, and estimate expenses.
- A budget analysis shows how planned spending (budget) compares to actual spending. Any differences are called variances.
- Manual and computerized recordkeeping methods will help you keep organized and prepare better financial records.
- A financial plan contains personal goals and financial goals that allow you to achieve personal goals.
- Five steps in financial planning are gathering information, analyzing information, setting goals, setting steps with a timeline, and implementing and evaluating the plan.

Key Terms

assets
budget
discretionary
   income
financial goals
financial plan
financial planner

financial resources
fixed expenses
identity theft
liability
net worth
opportunity cost

personal goals
phishing
trade-off
variable expenses
variances
wants

ACTIVITY 1
Review Key Terms

Use the key terms from Chapter 4 to complete the following sentences:

1. Your next best choice, called the _____, is what you give up when you make a decision to buy an item.

2. The amount of your assets minus your liabilities is called your _____.

117

3. _____ is the amount of money a person has to spend after needs are met.

4. A spending and saving plan based on expected income and expenses is called a(n) _____.

5. Rent or insurance payments are examples of _____ because they do not change each month.

6. An overall plan called a(n) _____ contains your personal and financial goals.

7. _____ are things you want to achieve.

8. A(n) _____ is a person who gives financial advice to individuals.

9. When you choose to give up one item to buy another, you are making a(n) _____.

10. Items of value that you own, called _____, may be appreciating or depreciating.

11. _____ are expenses that can go up and down each month.

12. Differences between planned and actual income or expenses are called _____.

13. _____ describe how you will pay for achieving your personal goals.

14. _____ occurs when a person's personal information is used without permission to commit fraud or theft.

15. A debt you owe, called a(n) _____, must be repaid.

16. _____ is a scam that uses an e-mail message to get a person to give out personal information.

17. Things we desire to buy, called _____, go beyond filling survival needs and basic comforts.

18. _____ are money and other items of value that can be used to acquire goods and services.

ACTIVITY 2
Math Minute

Complete these problems to build your math skills. You may use spreadsheet software or complete the problems manually.

1. Michael makes $127 a week and gets paid four times a month. What is his monthly pay? His yearly pay?

2. Rachelle makes $96 a week and gets paid 52 weeks a year. What is her yearly pay? Her monthly pay?

3. Maria's planned income for July was $539. The actual amount she earned was $522. Compute the variance amount and percent. Note if the variance is favorable (F) or unfavorable (U). Round to the nearest whole percent.

4. Chin's planned entertainment expense was $125. The actual amount he spent was $106. Compute the variance amount and percent. Note if the variance is favorable (F) or unfavorable (U). Round to the nearest whole percent.

ACTIVITY 3
Make a Financial Decision

  You belong to a school club that has ten members and two teacher advisors. The club members and advisors are planning to attend a conference in your state capital. Apply the decision-making process you learned in this chapter to help you decide how your club should travel to the conference. Work with a classmate to complete this activity.

1. Define the need clearly. Write a statement that says exactly what you need to decide.

2. List options for filling the need. What methods of transportation might your club use to reach the state capital? (If you live in the state capital, assume you will need to travel 20 miles to the meeting site.) Do research as needed to find the cost of each option. Remember to consider the distance both to and from the state capital. Record detailed notes to show how the cost for each item was calculated.

3. Compare the options you have identified. List the advantages and disadvantages of each one.

4. Make a decision based on your research and evaluation of the information you have gathered. Explain why you choose one option over the others.

5. Describe how you would take action based on your decision if this were a real situation.

ACTIVITY 4
Create a Household Budget

 In this chapter, you created a realistic budget that applies to your needs now. In this activity, you will pretend that you have graduated from high school and are living on your own. You will create a household budget that would provide for your needs in that situation.

1. Review the personal budget shown in Figure 4-2.2 on page 102. You will prepare a household budget for next month. Use spreadsheet software to prepare the budget, if it is available.

2. Use the budget in Figure 4-2.2 as an example of how to set up and format the document.

119

3. Assume you work 40 hours per week 4 weeks per month. You earn $8.00 per hour. Your take-home pay (after taxes and other deductions) is $224 per week. Calculate your monthly take-home pay. Enter this amount in the Income section of the budget. Enter **$60** per month that you earn doing odd jobs such as mowing grass or babysitting for a friend. Calculate the total income.

4. Enter an amount you want to save for the month. Use an amount that you think is realistic. You may need to adjust this amount later.

5. In the Expenses section, list your estimated expenses for one month. Think of all the expenses you would have if you were living on your own. Assume that health insurance premiums have been deducted from your paycheck. Also assume that the taxes you have withheld from your paycheck are all the taxes you have to pay. You do not need to list these items as expenses. A list of typical expenses for a household budget follows. You may add other items that you think would be realistic. You may leave out items that you think you would not want to have, such as satellite TV.
   o Rent
   o Car payment
   o Telephone
   o Cell phone
   o Electricity
   o Water
   o Groceries
   o Clothing and shoes
   o Internet access
   o Gasoline
   o Lunches at work
   o Satellite TV
   o Other entertainment
   o Car license and maintenance
   o Auto and renter's insurance
   o Miscellaneous

6. Do research to find typical monthly costs for these items in your area. For example, look at advertisements for apartments in a newspaper to find rent costs. Ask your parents or other adults how much they usually pay for items such as electricity and water. Calculate the total expenses.

7. Calculate the total savings and expenses. Is the budget in balance? If it is not, change the savings or expense amounts (within realistic limits) to make the budget balance. Some ideas to help balance your budget follow.
   o Can you find an apartment where the water or electricity is included in the rent?
   o Perhaps you cannot afford a car. If you take the bus to work and other places instead, you will not have a car payment, gasoline costs, or car insurance costs. Instead, add the cost of bus fares and an occasional taxi fare.

120

- Perhaps you cannot afford both a cell phone and a house phone. Can you do without one of them to save money?
- Consider getting a two-bedroom apartment and sharing it with a friend. Your friend would pay half of the rent, electricity, and water expenses.

ACTIVITY 5
Research Identity Theft

 INTERNET academic.cengage.com/school/pfl

1. Access the Internet. Using a search engine, search using the term *identity theft*.
2. Read several articles you find about identity theft.
3. Make a list of steps consumers can take to avoid being the victim of identity theft.
4. Make a list of steps consumers should take if they learn they are the victim of identity theft.
5. For each site you used to find information, list the article or Web page name, the Web site, the Web address, and the date you accessed the site. For example: "Welcome to the Federal Trade Commission, Your National Resource about Identity Theft," Federal Trade Commission Web site http://www.consumer.gov/idtheft/ (accessed May 12, 20--).

ACTIVITY 6
Evaluate a Financial Plan

 Critical Thinking

Take a look at the financial plan on the next page, and answer these questions:

1. Do you think the personal goals are realistic for a student who is currently a sophomore in high school?
2. Label each personal goal as short-term, intermediate, or long-term.
3. If this student gets a job, how much will she have to earn in take-home pay in order to meet her financial goals?
4. How can you add to or refine this plan to make it better?

121

GLORIA CADIZ FINANCIAL PLAN
Updated January 1, 20--

Net Worth on January 1, 20-- $150

Personal Goals	Financial Goals	Steps to Take	Timeline
1. Get a degree in landscape architecture	• Save $1,050 for college tuition, books, and fees	• Save $35 per month	• 30 months
	• Get financial aid to cover the balance	• Apply for financial aid	• January 20-- (next year as a junior)
		• Apply for a scholarship	• April 20-- (next year)
2. Own a car	• Save $500 for a car down payment	• Save $25 per month	• 20 months
	• Borrow money from bank	• Get a job so I will qualify for a loan	• Get a summer job and a part-time job by January 1, 20--
3. Take a vacation in Hawaii before starting college	• Save $1,500 for a vacation	• Save $50 per month	• 30 months
	• Buy new clothes for trip	• Make reservations early to get the best deal	• January 20-- (in 2 years)

© Getty Images/PhotoDisc

CHAPTER 5

Banking Procedures

Chapter 5 discusses banking activities for consumers and banking in the United States. Many benefits and services for consumers are available from financial institutions. Some accounts have fees or restrictions of which consumers should be aware. Banking in this country is centralized through the Federal Reserve System. In this chapter, you will explore how this system works and what it means to you as a consumer.

ONLINE RESOURCES

Personal Financial Literacy Web site:

- **Data Files**
- **Vocabulary Flashcards**
- **Sort It Out: Banking Procedures**
- **Chapter 5 Supplemental Activity**

Search terms:
- bank reconciliation
- online banking
- U.S. savings bonds
- Federal Reserve System
- monetary policy

Checking Accounts

OUTCOMES

- Explain the purpose and use of a checking account.
- Prepare a checkbook register.
- Write a check and prepare a deposit slip.
- Prepare a bank reconciliation.

INTRODUCTION TO CHECKING ACCOUNTS

Banks offer various types of accounts that consumers may find useful. Checking accounts, savings accounts, certificates of deposit, and money market accounts are popular choices. In this part of the chapter, you will learn about checking accounts. You will learn about other types of accounts in the next part of the chapter.

A **checking account** is a demand deposit account in a bank. Its purposes are to provide a safe place to keep money and to allow users easy access to the money in the account. The account holder may withdraw money from the account at any time. The account holder is also able to write checks on the account. A **check** is a written order to a bank to pay the stated amount to the person or business named on the check from an account. Checks can be used to pay bills by mail or to purchase items in stores. Writing a check for a major purchase is safer than carrying a large amount of cash to a store. A canceled check (one that has been cashed) also serves as proof of payment for bills or purchases.

A checking account provides a safe place to keep money. Checking accounts at banks generally are insured by the Federal Deposit Insurance Corporation (FDIC) up to the legal limit of $100,000 per depositor per bank. The FDIC is an agency of the federal government. By insuring deposits in banks, the FDIC helps to promote public confidence in the U.S. financial system. Consumers should confirm that a checking account will be insured by the FDIC before opening an account.

Opening a Checking Account

To open a checking account, the account holder will need some money (cash or checks). Often, as little as $50 or $100 is needed to open an account. The account holder will be given some checks when the account is opened. These checks have blank spaces in which to write information about the account. Personalized checks, which have the account holder's

Financial institutions offer checking accounts and many other financial services.

name and other data printed on them, are provided a short time later. A checkbook register and a checkbook cover are usually included with the checks. With a typical account, the account holder is charged a fee for the personalized checks. The account holder may also be charged a monthly fee for the account or for each check written. These fees may not apply if a certain minimum balance, such as $1,000, is kept in the account.

When opening a checking account, the account holder will need to provide personal data. An address, a phone number, and a Social Security number are usually required. The account holder may be asked to show a picture ID such as a driver's license for identification.

Some banks request that the account holder answer a security question, such as "What is your pet's name?" Others ask for a code word, such as your mother's maiden name. The purpose of a security question or code word is to identify the account holder when he or she calls on the phone.

The account holder will sign a signature card. This card provides an official signature that the bank can compare to the signature written on checks. A bank account can be a joint account owned by two or more people. Each person who is authorized to write checks on the account must have a signature card on file with the bank. The account holder should sign her or his name on the signature card the way it will appear on signed checks.

125

CHECK CASHING SERVICES

Exchanging a check written to you for money is called cashing the check. The money received can be in currency (bills and coins). It can also be a credit (increase) in your checking account if the check is deposited.

Some banks will not allow a person to cash a check unless he or she has an account with the bank. A very profitable business is cashing checks for people who may not have their own checking accounts. Check cashing businesses charge a fee for this service. Some states regulate the fees that may be charged. Fees vary by state and, in some cases, by the type of check being cashed. For example, the fee for a Social Security check might be 3 percent or $2, whichever is greater. The fee for a personal check might be 10 percent or $5, whichever is greater. If you have your own checking account, you do not have to use a check cashing service, and you can keep the full amount of the check.

Some check cashing companies also make short-term loans. An individual is given an advance, often called a payday loan, based on proof of employment. The borrower writes a check to the lender for the amount to be borrowed plus a fee.

The lender agrees to hold the check (not cash or deposit it) until after the borrower's next payday. A high fee is charged for this service. For example, to get an advance of $100 for 14 days, a borrower might have to pay a fee of $15. This fee is in addition to repaying the $100. In this example, the cost of the loan is a $15 finance charge at a 391 percent annual percentage rate.

Payday loans can be helpful to consumers. However, consumers should use this service sparingly. Getting payday loans regularly can lead to a cycle of borrowing money at a high cost. For example, a consumer may not have enough money to pay bills this month. A payday loan can help provide the money needed. However, the next month, the consumer may have even less money with which to pay bills. This happens because part of the money earned this month must be used to repay the loan from last month. The consumer is again short of money after repaying the loan. Borrowing money from other sources at a lower rate may be a better short-term solution for the consumer. Developing a budget that allows the consumer to pay all expenses with the available income is a better long-term solution.

Keeping a Checkbook Register

Keeping accurate records of checking account transactions is very important. Account holders should verify that the amounts deducted from the account and the amounts added to the account are correct. A **checkbook register** is a tool that can be used to track checking account transactions. The register can also provide a record of payments made for bills or purchases.

A **deposit** is money added to a checking or savings account. The money can be in the form of currency, checks, or electronic transfers. All deposits, checks, other withdrawals, and fees should be recorded in the checkbook register. The purpose of the transaction can also be recorded.

FIGURE 5-1.1

CHECKBOOK REGISTER

CHECK NO. OR TRANSACTION CODE	DATE	DESCRIPTION OF TRANSACTION	PAYMENT/ DEBIT (–)	FEE (–)	✓	DEPOSIT/ CREDIT (+)	BALANCE $800 00
581	7/1/--	Food Mart	$ 36 12	.20		$	36 32
		Groceries					763 68
DEP	7/15/--	Deposit Paycheck				220 50	220 50
							984 18
WD	7/16/--	ATM Withdrawal	20 00				20 00
							964 18
582	7/20/--	Bellvue Apts.	600 00	.20			600 20
		Rent					363 98
ON	7/22/--	Metro Gas & Electric	32 50				32 50
		Online Payment					331 48
SC	7/31/--	Monthly Account Fee		5.00			5 00
		July					326 48

A running balance in the register shows the amount of money in the account. By carefully entering all data related to the account into the register, you will be sure to know how much money is in your account at all times. A register can be kept manually or using a computer program such as *Excel* or *Quicken*. A manual register is shown in Figure 5-1.1.

Always complete the register entry for a check first. Then write the check. This process will help ensure that you do not forget to enter the item. Checking the balance in the account before writing a check is a good practice. You want to be sure you have enough money in the account to cover the check.

In the first column of the register, list the check number or a code to identify the transaction. For example, enter a code such as DEP to stand for *deposit*. Enter a code such as WD to stand for *withdrawal*. The check number, 581, is entered on the first line of the register in Figure 5-1.1.

In the Date column, enter the current date. (The characters -- are used in Figure 5-1.1 to represent the current year.) In the Description of Transaction column, enter the name of the person or business to which the check is written. You can also enter the purpose for the check. For example, Groceries is entered on line 2 of the register in Figure 5-1.1.

In the Payment/Debit column, enter the amount of the check or other withdrawal. If there is a check fee, enter that amount in the Fee column. In the register in Figure 5-1.1, $0.20 is entered as the check fee. When making a deposit, enter the amount in the Deposit/Credit column. Carry the amount of the payment plus any fee or the deposit to the Balance column. Subtract the payment or add the deposit amount to find the new balance.

CHECKS AND OTHER DEBITS

An advantage to a checking account is that the money is easy to access. The account holder can write checks to use money to pay bills or make purchases. Many banks offer debit cards that can also be used to make purchases or get cash. Automated teller machines (ATMs) are provided by many banks. Bank customers and others can use an ATM card to withdraw money from a checking account.

Some accounts offer the option of automatic withdrawals. With an **automatic withdrawal**, money is deducted from your account and

127

FIGURE 5-1.2

PERSONAL CHECK

Carley Jackson
Phone: 555-0100
4250 West 18th Avenue
Chicago, IL 60601-2180

581

July 1, 20 -- $\frac{2\text{-}74}{710}$

PAY TO THE
ORDER OF _Food Mart_ | $ _36.12_

Thirty-six and $^{12}/_{100}$ _____ DOLLARS

For Classroom Use Only

SKY CENTRAL BANK
Chicago, Illinois

MEMO _groceries_   Carley Jackson

⑈071000741⑈ 08⑈40⑈856⑈

transferred to another party. For example, insurance premiums could be deducted from your account and transferred to the insurance company. The main advantage is that you do not have to write a check each month to pay this bill.

Writing Checks

A check is a legal document used to transfer money. When you write a check, you are telling the bank to pay money to the person or company named on the check. This person or company is called the payee. The payee can cash the check or deposit it into a bank account.

Figure 5-1.2 shows an example check. Notice that the account holder's name and address are printed on the check. The check number, 581, appears near the top right of the check.

Checks should be written in ink. Use dark ink, such as navy blue or black. Write legibly so that your handwriting can be read. Fill in the spaces, and do not leave space before or after your writing. Follow these steps as you write checks:

1. Enter the current date. Checks should not be postdated. A **postdated check** is a check written with a date that will occur in the future. Banks will not hold postdated checks until the future date; they will process them at once without regard to the date.

2. Enter the name of the payee on the Pay to the Order of line. Do not leave this line blank. If you do so and lose the check, anyone can cash the check by simply writing the word *Cash* or her or his own name in the blank.

3. Enter the amount of the check in numbers after the dollar sign. Fill the space, separating dollars and cents clearly.

4. Write the dollar amount in words. Do not leave extra space anywhere on the line. Draw a line to the end if the space is not filled. Use the word *and* to separate dollars and cents, such as "Fifty-five and 35/100"_____ Dollars.

5. Sign your name exactly as you signed it for the signature card at the bank. Do not leave the signature line blank. An account holder authorized to write and sign checks is called a drawer.

6. Enter a note on the Memo line, if desired, to give the purpose of the check.

128

If you make a mistake when writing a check, begin again with a new check. On the check with the error, write VOID in large letters. In the checkbook register, write VOID over the entry in the Description of Transaction column. Draw a line through the check amount and the balance amount. Record the check data again, using the new check number.

Using Debit Cards and ATM Cards

A **debit card** allows the account holder to withdraw cash from an account at an ATM. The card can also be used to make purchases. The effect is the same as writing a check, but the withdrawal is made electronically. The money is taken out of the account very quickly. To use a debit card, the account holder passes the card through a card reader of some type. The account holder must also enter a personal identification number (PIN) or password. In some systems, a signature is also required. The PIN gives access to the account, so it should be guarded carefully.

An ATM card is similar to a debit card; however, the ATM card can be used only at an ATM. The account holder cannot make a purchase using an ATM card. At an ATM, the ATM card can be used to get cash from an account or to make deposits to an account.

Protecting Your Account Data

When someone alters a check to get money from another person's account, that is a crime called check fraud. When someone signs another person's name on a check, it is the crime of forgery. Identity theft occurs when someone uses your data without your permission to make purchases, withdraw cash, or borrow money. To help protect yourself from crime, take good care of your supply of checks. Keep them in a safe location. When using a debit card or an ATM card, protect your PIN or password and account number. Do not give out your bank account number unless you are sure the person or company receiving it is reputable.

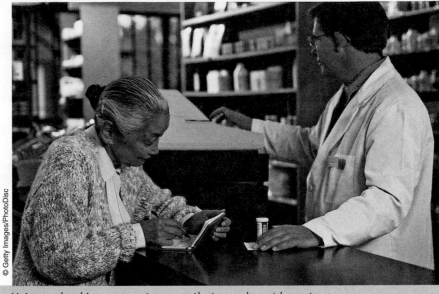

Using a checking account means that you do not have to carry as much cash.

Automated teller machines make personal banking easy and convenient.

MAKING DEPOSITS

A short time after opening an account, the account holder will usually receive personalized deposit slips, along with checks. Blank deposit slips, available at the bank, can also be used. Figure 5-1.3 on page 130 shows

FIGURE 5-1.3 **DEPOSIT FORM**

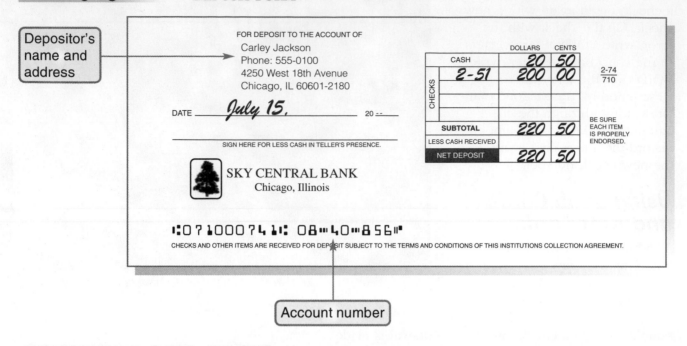

Depositor's name and address →

FOR DEPOSIT TO THE ACCOUNT OF
Carley Jackson
Phone: 555-0100
4250 West 18th Avenue
Chicago, IL 60601-2180

DATE _____ *July 15,* _____ 20 --

SIGN HERE FOR LESS CASH IN TELLER'S PRESENCE.

SKY CENTRAL BANK
Chicago, Illinois

⑆071000741⑆ 08⑈40⑈856⑈

CHECKS AND OTHER ITEMS ARE RECEIVED FOR DEPOSIT SUBJECT TO THE TERMS AND CONDITIONS OF THIS INSTITUTIONS COLLECTION AGREEMENT.

		DOLLARS	CENTS	
CASH		20	50	2-74/710
CHECKS	2-51	200	00	
SUBTOTAL		220	50	BE SURE EACH ITEM IS PROPERLY ENDORSED.
LESS CASH RECEIVED				
NET DEPOSIT		220	50	

Account number

a deposit slip for a checking account. Note that the depositor's name and address are printed on the slip. The account number appears at the bottom of the slip.

Checks that are to be included in a deposit must be properly endorsed. An **endorsement** is a signature or instructions written on the back of a check. It authorizes the bank to cash or deposit the check. If a check is not properly endorsed, it may be returned by the bank to the customer and not included in the deposit. Some endorsements provide more instructions than others. The most commonly used forms of endorsement are blank, restrictive, and special. Look closely at Figure 5-1.4 on page 131 as you read about each form of endorsement.

Many checks have an endorsement area printed on the back of the check. Be careful to write the endorsement within this area. If the back of the check is blank, place the check face up. Turn the check over, keeping the same edge at the left. Write an endorsement on the left edge of the check or other marked endorsement area.

For a blank endorsement, the signature of the payee is written on the back of the check. The signature must be in ink. This endorsement provides little protection. Anyone who has the check can cash it. This endorsement should be used only when you are at the bank ready to cash or deposit the check.

In a restrictive endorsement, the purpose of the transfer of the check is given. For example, *For deposit only* may be written on the check above the name of the payee.

In a special endorsement, the words *Pay to the order of* and the name of the person or company to which the check is being transferred are placed before the signature of the payee. In some instances, a special endorsement is referred to as an *endorsement in full*.

Once the checks are endorsed and the cash is totaled, you are ready to complete the deposit slip. Follow these steps to prepare a deposit slip. Refer to Figure 5-1.3 as you read the instructions.

FIGURE 5-1.4

Endorse Here	Endorse Here	Endorse Here
x *Sean Burns*	For deposit only Tony Cadiz	x *Pay to the order of* *Baylor Florist* *Drew L. Westwood*
Do not sign, write, or stamp below this line.	Do not sign, write, or stamp below this line.	Do not sign, write, or stamp below this line.
For financial institution use only	For financial institution use only	For financial institution use only
Blank Endorsement	Restrictive Endorsement	Special Endorsement

1. Enter the current date on the Date line.

2. Enter the amount of cash (bills and coins) in the Cash section.

3. Enter checks in the Checks section. Enter the bank's American Banking Association (ABA) number, shown at the upper-right-hand corner of most checks, beside each check. A deposit may contain more checks than can be listed on the front of the deposit slip. When this is the case, list the other checks on the back of the slip in the spaces provided. Carry the total of the checks to the front of the deposit slip.

4. Enter the total amount of cash and checks in the Subtotal section.

5. Enter the amount of cash received at the time of deposit, if any, in the Less Cash Received section, and sign on the line indicated.

6. Enter the total deposit amount in the Net Deposit section.

7. Make the appropriate entry in your checkbook register to record the deposit.

Deposits can be made at one of your bank's ATMs. If you make a deposit at an ATM, follow the instructions on the screen, and get a receipt. Verify that the receipt shows the correct amount of the deposit.

When checks are deposited in person, by mail, or at an ATM, it can take a few days for the deposit to be processed. The account holder may not have access to the money deposited for several days.

Automatic deposit is an option with many accounts. With **automatic deposit**, money is electronically placed in an account. Many people receive Social Security payments in this manner. Many businesses provide this service for their employees. If payday is the first of the month, the amount of the employee's net pay will be deposited electronically and is usually available on that day. The main advantage for account holders is that they have instant access to their money. This method is also safer and more convenient than carrying checks to the bank for deposit.

RECONCILING A BANK STATEMENT

Once a month, you will receive a statement from the bank. The statement may be on paper and arrive by mail, or it may be sent to you electronically. You may also receive cleared checks that your have written or photocopies of the checks. The statement will list checks, other withdrawals, and

131

deposits made to the account. It will show the account beginning balance and ending balance. Any service charges or other fees that have been debited (charged) to the account and any interest earned will also be listed.

When you get a bank statement, you should compare it to your checkbook register. You will adjust the balance shown in the checkbook register to record interest earned or fees charged. You will adjust the balance shown on the bank statement for checks or other withdrawals and deposits that have not yet been processed by the bank. After adjustments are made, the two balances (register and statement) should be the same. This process is called reconciling a bank statement. A form may be provided on the back of the bank statement for use in reconciling the account. You can also use programs such as *Excel* to prepare a reconciliation. A sample bank reconciliation is shown in Figure 5-1.5 on page 133.

Refer to Figure 5-1.5 as you read the following steps for reconciling a bank statement:

1. Enter the date of the reconciliation and the account number on the reconciliation form.

2. Enter the ending balance date and amount from the bank statement on the reconciliation form. The amount probably will not be the same as the balance shown in your checkbook register.

3. Compare your checkbook register with the bank statement. Verify that the amount of each deposit made is shown correctly on the bank statement. Place a check mark in the check mark (✓) column of the register by each deposit that is shown on the bank statement.

4. On the reconciliation form, list the date and amount of any deposits you made that do not appear on the bank statement. These are called deposits in transit. Total the amounts. Add the total deposits in transit to the bank statement ending balance. Place this amount on the Subtotal line.

5. Compare your checkbook register with the bank statement. Verify that the amount of each check you wrote and each ATM or debit card withdrawal you made is shown correctly on the bank statement. Place a check mark in the check mark (✓) column of the register by each check or other withdrawal that is shown on the bank statement.

6. On the reconciliation form, list the check number or code, date, and amount of any checks and other withdrawals you made that do not appear on the bank statement. Checks written that have not yet been processed by the bank are called outstanding checks. Total the amounts. Subtract the total from the Subtotal calculated in step 4. The amount left is called the adjusted bank balance.

7. Enter the balance date and amount shown in your checkbook register on the reconciliation form.

8. On the reconciliation form, list any fees or charges shown on the bank statement that are not recorded in the register. Total the amounts. Subtract the total from the checkbook register balance on the form. Record the fees and charges in your checkbook register, and update the balance.

9. On the reconciliation form, list any interest or other credits (additions) shown on the bank statement that do not appear in the register. Total the interest and other debits. Add this total to the amount calculated

132

FIGURE 5-1.5   **BANK STATEMENT RECONCILIATION**

RECONCILIATION OF BANK STATEMENT

Date   August 3, 20--

Account No.   942869

Bank Statement Balance on   July 31, 20-- $ 966.68

Add Deposits in Transit and Other Credits

Date	Amount
7/31/20--	220.50

Total Deposits in Transit/Credits   220.50

Subtotal   1,187.18

Deduct Outstanding Checks/Withdrawals

Check No.	Date	Amount
580	7/2/20--	20.00
581	7/29/20--	36.12
ATM	8/1/20--	40.00

Total Outstanding Checks/Withdrawals   96.12

Adjusted Bank Balance $ 1,091.06

Checkbook Register Balance on   August 3, 20-- $ 1,096.06

Deduct Bank Charges

Description	Amount
Service charge, monthly fee	5.00

Total Bank Charges   5.00

Subtotal   1,091.06

Add Interest or Other Credits

Description	Amount

Total Credits   0

Adjusted Checkbook Register Balance $ 1,091.06

133

in step 8. Record the interest or other credits in the register, and update the balance.

10. Compare the adjusted bank statement balance and the adjusted checkbook register balance. The two amounts should be the same. If they are not, complete the steps again and check your calculations carefully. If the numbers still are not the same, check your calculations in the checkbook register. If you find that a mistake has been made, add or subtract the amount of the mistake to correct the checkbook register balance.

11. In the checkbook register, enter a note in the Description column to indicate that the balance in is agreement with the bank balance on this date; for example, "Register and statement are in balance on August 3, 20- -."

12. Store the bank statement and the completed reconciliation form for future reference. Organize the documents by date so you can find a particular statement easily.

CHECKING ACCOUNT FEES

Some checking accounts do not have monthly service fees. To get this type of account, you may have to meet some criteria. For example, you may be required to keep a minimum balance in the account. Some checking accounts pay interest to you on the money you keep in the account. You might choose to have an account that pays a lower interest rate on the deposited amount in order to have no monthly fee.

Some accounts charge a fee for each check you write, such as 20 cents. In other accounts, you might be allowed ten checks at no charge and then have a set charge for each check after that. Fees and rules for checking accounts vary. Consumers should compare accounts and banks to find the best value for the type of account desired.

Credit unions are not-for-profit financial organizations. Members of a credit union may be offered free checking accounts with no minimum deposit. Some banks offer free checking accounts to senior citizens or others. Students or people under age 18 may also qualify. Accounts with monthly fees often cost $5 to $10 a month. This charge is in addition to charges for checks and fees for other services.

5-1 Activity 1 Can You Recall?

Answer these questions to help you recall what you have read. If you cannot answer a question, read the related section again.

1. What are the purposes of a checking account?
2. What information will a person typically be required to provide when opening a checking account? What form of identification and other information might also be required?
3. Checking accounts at banks generally are insured by the FDIC for up to how much?
4. What is the purpose of a signature card?
5. What does the term *cashing a check* mean?
6. Why should consumers use payday loans sparingly?
7. What is the purpose of a checkbook register? What types of data should be in a register?
8. List the six steps in writing a check.
9. What should you do with a check on which you make an error?
10. What is the difference between a debit card and an ATM card?
11. Why is it important to protect your bank account number and PIN or password?
12. What is the purpose of a check endorsement? How does a blank endorsement differ from a restrictive endorsement?
13. What procedure should you follow when completing a deposit form if you have more checks than can be listed on the front of the form?
14. What are some advantages for account holders of having automatic deposit for money received?
15. What is the purpose of completing a bank statement reconciliation?

5-1 Activity 2 Manage a Checking Account

Managing your checking account is a responsibility. You should write checks and complete deposit forms and the checkbook register carefully to avoid errors. In this activity, you will update a checkbook register, complete a deposit form, write checks, and reconcile a bank statement. Use the current year for dates. Refer to Figures 5-1.1, 5-1.2, 5-1.3, 5-1.4, and 5-1.5 for examples as you complete the activity.

1. Open and print the PDF file *CH05 Forms* from the data files. This file contains a deposit form and checks. It also contains a checkbook register.

135

2. Use the following information to complete the checkbook register and the deposit form. Remember to sign your name on the appropriate line to indicate that you received cash. Show how you would endorse the checks you are depositing using the space provided.
   - Date of the deposit: August 30, 20--
   - Items to be deposited:
     Currency   0
     Checks
     15-456 $108.66
     16-589 $ 50.00
   - Cash received from the deposit: $25.00

3. On August 30, write a check for $15.85 to Quick Pizza for food. Remember to complete the checkbook register before writing the check. Sign your name (first and last) to the check.

4. On August 31, complete the register and write a check for $12.35 to Fresh Cleaners for cleaning services. Sign your name to the check.

5. Open and print the PDF file *CH05 Statement* from the data files. This file contains a bank statement and a reconciliation form.

6. Reconcile the bank statement. Use the checkbook register you completed earlier. You can use the form provided or create a similar form using software such as *Excel*. Use September 3, 20--, as the date for the reconciliation.

7. Check your work. The adjusted bank statement balance and the adjusted checkbook register balance should be $382.29.

Savings Accounts

OUTCOMES

- Explain the purpose of savings.
- Compute interest on savings at a fixed interest rate.
- List savings options and their advantages.

THE PURPOSE OF SAVINGS

Saving money is important because it means you are providing for future needs and wants. A **savings account** is a demand deposit account that may have some restrictions about how quickly or easily the money can be withdrawn. When an account allows quick and easy access to the money in it, this is known as liquidity. Savings accounts are not as liquid as checking accounts. The purpose of a savings account is to accumulate money in a safe place for future use. Savings accounts at banks generally are insured by the FDIC up to the legal limit of $100,000 per depositor per bank.

Most savings accounts pay interest at a low rate. However, the rate is higher than on money in a checking account. Some banks allow depositors to link their savings and checking accounts. This allows the transfer of money back and forth (by phone or electronically) at the account holder's convenience.

Having a savings account helps you be prepared for emergencies and other unplanned spending. It gives you flexibility so that you can

Savings allow you to make purchases in the future.

make better buying decisions. For example, you may be able to buy items now at sale prices that will be used in the future. Buying at sale prices now saves money in the long run. Savings accounts allow you to accumulate money for large purchases, such a car or house. Setting aside money today for use later is a first step in becoming financially secure.

COMPUTING INTEREST

Money deposited in a savings account will usually earn a set rate of interest. Interest earnings are taxable when they are earned. The sum of money set aside on which interest is paid is called **principal**. Money earned on the principal is called interest. The higher the rate of interest, the more money the account earns.

When interest is computed on the principal once in a certain time period, this is called simple interest. The interest amount is not added to the principal. The simple interest method assumes that one interest payment will be made at the end of the period. Interest rates are usually given in yearly rates. However, the interest may be paid after a certain number of months. In this case, the months must be converted into a fraction of a year. The fraction is shown as a decimal amount in the formula. The formula for calculating simple interest and a sample problem are shown in Figure 5-2.1.

Another way of calculating interest is called **compound interest**. With this method, interest earned is added to the principal. Then, interest will be earned on the principal plus interest that was earned earlier. Figure 5-2.2 shows how interest compounds. The principal, $100, was put into savings at an annual rate of 6 percent. The interest was then compounded quarterly (4 times per year) for 3 years. An interest rate of 6 percent per year is 1.5 percent quarterly.

FIGURE 5-2.1

SIMPLE INTEREST EXAMPLE

SIMPLE INTEREST
Interest (I) = Principal (P) × Rate (R) × Time (T)
Interest = $1,000 × 6% annual rate × 6 months
$30 = $1,000 × 0.06 × 0.5

FIGURE 5-2.2

COMPOUND INTEREST EXAMPLE

138

			QUARTERLY COMPOUNDING (Annual Interest Rate 6%)				
			Quarterly Interest				
Year	Beginning Balance	Rate	1	2	3	4	Ending Balance
1	$100.00	0.015	$1.50	$1.52	$1.55	$1.57	$106.14
2	$106.14	0.015	$1.59	$1.62	$1.64	$1.66	$ 112.65
3	$ 112.65	0.015	$1.69	$1.72	$1.74	$1.77	$ 119.57

SAVINGS OPTIONS

Many people choose to save money using a savings account at the same bank where they have a checking account. This option provides some advantages. Using one bank for both accounts may be more convenient than using two or more banks. Having both accounts in one bank may allow you to use the savings account for overdraft protection. This means that if you write checks for more money than you have in your checking account, the bank will draw the money from your savings account or loan it to you. Without this protection, the check would be returned for non-sufficient funds (NSF). You would probably have to pay fees to your bank and to the person or business to which you wrote the check, as well as the original amount of the check.

Certificates of Deposit

Banks offer other savings options that you should consider in addition to a savings account. A **certificate of deposit**, called a CD, is a time deposit (rather than a demand deposit). This means that the money you deposit is set aside for a fixed amount of time. For example, you may put your money into a 6-month CD at a guaranteed rate of 5.25 percent. If you leave your money in the CD for the entire 6 months, you will earn the full 5.25 percent. If you withdraw part or all of it before the 6 months, you will be penalized. At some banks, you will lose part of your principal, as well as receive no interest on the money deposited.

Money Market Accounts

A **money market account** is another option offered by some banks. This type of account pays the market rate of interest on the money deposited. When interest rates are rising, a money market account will often earn more than a savings account or CD. When rates are falling, however, the interest earned may be less than that paid on a CD. A minimum balance, such as $1,000 or $5,000, is often required to open a money market account. Restrictions may apply to the account. For example, you may be able to write only two or three checks per month on the account. If you do not maintain the balance required, or if you write too many checks, you will be charged fees.

U.S. Savings Bonds

If you are able to commit your money for a longer period of time, you have other choices. One good long-term choice is a savings bond. A **U.S. savings bond** is a discount bond issued by the federal government. That means you pay less than face value. For example, you can purchase a $100 (face value) Series EE paper savings bond for $50. As interest is earned on the bond, it will grow to be worth the $100 (the maturity value).

U.S. savings bonds pay a guaranteed rate of interest if you keep the bond for a certain period of time. U.S. bonds are considered to be a safe form of saving. If you cash the

© Getty Images/PhotoDisc

A certificate of deposit or money market account provides a good way to save for education in the future.

139

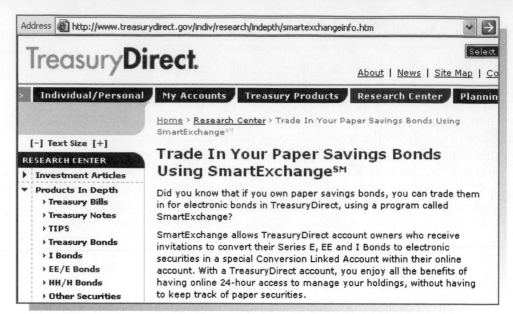

Source: TreasuryDirect, Converting Your Paper Savings Bonds Using SmartExchange, http://www.treasurydirect.gov/indiv/research/indepth/smartexchangeinfo.htm (accessed April 27, 2006).

bond before the time is up, the bond will earn a lower rate of interest. U.S. savings bonds can be purchased through banks or at the TreasuryDirect® Web site. You can also see the guaranteed rates currently being paid at the Web site. You can access the TreasuryDirect Web site using the link provided on the Web site for this textbook.

Once a savings bond has matured (has reached face value), it may continue to earn interest. In general, savings bonds earn interest for different lengths of time. Some types earn interest for up to 40 years. Others stop earning interest after 20 or 30 years. Information about the length of time a bond earns interest can be found on the TreasuryDirect Web site. When a bond stops earning interest, it should be cashed in or converted to another type of bond. Interest is not taxable until the bond is cashed in. If the bond is used for education expenses (for yourself or your children), the interest may not be subject to federal taxes. Look for more information about taxes on bonds at the TreasuryDirect Web site.

Individual Retirement Arrangements

Saving for retirement is an important goal for many people. One way to save for retirement is by creating an individual retirement arrangement (IRA). An IRA allows individuals to deposit money into an account during their working years. The money deposited may be tax-deductible. Taxes are paid on the money and interest earned when the money is withdrawn during retirement. Taxes paid then may be at a lower rate than the rate paid during working years.

IRAs can be set up at a bank or another financial institution. IRAs can also be set up through mutual fund companies, insurance companies, and stockbrokers. Different types of IRAs can be created. The amount of money that can be put in the account each year and other rules regarding IRAs are set by the federal government. More information about IRAs can be found in *Publication 590, Individual Retirement Arrangements (IRAs)* from the Internal Revenue Service. A link to the IRS Web site where you can search for this publication is provided on the Web site for this textbook.

Negotiation is the process of reaching an agreement that benefits you or enables you to get what is important to you. You have probably heard the expression "In life you don't get what you deserve; you get what you negotiate." It's true—people who have good negotiation skills get more of what they want!

The first step in negotiating is to understand your own position. What exactly do you want? In clear, unemotional words, be able to state your wants or needs. Have solid reasons for your choices.

The second step in negotiating is to understand your opponent's position. What exactly does he or she want? What needs and motives does this person have? When you know her or his needs, you can find ways to meet them while meeting yours, too.

Third, create a proposed solution. This usually means you give up something minor to get something important to you. It also means the other person will give up something to get what he or she wants.

People with good negotiation skills identify what is important to both sides and what they are willing to give up in order to reach an agreement. Both sides must feel good about what they are getting.

MEETING FINANCIAL GOALS

When choosing a savings option, consider your financial goals. How much money do you want to save and earn in interest for a particular purpose? How much time do you have in which to save? What interest rate can you earn on your savings?

All these factors should be considered when choosing a savings option.

The amount of time you have to save and the interest you can earn determine how much money you need to save each month or year to meet your goals. The amount of interest you can earn and the time the money must be left on deposit affect the savings option you should choose. For example, if you want to save $10,000 to buy a used car, a certificate of deposit might be a good choice. The CD would likely pay higher interest than a savings account, and you would not need immediate access to the money. A money market account might also be a good choice. This type of account typically earns higher interest than a savings account. A U.S. savings bond would probably not be a good choice in this situation. Savings bonds should be used to save for longer periods of time (20 or 30 years) to gain their full value.

A principle called the **Rule of 72** provides a quick way to see how long it will take to double money invested at a given rate. To apply the Rule of 72, simply divide the annual interest rate into 72. The answer is the number of years it will take at that rate to double the amount invested. For example, if $50 is invested at 6 percent interest, then it will grow to $100 in 12 years ($72/6 = 12$). At 4 percent interest, money invested will double in 18 years ($72/4 = 18$).

141

OTHER SERVICES AND FEES

Financial institutions offer a number of services. Some of these are included with a checking account. Others cost additional money, either once a year or as you use them.

Bank Services

Many banks rent safe deposit boxes as a service to customers. A safe deposit box is a secure container located in the bank vault. You can store important documents, such as deeds or stock certificates, there. The safe deposit box protects items from fire or theft. A safe deposit box usually costs from $35 to $100 a year, depending on the size of the box.

Overdraft protection can be a valuable service. If you write a check and your account does not have enough money to cover the check, the bank returns the check for non-sufficient funds. The check is commonly called a **bounced check**. The bank will charge you a fee when this happens—often $30 to $40, or more, per check. When a check bounces, the person or business that deposited it will also be charged a fee. You will be expected to pay that fee as well. A bounced check could cost you $50 or more! If you have overdraft protection, NSF checks will be paid rather than bounced. The money may come from a savings account you have at the bank. The money might also be paid by the bank as a short-term loan to you. You would have to pay the amount of the check plus a fee. However, the fee would be less than if the check bounced.

Ethics

WRITING BAD CHECKS

Having a checking account is not a right; it is a privilege. Banks, credit unions, and others make these accounts available to customers. Using a checking account is a very convenient way to manage money. You should monitor your account carefully. Be certain you have money in your account to cover checks you write.

When you write a check and you do not have money in your account to cover it, you are writing a *bad check*. This is also called a non-sufficient funds (NSF) check. If you do not monitor your account balance carefully, you might write a bad check by mistake. Knowingly writing a bad check is illegal and unethical. Criminal or civil charges can be brought against a person who writes bad checks. Writing bad checks can also affect your credit rating. You may have trouble borrowing money for purchases such as a car or getting a credit card if you have a poor credit rating.

Writing bad checks can be thought of as a form of stealing. Many merchants and individuals who are given bad checks never get the money that is due them. Merchants pass on some of the cost of bad checks to consumers in the form of higher prices.

You should write checks only when you have enough money in the account to cover the check. Do not write a check and plan to deposit money later to cover the check before the check is processed. Checks can be processed quickly. You should not expect that you will have time to deposit money before a check clears.

Another service provided by banks is called stop payment. With a **stop payment**, the bank is instructed not to honor a check you wrote or lost. The bank charges a fee for this service, often $25 or more per check. If the check has not already been processed, it will not be honored by the bank.

A **cashier's check** is a check issued against bank funds. When you buy a cashier's check, the money comes from your account to pay the bank. The money for the payee of the cashier's check comes from the bank's account. Some people prefer to receive a cashier's check rather than a personal check because a cashier's check is more secure. The check will not bounce because the money is set aside and waiting to be paid by the bank.

Some banks issue money orders. A **money order** is a type of check used to pay bills or make a payment for which the money is guaranteed. There is usually a fee for this service, based on the amount of the money order.

Some banks and credit unions also offer personal financial advising services. They look at your goals and resources and sell you financial products, such as mutual funds. Before investing, check options on your own. Be sure the funds and other products have been in existence for a long time and have performed well over time.

Banks offer loans to their depositors. Credit unions offer loans to their members. Because credit unions are nonprofit organizations, members may get lower interest rates on loans. Some examples of the types of loans provided by banks and credit unions are home mortgage loans, car loans, and personal lines of credit.

Technology Corner

INTERNET BANKING

Many banks allow their account holders to have Internet and telephone access to their accounts. An access code or PIN number along with a user name is needed. Customers can view their accounts at almost any time on any day. Banks typically will close access to accounts for several hours on the weekend so that they can update their systems. Accounts cannot be accessed during this time for online banking.

Internet banking may offer other services, such as those in the following list:

- Paying bills electronically
- Transferring money between accounts, such as from checking to savings

- Monitoring activity in an account
- Checking that deposits are posted
- Seeing which checks have cleared (have been processed)
- Seeing interest or fees that have been posted

Many people think that banking via the Internet is as safe as writing paper checks. When deposits and withdrawals are made electronically, nothing can get lost in the mail. Account holders can see when checks and deposits have been processed and exactly how much is in an account at any time.

143

Some financial institutions offer car buying services. For a fee of about $500, the company will find and buy the new or used car of your choice. This saves you the hassle of negotiating the price for the car. Basically, you are paying the company to negotiate on your behalf. In many cases, the bank or credit union is able to get a better price than you can.

Bank Cards

Banks and credit unions issue several types of bank cards. These cards have special features and are electronically coded. This allows you to use them for purchases, cash advances, and deposits.

Banks may issue credit cards to their customers who qualify and want this service. These cards often have interest rates that are both fixed and low. Because you are a customer, you may also be offered a high credit limit.

ATM cards and debits cards, discussed earlier in the chapter, are two other types of bank cards. Making a purchase with a debit card usually does not involve a fee. Using an ATM card may involve a fee. Many banks will allow you to use their own ATMs free of charge. If you use an ATM from another bank, however, the other bank will charge you a fee of $2 or more. Your own bank may charge you another fee of $2 or more.

Similar to debit and ATM cards, a smart card carries an electronic balance on the card. These cards can also be purchased at stores in the form of gift cards that can be renewed. You deposit money to the smart card electronically when you purchase or renew the card. When the money is spent, you can add more money to the card and continue using it. The advantage of a smart card is that it is not linked to your checking account, and if it is lost or stolen, the thief cannot access your account.

5-2 Activity 1 Can You Recall?

Answer these questions to help you recall what you have read.
If you cannot answer a question, read the related section again.

1. What is the purpose of a savings account?
2. What is the sum of money set aside on which interest is paid called?
3. What is the formula for calculating simple interest?
4. How does compound interest differ from simple interest?
5. How do a certificate of deposit and a money market account differ from a regular savings account? How are they the same?
6. Why is a U.S. savings bond considered a safe form of saving?
7. What is the purpose of an IRA? What types of companies offer IRAs?
8. How do the amount of time you have to save and the interest you can earn relate to achieving financial goals?
9. What is the Rule of 72 that is related to saving?
10. List some other services banks may provide for customers in addition to checking and savings accounts.

5-2 Activity 2 Compute Interest

1. Selena has placed $500 in an account that pays simple interest of 5 percent annually. How much interest will Selena have earned by the end of the year?
2. Suki has placed $800 in an account that pays 4 percent interest compounded quarterly. What will be the balance in the account at the end of 2 years (8 quarters)? How much interest will Suki have earned during that time? Round your answers to the nearest cent.
3. Jessica is considering putting her money ($50) into a $100 paper U.S. savings bond. Assume the guaranteed rate of interest is 4 percent. How long will it take for the money to double (reach $100)? Use the Rule of 72 to find the answer.

145

The Federal Reserve System

OUTCOMES

- Describe the purpose of the Federal Reserve System.
- Define *monetary policy* and discuss goals of U.S. monetary policy.
- Explain how the Federal Reserve System controls the banking industry.
- Identify the types of interest rates controlled by the Federal Reserve System.

INTRODUCTION TO THE FEDERAL RESERVE SYSTEM

The Federal Reserve System is the central bank of the United States. It is commonly called the Fed. The Fed was created by Congress in 1913. Its purpose is to provide the nation with safe, flexible, and stable monetary and financial systems. The system has a seven-member Board of Governors. Its headquarters is in Washington, D.C. The Fed also has 12 regional banks located in major cities across the United States. The 12 Federal Reserve districts are shown in Figure 5.3-1 on page 147.

The seven members of the Board of Governors are nominated by the President. They are confirmed by the U.S. Senate to serve 14-year terms of office. Members may serve only one full term. The President also chooses two members to be the Chairman and the Vice Chairman, for four-year terms. These terms may be renewed by the President.

ROLES OF THE FED

The Fed's activities are in four general areas as listed below. These areas are discussed in the sections that follow.

- Conducting monetary policy
- Providing financial services to the U.S. government, financial institutions, and the public
- Supervising and regulating banking
- Keeping the country's financial systems and markets stable

Conducting Monetary Policy

An important role of the Fed is conducting monetary policy. **Monetary policy** refers to actions of the Fed to influence money and credit conditions

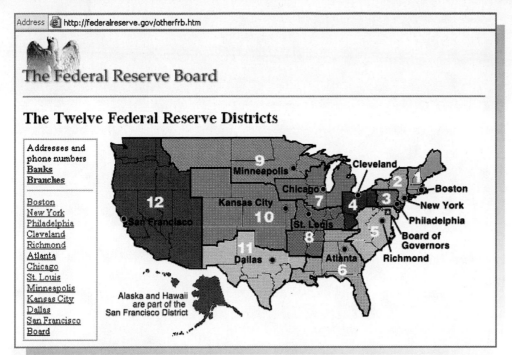

FIGURE 5-3.1

THE FEDERAL RESERVE SYSTEM DISTRICTS

Source: Federal Reserve Board, The Twelve Federal Reserve Districts, http://federalreserve.gov/otherfrb.htm (accessed April 27, 2006).

in the economy. These conditions affect employment levels and prices. The Fed tries to speed up or slow down the economy as needed to keep employment high and prices stable. The Fed watches the economy. When prices are rising too fast, it tries to slow down spending. This helps curb inflation. One way to slow down the economy is by raising interest rates. When interest rates rise, both individuals and businesses find it more expensive to borrow money to buy more goods and services. This slows down spending. (As you may recall from Chapter 3, demand-pull inflation is caused by spending in the economy.)

INTEREST RATES

Several types of interest rates are controlled by the Fed:

○ The **discount rate** is the rate that banks have to pay to borrow money from the Fed. Banks borrow money when they have the opportunity to make loans but do not have enough cash on hand. Banks are required to have a certain amount of cash on hand, called reserves. If these reserves go below the required amount, banks must borrow money.

○ The **federal funds rate** is the rate at which banks can borrow from the excess reserves of other banks. For example, if one bank has more money than it needs, it can loan that extra money to other banks.

○ The **prime rate** is the rate that banks charge to their most creditworthy business customers. When the discount rate increases, the prime rate also rises. The prime rate is often 3 percent (or more) higher than the discount rate or the federal funds rate.

When the Fed raises the discount rate, this causes interest rates to rise on all levels. For example, when the discount rate is 3 percent and the Fed raises it to 3.25 percent, the prime rate may go up from 6 to 6.5 percent or more. Consumers are charged higher interest rates (than the prime rate) on money they borrow. When the prime rate is 6 percent, consumers are probably paying 9 percent or more. Thus, with a 0.25 percent increase in

147

Interest rates on loans change as the Fed raises and lowers its rates.

the discount rate, the rate that consumers pay will likely rise from 9 percent to 12 percent. These interest rate increases have a slowing effect on borrowing and thus on spending.

The Fed affects the money supply by changing interest rates. The money supply, also called the money stock, is made up of currency (coins and bills) held by the public. It also includes deposits held by the public in banks and other institutions, money market funds, and other deposits.

When the federal funds rate falls, short-term market interest rates also fall. The short-term market interest rates may be below the rates paid on deposits at banks. This is because changes in bank rates tend to lag behind changes in market rates. The public tends to increase deposits at the banks to get the higher rates. This means the money supply increases. However, when the federal funds rate goes up, so do other short-term interest rates. The rates paid at banks become less attractive, and money growth slows.

OPEN-MARKET TRANSACTIONS

The Fed is also responsible for selling and buying back U.S. government securities such as government bills, notes, and bonds. This activity is called open-market transactions. Consumers can buy bills, notes, and bonds from the TreasuryDirect Web site.

Government bills, also known as Treasury bills, are short-term debt, up to 26 weeks. Buyers of these bills loan money to the federal government at a set interest rate. When the Fed sells Treasury bills to consumers, savings by consumers increase. In other words, people or businesses that buy Treasury bills are saving their money rather than spending it. This slows down the economy. When the Fed buys back Treasury bills, the money is available for spending. This speeds up the economy.

Treasury notes are medium-term debt. Notes are issued for 2, 3, 5, and 10 years. Treasury bonds (like savings bonds) are long-term debt (30 years) at fixed rates. Once again, selling Treasury notes and bonds takes money from the economy, and buying them back puts money into the economy. These open-market transactions are tools used by the Fed to regulate the economy.

Providing Financial Services

The Fed plays a major role in operating the country's payment systems. For example, the Fed is responsible for printing money. As bills get old and worn, they are destroyed, and new bills are printed.

The 12 reserve banks act as a clearinghouse for checks that are written on banks in the United States. Processing of checks is rapid. Today, you can expect that checks may clear your account the same day they are received by a business. Many businesses turn a check into an electronic deduction from your account. The Fed allows this to happen.

The Fed is in charge of our nation's money supply.

Regulating the Banking Industry

The Fed is empowered by Congress to control the banking industry. All banks that have interstate (in more than one state) operations are required to be member banks of the Fed. Banks that are intrastate (state-chartered) only do not have to belong to the Fed. However, all banks are subject to the rules and regulations of the Fed. These include credit policies, minimum payments, and other lending policies.

One important policy is called the reserve requirement. It means that banks must keep on hand a percentage of deposits by customers. When the reserve requirement is raised, banks have less money to lend. When the requirement is lowered, banks have more money to lend.

Maintaining Stability

Keeping the financial systems and markets in the United States stable is another role of the Fed. This role is carried out through the routine activities of the Fed. Supervising banks helps ensure that the banking system is safe and sound. This promotes consumer confidence in the system. The Fed operates key parts of the payment systems. It also oversees operation of the payment systems in general. This oversight helps keep the systems stable. The Fed uses monetary policy, as discussed earlier, to help keep the economy stable.

Actions of the Fed affect financial decisions made by consumers in this country. By raising and lowering interest rates, the Fed influences how willing people and companies are to buy goods. Will you buy a new car or house? Will you put savings in a bank, buy bonds, or invest

5-3   The Federal Reserve System

Good reading skills will help you be more productive at school, at work, and in personal activities. Comprehension is the ability to understand what you have read. Reading for comprehension is also called study reading. The goal of this type of reading is to learn and to remember what has been read.

To help improve reading comprehension, read slowly and think about what you are reading. Written material is divided into passages. A passage is a group of paragraphs. Paragraphs are used to introduce and explain ideas. Paragraphs often have a common structure. The first sentence of a paragraph is the topic sentence. It tells you what the paragraph is about. The middle sentences explain the topic. The last sentence of a paragraph sums up or draws a conclusion. To improve understanding as you read, think about the purpose of the paragraph and how it relates to the overall topic of the passage.

Many people take notes of major points in each paragraph. Underlining or highlighting can help identify key points when you are reviewing the material. Comprehension can be improved when you read passages more than once. The first time, look for main ideas and points being made. The second time, focus on vocabulary and details.

in the stock market? Will you start a new company? Will a business expand operations by building a new plant? The answers to these questions are affected by how costly it is to borrow money. They are also affected by what consumers and companies think about the economy. If they think the economy is stable and growing, they are more likely to spend on goods and services.

5-3 Activity 1   Can You Recall?

Answer these questions to help you recall what you have read.
If you cannot answer a question, read the related section again.

1. What is the Fed? When was it created, and what is its purpose?
2. The Fed's activities are in what four general areas?
3. What is the meaning of the term *monetary policy*?
4. What is the discount rate? The federal funds rate? The prime rate?
5. How does the Fed control the money supply in the United States?
6. How do open-market transactions for U.S. government securities affect the economy?
7. What types of banks must be members of the Federal Reserve System? Are banks that are not members also regulated by the Fed?
8. What is a bank reserve requirement?

5-3 Activity 2   The Fed

 academic.cengage.com/school/pfl

1. The Federal Reserve System requires national banks to be members. There are also state-chartered banks and credit unions that are not required to join the Fed. Even though non-member banks do not belong to the Fed, how are you (the depositor) protected at these banks?
2. Refer to Figure 5-3.1 on page 147. In which city is the Federal Reserve bank that serves the area where you live?
3. Who is the chairman of the Federal Reserve System? Access the Internet and search for this information if you do not know the answer.

151

Arts, A/V Technology & Communications

EXPLORING CAREERS IN ARTS, A/V TECHNOLOGY, AND COMMUNICATIONS

Do you have artistic or musical talent? Is performing on stage your dream? Do you like to write stories with complicated plots? Do you like to find interesting ways to share information in print or video? If the answer is yes, a career in arts, A/V technology, and communications might be right for you. Jobs in this area are varied. Some workers in this field use their talents and skills to write, sing, make music, or perform on stage. Others use print, video, and technology to share creative messages. Artists, sculptors, photographers, and animators also work in this career area.

Jobs in this career area are found in government and businesses. Many people in the visual arts field, such as painters, photographers, and animators, are self-employed. They work on a freelance basis and sell their services or products to businesses and consumers. The need for jobs in arts, A/V technology, and communications varies by career area. Employment in some jobs will grow; in others, it will decline.

Skills Needed

Some of the skills and traits needed for a career in arts, A/V technology, and communications include the following:

- Communications skills
- Computer/technology skills
- Creative writing ability
- Natural talent for performing arts
- Decision-making skills
- Problem-solving skills

Job Titles

Many jobs are available in arts, A/V technology, and communications. Some job titles for this career area include the following:

- Actor/actress
- Camera operator
- Desktop publisher
- Electrical engineer
- Graphic designer
- News reporter
- Playwright
- Sound technician
- Telecommunications equipment installer

Explore a Job

1. Choose a job in arts, A/V technology, or communications to explore further. Select a job from the list above, or choose another job in this career area.
2. Access the *Occupational Outlook Handbook* online. A link to the site is provided on the Web site for this textbook.
3. Search for more information about the job you selected to answer these questions:
   - What is the nature of the work this job involves?
   - What is the job outlook for this job?
   - What training or qualifications are needed for this job?
   - What are the median annual earnings for this job?

Summary

- A checking account is a demand deposit that allows you to access your money quickly and easily.
- A checkbook register is a record of checks written, deposits and other withdrawals made, and other charges to a checking account; it must be reconciled with the bank statement.
- Checks that are to be included in a deposit must be properly endorsed.
- Automatic deposits and automatic withdrawals are the electronic transfer of funds into or from an account.
- Fees charged on checking accounts include fees for ATM withdrawals, monthly fees, fees for checks written, and NSF check fees.
- To protect your account data, keep checks in a safe location. When making a purchase or withdrawing cash with a debit card or an ATM card, protect your PIN or password and account number.
- A savings account is a demand deposit that may have some restrictions about how quickly or easily money can be withdrawn.
- A certificate of deposit or money market account offers higher interest rates than a regular savings account, but it is also less liquid.
- A U.S. savings bond is a good way to save if you can invest the money for a long term.
- A sum of money set aside on which interest is paid is called principal. The Rule of 72 calculates how quickly principal earning interest at a certain rate will double.
- The calculation for simple interest is Interest = Principal × Rate × Time. With compound interest, interest earned is added to the principal and also draws interest.
- Banks may offer services such as safety deposit boxes, overdraft protection, stop payment, cashier's checks, money orders, loans, bank cards, car buying services, and financial advice.
- The Federal Reserve System (Fed) is the central bank of the United States. It controls the money supply in the United States and sets interest rates.
- The Fed sells and buys back U.S. government securities, including notes, bills, and bonds.
- The Fed regulates the banking industry, including credit and lending policies.
- The Fed sets the reserve requirement, which gives banks more money or less money to lend.

153

Key Terms

automatic deposit	compound interest	money order
automatic withdrawal	debit card	postdated check
bounced check	deposit	prime rate
cashier's check	discount rate	principal
certificate of	endorsement	Rule of 72
deposit	federal funds rate	savings account
check	monetary policy	stop payment
checkbook register	money market	U.S. savings
checking account	account	bond

ACTIVITY 1
Review Key Terms

Use the key terms from Chapter 5 to complete the following sentences:

1. Money electronically added to your checking account is called a(n) _____.

2. A bank card that allows the account holder to make purchases and to withdraw cash from an account at an ATM is called a(n) _____.

3. A math formula called the _____ is used to tell you how long it will take money earning a certain interest rate to double.

4. A demand deposit called a(n) _____ allows you quick and easy access to your money without penalties.

5. A discount bond issued through the United States government is called a(n) _____.

6. A(n) _____ is a convenient way to pay bills if you do not have a checking account.

7. _____ is interest earned on both principal and previous interest earnings.

8. A(n) _____ is a check issued by a bank against its own funds.

9. A bank service directing the bank not to honor a check is called a(n) _____.

10. The interest rate that banks charge to corporations, called the _____, is for the most creditworthy customers.

11. A record for keeping track of checks written and deposits made is called a(n) _____.

12. A check written with a future date is called a(n) _____.

13. The rate at which banks can borrow from the excess reserves of other banks is called the _____.

14. A(n) _____ is a signature or instructions written on the back of a check authorizing a bank to cash or deposit the check.

15. A savings option called a(n) _____ pays interest at the current market rate.

16. A(n) _____ is a written order to a bank to pay the stated amount to the person or business named from a certain account.

17. The _____ is the rate banks are charged to borrow money from the Fed.

18. A check returned by the bank, called a(n) _____, was returned because there was not enough money in the account.

19. Actions of the Fed to influence money and credit conditions in the economy are called _____.

20. A(n) _____ is money deposited for a fixed amount of time at a fixed interest rate.

21. An amount of money set aside (deposited or borrowed) on which interest is paid is called the _____.

22. A demand deposit called a(n) _____ may have restrictions and/or penalties for taking out money.

23. A(n) _____ is money added to a checking or savings account.

24. A(n) _____ deducts money from an account and electronically transfers it to another party.

ACTIVITY 2
Math Minute

When interest is compounded, interest earned is added to the principal before interest is calculated again. Use spreadsheet software to complete these compound interest problems, if it is available. If not, complete the problems manually. Round to the nearest cent.

1. Gloria has an account that draws interest at the rate of 6 percent per year, compounded monthly at 0.5 percent. The following amounts were deposited in the account in the current year. What is the balance in the account on December 31 of the current year?

June 1	$50
July 1	$50
August 1	$50
September 1	$50

2. Yoshi has an account that draws interest at an annual rate of 5 percent. The interest is compounded quarterly. The following amounts were deposited in the account in the current year. What is the balance in the account on December 31 of the current year (after four quarters)?

January 1	$450
April 1	$350
July 1	$200
September 1	$300

155

ACTIVITY 3
Checkbook Register

Open and print the PDF file *CH05 Register* from the data files. For each transaction, record the information in the register. Then write the check or complete the deposit slip if one is needed for the transaction. Use the current year in dates. Keep a running balance, and double-check your work. The ending balance should be $87.38.

1. Beginning balance $218.33
2. Check No. 401 on April 1 to Westside Services $15.00 for haircut
3. Check No. 402 on April 5 to J. Jill $28.50 for new shirt
4. Cash withdrawal at ATM for $20.00 on April 8
5. Deposit of $25.00 cash on April 10 (gift from uncle)
6. Debit card purchase (DC) of $19.50 on April 11 at Rowe's for food
7. Check No. 403 on April 15 to Bill Baxter $35.00 for loan payment
8. Cash withdrawal at ATM for $20.00 on April 18
9. Debit card purchase of $9.95 on April 25 at Aston Theater for movie
10. Bank service charge on April 28 for $8.00

ACTIVITY 4
Saving for the Future

Setting aside money (saving) for the future is known as deferred spending. You are setting aside money today so that you will have it when you need it. Most financial planners recommend you save 10 percent or more of your earnings. This is a good first step toward your retirement. Use spreadsheet software to complete the following problems if available, or complete them manually. Round to the nearest cent.

1. Assume you will earn $25,000 in gross pay the first year you work. Each year after that, you will get a 3 percent increase in pay. How much money will you have earned in 10 years?

2. Assume that during the 10 years discussed in problem 1, you set aside 10 percent of your earnings as savings. You estimate you can get an average of 5 percent (simple interest) yield per year return on your savings. How much money will you have saved in 10 years?

   Example:

Year	Earnings	Savings	Interest	Total Savings and Interest
1	$25,000.00	$2,500.00	$ 125.00	$2,625.00
2	$ 25,750.00	$ 2,575.00	$260.00	$5,460.00

156

ACTIVITY 5
Online Banking

  academic.cengage.com/school/pfl

Online banking is offered by many banks. Customers may have to pay a fee for online banking services. However, using online banking saves on postage and ensures that bills are paid on time—thus avoiding late fees.

1. Work with a classmate to complete this activity. Access the Internet and enter the term **online banking** in a search engine. This search should return a list of several banks that have online banking. You can also search using the name of a local bank to see if it has a Web site available.

2. Visit the Web sites for three banks or credit unions, and learn about their online banking. Answer the following questions about each bank or credit union:
   o What is the name of the bank?
   o Is online banking available?
   o Does the bank charge a fee for online banking? If so, how much is the fee?
   o What activities can the customer do through online banking?

3. Compare the results of your findings for the three banks. Which bank do you think has the best overall plan or services for online banking? Why?

ACTIVITY 6
Choosing an Account

 Read the following descriptions for two types of checking accounts. Which one would fit your needs better? Why?

Special Student Account
o No minimum deposit required
o No monthly service fee
o ATM card provided; no fee for use at this bank's machines; $2.00 fee for use at other ATMs
o 15-cent fee for each check processed
o $2.00 flat fee for talking with a bank teller

Interest Plus Account
o Minimum deposit $1,000.00
o No monthly service fee
o ATM/debit card provided; no fee for use at this bank's machines; $2.00 fee for use at other ATMs
o No per-check fee
o Pays current rate of interest (0.5 percent)
o Automatic paycheck deposit
o No charge for talking with a bank teller

157

ACTIVITY 7
Bank Reconciliation

Use the following information to prepare a bank reconciliation. Use a format similar to that in Figure 5-1.5 for the reconciliation.

Bank reconciliation date   4/4/20--

Account no.   589125

Bank statement balance on 3/30/20-- $629.64

Checkbook register balance on 4/4/20-- $687.50

Outstanding checks
4/1/20--	Check 498	$20.00
4/5/20--	Check 499	$28.50

Deposit in transit dated 4/2/20-- $97.36

Bank fee for checking account $9.00

ACTIVITY 8
Government Bonds

 academic.cengage.com/school/pfl

Government bonds can be researched and purchased on the TreasuryDirect Web site.

1. Visit the TreasuryDirect site. A link to the site is provided on the Web site for this textbook.

2. Find information for three types of bonds: I Bonds, EE Bonds, and HH Bonds. For each type, find the following information:
   o The bond name
   o A brief description of the bond
   o The current interest rate paid on the bond
   o The minimum purchase amount
   o The maximum purchase amount per year

PERSONAL RISK MANAGEMENT

© Getty Images/PhotoDisc

hapter 6 is about managing risks. In this chapter, you will learn about the risks you face, how serious they are, and what you can do about them. Buying insurance is one option you can choose to help protect against risks. When you decide the risk is serious and the possible losses are great, then you might choose to transfer the risk. Income protection is one type of insurance. Health and life insurance are two good ways to protect income. Property can also be protected. Homeowner's or renter's insurance protects against loss of your house and personal items. Car insurance protects you from losses that might occur to your car and because of your car.

ONLINE RESOURCES

Personal Financial Literacy Web site:

Vocabulary Flashcards

Beat the Clock: Risk Management

Chapter 6 Supplemental Activity

Search terms:
- risk
- insurance
- probability
- premiums
- liability insurance

Risk Assessment and Strategies

OUTCOMES

- Explain the concept of risk.
- List the three types of risk.
- Explain what is meant by *risk assessment*.
- Discuss four risk strategies.

WHAT IS RISK?

Risk is the chance of injury, damage, or economic loss. Driving a car and snow skiing are examples of behaviors that involve risk. When you are driving a car, an accident with another car might occur. This accident could cause personal injury and damage to the car. You might have an accident while snow skiing, such as breaking your leg. There are many types of risk you will face now and in the future. Some risks are avoidable and have a small chance of happening. Other risks are unpredictable and unavoidable. Some risky events may cause serious losses if they happen.

A **loss** refers to some type of physical injury, damage to property, or absence of property or other assets. The loss might be personal in nature, such as a broken leg or an illness. The loss could be damage or removal of money or property. For example, you might lose money or property as a result of theft. Losses could be major and could have a significant effect on your future. Losing your job could mean that you cannot make payments on your house or car. This event could cause you to lose your house or have your car repossessed.

The likelihood of a risk actually resulting in a loss is called **probability**. Just because you take a risk does not mean you will always suffer a loss, nor does it mean you can always avoid a loss. You must decide whether or not the risk and its possible outcome are serious. If the possible loss is serious, you may be able to take steps to lessen the risk or the resulting loss.

Personal Risk

Taking personal risk means you could lose something of personal value to you. For example, you might break your leg and then not be able to participate in an activity you really enjoy. Some personal risks are necessary. If you do not get out of bed in the morning, you can avoid many risks. However, not getting out of bed also means you will accomplish little. If you do not wear your coat and boots when it is cold and raining, you risk getting wet and cold. This may increase your chances of getting sick. The costs and outcomes of getting sick may not be serious if you are young and likely to recover quickly. For some people who have chronic illnesses, however, this personal risk must be taken seriously because the outcome can be deadly.

Risk of Financial Loss

Some risks will result in financial loss. Financial loss refers to a cost in terms of money. The loss can be big or small. Small possible losses should be assessed differently from large possible losses. For example, if you drive without a spare tire, you risk being unable to change a flat tire. Driving without a spare tire could be expensive if you have a flat and must pay someone to help you. The money you could lose must be compared to the cost of buying the spare tire. A large loss might result from driving without car insurance. If you get into an accident, the damage you could do to another vehicle or property could cost thousands of dollars. You might have to pay this money if you have no insurance. In some states, drivers are required to have insurance. If you drive without insurance, you risk being caught and having to pay a fine. Repeated offenses may result in losing your driver's license. Information about mandatory auto insurance for Washington state is shown in Figure 6-1.1.

Risk of Financial Resources

Risk of future resources is a serious kind of risk; it could jeopardize your future. With this type of risk, more than current income is threatened. You may lose your ability to earn in the future or assets you acquire in the future. For example, you might do something that causes an injury to another person. That person might sue you and win a financial judgment. This means that the court orders you to pay the person a certain amount of

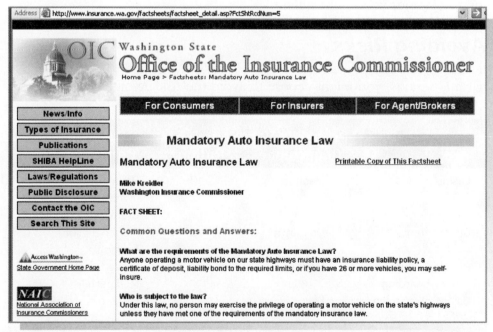

© Getty Images/PhotoDisc

Snow skiing involves risk of personal injury.

FIGURE 6-1.1

Many states require drivers to have automobile insurance.

Address http://www.insurance.wa.gov/factsheets/factsheet_detail.asp?FctShtRcdNum=5

OIC Washington State
Office of the Insurance Commissioner
Home Page > Factsheets: Mandatory Auto Insurance Law

News/Info
Types of Insurance
Publications
SHIBA HelpLine
Laws/Regulations
Public Disclosure
Contact the OIC
Search This Site

Access Washington
State Government Home Page

NAIC
National Association of
Insurance Commissioners

| For Consumers | For Insurers | For Agent/Brokers |

Mandatory Auto Insurance Law

Mandatory Auto Insurance Law   Printable Copy of This Factsheet

Mike Kreidler
Washington Insurance Commissioner

FACT SHEET:

Common Questions and Answers:

What are the requirements of the Mandatory Auto Insurance Law?
Anyone operating a motor vehicle on our state highways must have an insurance liability policy, a certificate of deposit, liability bond to the required limits, or if you have 26 or more vehicles, you may self-insure.

Who is subject to the law?
Under this law, no person may exercise the privilege of operating a motor vehicle on the state's highways unless they have met one of the requirements of the mandatory insurance law.

Source: Washington State, Office of the Insurance Commissioner, Mandatory Auto Insurance Law, http://www.insurance.wa.gov/factsheets/factsheet_detail.asp?FctShtRcdNum=5 (accessed May 3, 2006).

161

money. Because of the judgment, you could have your wages garnished or your assets taken away. This type of risk has a very grave outcome and should always be taken seriously.

RISK ASSESSMENT

The first step toward managing risks is assessing your risks. That means identifying what the risks are and deciding how serious they are. When you understand your risks and what you have to lose, you can make better choices. You may be able to take action to protect yourself from the serious outcomes that you could face.

To assess your risks, you must first understand them. Figure 6-1.2 shows an example of risk assessment. It lists the types of risks faced by Sally Edwards. It shows the probability of each risk, and each risk is rated in terms of seriousness. Finally, the chart lists the worst that could happen if the loss did occur.

RISK STRATEGIES

When the risk is serious, you will want to take some type of action to protect yourself. There are a number of ways to do this, such as reducing risk, avoiding risk, transferring risk, and self-insuring against risk.

Reducing Risks

The first strategy to consider is how you can lower the risk. Reducing risk means finding ways to change actions or events so that your chance for loss is less. For example, when you go snow skiing, you are taking a risk of personal injury. To reduce that risk, you could take skiing lessons. You could reduce your risk of financial loss by having health insurance to pay for any injuries you might suffer.

Avoiding Risks

If you decide that you cannot effectively reduce risk and that the potential harm is serious, you might choose to avoid the risk. Avoiding risk means

FIGURE 6-1.2

RISK ASSESSMENT FOR SALLY EDWARDS

162

Risk	Probability of Occurrence	Seriousness Rating*	Possible Consequences
Losing my job	Medium	10	Payments could be missed. Credit rating suffers.
Car accident	Unknown	10	Personal injury Lawsuit
Physical injury from snowboarding	Medium	3	Missed work time Medical bills
Having bike stolen	Low	2	Have to buy new/ used bike.

* 1 is a low risk; 5 is a medium risk; 10 is a high risk

you stop the behavior or avoid the situation that leads to the risk. In terms of snow skiing, you would choose not to take part in that activity. This would avoid the risk of injury from an accident.

Sometimes, however, avoiding the risk means that you must not do things you really want or need to do. In this case, you might consider other risk strategies.

Transferring Risks

When you face substantial risk that you cannot or do not wish to reduce or avoid, transferring risk is a good idea. You transfer the risk by buying insurance. The insurance company pays for the loss should it occur. Thus, you are transferring the risk of loss to the insurance company. For example, you could buy a homeowner's insurance policy that provides coverage against theft. If items are stolen from your home, you will be paid for the value of the items taken.

The price you pay for insurance is called a **premium**. The premium could be paid monthly, quarterly, semiannually, or annually. The premium is based on the possible loss to the insurance company. The more risk the insurer must take, the higher the premium. Sometimes the cost of the premium is very high, and you will look for ways to reduce the cost of insurance. For example, your homeowner's insurance premiums might be lower if you have a home security alarm system. Your car insurance premium might be lower if you choose to drive a reliable family car instead of a sports car.

Having a home security alarm system may reduce premiums on homeowner's insurance.

Assuming Risks

When the risk of loss is not great or when the cost of transferring the risk is too great in comparison to what you could lose, you might choose to **self-insure**. To self-insure means to set aside money to be used in the event of injury or loss of assets. Many people cannot afford to be totally self-insured. However, self-insurance is a good way for many people to assume responsibility for part of the risks they face. For example, you could choose not to have full-coverage automobile insurance on an old car. This will make your insurance premiums lower. If the car is destroyed in an accident that is your fault, you must pay to buy another car. However, your auto liability insurance would pay for damages to others that you cause in the accident.

Another option is to choose policies with high deductible amounts. The **deductible** amount is the money you must pay before your insurance company begins to pay. You could choose to have a health insurance policy with a high deductible. This would give you lower premiums. You would pay from your self-insurance fund for doctor visits or other routine care. However, if you have a serious illness that involves high medical expenses, your insurance policy would pay these bills. This allows you to assume the risk for small or routine expenses and have the insurance company assume the risk for large expenses.

163

Building Communications Skills

Reading speed affects how much material you can read in a certain amount of time. It also can affect how well you remember or comprehend what you read. To be an effective reader, you must read at a pace that allows you to cover material quickly and still comprehend what you are reading. Use these strategies to help you be a more effective reader:

- Select reading material carefully. Choose material that is likely to be of the most value for your purpose for reading.

- Preview the material before reading.

- Do not skim or skip passages. Read everything in a passage, chapter, or book.

- Read in the order the information is presented.

- Adjust reading speed to suit the material chosen. Technical material or material with a difficult vocabulary may require slower reading. Summaries, review sections, or passages with easy vocabulary allow faster reading.

- Read groups of words at a time.

- Use a pacer to focus your eyes on the page. A pacer is a tool such as a pencil or ruler that you move along under the words being read.

- Read in a quiet place where your concentration will not be interrupted.

6-1 Activity 1   Can You Recall?

Answer these questions to help you recall what you have read.
If you cannot answer a question, read the related section again.

1. What is risk?
2. What are the three general types of risk discussed in this chapter?
3. What is meant by *risk assessment*?
4. List four strategies for dealing with risk.

6-1 Activity 2   Assessing Risks

 Everyone faces risks—personal risks, financial risks, and resource risks. In this activity, you will think about some of the risks you may face.

1. Create a chart with the headings shown below. In the chart, list four risks that you face.

Risk	Probability of Occurrence	Possible Results	Ways to Reduce Risk

2. Estimate the likelihood of those events occurring. Add this information to the chart.
3. Think about and list the possible results if the risk events should happen.
4. Consider each possible risk that has serious consequences. List what you can do to (a) reduce risks, (b) avoid risks, (c) transfer risks, and/or (d) self-insure for the losses that you might suffer as a result of the risks.

Income Protection

OUTCOMES

• Explain the need for health insurance and the types of plans available.

• Describe types of coverage available in health insurance plans.

• List ways you can lower costs and manage health care spending.

• Explain the need for disability coverage and the types of plans available.

• Explain the need for life insurance and types of life insurance coverage.

HEALTH INSURANCE

Health insurance is a plan for sharing the risk of medical costs from injury or illness. People need health insurance to help pay high medical expenses. Many people cannot afford to pay medical costs without the help of insurance. Some people have group health insurance bought through their employers. Some people have individual policies.

Types of Plans

Three basic types of health insurance plans are available. Health insurance plans have many characteristics in common. The better the coverage, the higher the premiums will be. Some employers may pay for a part of medical insurance premiums. However, employees are often asked to pay part or all of the cost. This is because of high and rising costs for health care.

FEE-FOR-SERVICE PLANS

A fee-for-service plan allows patients to choose doctors and other providers for medical services. The insurance policy has a deductible. The insured pays expenses equal to the deductible amount. Then the insurance company pays a percent, such as 80 percent, for covered services. The insured must pay the remaining amount. For example, if a policy has a $150 deductible, that means the insured must pay the first $150 of medical expenses. Then the insurance company starts paying for part of the amount above the deductible.

A fee-for-service plan is often called unmanaged care. This type of coverage is often more expensive than managed care plans that offer fewer choices of doctors and other care providers.

PREFERRED PROVIDER ORGANIZATION PLANS

A preferred provider organization (PPO) is a group of health care providers (doctors, hospitals, clinics, and labs) that work together to provide health care services. Patients choose caregivers from approved lists. Lists include doctors, hospitals, clinics, and labs that will bill the PPO for services. If you use a doctor or medical facility that is not on the approved list, the plan may pay reduced benefits or no benefits. Thus, you should review the list of approved caregivers and facilities when considering a PPO. The PPO plan usually has a co-pay. A **co-pay** is an amount you must pay each time you use a medical service. Co-pays are often $15 to $30 per visit.

HEALTH MAINTENANCE ORGANIZATION PLANS

A health maintenance organization (HMO) is a managed care group plan that has prepaid medical care. HMOs usually have their own facilities (clinics and hospitals) and offer a full range of services. Patients must choose doctors on the HMO staff, including one doctor to be the primary care doctor. To see a specialist, patients must get a referral from the primary care doctor. HMOs usually do not have deductibles. Patients pay a co-pay for each visit.

Focus on . . .

BEING UNINSURED IN AMERICA

According to the U.S. Census Bureau, 45.8 million Americans did not have health insurance in 2004. That number is about 15.7 percent of the total population.[1] Those numbers are growing every year.

The percentage of working-age Americans with middle-range incomes without health insurance rose to 41 percent in 2005.[2] Many people who are not insured have problems paying medical bills. They do not have insurance companies with negotiated rates and contracts, so they pay higher fees than patients who have insurance.

The term *working poor* refers to Americans who spend some time working but whose incomes fall below the poverty level. Many of these people have no health insurance benefits. They do not make enough money to pay for health insurance. They do not have enough money to access adequate medical care. These people often work for an hourly rate at less than full-time jobs.

The uninsured often do not get adequate health care. They do not get regular screenings or checkups. They often do not take needed medicines because they cannot afford to buy them. Many of these people have chronic health conditions, such as asthma or diabetes.

When you begin to work and support yourself, make having health insurance a priority. This should be an important goal in your financial plan. Having health insurance is a good way to protect against loss from medical expenses and to be sure you can afford the medical treatment you need.

[1] Carmen DeNavas-Walt, Bernadette D. Proctor, and Cheryl Hill Lee, U.S. Census Bureau, *Income, Poverty, and Health Insurance Coverage in the United States: 2004* (Washington, DC: U.S. Government Printing Office, 2005), p. 16.

[2] MSNBC News Services, "Many Middle-Income Americans Lack Insurance," April 26, 2006, http://www.msnbc.msn.com/id/12480260/ (accessed May 8, 2006).

An advantage to HMOs is their emphasis on preventive care. Preventive care includes routine physical exams and wellness programs. The goal is to help keep people healthy. Examples of preventive care include regular exams, dietary counseling, and a focus on healthy living.

Many health plans have call-a-nurse programs. A skilled nurse is available by phone to answer health-related questions. This service helps people make good choices regarding health care. Some health plans also have education programs to inform people about ways to stay healthy.

Types of Health Coverage

Several types of health insurance plans are available. Some plans provide coverage for basic health care. Other plans provided coverage for serious injury or illness. Plans to help pay for dental and vision care expenses are also available.

BASIC HEALTH CARE

Basic health care coverage includes medical, hospital, and surgery services. It pays for doctor fees, office visits, and lab work. Approved hospital costs and surgeries are also covered. Cosmetic and elective surgeries are usually not covered. Elective surgery is surgery you choose to have that is not medically necessary. A face-lift to improve appearance and laser eye surgery to improve vision are examples of elective surgery.

MAJOR MEDICAL

Major medical coverage protects against very serious injury or illness. It pays for services beyond basic health care. The coverage often goes to $1,000,000 or more. Examples of procedures covered include bone marrow transplants, organ transplants, and other care that often costs $500,000 or more.

DENTAL AND VISION

Many group plans provide dental coverage. Dental plans often have deductibles and co-pays. They may have a total yearly benefit, such as $2,000. A typical plan includes services such as exams, x-rays, and fillings. Other services, such as crowns, bridges, and braces, often are covered at a lower rate or not at all. Cosmetic dental work is usually not covered.

Vision coverage often provides for an eye exam and part or all of the cost of glasses. The insurance pays for lenses and frames and may even allow for prescription sunglasses. Some policies cover the cost of contact lenses, but often on a limited basis.

Health insurance plans often include vision coverage.

© Getty Images/PhotoDisc

CATASTROPHIC ILLNESS

Catastrophic illness policies provide protection should you get cancer or some other disease or condition that might cost hundreds of thousands of dollars

168

to treat. If you have a family history of such a disease, you may not be able to get the insurance. You should buy this type of policy (and all policies) only from a well-known, reputable company. These kinds of policies are sometimes sold as scams. When you try to collect, you find that the company will not pay or no longer exists.

Managing Costs

The cost of health care is rising rapidly, making it difficult to pay rising premiums. Patients are paying higher co-pays and deductibles. Types of services provided are being limited. The cost of medicines is also rising. Many people are concerned about finding ways to manage the costs of health care. Whenever possible, patients should make sure medicines and treatments will be covered by their insurance before agreeing to use them. Some alternative or experimental treatments or medicines may not be covered.

DEDUCTIBLES AND CO-PAYS

When deductibles and co-pays are higher, premiums are often lower. Having higher deductibles and co-pays is one way to reduce health insurance premiums. Money must be set aside, however, to pay for expenses up to the deductible amount.

STOP-LOSS PROVISIONS

A **stop-loss provision** provides 100 percent coverage after a certain amount of money has been paid for medical expenses. For example, a policy may have a $5,000 stop-loss provision. This means that when you have paid $5,000 in deductible plus coinsurance payments in a year, your covered expenses are then paid at 100 percent. This amount is paid rather than the 80 percent or other rate the insurance company would otherwise pay. A stop-loss provision is a good feature to have in a health insurance policy.

HEALTH SAVINGS ACCOUNTS

A health flexible spending arrangement (FSA) allows people to set aside money to pay for qualified medical expenses. The money set aside is not included in the amount on which federal income taxes are paid. The plans are often set up by employers as an employee benefit. Deductions are made from the employee's pay to fund the account. The employer may also contribute. The employee files claims to be paid from the account for qualified expenses. Amounts not used by the end of the year are forfeited.

A health savings account (HSA) may also be set up individually rather than through an employer. This account is available to people with large deductibles, such as $1,000, on health care plans. The account holder puts money into an account (pretax). The money is then used to pay medical expenses. This reserve of money

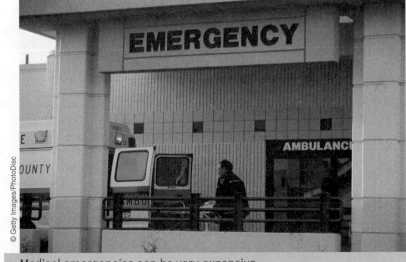

Medical emergencies can be very expensive.

is a form of self-insuring with a tax benefit. Money not used in one year is carried forward to the next year and continues to grow tax-free. The major advantage of this type of plan is that people manage their own health care dollars.

DISABILITY INSURANCE

Disability insurance provides money to replace a portion of normal earnings when the insured is unable to work due to an injury or illness that is not job-related. (If a person is injured at work or becomes ill because of work conditions, workers' compensation provides coverage.) If the disability is temporary, short-term disability insurance provides coverage. When the disability is for a longer period, long-term disability insurance provides coverage.

Short-Term Disability Insurance

Short-term disability insurance usually begins after a waiting period of 30 days. The disabled person receives a portion of regular pay (such as 75 percent) for a short period of time. This time usually is 6 months to 2 years.

Short-term disability insurance can be offered as a group policy. This type of coverage may be provided through an employer-sponsored health plan. It can also be bought as an individual policy. The coverage would likely be a part of a comprehensive health care package.

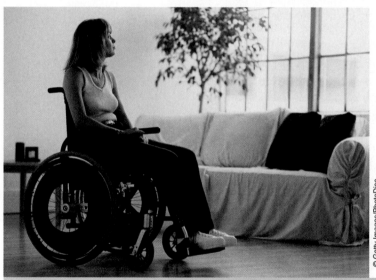

Being unable to work for a long time can cause financial hardship.

Long-Term Disability Insurance

Long-term disability coverage usually begins in 6 months to 2 years. It continues until retirement. It pays a percentage of regular pay, such as 60 percent. The smaller the payment percentage, the lower the premium will be. Premiums are based on the age of the employee and his or her salary. This insurance may be provided through an employer. Individual policies can also be purchased.

LIFE INSURANCE

Life insurance pays money when the insured person dies. The purpose of life insurance is to provide money to a **beneficiary**, the person designated to receive money. Some types of life insurance also build cash value, acting as a form of savings plan. Some reasons why people buy life insurance follow:

- To pay off a home mortgage and other debts at the time of death
- To provide money for a spouse and children to maintain their lifestyle

- To pay for education for children
- To make charitable bequests at death
- To accumulate savings
- To pay inheritance and estate taxes
- To provide cash value that can be borrowed later

Two common types of life insurance are term and permanent. Term life insurance provides a death benefit only. It does not build cash value. Permanent insurance provides a death benefit and builds cash value. An annuity can also be a type of life insurance policy. It may provide a death benefit, but it is really a type of investment plan.

Term Life Insurance

Term life insurance is a policy that provides a death benefit. It is in effect for a specific period of time, such as 20 years. The insured must continue to pay premiums to keep the policy in effect. When the time period is over, the policy is no longer in effect. Term insurance is also called pure insurance because it does not build a cash value. If you have a 20-year term policy, you will have life insurance for 20 years. If you die within that time, the policy pays the stated sum, called the **face value**, to the beneficiary. If you do not die during the 20-year term, no insurance protection remains at the end of the term.

Renewable term insurance is life insurance that can be renewed every year or for some other time period. The insured has the right to renew the policy until reaching a certain age, such as 93 or 95 years. The age limit can vary by the company and the type of policy. At each renewal, the premium goes up (because the risk of death increases).

With decreasing term insurance, the amount of coverage goes down each year. The premium remains the same. This type of insurance recognizes that as time goes by, the need for insurance is less. This may be because children are now adults, debts such as a home mortgage are paid, and there are fewer needs for the insurance benefit.

With level term insurance, the death benefit does not change. However, the cost of the premiums goes up each year. This is because the policyholder gets older, and the risk of death is greater.

An advantage to term insurance is lower premiums than for a permanent policy. A disadvantage to term insurance is that it does not build cash value that can be withdrawn or borrowed against. However, the policyholder could invest the amount saved on premiums. The money invested would likely grow at a faster rate and result in more savings than the cash value of a permanent policy.

Permanent Insurance

There are several types of permanent life insurance. **Permanent life insurance** provides a death benefit and builds cash value. When a life insurance policy has a cash value, the insured can borrow against the policy. With some policies, the insured can cash in the policy. This means that the policyholder will receive the cash value of the policy, and the insurance benefit will no longer be in effect.

WHOLE LIFE

A common type of permanent insurance is called whole life insurance. It is also known as straight life or ordinary life insurance. The insured pays

171

Life insurance can provide benefits for children when a parent dies.

premiums as long as the policy is in effect. There is usually an age limit, such as 93 or 95 years, for how long the policy will remain in effect. The policy pays the face value to the beneficiary at the death of the insured. Life insurance benefits are not taxable to the beneficiary.

The amount of the premium depends on the age of the insured at the time the policy is purchased. The premium is high enough to pay for the death benefit and also to add to the policy's cash value. The cash value can be borrowed against by the insured. This type of loan does not have to be repaid, but it lowers the death benefit when the insured dies. The insured can choose to repay the loan.

LIMITED-PAY LIFE

Limited-pay life insurance is a policy on which the insured pays premiums for a limited period of time, such as 20 years. At the end of the period, the policy is paid up. The insured pays no more in premiums, but the life insurance remains in effect until the age limit of the policy. The policy will pay the face value when the insured dies as long as it is in effect. This type of life insurance also builds cash value.

UNIVERSAL LIFE

Universal life insurance provides a death benefit. However, the premium and death benefit are not fixed. The policyholder can change the death benefit and the premiums during the life of the policy. The advantage of this type of plan is that it allows the policyholder to adjust the death benefit and premiums to fit changing needs.

VARIABLE LIFE

Variable life insurance is a form of permanent insurance that provides a death benefit and builds cash value. The premiums are fixed. Part of the premium is invested in securities chosen by the policyholder. The rest of the premium is used for life insurance. The advantage of this type of

172

policy is that the insured can decide how part of the premiums will be invested. The disadvantage is that the death benefit can vary depending on how well the investments do. However, a minimum death benefit is often guaranteed. Also, the insured cannot withdraw the cash value of the policy.

Group Life Insurance

When a life insurance policy is purchased through an employer or an organization, this is called **group life insurance**. Group life insurance has much lower premiums than individual policies. Individual policies are more expensive because there is more risk to the insurance company. With a group policy, a large number of people are insured. This lowers the risk to the insurance company and thus provides better coverage at lower prices.

Sometimes life insurance policies are portable. **Portable insurance** can be taken with you when you leave your job. In other words, the group policy becomes an individual policy at the same premiums. Having this feature makes it possible for people who would not otherwise qualify to have life insurance.

Success Skills

DEALING WITH PEOPLE IN DIFFICULT SITUATIONS

Whether you in a meeting, at a sporting event, or at a family gathering, you may find yourself in a situation in which someone is causing problems. Usually the problem is about attitude. One person does not want to cooperate or go along with the group activity. Instead, she or he wants to disrupt and ruin the activity for others.

Strategies for dealing with people in difficult situations start with focusing on the person causing the problem. First, consider who the person is. The person may be someone you do not have to see or deal with beyond the current situation. If this is the case, the best option may be simply to ignore the person's negative comments or bad behavior and continue with the activity. Is the person a customer, a neighbor, or a relative? If so, this should affect how you will approach the situation. You may have no choice but to deal with the person. Try to keep the goodwill of the person and continue the activity in spite of the person's poor behavior.

Regardless of who the person is, there are some techniques for dealing with people in difficult situations that work for everyone. Listen to what the person is saying, and repeat the concerns. Meeting the person in a private setting to discuss the issues may be helpful. Ignoring a problem does not make it go away. Deal with the issues head-on. This is a good way to keep the problem from getting worse. Ask the person to explain his or her position or situation. Ask for suggestions about how the problem could be resolved. Talk to others affected by the behavior. Find out what changes they would like to see. Bringing the situation to the front and dealing with it is often the best way to resolve it.

173

6-2 Activity 1   Can You Recall?

Answer these questions to help you recall what you have read. If you cannot answer a question, read the related section again.

1. Why do many people need health insurance?
2. What types of health insurance plans are available?
3. Describe the types of coverage available in health insurance plans.
4. What are some things you can do to help manage health care costs?
5. What is the purpose of disability insurance? How is short-term disability insurance different from long-term disability insurance?
6. List some reasons why people buy life insurance.
7. What is the main difference between term and permanent life insurance?
8. What is the face value of a life insurance policy?
9. Why are premiums for a group life insurance policy lower than for an individual life insurance policy?

6-2 Activity 2   Income Protection

You should consider several factors when deciding what type of insurance to buy. Read the following situations, and identify the type of insurance or insurance plan feature you think is right for each one.

1. You want a health insurance plan that will have low premiums and will allow you to self-insure for routine medical costs. What insurance plan feature should you request?
2. You want a health insurance plan that will pay 100 percent of covered medical expenses after a certain amount of money is paid toward medical expenses. What feature should you request?
3. You want a health insurance plan that will provide coverage should you get cancer or some other disease or condition that might cost hundreds of thousands of dollars to treat. What type of policy should you buy?
4. You want a life insurance policy on which the premiums will be as low as possible for the next 10 years. What type of insurance should you buy?
5. You want to choose how part of the premiums you pay for life insurance will be invested. What type of policy should you buy? What risk do you face with this type of plan?

174

6. You want a life insurance policy that will stay in effect for 10 years after you retire. However, you do not want to pay premiums after you retire. What type of policy should you buy?

7. You are considering whether to buy a whole life or a term life insurance policy. The death benefit will be the same for each policy. The premiums for the whole life policy will be $600 per year. In 40 years, you will be able to withdraw the cash value of $50,000 from the policy. The premiums for the 40-year term policy will be $200 per year. You can invest the money you save on premiums. You will receive an average annual return of at least 6 percent on the money you save for the next 40 years. Which option would you choose? Why?

Property Protection

OUTCOMES

- Explain the need for homeowner's insurance and the types of coverage provided.
- Explain the need for renter's insurance.
- Explain the need for automobile insurance and the types of coverage provided.
- Describe the purpose of an umbrella policy.

HOMEOWNER'S INSURANCE

A **homeowner's policy** protects the policyholder from risk of loss in the home. It covers the building and its contents. This includes personal property, such as furniture, appliances, clothing, and home decorations.

Types of Coverage

Policies can be purchased that provide fire insurance only. Most homeowners choose more than just protection from fire. Homeowner's insurance typically includes three types of coverage. This coverage is for fire and other hazards, criminal activity, and personal liability.

Read the homeowner's policy carefully to see the types of items and risks that are covered. Expensive items such as jewelry, furs, antiques, computers, and rare coins may not be covered or may have limited coverage. Earthquake, hurricane, and flood protection often is not included. A special provision, called a rider, can be purchased to provide more coverage for expensive items or special risks.

FIRE AND OTHER HAZARDS

Fire, water, wind, and smoke can damage a house and its contents. The risk of this type of loss is unpredictable, and the consequences can be very serious. For example, if your house burned and you had no insurance, you would still owe a mortgage payment, but you would have no house to live in. For this reason, you may be required to have insurance as part of a mortgage agreement.

Protection extends not just to your home but to a garage or shed, trees, plants, shrubs, and fences. The policy might also cover costs of lodging while your house is being repaired.

CRIMINAL ACTIVITY

Your house could be broken into, vandalized, or suffer damage as a result of other criminal acts. You may not be able to prevent these things from happening. However, you can reduce the risk by locking windows and doors. You might also get a security alarm system and put your lights on a timer. This type of risk is unpredictable, and the consequences can be expensive.

PERSONAL LIABILITY

If someone is injured on your property, you are responsible for her or his injuries. For example, a guest may break his leg while getting into your hot tub. Your homeowner's policy would pay medical and other costs.

ACTS OF NATURE

Some areas of the country can have hurricanes, floods, volcanoes, and earthquakes. These acts of nature can do a great deal of damage. Sometimes a private insurance company will provide coverage for these risks (at high premiums). You may also be able to buy insurance from the federal government to cover these risks. If you live in an area where you could suffer this type of loss, you should consider buying this type of coverage.

Home Inventory

Before buying a homeowner's policy, read it carefully to see how you will be paid for damages. You may be paid for the replacement cost of an item or for the actual cash value of the item. The payment depends on the language in the insurance policy. To ensure that you will be able to replace stolen or damaged items, choose a policy that covers replacement costs.

Homeowner's insurance protects you from losses as a result of fire.

When items are stolen from your home or destroyed or damaged, you must file a claim with the insurance company in order to be paid for the items. Could you name all the items in your home if it was destroyed by fire? Do you know the value of all the items? Many people would not be able to give an accurate record of home items from memory.

To be prepared in case you need to file a claim, you should create a home inventory. The inventory should list all the items of value in your home. Ideally, the inventory should include the number of items, when they were purchased, and the original cost. Record as much of this information as you can. Attach any receipts that you have for expensive items. Record serial numbers for items such as appliances and computers. The inventory should include a place to list the replacement cost of the item. That amount can be added just before a claim is filed so the price is current. Figure 6-3.1 on page 178 shows part of a home inventory. You may want to list items in alphabetical order; by room location; or by type, such as appliances, furniture, and so on. You may also want to take pictures of or videotape each room in your home to document the items it contains.

Once the inventory is complete, store it in a safe place, such as a fireproof box or a safe deposit box. You could also keep a copy at a

177

FIGURE 6-3.1

This home inventory was created using spreadsheet software.

	A	B	C	D	E
1	HOME INVENTORY				
2	Updated June 1, 20--				
3					
4	**Item**	**Number**	**Date**	**Original**	**Replacement**
5	**Description**	**of Items**	**Purchased**	**Cost**	**Value**
6	Air cleaner	2	2/12/2006	$110.78	
7	Ionic Pro Model CA-500B				
8	China, place setting including dinner	8	5/25/2000	$114.85	
9	plate, salad plate, cup, saucer,				
10	and bread plate. Pattern: Royal				
11	Albert Old Country Roses				
12	Computer monitor, 17-inch flat panel	1	3/18/2003	$635.25	
13	ViewSonic Model VA7000				
14	Sofa, Brown leather, 83 inches long	1	4/5/2006	$2,150.48	
15	Brand: Ethan Allen #28945				
16	Television, color, flat panel, 23 inches	1	4/23/2005	$989.56	
17	Sony Model KLV S23A10				
18	Serial # 700 4690				
19					

relative's home. Update the inventory regularly. Keeping the inventory in a spreadsheet or database program makes it easy to update. Special programs for creating home inventories are also available.

Reducing Costs

As with medical insurance, you can choose higher deductibles and save money on your property insurance. Of course, this means you are assuming more risk. Some people get discounts because they add security systems or have other features that reduce the risk to the insurance company.

Technology Corner

BUYING INSURANCE ONLINE

Consumers can shop online for almost any product or service. Insurance is no exception. When you are looking for property or income protection, the Internet is a good place to begin.

Many insurance companies have Web sites. Consumers can fill out applications and submit them online. In many cases, rate quotes are received in a few minutes. Consumers can compare prices of policies from different companies. They can buy insurance directly online and be assigned an online agent. Some companies also allow policyholders to file claims using the Internet.

Because consumers do not deal with an agent in person, the cost of these policies may be lower. Before buying insurance online, do research to be sure that the company is reputable and that you can count on it should you need to file a claim.

RENTER'S INSURANCE

Renter's insurance protects renters from the risk of losing personal property. Loss could occur from fire, smoke, theft, freezing, water damage, or other hazards. A renter's policy covers the cost of repairing or replacing personal property. As with a homeowner's policy, check carefully to see what items and risks are covered. Check to see whether the policy pays replacement costs or actual cash value. Purchase a rider if you need coverage for very expensive items, such as jewelry or fine art. Prepare an inventory of items to use if a claim must be filed.

As a renter, you are responsible for the inside of the apartment or house. If someone is injured, renter's insurance will pay for medical costs. Renter's insurance also protects your property in your car or at work. Renter's insurance is not expensive. It is a low-cost way to protect against loss of your personal property.

AUTOMOBILE INSURANCE

When you drive a car, there are serious risks to people and property. All states have financial responsibility laws. These laws require drivers to be prepared to pay for damages caused to others. One way to do so is to have automobile insurance. **Automobile insurance** protects the owner of a car from losses as a result of accidents. The cost of car insurance depends on many things, such as the model and style of car and the age and driving record of the insured.

If your car is stolen or you are in an accident, call the police right away. Get a copy of the theft or accident police report for use in filing a claim. Call your insurance company to begin the claim process. If your car is damaged but can be driven, you may be required to get estimates for the repair work.

Types of Coverage

If you have all of the following types of coverage, you have full coverage on your automobile. Unless you have a car loan, however, you are not required to have full coverage.

LIABILITY

Liability coverage protects against loss as a result of injury to another person or damage to that person's property. It pays nothing for the insured person's own losses. Liability coverage is usually expressed with three numbers, such as 100/300/50. The 100 stands for how much will be paid for injuries to one person ($100,000). The

Renters can buy insurance to protect their personal belongings.

179

Automobile insurance protects you from serious potential loss.

300 stands for the total that will be paid for all people in an accident ($300,000). The 50 stands for how much property damage will be paid ($50,000).

COLLISION

Collision coverage protects you from damage from being hit by another car or rolling over. It will pay for damage to your car if you are at fault. Collision coverage usually has a deductible. The deductible may be from $50 to $1,000. The higher the deductible, the lower the premium.

Some states have no-fault insurance laws. Under no-fault laws, your auto insurance company will pay for your damages (up to your policy limits), regardless of who was at fault for the accident.

COMPREHENSIVE

Damage to your car from causes other than collision or rolling over is provided by comprehensive coverage. Examples of this damage include fire, theft, hail, water, falling objects, and vandalism. This insurance also has a deductible that can save you money in premiums.

PERSONAL INJURY

Personal injury protection pays for medical, hospital, and funeral costs of the insured, that person's family, and passengers. Discounts are available if you have airbags and other safety devices to reduce injuries.

UNINSURED/UNDERINSURED MOTORIST

When another person is driving while uninsured or without enough insurance (underinsured) and causes an accident, this insurance pays your costs. In other words, the other driver is at fault in an accident with you. This driver has no insurance or not enough insurance. Your policy will then pay your damages. This insurance also covers you when you are a pedestrian and get injured by an uninsured vehicle.

TOWING/RENTAL CAR

Full coverage often provides for towing charges when your car is not in running order. While your car is being fixed, your insurance may also cover the cost of a rental car. These types of coverage cost extra, but the premiums are fairly low compared to other types of coverage.

Reducing Costs

As with other types of insurance, the higher your deductibles, the lower the premiums. Other things you can do to lower car insurance costs include the following:

○ Take driver training classes.
○ Maintain a good driving record.
○ Buy more than one insurance policy (both homeowner's and car insurance) from the same company.

- Get good grades in school.
- Have a car with a high safety rating.
- Install security devices on your car.
- Always pay your premiums on time.

You can also do other things to reduce risks. Drive while rested instead of when you are tired. Keep your car properly serviced to help prevent breakdowns. Avoid heavy traffic situations or driving in bad weather.

UMBRELLA INSURANCE

An **umbrella policy** provides coverage in addition to car and home insurance. It protects you from catastrophic losses. Policy limits are often $1,000,000 or more. Umbrella insurance pays for accidental injuries caused to other persons while you are driving or in your home. It protects you from extraordinary losses. For example, you may be in an accident in which costs for another person's injuries exceed $500,000. This amount might be more than is covered by your liability car insurance.

An umbrella policy is so named because it provides coverage above your other policies. You must have liability coverage on your home and car. When payment limits are reached on those policies, the umbrella policy takes over.

Ethics

DRIVING ACCIDENTS

Most states have financial responsibility laws. These laws may require that drivers be insured or that they be able to pay for damages caused to others. The minimum coverage required in many states is liability insurance. Liability insurance protects others from the results of negligence.

In spite of legal requirements, many people drive without insurance. Some cite the high cost of insurance as their reason. Others say that they are unable to buy reasonable coverage and they have to drive to get to work and other places they must go. There are so many uninsured motorists that drivers can buy extra coverage to protect against losses from an accident with one of them. Driving without insurance or without being able to pay for damages you cause to others is unethical.

When you injure another person in an accident, you can be sued for damages. Sometimes people demand money even though they have not been injured. They fake injuries in order to get money from the insurance company. This practice is both illegal and unethical.

There are people who stage accidents, causing your vehicle to rear-end theirs. When you hit another car from the rear, you are presumed guilty in many states. Always drive very carefully. Leave lots of room between you and the car in front of you. Defensive driving is a type of driving skill that helps you be aware of other vehicles and what might happen in traffic situations. Taking a defensive driving course can help to lessen the risk of loss from automobile accidents.

181

6-3 Activity 1 Can You Recall?

Answer these questions to help you recall what you have read.
If you cannot answer a question, read the related section again.

1. What is the purpose of homeowner's insurance?
2. Explain the provisions of homeowner's policies.
3. Why do renters need renter's insurance? How is renter's insurance different from homeowner's insurance?
4. Why should renters and homeowners prepare a home inventory?
5. Why do drivers need automobile insurance? What are the basic types of automobile insurance coverage?
6. What is the purpose of an umbrella policy?

6-3 Activity 2 Auto Insurance Quotes

Prices for auto insurance vary depending on the company, the age of the driver, the type of vehicle, and other factors. Descriptions of two drivers follow. For each driver, get an annual quote for full-coverage auto insurance. To find quotes, call a local insurance agent. Identify yourself as a student, and ask for a typical price for the driver described. You might also be able to find price quotes at insurance company Web sites.

Driver A
Sheila Roberts is 18 years old. She makes good grades in school and has taken a driver training course. She has had no auto accidents or tickets. The car she will drive is a 4-year-old midsize sedan in good working order. The car is owned by her parents. Sheila wants to be added to her parents' auto policy.

Driver B
Joe Chung is 19 years old. His college grades are a C average, and he has not taken a driver training course. He has had one traffic ticket for speeding. The car Joe will drive is a 2-year-old sports car. He owns the car. Joe wants to have his own insurance policy (not to be added to his parents' policy).

182

EXPLORING CAREERS IN INFORMATION TECHNOLOGY

Do you like to develop creative programs or multimedia games? Is creating Web pages your hobby? Are you the person friends come to with software or hardware questions? If the answer is yes, a career in information technology might be right for you. Jobs in this area are varied. Some workers create Web pages, games, or programs. Others design networks and oversee their use. Many equipment installers and repairers are also needed in this career area.

Jobs in this career area are found in government, education, and businesses. The need for jobs in information technology is expected to grow in the next several years. The outlook varies somewhat by job.

Skills Needed

Some of the skills and traits needed for a career in information technology include the following:

- Computer/technology skills
- Communications skills
- Math skills
- Science skills
- Decision-making skills
- Problem-solving skills

Job Titles

Many jobs are available in information technology. Some job titles for this career area include the following:

- Animator
- Computer programmer
- Computer software engineer
- Computer support specialist
- Database administrator
- Graphic designer (Web designer)
- Network administrator
- Technical writer
- Telecommunications equipment installer

Explore a Job

1. Choose a job in information technology to explore further. Select a job from the list above, or choose another job in this career area.
2. Access the *Occupational Outlook Handbook* online. A link to the site is provided on the Web site for this textbook.
3. Search for more information about the job you selected to answer these questions:
   - What is the nature of the work this job involves?
   - What is the job outlook for this job?
   - What training or qualifications are needed for this job?
   - What are the median annual earnings for this job?

Summary

- Everyone takes risks that have potential consequences that may be serious. Risks may involve personal or financial loss.
- Risk assessment is the process of identifying risks, their probability, their seriousness, and how to handle them.
- Risk strategies include reducing risk, avoiding risk, transferring risk, and assuming risk.
- Income protection is provided by health insurance, disability insurance, and life insurance.
- Health insurance can be purchased as a fee-for-service, PPO, or HMO plan.
- Types of health coverage include basic health care, major medical, dental and vision, and catastrophic illness.
- There are many ways to manage health care costs, including use of deductibles, co-pays, and health savings accounts.
- Disability insurance can be short-term (usually 6 months to 2 years) or long-term (to retirement).
- There are two basic types of life insurance: term and permanent.
- Term life insurance provides a benefit at the death of the insured. Permanent life insurance provides a benefit at the death of the insured and also builds cash value.
- Property insurance is for home and automobile protection.
- Homeowner's insurance covers fire and other hazards, criminal activity, and personal liability. Renter's insurance provides similar coverage on the contents of a home but not on the structure. It also includes liability protection.
- Automobile insurance may include liability, collision, comprehensive, personal injury, and uninsured/underinsured motorist coverage.
- Having high deductibles on policies and taking actions to reduce risks can help lower costs for all types of insurance.
- An umbrella policy protects you after your homeowner's or car insurance has paid the maximum amount.

Key Terms

automobile insurance	health insurance	probability
beneficiary	homeowner's policy	renter's insurance
co-pay	life insurance	risk
deductible	loss	self-insure
disability insurance	permanent life insurance	stop-loss provision
face value	portable insurance	term life insurance
group life insurance	premium	umbrella policy

Use the key terms from Chapter 6 to complete the following sentences:

1. Life insurance purchased through an employer is called
   _____.

2. The monthly, quarterly, semiannual, or annual payment for insurance
   is the _____.

3. The _____ is the amount you pay before insurance starts to pay.

4. A type of life insurance that provides a death benefit but no cash
   value is called _____.

5. _____ provides money to a beneficiary at the death of the
   insured.

6. Insurance to protect a tenant's possessions is called _____.

7. The stated sum, or _____, is the amount payable at the
   death of the insured.

8. Coverage for catastrophic expenses, in addition to car and home
   insurance, is provided by a(n) _____.

9. _____ provides income protection when you cannot work
   due to illness or injury.

10. Insurance you can convert to an individual policy when you leave
    your job is called _____.

11. Property insurance to protect the owner of a residence is called
    a(n) _____.

12. _____ protects the owner of an automobile for damage to
    the car and its occupants, as well as to other cars and their occupants.

13. The person to whom the face value of an insurance policy is paid is
    the _____.

14. Physical or monetary injury is called _____.

15. The chance that a personal or economic loss might happen is known
    as _____.

16. The amount a patient pays each time for using a medical service
    is called the _____.

17. _____ is a plan for sharing the risk of medical costs.

18. Life insurance that provides a death benefit and builds cash value is
    called _____.

19. The likelihood of risk actually resulting in a loss is known
    as _____.

20. When you _____, you set aside money to be used in the
    event of injury or loss of assets.

21. A(n) _____ is a feature of a health care plan that provides
    100 percent coverage after a certain amount of money has been paid
    for medical expenses.

185

ACTIVITY 2
Math Minute

1. Takashi Chan has health insurance that pays 80 percent of covered charges after a $150 deductible. He received a statement for $350 of covered charges. How much will Takashi have to pay?

2. Merl Jones has health insurance that pays 80 percent of covered charges after a $500 deductible. There is a stop-loss provision of $5,000. The insurance company has paid $16,000 (as 80 percent of the medical expenses after the deductible). Assuming all charges were covered, how much has Merl paid for medical costs?

3. Bob Scully has homeowner's insurance that pays 90 percent of the replacement cost of items damaged in a fire. He had a fire in his kitchen, and the electric stove was damaged beyond repair. Bob paid $350 for the stove 5 years ago. The cash value of the stove before the fire was $100. A new stove will cost $400. How much will his insurance company pay?

ACTIVITY 3
Research Financial Responsibility Laws

  academic.cengage.com/school/pfl

Financial responsibility laws vary by state. In this activity, work with a classmate to learn what the financial responsibility laws of your state require.

1. Access the Internet. In a search engine, enter your state name and the term **financial responsibility laws**.

2. Read the information you find about the laws for your state. Record the following information:
   o The name and address of the Web site(s) where you found the information
   o People to whom the financial responsibility laws apply
   o Methods that can be used to meet the requirements of the laws
   o Situations in which individuals may be required to offer proof that they are complying with the laws
   o The minimum amount of each type of insurance that must be carried if a person satisfies the laws by carrying insurance
   o Penalties for breaking the laws

186

ACTIVITY 4
Determine Insurance Needs

 Ramon Caldez needs your help in determining how much insurance and the types of insurance to buy. Read the information about Ramon and answer the questions that follow.

Ramon is 30 years old. He is married and has one son, who is 3 years old. Ramon's wife cares for their son and does not contribute to the family income. Ramon earns $40,000 a year in gross pay. He and his wife own their home, which is valued at $100,000. Ramon thinks the contents of their home would be valued at about $50,000. They have two cars. One car is 2 years old. The other car is 10 years old, but it is still in good condition.

1. What type of health insurance coverage would you advise Ramon to have for himself and his family?

2. Ramon has short-term disability insurance provided by his employer. Ramon wants to add long-term disability coverage. What amount of monthly benefit would you advise Ramon to have in the long-term disability policy?

3. Ramon's employer provides life insurance for Ramon equal to 1 year's gross salary. Ramon knows that he needs to buy additional life insurance to protect his family. Would you advise that he buy term life insurance or whole life insurance? Why? What do you think is the minimum amount of life insurance Ramon should purchase?

4. What step does Ramon need to complete before deciding how much homeowner's insurance he needs? Ramon's home is in an area with a high danger of flooding. Is flood protection likely to be covered in his homeowner's policy? How can he get flood protection?

5. Ramon has a car loan for his car that is 2 years old. He is required to carry full-coverage insurance on this car. Ramon owns the car that is 10 years old. What type of auto insurance would you recommend Ramon carry on this car?

ACTIVITY 5
Home Inventory

Once you own property, you should take steps to protect it from loss, theft, and damage. Review the example home inventory shown in Figure 6-3.1 on page 178.

1. Create an inventory similar to Figure 6-3.1 for the items in one room of your home. You can choose the room where most of your personal items are kept or another room, such as the living room or kitchen. Use spreadsheet or database software to create the inventory, if it is available.

2. If possible, take pictures of or videotape items in the room to supplement the inventory.

3. If your family does not have a complete home inventory, encourage your parents or other adults with whom you live to create one.

187

The FBLA Business Math Event and BPA Math Open Event allow students to demonstrate their ability to solve business math problems. Each contest consists of a test with various types of business math problems.

Evaluation

Students who take part in these events are judged on their ability to correctly solve the business math problems on the test. Read the following sample scenario and answer the related questions to practice solving business math problems.

Sample Scenario

Universe is a clothing store located in a college city. Most of the store's customers are college and high school students. Clothing sales for the store were $2.8 million last year. This year, sales have declined by 8 percent. One-eighth of annual sales are from blue jeans. The markup on merchandise purchased for sale is 250 percent. Universe marks down merchandise to 25 percent off the regular selling price after it has been in the store for 4 weeks. Merchandise is marked down to 50 percent off the regular selling price after 7 weeks and 75 percent off the regular selling price after 10 weeks. Salesclerks earn a commission of 12 percent of the selling price of items they sell.

Think Critically

1. What is the regular selling price of a shirt that the store buys for $20?
2. How much profit in dollars will the store make on a shirt it purchased for $20 when the shirt is marked down 50 percent on sale?
3. How much merchandise must an employee sell to earn $30,000 in commissions in 1 year?
4. What is the dollar amount of sales this year? What is the dollar amount of blue jeans sales?

PART 3

SPENDING AND CREDIT

OUTCOMES

After successfully completing this part, students should be able to:

* **Explain** the steps in a buying plan.
* **List** the sources and benefits of using credit.
* **Describe** the costs of using credit.
* **Compare** forms and methods of payment for credit.
* **Name** the types of consumer loans.
* **List** tips for using credit wisely.
* **Explain** how to avoid and resolve credit problems.
* **Identify** and discuss important credit reporting laws.

PART 3, SPENDING AND CREDIT, focuses on buying wisely. There are many benefits to using credit, such as building a solid credit history. Several credit sources are available to consumers, but some cost more to use than others. When you use credit, you may pay more for goods and services. The added cost can be major, especially when you make only minimum payments on a credit account. You can pay credit bills in many ways. Some ways are more convenient and less expensive than others. Unwise use of credit can lead to overspending and other problems. To avoid credit problems, you must understand and avoid the pitfalls related to using credit. You should also be aware of credit laws that help protect consumers.

© Rubberball Productions

CHAPTER 7

BUYING DECISIONS

© Digital Vision

Chapter 7 is about making good buying choices and using credit. Credit can be a helpful tool in managing finances. Misuse of credit, however, can lead to overspending and impulse buying. There are many sources of consumer credit. Some sources are inexpensive and easy to use. Others are restrictive and can lead to high payments and interest charges. High interest, fees, penalties, and rising rates are often imposed on those who do not use credit wisely.

ONLINE RESOURCES

Personal Financial Literacy Web site:

Data Files

Vocabulary Flashcards

Sort It Out: Buying Decisions

Chapter 7 Supplemental Activity

Search terms:
- annual percentage rate
- impulse buying
- line of credit
- variable interest rates
- principal
- finance charges

Buying Plans

OUTCOMES

- Explain the advantages of using a buying plan.
- List the steps of a buying plan.
- Set criteria for selecting one item over another to buy.
- Explain why comparison shopping leads to better buying decisions.
- Create a buying plan.

PURCHASING CHOICES

Buying goods and services can be a fun activity. Sometimes you are happy with your purchase, and it meets your needs and goals. Sometimes you are unhappy with a purchase and wish you had not bought that item.

When a purchase will affect you in the future, take some time to make the decision. Some people say that any purchase over $50 should be considered carefully. **Impulse buying** is when you do not think about a purchase ahead of time. You see an item that looks appealing and buy it right away. This type of buying often leaves the buyer feeling dissatisfied and wishing he or she had chosen more wisely.

Following a buying plan can help you make better buying choices. Using a buying plan, you can identify your needs and the items or services that can fill those needs. A plan can also help you avoid impulse buying.

A BUYING PLAN

A buying plan is a method for making good buying decisions. It will help you stretch your limited resources. It will also help prevent buyer's remorse, which is regret over a buying decision you have made. A buying plan may be a more detailed extension of a budget. For example, you may have allowed $500 in a yearly budget to buy a washer and dryer. In the buying plan, you will consider details of the purchase, such as features of the product and when to make the purchase.

Evaluate Wants and Needs

Items you buy should be selected to meet your wants and needs. By evaluating your wants and needs before you shop, you will be better prepared to make good buying decisions. This process is especially

Large purchases should be part of a buying plan.

important when buying items that cost a large amount of money. Because your resources will likely be limited, you should consider the opportunity cost of the item. What other items must you forgo buying in order to buy this item? Consider how the item relates to meeting the goals you have set in your budget or financial plan.

SET CRITERIA
Once you have decided to buy a good or service, you should set criteria for the item. **Criteria** are standards or rules by which something can be judged. In the case of an item to purchase, the criteria would be the features, functions, and quality of the item. To be sure the criteria are being met, list the features, functions, and quality that are required in an acceptable choice. Criteria are listed for the items in Kim Ono's buying plan, shown in Figure 7-1.1 on page 193.

SET A TIMELINE
For each item you want to buy, decide how soon you want to make the purchase. The timeline may depend on some activity, such as buying a new dress for graduation. It may also depend on someone else doing something. For example, you may wait to buy a particular item until a store places the item on sale. Putting a time frame on each planned purchase will help you prioritize. You may choose to drop some items from your list because buying them is not practical.

FIGURE 7-1.1   BUYING PLAN FOR KIM ONO

Need/Want	Item	Item Criteria	Timeline	Spending Limit
Washing clothes and linens at home rather than going to the laundromat (save time and money)	Washer and dryer (new or used)	Washer • Should be heavy-duty • Should have cycles for different kinds of items • Should allow adding bleach or fabric softener Dryer • Should have several heat settings for different types of items • Should use electricity (not gas)	1 year or sooner	$500
New clothes for spring prom	Suit or tuxedo (rent) Shirt (buy)	Dark blue suit or tuxedo White shirt in a good fabric that is wrinkle-resistant	By June 1	$100 rental fee for tux $25 to buy a shirt
Entertainment; music and movies at home	Large-screen TV	Clear picture No larger than 60 inches Should include DVD player	6 months	$750

SET A SPENDING LIMIT

A **spending limit** is the maximum amount you are willing to pay for an item. Based on the need or want that is being met, how much money are you willing and able to spend? By setting an amount, you know the spending limit. You will not be tempted to spend more than you have planned.

Gather Information

When you know what type of item or service you need to buy and how much you are willing to spend, you can start to gather specific information. You will want to know what products and services are available, along with their features and prices. You may find that you need to revise your spending plan. For example, you may learn that a product with the specific features you want is not available within your spending limit. You must change either the criteria or the spending limit.

COMPARISON SHOPPING

Comparison shopping leads to better buying decisions. You can make a better choice when you know all of the options available. Check several sources to find data on prices and features of the product or service. You may find that some items are on sale or offer rebates. A **rebate** is a refund of part of the purchase price of an item.

© Digital Vision

Take advantage of sales to get low prices for products.

193

You may also find a wide range of features available. The Internet is a good place to do product research. You can browse sites with product data at your own convenience and need not feel pressured to buy.

Compare the product or service features to the criteria you have set. Determine which product or service has all the features and the quality you need at the lowest price. Remember to add taxes, handling charges, and shipping fees when considering the total cost. Some catalog and Internet companies offer free shipping. You may not have to pay sales tax on some items purchased by catalog or on the Internet.

Be aware that the lowest price is not always the best price. Compare the warranties and return policies from the various sellers. On expensive items, having a good warranty can be an important criterion. Consider the seller. Is the seller a reputable and established company that you can expect to deal fairly with you? Be wary of buying at low prices from a seller you do not know much about. If the item is damaged or of poor quality, the seller may not allow a return or refund.

PAYMENT METHODS

Each purchase involves two choices—what to buy and how you will pay for it. Sometimes your only payment option is cash. At other times, you can choose among payment methods. You may be able to write a check or pay with a debit or credit card. You might choose to buy at one store instead of another because one store takes credit cards and the other does not.

Knowing in advance how you will pay for a product or service puts you in a better position to bargain. Some merchants will sell a product or service at a lower price if you pay in cash. For some items, such as a car, you may borrow money to pay for the purchase. This is often called financing the item. Always compare financing options that may be available through the seller with options from other sources. You will learn more about the advantages and disadvantages of different payment methods in Chapter 8.

Make the Purchase

Consider all the information you have gathered, and choose a product or service. Once you have decided on the product or service that will best meet your needs, it is time to buy. Check the item carefully to be sure it is in good condition. If the item is in a box, the box should be sealed. It should be clear that the box was not opened before and resealed. If the box has been resealed, take the item out and examine it.

Ask about warranties and return policies. Be sure to keep the receipt. Know the time within which a product can be returned should you find something wrong with it. Sometimes delivery will cost extra. You might be able to save money by picking up a product yourself.

Evaluate the Purchase

Once you get the product or service and try it out, you may feel differently about it. The excitement of buying is now gone. Ask yourself how satisfied you are with the purchase.

© Getty Images/PhotoDisc

Deciding how to pay for an item is part of the buying decision.

194

Did you follow a buying plan? Did you get good value for the money you spent? Does the product or service meet the want or need for which you purchased it? Are there ways you could have done a better job in selecting or buying? Learn from each buying experience so you can continue to make good buying decisions.

Building Communications Skills

INFORMAL SPEAKING

The purpose of informal speaking is to share information. Informal speaking often involves getting responses from others. Information is both given and received as other people interact with the speaker. Talking with another person and speaking with several people in a meeting or another group setting are examples of informal speaking. Follow these guidelines to help you communicate effectively in such situations:

- Express your ideas clearly. Do not assume that others will know as much about the topic discussed as you do.

- Speak clearly. Do not mumble or slur sounds. For example, say *nothing* instead of *nothin'*.

- Use standard English. For example, say *give me* instead of *gimme*.

- Use proper grammar. For example, say *she does not* instead of *she don't*.

- Use an appropriate tone. Tone is a manner of speaking that expresses your attitude or feelings. Make the tone of your voice match the topic being discussed. For example, use a light, friendly tone when talking about plans for an upcoming celebration. Use a more serious tone when discussing problems or serious issues.

- Speak at an appropriate volume level. Talk loudly enough to be heard but not so loud as to annoy others.

- Listen to others and give them time to respond.

7-1 Activity 1   Can You Recall?

Answer these questions to help you recall what you have read. If you cannot answer a question, read the related section again.

1. What are the advantages of using a buying plan?
2. How might a buying plan relate to your personal budget or financial plan?
3. What are the steps of a buying plan?
4. What does the word *criteria* mean? Why should you set criteria for evaluating a possible purchase?
5. Why does comparison shopping lead to better buying decisions?
6. What factors in addition to price should you consider when comparison shopping for an item?
7. Why is the Internet a good place to research products?
8. What can you do after a purchase to help ensure you make good choices in the future?

7-1 Activity 2   Create a Buying Plan

1. In this activity, you will make a buying plan. Begin by creating a table with five columns and four rows. Enter the following headings in the table:

Need/Want	Item	Item Criteria	Timeline	Spending Limit

2. Identify three needs or wants that you would like to purchase items or services to fill. List them in the table in the Need/Want column.
3. Identify items or services to fill each need or want. List them in the table in the Item column.
4. Identify the criteria that are important for each item or service. List them in the Item Criteria column in the table.
5. Select a time frame in which you want to make each purchase. List the time frames in the Timeline column of the table.
6. Select a price you are willing and able to pay for each purchase. List the prices in the Spending Limit column of the table.

Sources and Benefits of Credit

OUTCOMES

- Explain the purpose of credit.
- Compare sources of consumer credit.
- Complete a sample credit application.
- Describe the benefits of using credit.

SOURCES OF CREDIT

Credit is the ability to borrow money with the agreement to pay it back later. The repayment usually includes interest. The purpose of credit is to allow buyers to purchase items at the present time and pay for them in the future.

Several sources of credit are available to consumers. Once a consumer begins using credit, banks and other companies often offer to provide other sources or types of credit. The person who borrows money is called a debtor. In most cases, the debtor must fill out a credit application to be approved by the lender. The lender is also called the creditor.

On a credit application, the borrower provides data needed by the lender. Personal contact data, such as name, address, phone number, and date of birth, are given. The borrower's work information, other credit sources, and bank account information are also included. A sample application for credit is shown in Figure 7-2.1 on page 198.

When completing a credit application, give complete and honest responses. Read all the information carefully. The back of the application or additional pages may describe the terms of the credit agreement. Be sure you understand and agree to the terms before you sign and submit an application.

Service Credit

Service credit is the ability to receive services and pay for them later. Examples of service credit include the use of electricity, water, sewer, and other utilities. You may also receive service credit from doctors, dentists, and others. You may not think of it as credit, but you are receiving services now and paying for them later. Some companies that offer service credit require you to pay a deposit when you begin using the service. After your payment history is known, the deposit may be refunded to you.

Bank Credit Cards

Credit cards are available from banks and other companies. These cards are usually issued through a provider such as VISA® or MASTERCARD®. With a credit card, you can buy products or get cash at ATMs around the world.

FIGURE 7-2.1   **CREDIT APPLICATION**

CREDIT APPLICATION   PARNELL BANK

PERSONAL DATA

X Mr. ___ Ms. ___ Mrs. ___ Miss	First Name Raul	Middle B.	Last Name Cadiz

Home Address 248 Maple Lane	City Monticello	State KY	ZIP Code 42633-0345	How long? 10 years

Previous Address (If less than 2 years at present address)	City	State	ZIP Code

Home Telephone 606-555-0134	Business Telephone 606-555-0134	Date of Birth 10/12/75	No. of Dependents 1

Social Security No. 000-00-0000	E-Mail Address rcadiz48@providername.net

Are you a U.S. citizen? X Yes ___ No	If no, explain status.	Residence Situation ___ Own X Rent ___ Other	Monthly Rent or Mortgage $ 450.00

Employment

Employer Ready-Made Cabinets	Address 452 West Street	City Monticello	State KY	ZIP Code 42633-8741

How long? 5 years	Occupation Cabinet Finisher	Supervisor's Name Ben Bell	Yearly Gross Pay $ 20,000.00

Other Income Amount Source Amount Source $5,000 per year Summer job/Mowing lawns	Yearly Household Income $45,000.00

Other Credit Accounts

Type or Name	Account No.	Current Balance
Good Deal credit card	4589258-633	$ 450.53
Sears store account	632-569-4319	$ 750.23
Potter's Hardware store account	388-23-6	$ 145.89

Bank Accounts

X Checking Name of Bank First Bank	City Monticello	Account No. 3489541-12
X Savings Name of Bank First Bank	City Monticello	Account No. 3479542-16
___ Other Name of Bank	City	Account No.

Signature

I authorize Parnell Bank to check my credit record and verify my employment and references. I have read the information on the reverse side and agree to the credit terms. Under penalties of perjury, I declare the above statements to be true.

Raul B. Cadiz   Date *May 5, 20--*
Applicant's Signature

Bank credit cards are a type of revolving credit. With **revolving credit**, the account holder can charge to the account as often as desired, up to a certain dollar limit. The account holder makes payments, usually each month. The entire debt or part of the debt can be paid each month. This means that the account can have an ongoing balance. However, a minimum monthly payment is usually required. Interest is charged on outstanding balances. Interest on credit cards can be quite high. Bank cards also often charge an annual fee.

Store Accounts

Department stores, gas companies, and other retail merchants may offer their own credit accounts. The account holder may receive a credit card to use in making purchases. Unlike bank credit cards, **store accounts** allow you to charge items or services only at that store or with that merchant. These accounts often have high interest rates and require monthly payments. Using store accounts can lead to less comparison shopping when people simply buy where they have accounts.

Store accounts can be revolving credit accounts, or they can be installment plans. With **installment credit**, an amount is set for the purchase. Payments are made and the balance is paid off in a set period of time. For example, a customer might buy a refrigerator for $800 and agree to pay 18 percent yearly interest on a 3-year payment plan. Figure 7-2.2 shows the payments and interest for this plan.

Many types of credit cards are available to consumers.

Charge Cards

A charge card is a form of credit card because you buy now and pay later. With charge cards, however, you pay the balance in full each month. Because there is no interest or service fee, these cards often require a large annual fee ($50 to $100 or more). Examples of charge cards are American Express® and Diners Club®.

Loans

Banks and other companies loan money to consumers. Consumers can get different types of loans. An installment loan is similar to an installment plan for a store purchase. A set amount is borrowed at a certain interest rate for a set period of time. For example, a consumer might borrow $1,000 at 8 percent interest for 1 year. The debtor makes regular payments for the set period of time to repay the loan. The repayment includes the amount borrowed and interest. Handling fees may also be charged.

INSTALLMENT PAYMENT PLAN	
Initial Balance	$ 800.00
Monthly Payment	$ 28.92
Total Payments Amount	$1,041.19
Interest Paid	$ 241.19

FIGURE 7-2.2

INSTALLMENT PAYMENT PLAN

199

A single-payment loan also has a set amount borrowed at a certain interest rate for a set period of time. With this type of loan, however, the entire amount plus interest is repaid in one payment on a certain date.

The terms of a loan may allow the consumer to use the money borrowed as desired. Other loans may specify how the money is to be used. For example, the loan may be for home repairs or for the purchase of a car.

The lender may require the borrower to offer security for the loan. Property that can be used as security for a loan is called **collateral**. Land, a house, and a car are examples of items that can be used as collateral. The lender can sell the collateral to get the money due if the borrower does not repay the loan. If the borrower does not have the needed collateral, the lender may require that the loan have a cosigner. A cosigner is a person who signs the loan agreement along with the borrower. This person agrees to repay the loan if the borrower does not.

Lines of Credit

A **line of credit** is a preapproved amount that a debtor can borrow when needed. It is available through banks, credit card companies, and other lenders. The borrower must fill out a credit application. The maximum amount that can be borrowed is set. No interest is charged until the debtor uses the line of credit. A line of credit is a good thing to have so you know how much you can borrow for something such as a car or a remodeling project.

Focus on . . .

CREDIT IN AMERICA

Credit today is easy to get, and many creditors want your business. Merchants encourage their customers to use store credit. They offer discounts and price reductions to get customers to open and use a credit account.

The ease of buying over the Internet has opened new uses of credit. Online purchases at reputable sites are fairly secure and no more risky than in-person purchases. Either way, you are vulnerable. Dishonest people can get your private data and use the data to steal in your name.

As long as you maintain a good credit record, you will receive many credit offers. These offers will come from established as well as new companies. Credit offers may

also pose a security threat. If someone steals your mail, she or he can open accounts in your name and charge products. You will then have a serious problem.

If you do not manage your credit responsibly, you will find the electronic age to your disadvantage. For example, if you make a late payment to one creditor, other creditors may learn about it. Other lenders may be less likely to extend credit to you. Once you are refused credit at one company, this is a signal to others that you are not a good risk. If you use credit too freely and cannot make the payments you owe, you will soon find it very hard to get or use credit. Manage your credit wisely so you will have it when you need it.

BENEFITS OF CREDIT

People use credit for a variety of reasons. Using credit has both benefits and costs or advantages and disadvantages. In this part of the chapter, you will learn how consumers can use credit to take advantage of its benefits. You will learn about the costs of credit in the next section.

Convenience and Rewards

Credit cards and store accounts offer convenience to consumers. Many people prefer to use credit cards for purchases instead of carrying large amounts of cash. Some companies to which consumers make regular payments accept credit cards. The account can be set up to be billed to a credit card each month. Utility companies and Internet service providers are examples of businesses that offer this option. Paying one credit card bill each month is easier than paying several bills to different companies. Consumers can get cash advances with some credit cards. This is convenient for consumers traveling far from home.

Many bank credit cards and store accounts have rewards features. With a rewards program, you get points or other bonuses, such as cash back, when you use the card. Points can be redeemed for merchandise or other goods or services.

Increased Spending Power

Without credit, many people would have lower standards of living. They would have to wait to buy things that can save them time and money. For example, a consumer might have to save money for a year to have the purchase price of a washer and dryer. By using credit, the consumer can purchase the washer and dryer when needed. A small down payment might be required. The remaining cost, along with interest, can be repaid over the course of a year or two. During this time, the consumer is able to use the washer and dryer.

Using credit allows some people to buy expensive items that they might never save enough to pay for at once. For example, many people do not have enough money to pay the full purchase price of a house. Having a home loan, called a mortgage, allows these people to buy a home.

Records and Protection

Credit card receipts provide you with records of what you have bought using the card. You can use receipts for returning goods, as well as getting adjustments. Having the receipts also allows you to verify your purchases against the credit card statement.

Using credit gives you advantages when resolving some disputes with merchants. For example, suppose you purchased an item on the Internet. The seller says you can expect delivery within two weeks. Five weeks go by, however, and you have not received the item. When your credit card bill arrives, you find you have been charged for the item. Because you have used a credit card as payment, you can dispute the charge with your credit card company.

© Stockbyte

Credit card receipts offer proof of purchase.

The credit card company must resolve the dispute within a certain time. You can withhold payment of the disputed amount during the investigation.

Some credit card companies offer various benefits or protections against risks. The following list gives several examples:

- You pay no charges for any fraudulent use of the card. You do not have to pay for any online purchases made without your knowledge.
- You can withhold payment for disputed items while the dispute is being investigated.
- If a store refuses to refund the price of a returned item within 90 days of purchase, the credit card company will refund the purchase price up to a dollar limit (such as $500) per eligible item.
- If goods are damaged or stolen within 90 days of purchase, the credit card company will replace or refund eligible items.
- You can receive an emergency replacement for a lost card quickly, often within 24 hours.

Success Skills

MANAGING PROJECTS

Most people have projects for school, home, or work that they should or would like to complete. Some projects are small, such as painting a porch. Others are large, such as planning a two-week vacation. Whatever the time or dollar value, all projects can benefit from planning. Large projects can be especially overwhelming without a plan for completion. Follow these guidelines to help you manage a project successfully:

1. Define the overall objective of the project. State clearly what you want the completed project to be or do.

2. If the project is large, divide it into smaller, more manageable parts.

3. Set a completion time for each part and for the overall project. By looking at the different parts of the project and how long they will take, you can coordinate activities.

4. Identify the resources needed to complete each part. What items, money, people, or other resources do you need to complete the project? List each one.

5. If other people will help with the work, decide who will do each task or part. Some tasks can be delegated. Some

items need to be purchased. Some tasks need to completed before others can be done.

6. Seek approvals, if needed. For a work project, you may need the approval of your boss. For a school project, you might need a teacher's approval. For a home remodeling project, you might need a building permit. If you live in an area with historic houses or zoning restrictions, you might need the approval of some committee. If you must borrow money to pay for the project, you may need to have the plans approved by the lender.

7. Monitor each part of the project as work progresses. Problems may arise. Some tasks may take longer or cost more than planned. When this happens, reevaluate your plan and take steps to get back on schedule.

8. Review the completed project. Does it achieve the goal you set at the beginning? Share the credit. Thank those who helped make the project a success. Review the process you used to complete the project. Note tasks or steps you could do differently to improve on future projects.

7-2 Activity 1   Can You Recall?

Answer these questions to help you recall what you have read.
If you cannot answer a question, read the related section again.

1. What is the purpose of using credit?
2. List several sources of consumer credit.
3. What types of information are asked for on a typical credit application?
4. How are store credit accounts different from bank credit card accounts?
5. How are credit cards different from charge cards?
6. How is a single payment similar to an installment loan? How is it different?
7. Give two examples of collateral that might be used to secure a loan.
8. What is the responsibility of a cosigner of a loan?
9. How is a line of credit different from other types of loans?
10. List several benefits of using credit.

7-2 Activity 2   Credit Application

 To get a credit card or open a store account, consumers typically must fill out a credit application. Although you may not be ready to apply for credit for a few years, you will practice completing an application in this activity.

1. Open and print the PDF file *CH07 Credit App* from the data files.
2. Use the following information to complete the credit application. Print the data neatly and clearly on the form.
3. Use your title, name, address, and home phone number.
4. For a business phone, write **606-555-0132**.
5. For the date of birth, write **August 1, 1980**.
6. Enter **0** for the number of dependents.
7. For a Social Security number, write **000-111-0000**.
8. For an e-mail address, write **myname@provider.com**.
9. Indicate that you are a U.S. citizen.
10. Indicate that you rent your residence and you pay **$600** per month in rent.
11. For your employer, enter the name of a business in your area. Use the real address of the business or make up an address.

203

12. In the Occupation box, enter a job that would be found at this business. Indicate that you have worked there for 4 years.

13. For the name of a supervisor, enter **Emily Gale**.

14. You earn $10 per hour, working 40 hours per week for 50 weeks a year. Compute your gross pay, and enter it in the Yearly Gross Pay box. Enter the same amount in the Yearly Household Income box.

15. Enter **None** in the Other Income box.

16. In the first Other Credit Accounts box, write **Sears store account** in the Type or Name box. Enter **34289-10** for the account number. Enter **$250** for the current balance.

17. Under Bank Accounts, place a check mark to indicate that you have a checking account. Write the name of a local bank. Write the name of your city or a nearby city. For the account number, write **45892-4509**.

18. Indicate that you have a savings account at the same local bank. For the account number, write **45892-4510**.

19. Sign your name and enter the current date at the bottom of the form.

7-3

Costs of Credit

OUTCOMES

- List costs associated with using credit.
- Explain the difference between fixed and variable interest rates.
- Use three different methods for computing finance charges.
- Describe penalties and fees imposed by credit card companies.
- Compare credit card offers.

CREDIT COSTS

Although using credit can have benefits, it can also have disadvantages and costs. Unwise use of credit can lead to overspending. If you do not make payments on credit accounts on time, your credit rating will suffer. This may mean that you cannot get credit when you need it in the future.

If you use credit wisely, costs can be kept to a minimum. For example, credit card companies charge interest on outstanding balances. If you pay the full amount owed on your credit card each month, you can avoid paying interest charges. Using this strategy, you can enjoy the benefits of using credit with little cost. However, you may have to pay a yearly fee for the privilege of using the card.

Interest and fees you pay are also called finance charges. These charges have the effect of increasing the cost of items you purchase on the credit account. There are several different ways of computing interest for credit. Whatever the method used, you will pay interest if you carry a balance on the account.

Fixed and Variable Rates

A credit account may have a fixed annual rate of interest. With a **fixed rate**, the interest rate is set and does not change each month or year. However, even with a fixed rate, the credit card company can, with 30 days' written notice, raise the fixed rate of interest. You can refuse to accept this new rate; but if you do, the company will close your account. When an account is closed, you can pay it off at the old rate, but you can no longer make charges to the account. The daily interest rate and the corresponding annual interest rate are shown on the partial credit card statement in Figure 7-3.1 on page 206.

With a **variable rate** of interest, the lender or credit card company can change the rate often. Variable rates tend to rise fast when interest rates in general go up. However, rates go down very slowly. Credit cards

Summary of Transactions

Previous Balance	Payments and Credits	Cash Advances	Purchases and Adjustments	Finance Charges	New Balance Total
$2,102.42	$2,144.81	$0.00	$1,259.61	$0.00	$1,217.22

Finance Charge Schedule

Category	Periodic Rate	Corresponding Annual Rate	Balance Subject to Finance Charge
Cash Advances			
A. Balance Transfers, Checks	0.043753% Daily	15.97%	$0.00
B. ATM, Bank	0.043753% Daily	15.97%	$0.00
C. Purchases	0.043753% Daily	15.97%	$0.00

Total Minimum Payment Due

Past Due Amount	Current Payment	Total Minimum Payment Due
$0.00	$15.00	$15.00

with variable interest rates should be used sparingly. You do not want to get caught with a large balance when interest rates are rising. When the rates for two cards are the same or close to the same, choose a card with a fixed rate instead of a card with a variable rate.

Methods of Computing Interest

Three basic methods are used to compute interest on revolving credit accounts. These methods are the adjusted balance method, the previous balance method, and the average daily balance method. Most creditors use one of these methods or a method that is similar. The three methods can result in different interest charges. For example, suppose an account has a $500 previous balance. During the month, charges of $30, $50, and $80 are made. A payment of $100 is made. Using the adjusted balance method, the interest charged is $8.40. Using the previous balance method, the interest is $7.50. Using the average daily balance method, the interest is $8.46. Each of these methods is explained in the following sections.

ADJUSTED BALANCE METHOD

With the **adjusted balance method**, the balance at the beginning of the period is added to charges made during the period. The payment received is subtracted from this amount to find the adjusted balance. The adjusted balance is multiplied by the interest rate and the time to find the interest amount. The interest amount is added to the adjusted balance to find the new balance (amount owed). Figure 7-3.2 on page 207 shows how to calculate interest using this method.

PREVIOUS BALANCE METHOD

With the **previous balance method**, interest is calculated using the outstanding balance at the end of the previous billing period. Charges

206

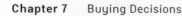

FIGURE 7-3.2

ADJUSTED BALANCE
METHOD

ADJUSTED BALANCE METHOD

Previous Balance		$500.00
Charges	$30.00	
	$50.00	
	$80.00	
Total Charges		$160.00
Payment		$100.00
Adjusted Balance		$560.00
Interest (18% yearly for 1 month)		$8.40
[$560 x 18% x 30/360]		
New Balance (Amount Owed)		$568.40

FIGURE 7-3.3

PREVIOUS BALANCE
METHOD

PREVIOUS BALANCE METHOD

Previous Balance		$500.00
Interest (18% yearly for 1 month)		$7.50
[$500 x 18% x 30/360]		
Charges	$30.00	
	$50.00	
	$80.00	
Total Charges		$160.00
Payment		$100.00
New Balance (Amount Owed)		$567.50

in the current billing period are not included. Interest is calculated by multiplying the previous balance times the interest rate times the time. The new balance is the previous balance plus interest plus charges minus any payments made. See Figure 7-3.3.

AVERAGE DAILY BALANCE METHOD

With the **average daily balance method**, an adjusted balance is computed for each day of the month. The adjusted balance is the balance from the previous day plus charges and minus payments received on that day. The adjusted balances for all days are added and then divided by the number of days. This amount is the average daily balance. The amount

207

FIGURE 7-3.4

**AVERAGE DAILY
BALANCE METHOD**

AVERAGE DAILY BALANCE METHOD

	Previous Balance	Charges	Payments	Adjusted Balance
Previous Balance	$500.00			
Daily Balances				
Day 1	$500.00	$0.00	$0.00	$500.00
Day 2	$500.00	$0.00	$0.00	$500.00
Day 3	$500.00	$0.00	$0.00	$500.00
Day 4	$500.00	$0.00	$0.00	$500.00
Day 5	$500.00	$30.00	$0.00	$530.00
Day 6	$530.00	$0.00	$0.00	$530.00
Day 7	$530.00	$0.00	$0.00	$530.00
Day 8	$530.00	$0.00	$0.00	$530.00
Day 9	$530.00	$0.00	$0.00	$530.00
Day 10	$530.00	$50.00	$0.00	$580.00
Day 11	$580.00	$0.00	$0.00	$580.00
Day 12	$580.00	$0.00	$0.00	$580.00
Day 13	$580.00	$0.00	$0.00	$580.00
Day 14	$580.00	$0.00	$0.00	$580.00
Day 15	$580.00	$80.00	$0.00	$660.00
Day 16	$660.00	$0.00	$0.00	$660.00
Day 17	$660.00	$0.00	$0.00	$660.00
Day 18	$660.00	$0.00	$0.00	$660.00
Day 19	$660.00	$0.00	$100.00	$560.00
Day 20	$560.00	$0.00	$0.00	$560.00
Day 21	$560.00	$0.00	$0.00	$560.00
Day 22	$560.00	$0.00	$0.00	$560.00
Day 23	$560.00	$0.00	$0.00	$560.00
Day 24	$560.00	$0.00	$0.00	$560.00
Day 25	$560.00	$0.00	$0.00	$560.00
Day 26	$560.00	$0.00	$0.00	$560.00
Day 27	$560.00	$0.00	$0.00	$560.00
Day 28	$560.00	$0.00	$0.00	$560.00
Day 29	$560.00	$0.00	$0.00	$560.00
Day 30	$560.00	$0.00	$0.00	$560.00
Average Daily Balance				$563.67
Interest (18% yearly for 1 month)				$8.46
[$563.67 x 18% x 30/360]				
New Balance (Amount Owed)				$568.46

is multiplied by the interest rate and the time to find the interest amount. The interest is added to the balance on the last day of the billing period to find the new balance (amount owed). Figure 7-3.4 shows how to calculate interest using this method.

Minimum Payments

The minimum payment is how much you must pay each month on a credit account. If you pay only the minimum, it could take many years to pay off a balance. The interest charges could cost you more than the purchase itself.

Minimum payments usually are 3 to 5 percent of the balance owed. Thus, if you owe $1,000, your monthly payment would be $30 to $50.

Chapter 7   Buying Decisions

This payment includes both principal and interest. Higher minimum payments help you pay off debt sooner. However, higher payments also give you less flexibility in managing your budget.

The minimum payment can be changed at any time. The creditor may decide to increase the minimum, and you will have to pay that amount. This could be difficult if your budget is already tight.

Penalties and Fees

If you make a late payment, you will typically be charged a penalty. A **penalty** is a fee charged for violating the credit agreement. A late penalty is often $35 or more. Late payments can also cause your interest rate to rise. Many credit agreements state that if you are late with a payment or miss a payment, your interest rate will increase.

Many credit card accounts have a set limit to the amount you can charge at any one time. If you try to charge more than your limit, the charge may be refused. In others words, your purchase is not approved at the time you check out and try to pay using the credit card. The credit card company may approve the charge even though it is over your limit. You will then be charged an **over-the-limit fee**. This is another type of penalty, and it can also cause your interest rate to rise. You may have to pay the fee every billing period until the outstanding balance falls below your credit limit.

© Digital Vision

Credit limits on some cards can be high enough to make expensive purchases, such as buying a car.

Some credit card agreements have a termination penalty. This penalty may apply if you close the account before a stated time, such as 1 year. Often, the penalty involves raising the interest rate to the highest rate allowed by law. This rate is often more than 20 percent per year. The penalty may apply to cards that offer low introductory rates. It discourages you from closing the account at the end of the low-rate period.

SPECIAL RATES

Credit card interest rates are expressed as annual percentage rates. By law, creditors must clearly state the rate of interest on all credit offers. Variable rates are often tied to the prime rate. Typically, it would be the prime rate plus some percentage, such as 5 percent.

Low introductory interest rates often last 6 months to a year. These temporary rates are then replaced with variable or fixed rates. The purpose of these rates is to get you to switch to a new credit card. Be cautious, however, because the regular rate may be higher than the rate for your previous card. Figure 7-3.5 on page 210 shows an example of introductory rates from a credit card application.

When you get a new credit card, you can transfer the balance of what you owe on an old card to the new card. Balance transfer rates are sometimes 0 percent. These low rates are offered to entice you to change cards.

FIGURE 7-3.5   **CREDIT CARD RATES**

Details of Rates	
Annual Percentage Rate (APR) for Purchases	**7.9%** for Gold accounts or **13.99%** for Silver accounts The account you receive is determined based on your creditworthiness.
Introductory Rate	**3%** Introductory APR for balances through your first 12 statement closing dates After that, the standard APR of **7.9%** for Gold accounts or **13.99%** for Silver accounts applies. The Introductory APR may end sooner if your payment is late.
Balance Transfers and Cash Advance Checks	**0%** Introductory APR for balance transfers and cash advance checks through your first 12 statement closing dates After that, the standard APR of **7.9%** for Gold accounts or **13.99%** for Silver accounts applies. The Introductory APR may end sooner if your payment is late.

However, the rates usually apply to the balance from the old card only and only for a short period of time.

Sometimes credit card companies provide access checks. These checks look like regular checks, but they are used to borrow money. When you use a check to buy goods or to pay off another credit card, you are transferring the balance to your credit card.

When you have more than one rate being charged, credit card companies apply your payment to the balance with the lowest rate first. This means you will pay an overall higher rate than the balance transfer rate.

Technology Corner

APPLYING FOR CREDIT ONLINE

Today you can find major creditors, even mortgage lenders, and apply for credit online. In some cases, you can get a decision on whether the loan is approved in just a few minutes.

Online applications will require sensitive personal data. You will be asked for your address, Social Security number, income, and bank account numbers. The creditor will need to be sure that the person applying is really you. You may be asked to verify data that others would not know, such as your place of birth. Be careful that you are using a secure site anytime you give out this type of information.

When applying online, do not respond to credit offers sent to you. They may be scams. Instead, only apply when you initiate the contact. If you want to apply online, first do research to be sure the site is the real one for a reputable company. You can also call a reputable lender and ask for its Web site address.

CHECKING CREDIT STATEMENTS

When you receive a credit account statement, you should check it carefully. You want to be sure that the charges, payments, interest, fees, and new balance are correct. Follow these steps to check a credit statement:

1. Compare the charges listed on the statement with your sales receipts and records of online or telephone purchases. Make sure the amounts are the same.

2. Verify that payments you have made are shown on the statement.

3. Verify that credits (such as for returned items) are shown on the statement.

4. Take note of any fees or penalties you have been charged. Determine whether the creditor is allowed to charge these fees according to the credit agreement.

5. Verify that the interest amount and the new balance (amount owed) are correct.

If you find what you think are errors on the statement, contact the company using the method given in the credit agreement. You will typically be required to make the complaint in writing. A form may be provided on the back of the statement to use in filing complaints. You will learn more about consumer rights regarding credit and credit disputes in Chapter 9.

Ethics

CREDIT CARD FRAUD

Creditors (lenders) are in business to make a profit. They provide a valuable service to consumers by allowing them to charge purchases and pay for them later. They are entitled to good-faith use of credit and payment for its use.

Using a credit card that does not belong to you to charge purchases is both unethical and illegal. This crime is called credit card fraud. Credit card fraud costs businesses a great deal of money. This results in higher charges for all consumers.

You can help prevent credit card fraud by closely guarding your cards and card numbers. Some precautions you can take follow:

- Sign your cards in ink as soon as you receive them.

- Be sure your card is returned to you by the salesperson after each purchase.

- Carry only one or two credit cards at a time. This gives you fewer cards to report if the cards are lost or stolen.

- Record the telephone numbers for reporting lost or stolen cards, and report lost or stolen cards right away.

- When you keep cards at home, store them in a safe place that will not be quickly located by a burglar.

- Guard your purse or wallet when away from home.

- Do not lend your cards to anyone. If you want to help someone buy an item, make the purchase yourself.

- When you need to throw away a card, cut it into several pieces.

- Tear credit card receipts into small pieces before throwing them away.

211

7-3 Activity 1   Can You Recall?

Answer these questions to help you recall what you have read. If you cannot answer a question, read the related section again.

1. List some costs associated with using credit.
2. Explain the difference between accounts that have fixed interest rates and those that have variable interest rates.
3. Describe how finance charges (interest) may be computed on credit cards using three common methods.
4. What does the minimum payment amount on a credit card statement indicate?
5. Describe fees and penalties charged by credit card companies.
6. Why do credit card companies offer low introductory annual rates for purchases and account balance transfers?
7. What items should you verify when you receive a credit card statement?

7-3 Activity 2   Credit Card Offers

 academic.cengage.com/school/pfl

Credit card offers can vary considerably. Some credit cards have annual fees; others do not. Some have variable interest rates; others have fixed rates. Some have high minimum payments of 5 percent or more. Others have low minimum payments of 1 percent or less. Most credit card accounts charge you for balance transfers (to pay off other accounts). Some provide access checks with which you can easily borrow cash. Some offer rewards programs with points or other bonuses for money you spend.

Shopping for a credit card involves decisions similar to those involved in making purchases. You should follow the same steps as in a buying plan. First, think about why you want or need a credit card. Next, consider how you will use it. Set criteria that you want the credit card agreement to meet. Then, do comparison shopping to find the card that most closely matches the criteria you have set.

1. Pretend that you are ready to apply for a credit card. You will use the card to make shopping more convenient. You plan to pay the entire balance each billing period to avoid paying interest charges.

2. You have thought about the criteria for the card you want. The card should have:
   o A low annual fee ($50 or less) or no annual fee
   o A reasonable annual interest rate
   o A low introductory annual interest rate
   o A rewards program that interests you

3. Access the Internet. Search the Web using terms such as **low credit rates**, **credit card offer**, or **credit card application**.

4. Visit several sites that provide information about credit card offers. Read the information about fees and interest rates. Find a card that meets the criteria listed in step 2.

5. Record the name of the card, the annual fee, the introductory annual interest rate, and the regular annual interest rate. Describe the rewards program the card offers. Explain why you selected this card over other cards you considered.

213

Business, Management & Administration

EXPLORING CAREERS IN BUSINESS, MANAGEMENT, AND ADMINISTRATION

Does the world of business interest you? Would you enjoy creating plans and managing people, projects, and resources? Do you want to own your own business someday? If the answer is yes, a career in business, management, and administration might be right for you. This career area includes a wide variety of jobs. Workers in human resources, sales, marketing, accounting, customer support, and business communications are all part of this career area. These workers, along with managers of many types and support personnel, are all needed to make businesses run smoothly.

Jobs in business, management, and administration are found in government and in private companies. This job area also includes entrepreneurs. Many small business owners create plans, promote and sell products, hire employees, and handle the daily management of their companies. The need for jobs in this area is expected to grow. The outlook varies by job.

Skills Needed

Some of the skills and traits needed for a career in business, management, and administration include the following:

- Knowledge of business operations
- Management skills
- Communications and math skills
- Computer skills
- Problem-solving skills
- Leadership skills

Job Titles

Many jobs are available in business, management, and administration. Some job titles for this career area include the following:

- Accountant
- Benefits manager
- Financial analyst
- General manager
- HR assistant
- Real estate agent
- Receptionist
- Salesperson
- Trainer

Explore a Job

1. Choose a job in business, management, and administration to explore.
2. Access the *Occupational Outlook Handbook* online. A link to the site is provided on the Web site for this textbook.
3. Search for more information to answer these questions:
   - What is the nature of the work this job involves?
   - What is the job outlook for this job?
   - What training or qualifications are needed for this job?
   - What are the median annual earnings for this job?

Review

Summary

- Following a buying plan can help you make better buying choices. It helps you identify your wants and needs and the items or services that can fill those wants and needs.
- Impulse buying brings little or no satisfaction and often results in buyer's remorse.
- Buying criteria are features that you want in products or services you have decided to buy.
- Gathering information is the second step of a buying plan; it begins with comparison shopping.
- Making a purchase involves careful checking and asking questions, keeping receipts, and knowing about warranties and return policies.
- Evaluating a purchase will help you make better choices in the future.
- Credit is the ability to borrow money with the agreement to pay it back later. The repayment usually includes interest.
- The purpose of credit is to allow buyers to purchase items at the present time and pay for them in the future. Use of credit allows consumers to buy products that they otherwise could not purchase.
- In most cases, the borrower must fill out a credit application to be approved by the lender.
- Bank credit cards are a type of revolving credit. The account holder can make charges up to a set credit limit and make periodic payments.
- Store accounts can be revolving credit accounts, or they can be installment plans. With installment credit, an amount is set for the purchase. Payments are made and the balance is paid off in a set period of time.
- Charge cards are a type of credit, but the balance is paid in full each month.
- Using credit has many advantages, such as convenience and increased spending power. Credit receipts and statements provide good records of purchases made.
- Property that can be used as security for a loan is called collateral.
- Interest and fees you pay for the use of credit are called finance charges.
- A fixed rate of interest does not go up and down frequently, but it can change with proper notice to customers.
- A variable rate of interest goes up and down at the discretion of the creditor.
- Three basic methods are used to compute interest on revolving credit accounts. These methods are the adjusted balance method, the previous balance method, and the average daily balance method.
- Borrowers are charged penalties and fees for violating any term of the credit agreement, such as for making a late payment or spending over the credit limit.
- When you receive a credit account statement, you should check to be sure that the charges, payments, interest, fees, and new balance are correct.

215

Key Terms

adjusted balance
  method
average daily
  balance method
collateral
credit
criteria
fixed rate

impulse buying
installment credit
line of credit
over-the-limit
  fee
penalty
previous balance
  method

rebate
revolving
  credit
service credit
spending
  limit
store accounts
variable rate

ACTIVITY 1
Review Key Terms

Use the key terms from Chapter 7 to complete the following sentences:

1. A fee called a(n) _____ is assessed to customers who go over their credit limit.

2. Credit offers through individual stores, companies, or other merchants are called _____.

3. _____ is the practice of buying first and thinking about it later.

4. With a method of computing finance charges called the _____, charges and payments are applied first, and then interest is calculated.

5. An interest rate that changes at the discretion of the creditor is called a(n) _____.

6. Property that can be used as security for a loan is called _____.

7. Money borrowed now with the agreement to pay it back later is called _____.

8. A partial refund of the purchase price of an item is a(n) _____.

9. An interest rate on credit that remains the same each month is called a(n) _____.

10. The use of electricity, water, and other utilities that you will pay for later is called _____.

11. A method of computing finance charges in which interest is calculated using the average daily balance for all the days of the billing cycle is called the _____.

12. A type of credit in which you repay a fixed balance with periodic payments is called _____.

13. With the type of credit called _____, you make payments and continue charging to the account.

14. The maximum amount you are willing to spend for an item is called your _____.

15. Standards or features used to judge an item you want to purchase are called _____.

16. A fee charged for violating a credit agreement is called a(n) _____.

17. A method of computing finance charges in which interest is calculated using the final balance from the previous period is called the _____.

18. A preapproved amount that can be borrowed is a(n) _____.

ACTIVITY 2
Math Minute

Use spreadsheet software, if available, to complete these problems, or do them manually. Round to the nearest cent.

1. The following table shows the activity on your credit card for the past month. What is the new balance using the adjusted balance method of computing interest?

2. Using the same information, what is the new balance using the previous balance method for computing interest?

3. Using the same information, what is the new balance using the average daily balance method for computing interest?

Credit Card Activity		
Previous Balance	$800.00	
Charges	September 5	$35.78
	September 18	$124.87
	September 21	$528.00
Payments	September 22	$750.00
Annual Interest Rate	14%	

ACTIVITY 3
Comparison Shopping

  academic.cengage.com/school/pfl

Comparison shopping leads to better buying decisions. You can make a better choice when you know all of the options available. Work with two classmates to complete this activity.

1. As a group, identify a product you would like to buy that you think costs between $100 and $500. Ask your teacher to approve your choice.

217

2. Make a list of criteria that the product should have.

3. Each team member should search the Internet, catalogs, sales brochures, or other sources. Find the following information about the product from at least two stores or Web sites:
   - Product name or brand
   - Product make or model number
   - Criteria on your list that this product meets
   - Price of the product
   - Other costs that will apply, such as taxes or shipping charges
   - Product rebates or other special offers
   - Product warranty
   - Store return policy

4. As a group, compare the information from all the sources. Consider product prices and other charges. Remember that the lowest price is not always the best price. Discuss whether each product meets the criteria you listed. Compare the warranties and return policies from the various sellers.

5. As a group, decide from which source you would buy the product. Give reasons why you selected this source.

ACTIVITY 4
Evaluate Credit Terms

1. Credit card companies offer different rates, fees, penalties, and other terms. Study the two examples of credit card terms that follow.

2. Evaluate these two credit card offers. Which one would you choose? Why?

Credit Card A

Credit Card A has a fixed annual interest rate of 8.9 percent. It also has an over-the-limit fee of $50. If you are late for even one payment, the interest rate rises to 19.99 percent. If you have two or more offenses (such as an over-the-limit fee and a late payment), the interest rate rises to 29.99 percent.

Credit Card B

Credit Card B has a variable annual interest rate of 4.9 percent for 1 year. After that, the rate is based on the prime rate plus 6 percentage points. This card has an over-the-limit fee of $35. If you are late making a payment, the interest rate will rise to 9.9 percent plus the prime rate.

218

ACTIVITY 5
Reconcile Credit Records

 You should check credit statements carefully when you receive them. You want to reconcile (make sure there is agreement between) your credit receipts and records and the information shown on the credit statement.

1. Open and print the PDF file *CH07 Statement* from the data files. This file contains a credit card statement and charge and payment records for 1 month.

2. Compare the charges listed on the statement with the list of receipts. Which, if any, amounts are different?

3. Are any payments that were made shown on the statement?

4. Are any credits (such as for returned items) shown on the statement?

5. Are any fees or penalties shown on the statement? If so, what is the reason for them?

6. Are the interest amount and the new balance (amount owed) correct?

7. What should you do if you find what you think is a mistake on a credit account statement?

219

CHAPTER 8

PAYING FOR CREDIT

© Getty Images/PhotoDisc

hapter 8 discusses paying for credit, types of loans, and managing credit wisely. You will learn about payment options and their advantages and disadvantages. You will discover the various types of consumer loans and debt options. You will also take a careful look at some tips for using credit wisely.

Payment Methods

OUTCOMES

- Describe manual and electronic options for making payments.
- Explain the advantages and disadvantages of manual payment options.
- Explain the advantages and disadvantages of electronic payment options.
- Name the primary advantage of wire transfers.
- Discuss prepayment penalties and why a loan might be repaid early.

MANUAL PAYMENTS

When you use some form of credit, you must decide how you will make payments on the account. When you make a payment on an account, you are reducing the amount you owe. Several payment options can be used. Each payment method has advantages and disadvantages.

Cash

Cash is a traditional payment option. Many people prefer to deliver cash to local stores and banks rather than mail a check. An advantage to using cash is that cash is accepted everywhere for payments. Be sure to get a receipt for any payment you make in cash. The receipt serves as proof of payment and is another advantage to this payment method. A disadvantage to paying with cash is that carrying large amounts of cash can be unsafe. You may be robbed, or you may lose the money. Another disadvantage is that the cash must be delivered in person. Never send cash through the mail.

Personal Checks

A personal check is another traditional payment option. The check can be mailed or delivered in person. Before you write the check, compare the bill with your receipts to be sure everything is correct. For revolving credit accounts, pay the outstanding balance if you can. If not, choose a payment amount that is more than the minimum required, if possible.

Paying by check has some advantages. Checks are easy and inexpensive to use. Mailing checks is relatively safe. Cancelled checks or bank statements showing checks that have been processed provide proof of payment. A disadvantage of paying by check is that the check can get lost or delayed in the mail. If the check does not reach the creditor before the due date, you may be charged a late fee. You can explain that the check was delayed in the mail and ask to be excused from paying the late fee. However, the creditor may not accept this excuse. Some creditors will waive at least one late fee.

When paying by check, you should plan ahead so that checks are written and mailed in time to reach the creditor by the due date. Be sure to mail payments from a secure location. Leaving mail in the unlocked box outside your house may not be a safe option. Instead, you can take the mail to a post office or mailbox that is secure.

Be sure to verify charges before you pay credit bills.

Money Orders

A **money order** is a type of check that directs payment of a sum of cash to a payee (a person or company). A money order typically has two parts. One part is the check that is sent to the payee. The other part is a receipt keep by the person buying the money order. The amount of the money order is printed on both parts. Money orders can be purchased at banks, U.S. post offices, and some stores. There may be a limit to the amount for which the money order is issued. For example, a postal money order may be limited to $1,000.

An advantage to using a money order is that it is prepaid. The payee is guaranteed payment because this type of check cannot bounce. A money order can also be sent safely by mail.

A disadvantage to using money orders is that getting one can be inconvenient. At some locations, you may have to stand in line and pay for the money order using cash. At other locations, you may be able to pay by personal check. Another disadvantage is that you must pay a fee for the money order. Often the fee is based on the amount of the money order. For example, a $100 money order might cost $5 (or more) for a total of $105.

Money orders can also be purchased on the Internet. To find a Web site that sells money orders, search using the term *money order*. At the Web site, you will need to enter the amount of the money order and select a delivery method, such as U.S. mail. You will also need to enter the recipient's name and address. Then you enter your name, address, and credit card information. Fees for buying a money order online are about the same as when buying one in person. For example, a $100 money order might cost $6.48 for a total of $106.48.

Money orders can be purchased at banks and other locations.

222

Bank Checks

A cashier's check is another payment option. You can purchase a cashier's check at a bank or credit union. You can pay for the check in cash or have the money taken from your account with the bank. An advantage to using a cashier's check is that it is prepaid. The payee is guaranteed payment. Unlike a money order, a cashier's check can be written for large amounts. A cashier's check can also be sent safely by mail. A disadvantage to this payment option is that you may have to pay a fee for the cashier's check. Some checking accounts include this service as a part of the account.

A **certified check** is a personal check for which payment is guaranteed by the bank on which it is drawn. To use this payment option, you write a check and have the bank certify it. The bank sets aside from your account the amount of the check. This amount will be used only for payment of the certified check. When the check is presented for payment, the money is waiting. An advantage to using a certified check is that it is prepaid. The payee is guaranteed payment. A certified check can also be sent safely by mail. A disadvantage to this payment option is that you may have to pay a fee for having a check certified. It may not be convenient to go to the bank and wait for service.

ELECTRONIC PAYMENTS

Using your checking account, you can set up electronic payments for some credit accounts. There are several types of electronic payments, such as online payments, online banking, payment by telephone, and automatic withdrawals. Electronic payments have several advantages. All of these methods save you postage. Once set up, they are quick and easy to use. Many people make most of their payments in this manner.

Electronic payments also have disadvantages. You will be charged fees for using some types of electronic payment services. You must monitor the balance in your checking account carefully. Be sure enough funds are available to cover the electronic payments. Otherwise, you may have to pay overdraft fees. If funds are not available, the bank might refuse the payment. Then you would have to pay late fees to the creditor.

Online and Telephone Payments

You may be able to make payments online at the creditor's Web site. At the Web site, you access your account with a user name and password. Then you enter your bank account information. This includes the bank routing number and checking account number. A sample screen for entering data is shown in Figure 8-1.1 on page 224. Now you are set to make online payments. When you want to make a payment, you authorize a withdrawal from your checking account. There usually is no fee for this service. You can choose the date the money is withdrawn from your account.

Some creditors allow you to authorize payments from a checking account by telephone. You must supply information such as your account number with the creditor. You will also need to give the creditor the bank routing number and your checking account number. Some banks allow

223

FIGURE 8-1.1

*You must enter
your bank account
information to set up
online payments.*

Bank Information

Enter your bank account information. You must use a checking account at your bank, credit union, or savings and loan. You must be authorized to sign checks on this account.

Nine-Digit Routing and Transfer Number:

Checking Account Number:

Reenter Checking Account Number:

Click NEXT to continue.

Next

you to make payments and manage your account using the telephone. A fee may be charged for this service, especially if you must speak to a person who assists you with the process.

Online Banking

Another type of online payment is made through your bank or credit union. This service, called **online banking**, allows you to make payments and manage your account using the bank's or credit union's Web site. Convenience is the main advantage to online banking. A disadvantage is that banks or credit unions may charge a monthly fee based on the number of payments you make. A major drawback to this method is that all of your creditors may not be set up to receive electronic payments. In this case, the bank creates a check and mails it to the creditor. In order to avoid late fees, you must allow mailing time when you authorize the payments.

Automatic Payments

Automatic payments occur when you ask the bank to transfer money electronically from your checking account to some other account. For example, many people choose to pay their car insurance premiums with automatic payments. The payment is made automatically each billing period. An advantage to this option is convenience. You do not have to remember to pay the bill each month. Another advantage is that you may get a discount for using this payment method. A disadvantage to this method is that you must be sure to keep enough money in the account to cover the automatic payment. If you do not, you may have to pay overdraft or late fees.

Wire Transfers

A **wire transfer** is the process of sending money electronically rather than using paper checks. This service is available from companies such

as Western Union. Banks and other financial institutions also do wire transfers for their customers. The sender pays the amount of the money transferred plus a fee. The money is delivered to a designated location where the recipient can collect it. For example, Western Union has sites called agent locations. They are businesses such as grocery stores, drugstores, and travel agencies. Customers can send a wire transfer or receive money from a wire transfer at these locations. The fee for this service depends on the amount of the transfer. For a wire transfer of $100, the fee could be $15 or more.

An important advantage to using wire transfers is that the transaction is completed very quickly. Money is transferred in just minutes, and you are assured that it arrives safely. A disadvantage to using wire transfers is that they can be inconvenient to purchase in person. You have to go to a bank or business that offers wire transfers. At some locations, you may have to pay cash for the amount being wired.

Wire transfers can also be arranged online and by telephone. Companies such as Western Union have Web sites and telephone numbers you can use to make a wire transfer. You pay for the transfer using a credit or debit card. This method may be more convenient than visiting a business to complete the transfer.

PREPAYMENT PENALTIES

Some types of loans may have penalties for early repayment. A **prepayment penalty** is a fee charged when you repay a loan before the agreed-upon time. For example, suppose you borrow money and agree to repay the loan over a 15-year period. A short time later, you decide to pay the entire loan balance. The loan agreement may specify a 30- to 90-day interest penalty. The lender has certain costs related to setting up the loan. These costs are spread over the life of the loan. If the loan is repaid early, the lender charges a penalty fee to cover these costs.

An example of a 60-day interest penalty on a $10,000 loan that is paid off after one year is shown in Figure 8-1.2.

Repaying a debt early may be a wise choice, even with a prepayment penalty. If the penalty amount is less than the interest you would pay if you paid on the original schedule, paying off the debt would be to your advantage.

FIGURE 8-1.2

PREPAYMENT PENALTY EXAMPLE

INSTALLMENT PAYMENT PLAN	
Terms: $10,000, 5-year loan at 8% interest, with a 60-day interest penalty for early repayment	
Initial Balance	$10,000.00
Monthly Payment	$ 202.76
Current Loan Balance	$ 8,305.60
(at payoff after 1 year)	
60-Day Interest Penalty	$ 110.74
Balance to Be Paid	$ 8,416.34

225

Building Communications Skills

The purpose of a formal speech is to convey information, to entertain, or to persuade. When preparing a speech, begin with a clear statement of the goals you want to accomplish. These goals will guide you as you prepare the content of the speech.

Use an outline to develop the content. The outline should have three main parts: the introduction, the body, and the conclusion. The introduction briefly explains your topic. The body gives the details or substance of the speech. The conclusion is a summary or request for action.

As you develop the content, consider the listeners who will hear the speech. Why will these people be listening? What do they have in common (age, place of work or residence, hobbies, other interests)? How much do they already know about the topic? Answering these questions will help you create content that will accomplish your goals.

Many formal speeches are presented using electronic slides. Projection equipment and software such as *Microsoft PowerPoint*® are often used. The slides help illustrate points and add interest to the speech. Slides should list only the main points being covered. If more detailed information must be shared, use a handout for that material.

A time limit is often set for formal speeches. Practice delivering the speech so you can stay within the required time limit. As you deliver the speech, make eye contact with members of the audience. Use an appropriate tone, rate, and volume. Speaking with confidence and enthusiasm will help you keep the audience interested. Pause briefly after important points to allow listeners to think about the point.

Effective formal speaking often takes lots of practice and refining of skills over time. After you make a speech, evaluate yourself. Think about what you did well and what you could do better the next time. You may also want to ask the audience to evaluate the speech.

8-1 REVIEW

8-1 Activity 1 Can You Recall?

Answer these questions to help you recall what you have read.
If you cannot answer a question, read the related section again.

1. List four types of manual (not electronic) ways to make payments on a credit account.
2. What are the advantages and disadvantages of making payments using cash?
3. What are the advantages and disadvantages of making payments using a personal check?
4. What is a money order? What are the advantages and disadvantages of making payments using a money order?
5. How is a cashier's check different from a certified check? What are the advantages to using these methods of payment?
6. What are some advantages of using electronic payments? What are some disadvantages?
7. What types of activities can customers do using online banking? Give one advantage and one disadvantage to making payments using online banking.
8. What types of information must customers provide to set up online payments at a creditor's Web site?
9. What is a wire transfer? What is its primary advantage?
10. What is a prepayment penalty? Why might you still wish to pay off a loan early, even when there is a prepayment penalty?

8-1 Activity 2 Payment Options

 Assume the following options are available to you for paying bills:

- Pay in person with cash.
- Send a personal check by mail.
- Make an online payment (at the creditor's Web site).
- Use the online banking payment system (at your bank's Web site).
- Set up a monthly automatic payment from your account.
- Buy and mail a money order.
- Secure and mail a cashier's check.
- Send a wire transfer.

227

What payment method would you choose for each of the following payments and why?

1. Monthly cell phone bill
2. Monthly electric utility bill
3. Monthly credit card bill
4. Monthly loan payment to your credit union
5. An online purchase of a book from a merchant with whom you are not familiar
6. $100 cash for your brother who is in another town and needs the money right away

Most secured loans also have closing costs. **Closing costs** are expenses you must pay in order to get a loan. They include charges for items such as appraisal fees, credit report fees, loan origination fees, recording costs, and inspection fees. Closing costs can be hundreds or even thousands of dollars. Before agreeing to a loan, be sure to ask about all the costs you will be expected to pay to get the loan.

If a mortgage is for more than 80 percent of the value of the home, the borrower is typically required to purchase mortgage insurance. This insurance will pay the lender if the borrower does not repay the loan. The loan agreement may also require the borrower to carry a homeowner's insurance policy.

Many people who buy houses finance the purchase with a mortgage loan.

AMORTIZATION

Repaying a debt by making regular payments of principal and interest over a period of time is called **amortization**. A formula can be used to calculate payments on an amortized installment loan. The formula is more complicated than the formula you learned earlier for simple interest. This is true because payments reduce both the principal and the interest amounts. Interest is charged on the outstanding balance, which decreases over the life of the loan. Amortization tables and calculators are available on the Internet. An example calculator is shown in Figure 8-2.1. These tools can help you quickly calculate loan payments. The payment is based on the principal, interest rate, and number of monthly payments.

FIGURE 8-2.1

MORTGAGE CALCULATOR

Mortgage Calculator

Loan Balance	$150,000
Yearly Interest Rate	9%
Loan Term in Years	20
	Calculate
Monthly Payment Required	$1,349.59

231

When you have credit standing by in case you need it, it can actually cost you in ways you never suspected. For example, you may have five or six credit cards with zero balances. On the surface, this seems to be a very good thing. Lots of credit is available to you, but your outstanding debt is zero.

Suppose you now apply for a loan for a car or another large purchase. Because you have five or six credit cards with potential for debt of $25,000 or more, the lender may be reluctant to extend more credit to you. The lender may ask you to close several of those unused credit accounts. Then the lender will feel more secure about your ability to repay the loan.

Having some credit available is useful. If you have too much, however, you may find yourself at a disadvantage when applying for a loan.

A mortgage calculator can also be used to show how much of each payment made goes toward repaying the principal and how much goes toward paying interest.

You may see two different rates given for a loan offer. The loan interest rate is used to compute monthly payments on the principal borrowed. The term *annual percentage rate* (APR) takes into account the other loan fees, such as closing costs, that the borrower must pay as part of the loan payments. Comparing the APRs for two different loans gives you a better picture of the total charges you must pay for each one. When comparing the APRs for loan offers, be sure the same fees are covered in the APR numbers. APR calculators are available on the Internet.

Student Loans

A **student loan** is debt that is used to finance education costs. Student loans can be secured from banks and other financial institutions. Students who meet certain criteria can also get student loans from the U.S. government. On some student loans, called subsidized loans, interest is paid by the federal government while the borrower attends school at least half-time. The borrower repays the loan after finishing or leaving school. To qualify for student loans, you must fill out a loan application. If you live with your parents, they will also have to fill out paperwork showing income and assets. To get a subsidized loan, the borrower must show proof of financial need. Other loans are available and are not related to financial need. The borrower must pay all interest on these loans.

Many students take out several student loans to pay for attending college or other schools. After they complete their education, they often have these loans consolidated. Several loans are rolled into a single loan with one payment. This makes it easier to pay off the debt over a long period of time.

If you decide to get a student loan, compare the terms for loans from various sources. Information about student loans from the U.S. government

232

FIGURE 8-2.2

Student loans are available for those who qualify.

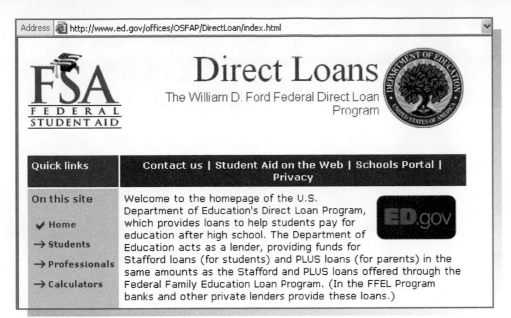

Source: U.S. Department of Education, Federal Student Aid, Direct Loans, http://www.ed.gov/offices/OSFAP/DirectLoan/index.html (accessed June 5, 2006).

and other sources is available online. Figure 8-2.2 shows the Web site for the Direct Loan program. The National Student Loan Data System for Students Web site is also provided by the U.S. Department of Education. This site is a central database of information for student aid. The site will help you compare sources of loans and grants for education. Links to both sites are provided on the Web site for this textbook.

LEASE/RENT-TO-OWN

Another way of buying is by leasing or renting to own. You select an item, such as a television. You take the item home and use it just as if you had purchased the item. Each week or month, you make rent payments. At this point, you do not own the item. However, the rent-to-own agreement may state that if you make a certain number of payments, you will then own the item.

There are advantages to this type of agreement. You do not have to make a large down payment at the time of purchase. Some lease or rent agreements require that no cash be paid at the time you sign the agreement. You can try the item before you buy it. If you decide you do not want the item, you can return it and end the rent agreement according to the terms of the contract. The contract also provides you with a guaranteed price that will not go up later.

The disadvantages of this option usually outweigh the advantages. You may not have much choice in the models or features available for items. If you decide not to buy the item, no part of your rent payments is returned to you. The main disadvantage, however, is that the total price you will pay for the item if you make payments until you own it is often much higher than if you buy the item outright. For example, suppose you rent-to-own a television that sells for $220. You make weekly payments of $10. After making 78 weekly payments, you own the television. You will have

233

paid a total of $780 for an item that sells for $220. This amount compares to paying a loan interest rate of 220 percent. A better option would be to take out a personal or secured loan at a bank to get money to buy the television. You could also charge the purchase on a credit card. In both cases, the interest rate would be much lower.

Success Skills

BUILDING A POSITIVE REPUTATION

Your personal behavior can have a big effect on the success of your personal relationships and activities. Your behavior also affects your success at school and work. *Reputation* is a word that means the opinion others have of you, especially as it relates to character or personal behavior. People form opinions about you, in part, from seeing the way you behave. They also form opinions from what others say about you. For example, a classmate may tell another person that you are prompt after noticing that you always come to class on time. Another person may notice that you did not do your part of a group task. This person may think that you are lazy or not cooperative.

Building a positive reputation is an important success skill. People may form opinions about you based on your reputation even before they meet you. This can be good or bad, depending on your reputation. Suppose you have a reputation for being a hard worker and treating others fairly. People will likely welcome you to their group or team. You will have a better chance of getting a job than another person with similar skills who has a poor reputation. Suppose you have a reputation for submitting work late that is poorly done. Others may not want to be on your team. You may find it difficult to get a good recommendation from former teachers or employers. This might keep you from getting a job or from being accepted to a college.

Follow these suggestions to build a positive reputation and be successful in your relationships:

- Treat others with courtesy and respect.

- Be fair and honest in your dealings with people.

- Be courteous to everyone, but choose your friends carefully.

- Be reliable. Always be on time for classes and appointments. Complete work or projects on time.

- Be willing to listen to new ideas and learn new skills.

- Show appreciation for the talents and accomplishments of others.

- Do your best whatever the task, but be willing to admit that you do not know all the answers all the time. Ask for help when you need it.

- Show maturity. For example, a mature person can admit that he or she made a mistake. A mature person can also accept disappointments or criticism tactfully.

- Be a team player. Do your share and be willing to help others.

8-2 Activity 1   Can You Recall?

Answer these questions to help you recall what you have read. If you cannot answer a question, read the related section again.

1. What is a personal loan? What factors affect the amount of a personal loan for which you may be approved?
2. How is a secured loan different from a personal loan? Give two examples of secured loans.
3. Explain how a fixed rate mortgage differs from an adjustable rate mortgage.
4. What is a balloon payment? Why might this type of payment be included in a loan agreement?
5. What types of fees are typically included in loan closing costs?
6. What is the purpose of a mortgage calculator?
7. What is the purpose of a student loan? From what sources are student loans available?
8. Describe how a rent-to-own agreement works. What are the advantages and disadvantages of this purchase method?

8-2 Activity 2   Compare Buying and Leasing Options

Consumers often do not have enough money to pay the full price of items they want or need to buy. Using credit makes buying these items possible. Different forms of credit have different costs. In this activity, you will compare paying for an item using a credit card, renting to own an item, and leasing an item.

1. You have decided you need a laptop computer. The purchase price of the computer is $1,200. You can charge this item on your credit card and pay for it over the course of 1 year. The interest rate is 18.99 percent. Each month for 11 months, you will pay $110. In the last month, you will pay the remainder of the outstanding balance. (For the purposes of this problem, assume there will be no other charges or fees on the credit card bill.) The credit card company uses the adjusted balance method to compute interest. What is the total amount (purchase price plus interest) that you will pay if you use this method to buy the computer?
2. Another option for buying the computer is to get it from a rent-to-own company. With this type of arrangement, you pay fixed monthly rental payments. At this point, you are renting the computer; you do not own it. You can stop renting and return the item at any time.

235

If you continue renting until you have paid a certain set amount, you will own the computer (and make no more rental payments). You must pay a monthly rental fee of $200. You will own the computer after you make 12 payments. What is the total you will pay for the computer using this option?

3. Another option you can choose is to lease a computer for 1 year. You will be required to make monthly payments of $125 for 1 year. At the end of that time, you can return the computer to the leasing company, lease it for another year, or lease a newer computer instead. What is the total amount that you will pay for 1 year if you choose this option?

4. Which of the three options—charge to a credit card, rent-to-own, or lease—would you choose? Why would you choose this option?

Credit Tips

OUTCOMES

- Explain why using credit may tie up future income.
- Discuss why you should consider the state of the economy when planning credit purchases.
- List the terms typically included in a credit offer.
- List ways you can reduce and avoid credit costs.

USING CREDIT WISELY

When you begin using credit, plan to use it wisely. Go slowly; do not use too much credit at first. It is very important to establish credit when you do not need it so that it will be available to you when you do. Build a solid credit history by paying all credit bills on time. Later, when you want to use credit, you will be considered a low (good) risk. You may also be able to borrow at lower interest rates than someone who is considered a high (bad) risk.

Buying items using credit can tie up future income. For example, suppose you buy an item for $500 using a credit card. If you pay the entire amount in one billing cycle, future income is not tied up with this debt. However, suppose you pay the $500 plus interest over six billing cycles. Part of your income for the next 6 months must be used to pay for the item you purchased this month. You may have to forgo buying some items you want or need during the next 6 months because the money must be used to pay an existing debt.

As your earnings go up over time, save more money rather than spending the full amount of the pay increase. Think about future needs rather than only things you might want, but not need, in the present.

You may feel secure in your job and your prospects for the future. However, you should always have a back-up plan for handling expenses if you are out of work for a time. Save a cash fund, and have some unused credit available. If the worst happens, you will have money to pay bills until you begin earning money again. You will also have some credit available to make purchases.

Consider the Economy

When the economy is doing well and people can get jobs easily, consumers may feel optimistic about the future. This optimism often leads to increased

Using credit to buy items can tie up future income.

buying. When credit is used to buy more items, future income may be tied up as well. During good economic times, interest rates are usually rising. Thus, rather than buying on credit, this could be a good time to save money.

The opposite is true when the economy is slowing down. People are being laid off, and jobs are scarce. People may feel pessimistic, and this can lead to decreased buying. Because people are buying less, prices may be dropping. Thus, this could be a good time to buy because you can get better values. If you do not spend all of your money (and credit) during the optimistic stage, you will have money available to spend when prices may be more favorable.

Study Credit Offers

If you are like many people, you will receive credit offers soon after you begin working. These offers are mailed, e-mailed, or found in advertisements. Carefully examine each offer and compare the terms and conditions if you are considering the offer. A credit offer typically includes these terms:

○ **Interest rates.** Are they fixed or variable? How often can they change? What will cause them to change? Fixed rates often do not stay fixed and can be changed with some notice from the creditor. However, they are usually better than variable rates, which can rise without advance notice.

○ **The grace period.** The **grace period** is the amount of time you have before a credit card company starts charging you interest on your new purchases. Most credit offers allow for a grace period of at least 20 days. The longer the grace period, the longer you have to pay without being charged interest on the purchase amount.

○ **Method of computing interest.** Many creditors use the two-cycle average daily balance method. This means if you have a balance any-time during the two-cycle billing period, you will be charged a finance

238

charge. A billing cycle is typically about 1 month. This method is not good for consumers.

- **Annual fee.** Some credit cards charge an annual fee or a membership fee. This fee can be $25 to $50 or more. Once your credit is established, you should be able to find a credit card offer that does not require an annual fee.
- **Minimum finance charge.** Some credit cards require a minimum charge of $1 or more for each billing period.
- **Transaction fees.** If you transfer balances from other credit accounts, you may be charged a transaction fee. This fee is usually a percentage, such as 3 percent of each transaction. There is often a minimum of $5 and a maximum of about $75.

Technology Corner

APPLYING FOR A LOAN ONLINE

Getting a loan online can be a very attractive option. You give personal information and fill out an application. When you submit the application electronically, you may have an answer quickly. You can fill out the application in the privacy of your own home and at a time that is convenient for you.

Be cautious about applying for a loan online. Deal with lenders you know. Do not respond to online offers. Instead, go to the Web site of a reputable lender by keying a URL in the browser's address box. If you do not know the URL, call the lender and ask for this information. You may be required to create an account with a user name, password, and other data before you can fill out an application. A sample screen for entering information to set up an account is shown in Figure 8-3.1 on page 240.

You will need the same type of information as you would to complete a paper application. Thus, you need to gather all the data and have the data ready. You will need to give very sensitive and private information in the credit application. Be sure the Web site is secure to lessen the chances that your information will be stolen. A secure Web site will have a message to tell you that the site is secure. The message is often next to a padlock icon. You may be required to provide written documents, such as pay stubs, to verify the information in the loan application.

Before accepting the loan, read the entire contract. Study the conditions, rates, and other items in the agreement. Print everything so that you will have a complete copy of the application and all of the loan documents. Some lenders will assign a loan advisor to your account. You can contact this person by phone or e-mail to ask questions about the loan or the application process.

Once your loan is approved by the lender and you agree to the loan terms, you must sign the loan papers. Some lenders have an online process in which borrowers can provide an electronic signature. Figure 8-3.1 shows a Web page at which students can learn about using an electronic signature when applying for a loan. Some lenders will send a notary public to an agreed-upon location, such as your home or work site. This person will witness you signing the documents and will return them to the loan company. Once the loan documents are signed, the funds are released to you.

239

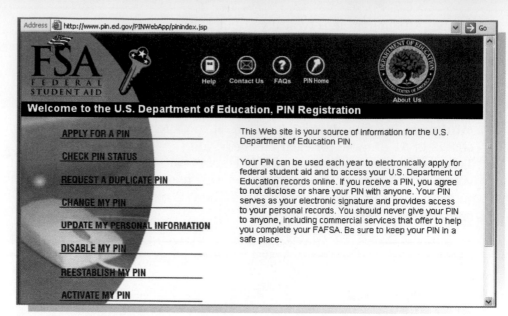

Source: U.S. Department of Education, Federal Student Aid, PIN Registration, http://www.pin.ed.gov/PINWebApp/pinindex.jsp (accessed June 12, 2006).

○ **Cash advance fees**. Some credit cards allow you to take cash advances at ATM machines and at banks. There is often a fee for this type of transaction. It is usually a percentage, such as 3 percent with a minimum amount of $5 or more.

○ **Late fees and over-the-limit fees**. The fee for late payments can be $15 to $50 or more. The fee may depend on the balance on your card. The over-the-limit fee is usually a flat amount, such as $35 or more. Having late fees or over-the-limit fees can cause the interest rate you are charged to rise.

Some credit card offers state that the company reserves the right to change the account terms at any time for any reason. This includes raising interest rates. When an interest rate goes up, you must accept the change or cancel the card. Thus, being in a flexible position is important. You want to avoid being in the position of having to accept higher rates and fees.

REDUCE AND AVOID COSTS

When you use credit, there is usually a cost. You may want to pay cash for small purchases instead of using credit to avoid credit costs. When you do use credit, try to pay the full account balance each billing cycle. If you do, you will not have to pay any interest. Here are several other ways you can reduce your costs:

○ Keep the number of credit cards and accounts you have to a minimum. Avoid having an account at every store in town and with every bank card available. Only carry with you the cards you will be using. Having a bank card is a good idea because it is accepted at many different businesses. Using a bank card also eliminates the need to have several individual store accounts.

240

The method used to pay for a large purchase is as important as the item being purchased.

- Comparison-shop when getting a loan. Compare the costs of credit from at least three different sources. When planning a large purchase, such as a car, arrange the financing ahead of time. That way, you will know the dollar amount you can spend and the interest rate you can get. You can then compare any offers that the seller might have.
- Consider financing and special deals arranged by the seller. A **sales finance company** is a type of lender that makes loans for the purchase of consumer goods, such as cars or household appliances. The finance company may also purchase time-sales contracts from merchants. The finance company often works closely with the seller. This makes it easy for customers to arrange financing at favorable terms. For example, GMAC (General Motors Acceptance Company) is a sales finance company. One of the services offered by GMAC is loans for the purchase of automobiles. When buying a car, you may be offered a sales incentive, such as 0 percent interest on a loan or $2,500 cash back on a purchase. These deals are worth considering.
- Use credit to take advantage of sale prices. With the help of credit, you can buy things on sale that you would not buy if cash were your only option. Thus, you can avoid higher prices and save money.
- Time your credit purchases. If you buy right after the closing date of your billing cycle, you may be able to delay payment for 2 months after the purchase. Most credit accounts have a 25- to 30-day billing cycle.
- Take advantage of cash rebates and rewards. Many credit cards offer rebate programs. A rebate is a partial refund of the purchase price

241

of an item. For example, a 5 percent rebate would give you back 5 percent of the purchases you made during the month or year. This increases your spending power. Be careful, however, not to overspend because of this reward. Some credit accounts also offer gift certificates and other incentives. Choose the reward that benefits you the most, and use cards that have rewards rather than those that do not.

Ethics

UNETHICAL LOAN PRACTICES

Some people use unethical loan practices. They take advantage of people who can least afford to pay. Because some people have poor credit ratings or have not used credit wisely in the past, they may not be able to get loans from legal sources. They may decide to take out illegal loans, and the interest may be very high.

A loan shark is one source of illegal loans. A loan shark is a person who offers illegal unsecured loans at very high interest rates. Because the borrower is desperate, she or he borrows the money. At such a high rate, however, the debt grows rapidly and is very difficult, if not impossible, to repay. The borrower may receive threats of violence if the loan is not repaid.

Many people have lost money in advance-fee loan scams. In this type of scam, a lender agrees to make a loan if the borrower pays an up-front fee. The lender may promise to refund the fee or to apply it to loan payments once the loan has been secured. The fee may be several hundred dollars. The borrower may have a bad credit history and may be desperate for the loan, so he or she agrees and pays the fee. Later, the borrower learns that the lender is not reputable. The borrower may be told that the loan has been denied and that the

fee will not be refunded as promised. In some cases, the borrower may not hear from the lender again. However, money may be illegally withdrawn from the borrower's bank account using information provided on the loan application.

An unethical practice related to home mortgages is called equity stripping. In this situation, a person with a home needs money. A lender points out that the person has built equity (monetary value) in the home. A loan is arranged using the home as collateral. The borrower may not have enough monthly income to make the loan payments. However, the lender approves the loan anyway. The lender may even encourage the borrower to overstate her or his income to get the loan. Once the borrower starts missing payments, the lender will foreclose and take the home.

These examples are just a few of the ways you can be deceived by unethical or illegal lenders. Whenever you come upon a deal that sounds too good to be true, it probably is. There are always people looking to take advantage of others. Beware of offers for loans with terms that sound unreasonable. They may sound good, but in reality they are deceptive, unethical, and sometimes illegal.

8-3 Activity 1 Can You Recall?

Answer these questions to help you recall what you have read.
If you cannot answer a question, read the related section again.

1. Explain why using credit may tie up future income.
2. Explain how your credit history relates to the interest rate you may have to pay for credit. Why are some people who really need credit unable to get it?
3. Why should you consider the economy when planning credit purchases?
4. List the terms typically included in a credit offer.
5. Why is it important for you to be able to cancel a credit card whenever you wish?
6. List three ways you can reduce or avoid credit costs.
7. Describe one unethical loan practice.

8-3 Activity 2 Research Loan Offers

1. Find three advertisements of offers for loans. The loans can be personal loans, secured loans, or student loans. Newspapers, magazines, and the Internet are places where you may find loan offers. You could also ask about loans available at local banks or credit unions.
2. Find the following information for each loan offer:
   ○ Type of loan (secured, unsecured, or student loan)
   ○ Interest rate charged
   ○ Length of the loan in months or years
   ○ Application fees, closing costs, and other fees
   ○ Penalties that may apply, such as a prepayment penalty
3. Evaluate each offer. Do you think the lender is reputable? Are any of the terms questionable? Which offer has the most favorable terms for the borrower?

EXPLORING CAREERS IN HEALTH SCIENCE

Do you enjoy working with other people? Are you interested in helping people stay healthy? Do you like to analyze problems and search for solutions? If the answer is yes, a career in health science might be right for you. Jobs in this area are varied. Some workers, such as nurses, work directly with patients to provide health care. Others are employed in labs or research facilities to run diagnostic tests or develop new drugs. Support staff are needed in hospitals, labs, and other places to make patient care possible.

Jobs in this career area are found in government and businesses. Health care is one of the largest and fastest-growing industries in the United States. The need for jobs in health science is expected to grow. Job outlook varies by job.

Skills Needed

Some of the skills and traits needed for a career in health science include the following:

- Math and science skills
- Communications skills
- Computer/technology skills
- Ability to work well with others
- Decision-making skills
- Problem-solving skills

Job Titles

Many jobs are available in the health science field. Some job titles for this career area include the following:

- Billing clerk
- Clinical laboratory technician
- Dietitian
- Medical records technician
- Medical scientist
- Paramedic
- Pharmacist
- Physician
- Registered nurse

Explore a Job

1. Choose a job in the health science field to explore further. Select a job from the list above, or choose another job in this career area.
2. Access the *Occupational Outlook Handbook* online. A link to the site is provided on the Web site for this textbook.
3. Search for more information about the job you selected to answer these questions:
   - What is the nature of the work this job involves?
   - What is the job outlook for this job?
   - What training or qualifications are needed for this job?
   - What are the median annual earnings for this job?

Summary

- Cash, personal checks, money orders, and bank checks are manual or traditional methods of making payments.

- An advantage to using a money order or a bank check is that the payee is guaranteed payment.

- Online payments can be made at some creditors' Web sites. Online banking, payment by telephone, and automatic withdrawals are available for some accounts.

- A wire transfer is the process of sending money electronically rather than using paper checks.

- A prepayment penalty is a fee charged when you repay a loan before the agreed-upon time. Repaying a loan early may be to your advantage even when there is a prepayment penalty.

- An installment loan is a type of debt in which you borrow money for a period of time. The loan has an agreed-upon interest rate and repayment plan. Personal loans, secured loans, and student loans are three types of installment loans.

- A personal loan is granted based on your creditworthiness. A secured loan is a debt agreement in which the borrower pledges property of value as security for the loan.

- Many mortgages have fixed interest rates and payments over the life of the loan (typically 10 to 30 years). An adjustable rate mortgage has a variable interest rate that goes up or down at the discretion of the lender.

- A student loan is debt used to pay for education. You must qualify based on creditworthiness. For some student loans, you must also qualify based on need.

- Lease or rent-to-own agreements are another option for buying items. The total price you will pay for the item if you make payments until you own it is often much higher than if you buy the item outright.

- It is very important to establish credit when you do not need it so that it will be available to you when you do. Build a solid credit history by paying all credit bills on time.

- Buying items using credit can tie up future income if the debt is paid over several months or years.

- During good economic times, interest rates are usually rising. This could be a good time to save money. When the economy is slowing down, prices may be dropping. This could be a good time to buy because you can get better values.

- Carefully study and compare credit offers. Fixed versus variable rates, the method of computing interest, all types of fees, and grace periods are some items that should be carefully examined.

- To reduce and avoid costs, keep the number of credit cards and accounts you have to a minimum. Comparison-shop for loans and other types of credit. Use credit to take advantage of sales. Use credit cards that have rebate or rewards programs.

245

Key Terms

adjustable rate
  mortgage
amortization
automatic payments
balloon payment
certified check
closing costs

cosigner
grace period
installment loan
money order
mortgage
online banking
personal loans

prepayment penalty
sales finance
  company
secured loan
student loan
wire transfer

ACTIVITY 1
Review Key Terms

Use the key terms from Chapter 8 to complete the following sentences:

1. A type of mortgage loan called a(n) _____ has an interest rate that can change over time, at the discretion of the lender.

2. A debt instrument called a(n) _____ is used to secure financing of a house purchase.

3. A loan for which property has been pledged as collateral called a(n) _____ .

4. A large payment, called a(n) _____ , is much larger than other loan payments and must be paid at a set time, often as the last loan payment.

5. _____ are loans that are based on personal creditworthiness (that have no collateral).

6. A(n) _____ is the process of sending money electronically rather than using paper checks.

7. The amount of time you have before a credit card company starts charging you interest on your new purchases is called the _____ .

8. A type of lender that makes a loan for the purchase of consumer goods, such as cars or household appliances, is called a(n) _____ .

9. A personal check for which payment is guaranteed by the bank on which it is drawn is called a(n) _____ .

10. A service that allows you to make payments and manage your bank account using the bank's Web site is called _____ .

11. A(n) _____ is a type of prepaid check that directs payment of a sum of cash to the payee.

12. A fee charged for repaying a loan before the agreed-upon date is called a(n) _____ .

13. A(n) _____ is debt used to finance education costs.

14. Payments that are made by transferring money electronically from a checking account to another account (such as a creditor's) every billing period are called _____.

15. Expenses the borrower must pay to get a loan, such as appraisal fees, credit report fees, recording costs, and inspection fees, are known as _____.

16. A(n) _____ is a person who agrees to repay a loan if the borrower does not repay it.

17. A type of debt in which you borrow money for a period of time with an agreed-upon interest rate and repayment plan is called a(n) _____.

18. Repaying a debt by making regular payments of principal and interest over a period of time is called _____.

ACTIVITY 2
Math Minute

1. The following charges are part of the closing costs for a loan. What is the total amount of the closing costs?

Appraisal fee	$500.00
Lender's inspections fee	$250.00
Credit report fee	$ 50.00
Loan origination fee	1 percent of the loan amount of $250,000.00
Notary public fee	$ 60.00
Document recording fees	$ 75.00
Title search	$250.00
Survey fee	$250.00
Flood certification	$ 30.00
Buyer's attorney fees	$750.00
Mortgage insurance	0.5 percent of the loan amount of $250,000.00

2. Albert Morrison took out a loan for $90,000.00 at 10 percent interest for 15 years. Albert's monthly payments are $967.14. Part of each payment is applied to the loan balance, and part is for interest. He has made payments for 2 years (24 payments). He now wants to repay the loan early. The current principal balance owed is $84,257.19. The loan has a $468.00 interest penalty for early repayment. Will Albert save money by repaying the loan (current balance plus penalty) at this time? If so, how much will he save?

3. Sue Thomson bought a house for $178,750.00. She is getting a mortgage for $145,000.00. If a mortgage is for more than 80 percent of the value of the home, Sue's lender requires that the borrower purchase mortgage insurance. Will Sue have to purchase mortgage insurance?

247

ACTIVITY 3
Mortgage Payments

1. Open the *Excel* file *CH08 Loan Payment Calculator* from the data files. Read the instructions provided in the file for using the loan payment calculator. (If you do not have *Excel*, search for a mortgage calculator on the Internet.)

2. Joe Chin bought a house for $180,000.00. He made a 20 percent down payment. Joe secured a loan for the balance of the purchase price at 6.5 percent interest for 30 years. What will the monthly payments on the loan be?

3. Louisa Perez bought a house for $300,000.00. She made a 10 percent down payment. Louisa secured a loan for the balance of the purchase price at 5.95 percent interest for 30 years. What will the monthly payments on the loan be?

4. Mary Roberts bought a house for $255,000.00. She made a 5 percent down payment. Mary secured a loan for the balance of the purchase price at 6.75 percent interest for 15 years. What will the monthly payments on the loan be?

ACTIVITY 4
Group Presentation

   academic.cengage.com/school/pfl

1. Work with two or three classmates to complete this activity.

2. Choose a topic related to using credit, and get approval of the topic from your teacher. A few suggested topics follow:
   o The housing market in your local area or state
   o The employment market in your local area or state
   o The new and used car markets in your local area or state
   o Interest rates in the economy
   o Loan scams or deceptive practices
   o Making payments online or online banking
   o Comparison of interest rates and other credit terms for different lenders in your area

3. As a group, do research on your topic. Use local newspapers, magazines, and the Internet.

4. As a group, create an outline of the main points you want to include in your presentation. Then write down the details you want to cover. Include how the information you found could or should affect use of credit by consumers in your area.

5. Prepare electronic slides, transparencies, posters, handouts, or other visual aids that you can use during the speech delivery.

6. Decide which person will present each part of the speech. Practice as a group. Review the Building Communications Skills: Formal Speaking feature in this chapter to help you prepare.

7. Deliver the presentation to your class.

248

ACTIVITY 5
Reducing Credit Costs

Critical Thinking → Enrique is thinking about buying a large, flat-panel television. He will need to borrow money to make the purchase. He can arrange the financing ahead of time, or he can use the installment sales plan at the store.

1. What steps can Enrique take to minimize his total costs when choosing the television?

2. What steps can Enrique take to minimize his total costs when choosing a source of credit?

3. What steps related to his credit account can Enrique take to minimize his costs following the purchase?

249

CHAPTER 9

CREDIT PROBLEMS AND LAWS

© Andreas Pollok/Stone

Chapter 9 is about resolving problems with credit. In this chapter, you will learn about ways to avoid credit problems and how to resolve credit problems. You will also learn about bankruptcy and its purposes. You will study credit reporting and related laws. These laws protect both consumers and creditors in credit reporting, billing, collections, and granting or denying credit.

9-1

Resolving Credit Problems

OUTCOMES

- Explain how to dispute an error on a credit statement.
- List ways to prevent credit card fraud.
- Describe the purpose of consumer advocacy groups.
- Explain how government consumer protection services help consumers.
- List ways to prevent garnishment and repossession of assets.

ERRORS AND FRAUD

When buying goods and services, there may be times when you think that you were cheated or that an error has been made. You may be due some type of adjustment to your account or the amount you owe. This remedy for unfair treatment is often called **recourse**. Your recourse may be returning damaged goods for a credit to your account. The recourse could be having an amount on your account reduced to reflect a correct price. You may get recourse in some other way to compensate you for errors or fraud. To get recourse, you must take action.

Disputing Charges

When you receive a credit account statement, compare the charges to your receipts. If you find a charge on the statement that you did not make or that is incorrect, take action right away to dispute the charge. Disputing a charge is the process of informing the credit company of the mistake.

Disputing charges usually begins with a telephone call or a visit in person to report and discuss the problem. Always follow up with a written letter explaining what happened. When you keep good records, you have **documentation** that can help support your claim that the bill has an error or a false charge. Always keep receipts, statements, and other credit records you receive. Whenever you talk to a person about a dispute, write down the date, the person's name and title, the phone number, and the details discussed. Then you will have a record of what has happened and the steps you have taken.

Figure 9-1.1 on page 252 shows a letter of complaint written to dispute an incorrect charge on an account. A dispute letter should begin with your return address and the date. Read the credit account information to find the proper address to which you should send a dispute letter. Often, the address is not the same one you use for payments. Key the correct address

FIGURE 9-1.1   **LETTER OF DISPUTE FOR CREDIT CARD CHARGES**

4550 Bay View Road
Hamburg, NY 14075-4450
April 7, 20--

Credit Company
P.O. Box 87483
Wilmington, DE 19850-7483

Dear Sir or Madam

DISPUTE ON ACCOUNT 2444 2344 2317 3243

Please register this dispute of a charge on my recent credit statement, which
is dated April 2, 20--. The incorrect charge is circled on the enclosed copy of
the statement.

I called to report this error today and talked to Melanie Smith in your
Customer Service Department. The charge is for $46.42 for the purchase of
gasoline in Houston, Texas, on March 20, 20--. I did not make this purchase.
I have never been to Texas. I have not loaned my card to another person or
given permission to anyone to use my account. I have had my card with me
at all times, and it is not lost or stolen.

Please remove this incorrect charge from my credit account. If you have any
questions about this dispute, please call me at 716-555-0134.

Sincerely

Joy B. Adams

Joy B. Adams

Enclosure: Credit Statement

252

in the letter and on the envelope. Include your credit account number in a subject line in the letter. State the problem with the account clearly. Give all the details needed to make the problem easy to understand. State any earlier steps you have taken related to the problem. For example, describe any phone calls you made regarding the error. State clearly the action you want the company to take, such as removing a charge. Indicate that you are enclosing a copy of the statement that contains the error, and place an enclosure notation at the end of the letter. Continue to communicate with the credit company until the dispute is resolved.

Credit Card Fraud

You may have improper charges made to your store or credit accounts. When someone intentionally uses your credit account to steal money or goods, this is a crime called **credit card fraud**. Credit card fraud is a felony (a serious crime). If you are a victim of credit card fraud, notify the creditor as soon as possible. Take steps such as these to help prevent credit card fraud:

- Carry only the cards you need.
- Keep a list of credit card account numbers and phone numbers to call so you can rapidly report a card that is lost or stolen.
- Verify purchases and account balances when you receive a statement.
- Shred receipts and statements that show your account number when you are finished with them.
- Do not loan your credit card to others.
- Know where your credit cards are at all times.
- Close inactive accounts because they are often targeted by thieves.
- Have mail delivered to a post office box or a secure mailbox.
- Mail bills only from a secure mailbox or a post office.
- Use only secure Web sites, and buy online only from reputable companies you know.
- Do not give out credit card or other private information over the telephone or by e-mail to people who say they are calling from your bank or credit card company.

CONSUMER ADVOCACY GROUPS

Consumer advocacy groups are organizations that promote consumers' rights. They often provide information about laws related to consumer rights. Some groups also seek to have laws passed that will be beneficial to consumers. Some groups focus on a single area, such as food safety. Other groups address a wide range of issues.

Several groups deal with consumer issues related to using credit. You can visit their Web sites to learn about the latest frauds and about how to protect yourself. These Web sites are a good place to do research before you accept some offer that sounds suspicious. Remember, when an offer sounds too good to be true, it probably is. Figure 9-1.2 on page 254 shows a list of consumer advocacy groups. Links to the Web sites for many of these groups are provided on the Web site for this textbook.

Web sites such as the Fraud Bureau and the Independent Consumer Complaint Network allow users to log complaints about company practices

253

CONSUMER ADVOCACY GROUPS

Better Business Bureau	Promotes responsible business practices
Consumer Action	Promotes consumers' rights and advocates for consumers in the media and before lawmakers (a nonprofit organization)
Consumer Federation of America	Advocates for consumers through legislation
Consumers Union	Publishes *Consumer Reports*
	An independent, nonprofit testing and information organization that provides advice about products and services
National Consumers League	Sponsors the National Fraud Information Center and addresses a wide range of issues
Public Citizen	Addresses issues such as the right of consumers to seek redress in the courts; clean and safe energy sources; and strong health, safety, and environmental protections

FIGURE 9-1.3

FIND-IT! CONSUMER WEB SITE

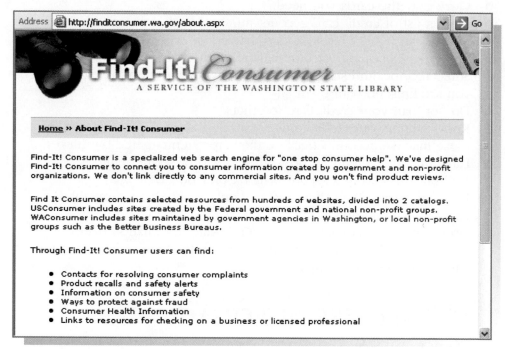

Source: Washington State Library, Find-It! Consumer, http://finditconsumer.wa.gov/about.aspx (accessed June 20, 2006).

or frauds and read complaints posted by others. Find-It! Consumer, shown in Figure 9-1.3, is a Web site that allows you to search for consumer information provided by government and nonprofit groups. This site is a service of the Washington State Library.

GOVERNMENT CONSUMER PROTECTION SERVICES

Numerous federal and state agencies assist consumers. These agencies regulate trade, investigate crimes, and enforce laws. They test drugs, food, and other products for safety and to see if they live up to their claims.

Federal Agencies

There are many agencies that protect and help consumers. The U.S. Consumer Product Safety Commission (CPSC) is one such agency. The CPSC is charged with protecting the public from unreasonable risk of death or injury from thousands of consumer products. The agency issues consumer recalls or alerts for products that are considered unsafe.

The U.S. Food and Drug Administration (FDA) is one of the nation's oldest health agencies. It is a science-based law enforcement agency. Its mission is to protect public health and safety related to certain areas. The FDA ensures that foods, cosmetics, and medicines are safe. It investigates complaints, tests products, and allows safe products in the marketplace. The FDA also removes products that are not safe.

The Federal Trade Commission (FTC) deals with issues that affect the U.S. economy. One of its goals is to keep a competitive marketplace for businesses and consumers. The Bureau of Consumer Protection is a part of the FTC. This bureau seeks to protect consumers against unfair, deceptive, or fraudulent practices. The FTC also provides consumer education. It publishes tips for avoiding scams and rip-offs and provides a place to file complaints online. A link to the FTC site is provided on the Web site for this textbook.

The Federal Bureau of Investigation (FBI) is a part of the U.S. Department of Justice. The FBI investigates fraud and other crimes. It also publishes information on issues such as identity theft. The FBI's Web site lists current scams and tells you how to avoid them. Consumers can file a complaint online at several government sites as shown in Figure 9-1.4. Links to the U.S. Department of Justice and FBI Web sites are provided on the Web site for this textbook.

State Agencies

State governments also have consumer protection services. Consumers can read the latest information about products and crimes, file reports, and ask

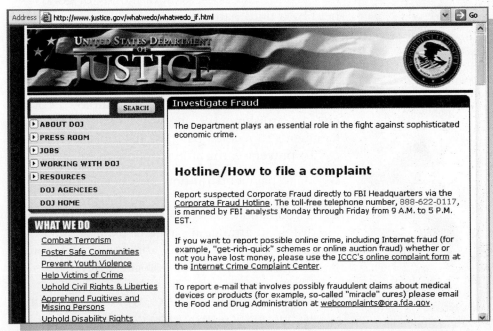

FIGURE 9-1.4

Consumers can file complaints online at government Web sites.

Source: U.S. Department of Justice, What We Do: Investigate Fraud, http://www.justice.gov/whatwedo/whatwedo_if.html (accessed June 20, 2006).

questions. Many counties and cities provide consumer alerts and support as well. District attorneys' offices and nonprofit groups serve as places to get information. City and county government offices and local offices of consumer groups can be found using the Internet and the telephone book.

CREDIT DELINQUENCY

Delinquency means the failure to do what your duty or the law requires. When the term is used with regard to credit, delinquency means an overdue debt. A credit contract requires that you make payments on time. When you do not make payments on time, your account is in delinquency. As soon as you find you are unable to make payments as agreed, contact your creditors and explain the situation. Many creditors are willing to work with you so that you can pay your account. They will often reduce or postpone payments, reduce interest, or make special arrangements so you can avoid penalties for late payment.

Collection Agencies

If payments on your credit account are overdue, your account may be turned over to a collection agency. Collection agencies legally have the right to represent the creditor to collect the amount due. If you do not pay your debt, they may file a lawsuit to get a judgment against you. A judgment is a ruling of a court of law. The judgment may give the collection agency the legal right to take assets away or to garnish your wages. This is a situation you want to avoid. A judgment is likely to have a bad effect on your credit rating. You may have to pay certain fees to the collection agency, as well as the debt amount owed.

Garnishment

Garnishment is a proceeding in which a creditor may legally take possession of money or goods held by a third party in payment of a borrower's debt. For example, a creditor may take money from a worker's pay each month to pay a debt the worker owes. The money is paid directly from the employer to the creditor. Because the creditor has a legal garnishment order, the employer cooperates. Garnishment is one way creditors enforce judgments to receive payment for a debt.

To prevent garnishment, follow these steps:

- Make payments on time as stated in the loan agreement.
- If you cannot pay, contact your creditor immediately to arrange a payment plan.
- Be up-front and truthful about your situation.
- Keep good records so you can defend your actions.
- Ask to negotiate claims to avoid having your account turned over to a collection agency.
- Respond to all legal documents; stay current in paying claims.

© Digital Vision

Keep your creditors aware if you are having problems making payments.

Your car may be repossessed if you do not make your car loan payments on time.

Repossession and Foreclosure

A loan that has collateral pledged for repayment is called a secured loan or debt. If the borrower does not make payments as agreed on a secured loan, the property used as collateral can be taken away to pay the debt. **Repossession** is the process of taking an asset used for collateral, such as a car, and selling it to pay a debt. Having an item repossessed hurts the borrower's credit rating.

Foreclosure is a legal proceeding a creditor can use when a borrower does not make mortgage payments. The creditor may be able to force a sale of the property. Money from the sale is used to pay the mortgage. Debtors may lose the money they have paid so far as mortgage payments. They also may have to pay foreclosure costs. Foreclosure costs can include attorneys' fees, court costs, and interest charges. Foreclosure also hurts one's credit history.

The best way to avoid repossession or foreclosure is to be very careful when buying. Know what you can afford in a monthly payment. Do not take out a loan unless you are reasonably sure you can make the payments. If you find you cannot make payments as agreed, talk to the lender immediately. Work out an alternate arrangement, give back the asset, or find another way to resolve the problem.

257

9-1 REVIEW

9-1 Activity 1   Can You Recall?

Answer these questions to help you recall what you have read. If you cannot answer a question, read the related section again.

1. Explain how to dispute an error on your credit statement.
2. List ways you can protect yourself from credit card fraud.
3. Explain the purpose of consumer advocacy groups.
4. List three federal government agencies that help protect consumers. Give a brief description of what each agency does to help consumers.
5. What does the term *delinquency* mean as it relates to a credit account?
6. What is a collection agency? Why might your credit account be turned over to a collection agency?
7. Describe what you can do to prevent garnishment or repossession of assets.

9-1 Activity 2
Research Consumer Advocacy Groups

 academic.cengage.com/school/pfl

Consumer advocacy groups have many different goals. They provide information to consumers. They may seek to have laws passed that help consumers. They may provide reports on companies or products or a place to file complaints. In this activity, you will learn more about one consumer advocacy group. You will present the information you learn to the class.

1. Select a consumer advocacy group from Figure 9-1.2 or another group approved by your teacher.
2. Search the Internet or other sources to find information about this group. You may find a Web site sponsored by the group or articles written about the group.

3. Write a summary of the information you find about the group. Include the points listed below and other information you think would be helpful for your classmates to know about the group.
   o The group's name
   o The main activities or mission of the group
   o Services offered to consumers by the group
   o Publications or Web sites published by the group
   o When the group was founded
   o Whether the group is a nonprofit organization
4. Give a short talk to the class to present the information you learned about this group.

Bankruptcy

OUTCOMES

- Explain the purposes of bankruptcy.
- List strategies to help avoid bankruptcy.
- Describe Chapter 7 Liquidation bankruptcy.
- Describe Chapter 13 Wage Earner Plan bankruptcy.
- Explain bankruptcy exemptions and how they affect consumers.

AVOIDING BANKRUPTCY

Credit that is used wisely can be a valuable tool in reaching financial goals. When credit is not used wisely, however, the consumer may build debt to the point where it can never be repaid. **Bankruptcy** is a legal procedure to relieve a person who cannot pay his or her debts of those debts. The person may be relieved of (not have to pay) most debts or may be allowed to repay some debts over a set period of time. This depends on the type of bankruptcy granted. Bankruptcy must be granted by a federal court. The person may have to surrender assets to be sold to help pay debts. In a voluntary bankruptcy, the individual asks the court to declare bankruptcy. Creditors or lenders can also ask the court to declare bankruptcy for a debtor. This situation is called involuntary bankruptcy.

Some common reasons why debtors cannot pay their bills and seek bankruptcy are listed below.

- Excessive medical bills (even with insurance coverage)
- Small business failure (half of all small businesses fail each year)
- Overspending and unwise use of credit
- Losing employment and being overextended
- Having no savings when unexpected events (losses) occur

Consumers should try to avoid bankruptcy, if possible. Bankruptcy damages a person's credit rating. It stays on the credit record for 10 years. It prevents the consumer from getting low interest rates on credit accounts or loans. Bankruptcy can make it difficult to obtain credit, buy a home, get life insurance, or sometimes get a job. The consumer may be left with very little property. Thus, it pays to try to find other ways to solve debt problems rather than seeking bankruptcy. Credit counseling, debt management, and debt consolidation are three strategies consumers may be able to use to avoid bankruptcy.

FIGURE 9-2.1

Source: U.S. Department of Justice, U.S. Trustee Program, http://www.usdoj.gov/ust/eo/bapcpa/ccde/cc_approved.htm (accessed June 27, 2006).

Credit Counseling

Credit counseling is available through nonprofit groups and other organizations. They work with debtors to arrange a payment plan for debts. They also provide lifestyle counseling to help people avoid credit problems in the future. Sometimes, these counselors are able to negotiate lower interest rates with creditors so that debt can be paid off sooner. This type of service allows people to pay their debts and get back on track with financial plans. Debtors must get credit counseling from a government-approved organization within 6 months before filing for any bankruptcy relief. You can find an approved credit counseling agency in your area on the U.S. Trustee Program Web site as shown in Figure 9-2.1.

Debt Management

A debt management service works with you and your creditors to create a workable plan for paying off debt. Debt management begins with a careful look at each credit balance. Its interest rate, minimum payments, and how soon it will be paid off are considered. This service often involves turning over your checking account and your bills to the debt manager. It also requires that you have sufficient income to be able to pay the outstanding debt. There is usually a fee or a commission charged for this service. You give up your credit cards and live on an allowance. At the end of the agreed-on period of time (usually 3 to 5 years), your debt has been repaid. With education in how to prevent credit problems from happening again, you then have a fresh start.

Some debt management services that claim to be nonprofit charge unreasonably high fees. Many reputable services are accredited through

261

A cosigner is a person who guarantees the debt of another person. In many cases, a person who does not have credit established will have a hard time getting a loan. The lender needs some assurance that the debt will be paid. A cosigner is a person with good credit or assets that can be used as collateral. The cosigner vouches for the person who needs credit.

The cosigner must repay the loan if the debtor does not repay the loan as agreed. The cosigner's credit rating will also be affected by a delinquency. On credit reports, cosigning for a loan has the same effect as taking out a loan yourself. In other words, creditors will count it as existing debt to the cosigner.

Before you cosign for a loan, be sure to understand your position. Be prepared to repay the debt at any point in time. Some cosigners find it a good idea to make one payment in advance. This helps avoid having a late payment if the borrower does not pay on time.

the Association of Independent Consumer Credit Counseling Agencies or the National Foundation for Credit Counseling. Check with these organizations for information about a debt management company you are considering using.

Debt Consolidation

Debt consolidation is the process of getting one loan to pay all your debts. Then a single monthly payment is made to repay that loan. The single payment is usually much less than the minimum payments on a number of loans or debts.

Consolidation loans are available through banks and other financial institutions. There are finance companies that specialize in loans to pay off credit card debt. Many debt consolidation loans require collateral to secure the loan. If you are making payments on a house, this would be in the form of a second mortgage. An **equity loan**, or second mortgage, is secured by the value of your home. For example, if your house is valued at $150,000 and your mortgage is $120,000, then you have equity of $30,000. This amount could be borrowed to pay off high-interest credit cards and accounts. The interest rate is generally much lower, and the debtor can afford the payments.

PURPOSES AND TYPES OF BANKRUPTCY

There are two purposes of bankruptcy law. One purpose is to give a debtor a fresh start. A fresh start is needed when bills are so high that they could never be repaid. The second purpose is to ensure fair treatment for creditors. Bankruptcy laws are there to help people in hopeless situations

FEDERAL BANKRUPTCY EXEMPTION EXAMPLES	
Exemption	**Amount**
Motor vehicle	$ 2,400
Household goods ($400 limit for a single item)	8,000
Jewelry	1,000
Tools (for debtor's trade)	1,500
Personal injury compensation payments	15,000
Other property	800
Public assistance	
Social Security benefits	
Veterans' benefits	

Source: U.S. Congress, *United States Code*, "Title 11—Bankruptcy, Chapter 5—Creditors, the Debtor, and the Estate, Subchapter II—Debtor's Duties and Benefits," GPO Access, http://frwebgate3 .access.gpo.gov/cgi-bin/waisgate.cgi?WAISdocID=0030315692+4+0+0&WAISaction=retrieve (accessed October 4, 2006).

FIGURE 9-2.2

A bankruptcy exemption is property that a debtor does not have to give up to pay off creditors.

get back on their feet. Bankruptcy was never intended to be used for reckless spending and avoiding responsibility.

There are different types of bankruptcy. For example, Chapter 7 Liquidation and Chapter 13 Wage Earner Plan are for individuals. Chapter 11 is for businesses. Bankruptcy immediately stops all collections. This stay is automatic. When a debtor files for bankruptcy, all accounts and contracts are frozen. That means no further action, including lawsuits, can be taken.

Chapter 7

Also known as straight bankruptcy, **Chapter 7 Liquidation** is used when an individual seeks to have her or his debts discharged. A **discharge** is a court order that pardons the debtor from having to pay debts. Chapter 7 bankruptcy is also called liquidation. The debtor's assets are sold (liquidated), and the money is used to repay as much of the debt as possible. Then all remaining debts (with a few exceptions) are discharged.

Most debts can be discharged. This includes credit card balances, bank loans, medical bills, and court judgments. There are some types of debt, however, that are not discharged by bankruptcy, such as tax debt, student loans, government fines for criminal charges, child support, and spousal support.

Before filing a Chapter 7 bankruptcy case, the debtor must get credit counseling and satisfy a means test. This test requires the debtor to confirm that his or her income does not exceed a certain amount. The amount varies by state.[1]

Under Chapter 7, many debtors do not lose all of their property. This is because there are exemptions. An **exemption** is property that a debtor does not have to give up to pay off creditors. For example, there is a homestead (housing) exemption that allows the debtor to keep $15,000 worth of equity in a home. If the debtor's equity is that amount or less, the debtor can keep the home.

Examples of other federal bankruptcy exemptions are shown in Figure 9-2.2. This is not a complete list. Amounts are adjusted periodically,

263

---

[1] *Facts for Consumers: Knee Deep in Debt*, Federal Trade Commission, http://www.ftc.gov/bcp/ conline/pubs/credit/kneedeep.htm (accessed June 24, 2006).

and current amounts may be different from the ones shown here. Many states also have bankruptcy laws that affect the exemptions allowed.

Chapter 13

Another form of bankruptcy for individuals is the **Chapter 13 Wage Earner Plan**. This type of bankruptcy is for debtors who have a good source of steady income. It is designed mostly for homeowners and working people. The debtor selects exemptions just as in Chapter 7. Rather than liquidate assets, debtors follow a plan to pay back as much debt as they can over a 3- to 5-year time period. After that time period, their debts are discharged.

Chapter 13 forces creditors to stop interest and late penalties. While a Chapter 13 plan is in effect, creditors cannot start or continue collection efforts. They must accept what the bankruptcy court decides will be their settlement. In some cases, creditors who have made unsecured loans receive no more than 10 to 30 percent of the amount owed to them.

New Bankruptcy Legislation

The Bankruptcy Abuse Prevention and Consumer Protection Act was approved by Congress in April 2005 and signed by President George W. Bush. Most parts of the law apply to cases filed on or after October 17, 2005. The law seeks to make

Chapter 13 bankruptcy is for people who have a good source of steady income.

© Getty Images/PhotoDisc

Ethics

BANKRUPTCY FRAUD

Bankruptcy fraud is the use of bankruptcy laws to take advantage of others or to make false claims. Bankruptcy fraud is a serious federal crime (a felony). People who try to hide assets from the bankruptcy court are committing bankruptcy fraud. Assets must be disclosed so that creditors can receive a fair share in the payment of debts.

Creating debts with the intent of denying creditors payment for goods and services is also illegal and unethical. It is abuse of bankruptcy laws to plan a bankruptcy with overspending and staying just below the exemption allowances. If the court suspects that a person is committing bankruptcy fraud, it may dismiss the bankruptcy and prosecute for fraud.

264

it more difficult for consumers to erase all debt by requiring more people to file under Chapter 13 rather than under Chapter 7 bankruptcy.

Some debtors who want to file under Chapter 7 must first complete a means test. This test is to see whether they have enough disposable income to repay debts under a Chapter 13 plan. The test compares the debtor's gross income to the median income in the state. Debtors who earn less than the median income in their state typically qualify for Chapter 7 bankruptcy. Other debtors may or may not qualify depending on other factors.

Debtors who do not qualify for Chapter 7 bankruptcy may file for Chapter 13 bankruptcy. They will be required to repay some or all of their unsecured debt. The court can also convert a Chapter 7 case to a Chapter 13 case or dismiss the case (not allow bankruptcy).

The new law requires most debtors to receive credit counseling at least 6 months before filing for bankruptcy. Debtors may also have to take a class on debt management techniques.

Building Communications Skills

PERSUASIVE SPEAKING

The focus of public speaking is often to convince people to take action or support an idea or position. To be effective, the speaker must be believable. Persuasive speaking is challenging because you may have to change people's minds. You may also have people in the audience who are biased against your ideas or position. Giving public speeches means you are often speaking to people you do not know. You are presenting a message and hoping for their support. For example, people who run for public office must prepare persuasive speeches.

Effective persuasive speeches are relevant, interesting, and decisive. You will need to capture the listeners' attention and hold it as you present information and logical conclusions. When giving a persuasive speech, open with remarks that will get the attention of the audience. Clearly state the position or action you want the listeners to support. Give supporting data or quotes that will strengthen your position. When preparing the speech, think about negative reactions or questions the listeners may have. Prepare answers to have ready for these questions.

The next time you hear a campaign speech, listen carefully to what is being said. Also listen to the techniques used in presenting the speech. How did the person get your attention? What problems were discussed? What solutions were proposed? Was the speaker believable? Apply the techniques that you think were effective to your next speech.

9-2 Activity 1   Can You Recall?

Answer these questions to help you recall what you have read.
If you cannot answer a question, read the related section again.

1. What are some reasons people get into extreme debt and seek bankruptcy?
2. Explain how credit counseling can help to avoid bankruptcy.
3. How is debt management different from debt consolidation?
4. What are the two purposes of bankruptcy law?
5. Why is Chapter 7 bankruptcy also called liquidation?
6. What are bankruptcy exemptions?
7. How is Chapter 13 bankruptcy different from Chapter 7 bankruptcy?
8. What is meant by bankruptcy fraud?

9-2 Activity 2   Credit and Bankruptcy Advice

 academic.cengage.com/school/pfl

When consumers have serious problems making payments and managing their debt, they may seek advice. Some credit counseling agencies offer free advice; others charge a fee. In some cases, bankruptcy may be the only course available. Consumers may seek legal advice in filing for bankruptcy. Some bankruptcy lawyers will give an initial consultation that is free. In this free session, the client explains her or his situation, and the attorney evaluates the options.

1. Visit the U.S. Trustee Program Web site. A link to the site is provided on the Web site for this textbook. You can also search the Web using the term **approved credit counseling agencies**.
2. Find a credit counseling agency that is approved for residents of your state. Give the agency name and address.
3. Look in the Yellow Pages or search online using the term **bankruptcy attorney**. Find ads or Web sites for bankruptcy attorneys. Review at least two ads or Web pages.
4. What types of claims do the attorneys make about bankruptcy? What kinds of fees do they charge? Is there a free initial consultation?

Consumer Protection and Laws

OUTCOMES

- Explain the purpose of a credit report and credit score.
- Explain consumer rights related to denied credit.
- State the purposes of several consumer protection laws.
- Explain the process of alternate dispute resolution.
- Describe the process of resolution through filing a lawsuit.
- List credit scams and ways to protect yourself from them.

CREDIT REPORTS AND SCORES

Every person who has a Social Security number also has a credit file. Data in your credit file are shared with interested parties in a **credit report**. The purpose of a credit report is to give lenders and others information about your credit history and current status. A credit report contains a listing of your current credit accounts and their balances. Accounts you have had in the past may also be listed. If you have defaulted on a loan or made late payments, that is reported. The report contains personal data such as your address, phone number, Social Security number, and date of birth. It may include where you work and how much you earn.

The three major credit bureaus are Equifax, TransUnion, and Experian (TRW). Each of these bureaus collects and analyzes data about you and assigns a number called a credit score. The purpose of a credit score is to rate whether you are a good or poor credit risk. Example credit scores are shown in Figure 9-3.1 on page 268. The higher the score, the lower the risk. Many lenders use these scores provided by credit bureaus. Some lenders compute their own scores. There is no single cutoff score used by all lenders. The scores shown are examples only.

Consumers can get their credit scores from the credit bureaus, usually for a charge. Newly passed laws allow you to view your credit reports once a year free. However, the score itself will probably cost you $30 or more. Follow these suggestions to improve your credit score:

- Pay all debts on or before the due dates.
- Pay more than minimum payments.

FIGURE 9-3.1   EXAMPLE CREDIT SCORES

Credit Score	Description
Up to 499	Unacceptable. Debtor has no credit established or has a previous bankruptcy or current delinquencies. (Credit requests would be denied.)
500–599	Poor. Risk is high. Debtor is improving but had too much credit or too many collections in the past. (Credit requests are denied or carry very high interest rates to cover high risk.)
600–699	Fair. Medium risk. Debtor has too much credit and too many payments but is not currently delinquent or in collection; credit history is not perfect. (Credit requests are granted with medium interest rates and lower limits.)
700–749	Good. Lower risk. Debtor has a fair load of debt not exceeding recommended levels; payment record is good. (Credit requests are granted with low interest rates and good limits.)
749–799	Very good. Low risk. Debtor can take on more debt without a problem; payment history is very good. (Credit requests are granted with low interest rates and high limits.)
800+	Excellent. Risk is minimal. Debtor has very little debt and usually pays off balances in full each month. (Credit requests are granted with lowest rates and highest limits.)

- Keep your debt as low as possible.
- Do not charge more than 50 percent of the credit line available to you.
- Pay off credit card balances when possible.
- Have a good job with solid income.
- Stay in the same job for several years.
- Own your house rather than rent.
- Check your credit report regularly to be sure it contains correct information.

CONSUMER RIGHTS

A number of laws protect consumers from unfair credit practices. These laws help consumers as well as outline their responsibilities. The laws cover topics such as credit reports, reasons a person may or may not be denied credit, and ways disputes can be resolved.

When You Are Denied Credit

If you are denied credit, it may be because there is inaccurate information in your credit file. The **Fair Credit Reporting Act** gives you the right to know what is in your credit file. You can also find out who has seen your file. You may see your file at no charge within 30 days of a credit denial. You have the right to have inaccurate data investigated, corrected, and deleted from your file. The three national credit bureaus are required to furnish a new report. If information is correct, you can write your own statement giving your side of the issue. This statement must be added to the file and made available to lenders and others who see your credit report.

268

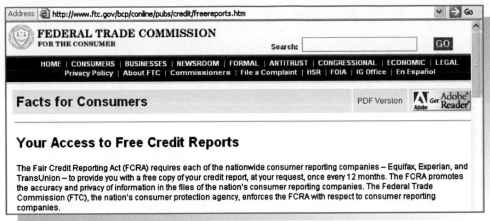

The Federal Trade Commission Web site provides information about credit reports.

Source: Federal Trade Commission, *Facts for Consumers*, http://www.ftc.gov/bcp/conline/pubs/credit/freereports.htm (accessed June 29, 2006).

Reviewing Your Credit Report

Consumers have the right to see one free copy of their credit reports annually. You can learn more about free credit reports on the Federal Trade Commission Web site, as shown in Figure 9-3.2. Consumers should check their credit files regularly to be sure there are no errors. When an error is discovered, it can be corrected before it results in denial of credit. Checking the report often can also help protect against credit card fraud.

Technology Corner

GETTING A CREDIT REPORT ONLINE

You can order a credit report online by going directly to the Web site of a credit bureau. You can also get your credit score. You may have to pay a fee to see your credit score. However, you can get a free credit report once a year. AnnualCreditReport.com is a Web site that allows you to request a free credit report once every 12 months. Using this site, you can get a free report from each of the major consumer credit reporting companies: Equifax, Experian, and TransUnion.

To get a report, you will have to give personal information. A telephone call may be required to verify your identity.

The entire process is relatively quick and easy. Within minutes, you can find out what is in your report.

You can also enroll for credit protection services. For an annual fee that is often $50 or more, consumers will be notified of changes to their credit files. They can see who is looking at their files. They are able to monitor any changes and check the accuracy of the file. This type of service is offered by credit bureaus, credit card companies, and others. It is considered by some people to be a good defense against credit fraud and identity theft.

269

Being Fully Informed

The Consumer Protection Act of 1968 is also known as the **Truth-in-Lending Act**. This act requires that consumers be fully informed about the cost of credit. Before a credit agreement is signed, a lot of information must be given, in writing:

○ Cash price of the item being purchased
○ Down payment or trade-in price
○ Amount financed
○ Any service fees or other costs being added to the price
○ Finance charges
○ Annual percentage rate
○ Deferred payment price
○ Amounts and dates of payments
○ Description of the item being purchased
○ Method of computing finance charge in case of early payoff

Truth-in-Lending limits a person's liability to $50 after a credit card is lost or stolen. There is no liability when a card is reported lost before its illegal use. The law requires that consumers be given a grace period of 3 days to change their minds about a credit contract in which their home is used for security. During those 3 days, consumers can change their minds and cancel a credit sale.

Resolving Errors

The **Fair Credit Billing Act** protects consumers who have billing disputes. The law applies to open-end credit, such as store or credit card accounts. It does not apply to installment loans. A consumer has 60 days from the day the bill is received to file a dispute. Then, the creditor has 30 days to respond to the complaint. Within 90 days after receiving your complaint, the creditor must either correct the error or show why the bill is correct. This law helps consumers resolve errors on their accounts in a timely manner. When an amount is in dispute, the creditor cannot charge interest on that amount. The creditor also cannot try to collect that amount.

All credit card companies must have credit policies. They must tell their customers how to report errors. Figure 9-3.3 on page 271 shows an error correction policy for a credit card company.

Discrimination

The **Equal Credit Opportunity Act** protects consumers from discrimination in the granting or denying of credit. The act makes it illegal to discriminate on the basis of these factors:

○ Gender
○ Marital status
○ Religion
○ National origin
○ Race
○ Color
○ Age

In addition, credit cannot be denied because the person receives government payments, such as unemployment or Social Security

FIGURE 9-3.3   **ERROR CORRECTION POLICY**

IN CASE OF ERRORS OR INQUIRIES ABOUT YOUR BILL

The Fair Credit Billing Act requires prompt resolution of errors. To preserve your rights, follow these steps:

1. Do not write on the bill. On a separate piece of paper, write a description as listed below. A telephone call will not preserve your rights.
   a. Your name and account number
   b. Description of the error and your explanation of why you believe there is an error (Send copies of any receipts or supporting evidence you may have; do not send originals.)
   c. The dollar amount of the suspected error
   d. Other information that might be helpful in resolving the disputed amount
2. Mail your letter as soon as possible. It must reach us within 60 days after you receive your bill.
3. We will acknowledge your letter within 30 days. Within 90 days of receiving your letter, we will correct the error or explain why we believe the bill is correct.
4. You will receive no collection letters or collection action regarding the amount in dispute, nor will it be reported to any credit bureau or collection agency.
5. You are still responsible for all other items on the bill and for the balance less the disputed amount.
6. You will not be charged a finance charge against the disputed amount unless it is determined that there is not an error in the bill. In this event, you will be given the normal 25 days to pay your bill from the date the bill is determined to be correct.

payments. Certain questions cannot be asked, such as which church you attend. The law benefits consumers because only the consumer's credit standing may be used when evaluating whether or not to grant credit.

Debt Collections

The **Fair Debt Collection Practices Act** protects consumers from abusive practices related to collecting debt. For example, threats and intimidation are not allowed. Debtors cannot be called at certain places, such as at work. The time of day is also important. Collection calls may not be made after 9 p.m. Collectors cannot call repeatedly throughout the day. Also, debt collectors must be sure the bill is accurate and allow the consumer to dispute it. Any disputed amounts must be resolved before they can be collected.

GETTING RECOURSE

A consumer may have trouble settling a dispute with a creditor. Rather than give up, the consumer can seek alternate dispute resolution. If that method does not settle the dispute, the consumer might file a lawsuit.

Alternate Dispute Resolution

Alternate dispute resolution (ADR) is a method of settling a dispute using a neutral third person. ADR is much less expensive than going to court. It is usually much faster also.

Negotiation occurs when two people get together, with or without a neutral third party, to come to an agreement. Both people talk about their point of view and how they want to see the issue resolved. They listen to each other and come to some type of agreement. The agreement usually involves both sides giving something and getting something in return.

Mediation, the next level of resolution, involves using a neutral third party to guide the process. The mediator talks to both parties and hears both sides of the issue. The mediator may allow the parties to talk to each other. The mediator then makes a proposed settlement.

Arbitration is the highest level of resolution. A third party, called an arbitrator, listens to both parties and then makes a decision. The decision may be binding on both sides. Arbitration may take several months. Both sides present their case formally, and rules of law are followed. The arbitrator is a professional who knows the law and is able to understand the issues.

Filing a Lawsuit

When attempts to resolve a dispute have failed, a consumer may decide to file a lawsuit. Filing a complaint in small claims court is a simple and quick method of resolving a matter involving a small amount (usually less than $5,000). The plaintiff files a document called a complaint. The complaint is served on the defendant. The two parties appear before a judge, whose decision is final. This process usually takes from a few weeks to 2 months. Attorneys do not participate in small claims court.

For larger dollar amounts, regular trial courts settle disputes. Attorneys represent each side. The first step is hiring an attorney to represent you. The attorney tries to negotiate a settlement for you. If that fails, a lawsuit is filed. The case goes to trial, and the judge or jury makes a decision (called the verdict). If you win the lawsuit, you get a judgment against the defendant. This process often takes many months. It may also cost hundreds or thousands of dollars in attorneys' fees.

Credit disputes can often be resolved by negotiation.

© Getty Images/PhotoDisc

272

Many people have trouble dealing with change. Even changes that a person thinks are good can cause stress. Why is change stressful? Changes at home, school, or work may mean that you have new duties or tasks to complete. You may feel uncertain about whether you can do these new duties or tasks well. You may think that they will take too much of your time or effort. You might feel uneasy because you do not know how the changes will affect your relationships with others. For example, if you attend a new school, will you still see your friends from your old school? You may worry that you are not making the best decision related to a change. For example, if you take a new job that pays more money, will you like the work you do? Such thoughts, feelings, and questions can cause a person to experience stress.

One thing is certain: changes will come throughout life. Learning to deal with change and the related stress is an important success skill. In some cases, you can choose to ignore or resist change. However, this may create even more stress. It may also have other negative effects. For example, if you refuse to change work methods, you could lose your job. If you ignore changes in your health, you could become seriously ill. In many cases, the only reasonable choice is to accept change and to make the best of it. Some of the following suggestions can help you deal with change in a positive way:

- Learn as much as you can about how the change will affect you.

- Keep a positive attitude. Try to see something good or helpful in the change.

- Be objective. Do not let fears or bias rule your actions.

- Create a plan. List small steps you can take that will lead you through the change process.

- Get help, support, or counseling, if needed, to help you deal with making a change.

- Take care of your health. Eat a balanced diet, exercise, and get enough sleep. Take some time to relax. You will be better able to deal with stress if you are healthy and rested.

- Build your self-esteem. Have confidence that you will be able to deal with a new situation, coworker, or task.

- Expect change to be a part of your life. Look at every change as an opportunity to build new skills or relationships.

In a class action lawsuit, a group of people file a claim together. One attorney or law firm represents all the plaintiffs. Any judgment is then split among the plaintiffs, who may also share attorneys' fees.

CREDIT SCAMS AND RELATED CRIMES

A **scam** is a fake offer, sale, or other gimmick that will cost you money if you agree to it. Every year, millions of American consumers lose money in scams. The scam may allow thieves to access their bank or credit accounts or to steal from them in other ways. For example, a disreputable lender

273

may offer a loan to a borrower who has a poor credit history and no assets to use as collateral. All the borrower has to do is a pay a large, up-front loan application fee. The loan is then denied, and the application fee is not returned.

A common scam is carried out by thieves from foreign countries. They ask you to transfer money through your bank account and keep a portion of the money for your fee. They send you a check, which you deposit. The check appears to be good. You wire the money to an address provided. However, the original check is later found to be worthless. You lose the money you wired to the thief, and you may have to pay a fee to the bank for depositing a bad check.

Credit repair scams are also common. The company claims to be able to replace your poor credit history with a good one. No one can "fix" bad credit. The services provided (for a fee) by such companies are nothing more than what you can do for yourself. They cannot take true information from your file. They cannot change your credit rating. Any advice they give is available to you free of charge from various government and nonprofit agencies.

New scams are being developed daily. When in doubt, do not agree! Ask questions and research offers and companies to avoid being caught in a scam.

Identity Theft

Identity theft occurs when someone uses your personal information without your permission to commit fraud or other crimes. According to the U.S. government, identity theft is one of the fastest-growing crimes in America. When a thief has your Social Security number, it can be used to get other personal data. The data may be used to apply for credit in your name. The credit card or loan is used to buy goods, but the credit bills are not paid. The account may have false address information, so the bills do not come to you. For this reason, you may not find out for some time that you are a victim of identity theft.[2]

Identity thieves may also open a bank account in your name and then write bad checks against the account. They may open service accounts in your name, such as for telephone or cable TV service, and not pay the bills. They may even take a job and file tax returns using your name and personal data.

One reason this crime is on the rise is because identity can be stolen without any contact with the thief. It can happen even if the victim does not make a purchase or do anything risky. Simple acts, such as giving personal information to an employer, can expose you to identity theft. Your information may be stolen from your employer's records. Your data can also be stolen from your mail, such as credit card statements.

If you find that your identity has been stolen, or if you lose items that show your personal data, take the following steps quickly:

- Close credit and bank accounts. Open new accounts with new passwords and credit alerts.
- Have a fraud alert placed on your credit reports. This can help stop someone from opening a credit account in your name.

274

[2] *Identity Theft and Your Social Security Number,* Social Security Administration, SSA Publication No. 05-10064, January 2006, http://www.ssa.gov/pubs/10064.html (accessed June 23, 2006).

An identity thief may open an account in your name and write bad checks.

○ Contact the government agencies that issued your identification documents, such as a driver's license. Follow the agency's procedure to get a replacement document, if needed. Ask the agency to place an alert in your file so that another person cannot get an identification document in your name.

Phishing

Phishing is a common Internet scam. The thieves use e-mail messages and Web sites designed to look like the sites of real companies. They appear to be real businesses, banks, and government agencies. Consumers are deceived into giving account information and personal data, such as user names and passwords. The phishers then use that information to steal money from accounts and for identity theft. If you think that a message regarding your bank account or other financial matters may be real, contact the bank or other business by phone. Ask if there is a problem with your account. Do not reply to the e-mail message or go to the link provided.

275

9-3 Activity 1   Can You Recall?

Answer these questions to help you recall what you have read. If you cannot answer a question, read the related section again.

1. What is the purpose of a credit report? What kind of information does a credit report contain?
2. What is the purpose of a credit score? How can you find your credit score?
3. What can you do if you are denied credit?
4. How often can you see your credit report (without charge)? What Web site can you use to get a free credit report?
5. List the basic provisions of the Truth-in-Lending Act.
6. Explain the procedures for resolving errors under the Fair Credit Billing Act.
7. List the items that cannot be the basis for discrimination in the granting or denial of credit.
8. List some activities that the law does not allow in the collection of credit debts.
9. Describe three types of alternate dispute resolution.
10. Describe the process of going to court to file a lawsuit to settle a dispute.

9-3 Activity 2   Taking Action

Write a few sentences for each of the situations below, telling what would you do to resolve it. Be sure to include any outside source of information or support you would contact.

1. You tried to use your credit card, and it was rejected. When you called your credit card company, you were told that your balance is over the limit. You have not used your card in the last week. There should be well over $1,000 worth of credit available on it. What do you do?
2. A representative from your bank called and told you about a special offer—a free safe deposit box and a $50 gift—if you upgraded your account. You verified your personal information with the caller. After the call, you phoned the bank to ask a question about the deal, but you found that no one from the bank had called you. What do you do?
3. You took your car in to have the brakes replaced. When the mechanic did the job, he also found that your muffler needed replacing. You authorized him to do the work. After you got home, you noticed a bill that shows your spouse had the muffler replaced 2 weeks earlier. What do you do?

Chapter 9   Credit Problems and Laws

EXPLORING CAREERS IN ARCHITECTURE AND CONSTRUCTION

Are you fascinated by long bridges and tall skyscrapers? Do you like to take apart and rebuild machines to see how they work? Are you interested in measuring and mapping the earth's surface? Would you enjoy planning the location of buildings, roads, and walkways and the arrangement of flowers, shrubs, and trees? If the answer is yes, a career in architecture and construction might be right for you. Jobs in this area are varied. Some workers in this field design buildings or outdoor spaces such as parks. Others are engineers who develop solutions to environmental problems or design and test tools, engines, and machines. Surveyors, carpenters, electricians, highway builders, heavy equipment operators, and metalworkers are also part of this career area.

Jobs in this career area are found in government and businesses. Many general contractors and architects are entrepreneurs and have their own businesses. The need for jobs in this area is expected to grow.

Skills Needed

Some of the skills and traits needed for a career in architecture and construction include the following:

- Math and science skills
- Communications skills
- Computer/technology skills
- Decision-making skills
- Problem-solving skills
- Leadership skills

Job Titles

Many jobs are available in architecture and construction. Some job titles for this career area include the following:

- Architect
- Carpenter
- Equipment operator
- Electrician
- Engineer
- Iron/metal worker
- Landscape architect
- Mechanical engineer
- Surveyor

Explore a Job

1. Choose a job in architecture and construction to explore further.
2. Access the *Occupational Outlook Handbook* online. A link to the site is provided on the Web site for this textbook.
3. Search for more information to answer these questions:
   - What is the nature of the work this job involves?
   - What is the job outlook for this job?
   - What training or qualifications are needed for this job?
   - What are the median annual earnings for this job?

Summary

- Errors in your credit accounts and in your credit report can be corrected.
- Mistakes or false charges to a credit account should be disputed in writing.
- To avoid credit card fraud, the consumer must take precautions, such as shredding receipts and checking bills.
- Consumer advocacy groups and governmental agencies provide information and help for consumers who are victims of crime.
- Credit delinquencies can have serious outcomes. Your account may be turned over to a collection agency. Your earnings may be garnished. Items bought on credit, such as a car, may be repossessed. If you do not make mortgage payments, the creditor may be able to foreclose on the property.
- Bankruptcy is a legal procedure to relieve a person who cannot pay his or her debts of those debts. The person may be relieved of most debts or may be allowed to repay some debts over a set period of time. Bankruptcy should be used only as a last resort.
- Credit counseling, debt management, and debt consolidation are ways of avoiding bankruptcy.
- Chapter 7 Liquidation is also known as straight bankruptcy; the debtor gives up property and has many debts discharged.
- Chapter 13 Wage Earner Plan is bankruptcy for people who have a regular source of income. They pay off debts for 3 to 5 years, and some remaining debts are discharged.
- Credit reports are maintained for all people using credit. Consumers have the right to view and challenge items in a credit report.
- Truth-in-Lending is a law requiring full disclosure of all costs of credit. The law requires that consumers be given a grace period of 3 days to change their minds about a credit contract in which their home is used for security.
- Errors in credit accounts must be investigated and adjusted; time limits are imposed by the Fair Credit Billing Act.
- Discrimination is not allowed in the granting or denial of credit.
- Alternate dispute resolution and lawsuits are ways for consumers to get recourse in credit disputes.
- Every year, millions of American consumers lose money in scams related to credit or identity theft. Consumers should ask questions and research offers and companies to avoid being caught in a scam.

278

Key Terms

bankruptcy
Chapter 7
   Liquidation
Chapter 13 Wage
   Earner Plan
credit card fraud
credit report
debt consolidation
delinquency

discharge
documentation
Equal Credit
   Opportunity Act
equity loan
exemption
Fair Credit Billing Act
Fair Credit Reporting
   Act

Fair Debt Collection
   Practices Act
foreclosure
garnishment
recourse
repossession
scam
Truth-in-Lending
   Act

ACTIVITY 1
Review Key Terms

Use the key terms from Chapter 9 to complete the following sentences:

1. Getting a loan to pay off other debts is called _____.

2. The _____ is a federal law requiring creditors to resolve disputes in billing within a specified period of time.

3. _____ is a legal procedure to relieve a person who cannot pay debts of those debts or to create a payment plan for paying some of the debts.

4. A federal law that makes discrimination in the granting or denial of credit illegal is the _____.

5. The _____ is a federal law giving consumers the right to know what is in their credit file and to challenge information in the file.

6. In a type of bankruptcy called _____, the debtor repays part or all of the unsecured debt over 3 to 5 years.

7. A remedy or action taken to seek aid, such as for the correction of an error in a credit account, is called _____.

8. A court order called a(n) _____ pardons a debtor from paying debts.

9. A proceeding in which a creditor may legally take possession of money or goods held by a third party in payment of a borrower's debt is called _____.

10. A(n) _____ is property a debtor is allowed to keep in a bankruptcy proceeding.

11. When someone intentionally uses another person's credit card to steal money, that is called _____.

12. A federal law, the _____, prohibits abusive practices when collecting debt.

13. A type of bankruptcy called _____ is also known as straight bankruptcy.

14. When a debtor gets behind in making payments, the account is said to be in _____.

15. Records that can be used to support a claim, also known as _____, can help win an adjustment to a credit account.

16. Borrowing money using the equity in your home as security is getting a(n) _____.

17. A fake offer, sale, or other gimmick, called a(n) _____, is designed to cheat consumers.

18. A document that gives a person's credit history and current status with regard to credit and income is called a(n) _____.

19. The _____ is a federal law that requires that consumers be fully informed about the true cost of credit.

20. A legal process a creditor can use to force the sale of mortgaged property to repay the mortgage when a borrower does not make mortgage payments is called _____.

21. The process of taking an asset used for collateral, such as a car, and selling it to pay a debt is called _____.

ACTIVITY 2
Math Minute

1. Juan Martinez has a house valued at $250,000. His mortgage is for $180,000. How much money can he borrow if the company will lend 80 percent of the equity in the home?

2. Joe Patel has a house valued at $180,000. His mortgage is for $150,000. How much money can he borrow if the company will lend 70 percent of the equity in the home?

3. Jeff Wong has a house valued at $200,000. His mortgage is for $190,000. How much money can he borrow if the company will lend 85 percent of the equity in the home?

4. Your credit card was stolen. You reported the theft within 24 hours. Before the theft was reported, the thief charged $2,450 at a jewelry store and $1,245 at an electronics store. How much of the fraudulent charges will you have to pay?

5. Gloria Perez owes a balance of $5,000 on one credit card that charges 19 percent interest. She can pay off the balance in 2 years making monthly payments of $252.02. She has another credit card with a balance of $7,500 that charges 20 percent interest. She can pay off the balance in 2 years making monthly payments of $381.72. Gloria owns a home valued at $150,000. She can get a home equity loan for $12,500 at 8 percent interest. Gloria can repay the loan in 2 years

making monthly payments of $565.34. How much money will Gloria save if she takes out a home equity loan to pay off the credit card balances?

ACTIVITY 3
Filing Complaints

  academic.cengage.com/school/pfl

1. Work with two classmates to complete this activity.

2. Review the information presented in this chapter, and search the Internet if needed. Find out where or how you could file complaints in the following situations:

   a. You were the victim of a telemarketing scam. The caller offered to send you money if you provided your Social Security number and bank account number.

   b. You bought items from a business on the Internet. The company did not send the merchandise that was ordered.

   c. An investment scheme promised you a 50 percent return on your money in less than a year. You invested $1,000, and you have not heard from the company since.

ACTIVITY 4
Letter Disputing a Charge

Upon checking your credit card statement, you see that you were charged $85 for the purchase of a hat at the Mad Hatter Shop on May 8, 20--. You have a receipt that shows a $58 purchase at the Mad Hatter Shop on that date. Write a dispute letter to the credit card company to report this error. Review Figure 9-1.1 for the format and content of a dispute letter.

1. Use your return address. Use May 12, 20--, as the letter date.

2. Use this letter address and an appropriate salutation:
   Credit Company
   P.O. Box 87483
   Wilmington, DE 19850-7483

3. Use a subject line that indicates you have a dispute on Account 2444 2344 2317 1111.

4. State that you are registering a dispute. Explain the problem and ask for a credit of the extra amount charged on your statement. Indicate that you are enclosing a copy of the statement and a copy of your receipt.

5. Use an appropriate letter closing and your full name. Add an enclosure notation at the end of the letter.

6. Proofread the letter carefully and correct all errors. Print the letter.

ACTIVITY 5
Handling Credit Problems

 In each of the following situations, explain what you would do or the advice you would give:

1. Jim and Fran have decided to get help with their credit problems rather than file for bankruptcy. They want more time to pay loans, and they have several credit card debts with high interest rates. What would you suggest?

2. Ramon is deeply in debt. He knows that he will not be able to pay all his debts. He wants to be fair to the creditors, but he also needs a fresh start. He has a good job with a steady income. Explain to him the differences between Chapter 7 and Chapter 13 bankruptcy. Which one do you think would be appropriate for Ramon?

3. Alicia is having trouble paying her bills. She is working two jobs and still cannot make all the payments. She has a very large medical bill (exceeding $400,000) as a result of an illness 2 years ago. Because of the interest rate of 18 percent, she is making little progress in paying it off. What do you suggest?

282

PUBLIC SPEAKING EVENT

The FBLA Public Speaking I Event and BPA Prepared Speech Event focus attention on current business topics. Students must prepare a 4-minute speech for FBLA and a 5- to 7-minute speech for BPA using an effective business style. Facts and working data that are used for the speech may be secured from any source. The speech should be well organized. Sources used for facts, quotes, or other data should be provided. Students may use notes to deliver the speech; however, no visual aids may be used. Points may be deducted if the speech does not keep to the set time frame.

Evaluation

Students who take part in these events are judged on their ability to:

- Clearly state the goal of the speech.
- Develop the topic thoroughly.
- Present a logical sequence of ideas or facts.
- Present accurate information backed by current sources.
- Demonstrate effective public speaking skills.
- Present an informative speech.

Sample Scenario

You have been asked to prepare a speech on identity theft. Identity theft occurs when someone uses your personal information without your permission to commit fraud or other crimes. The number of identity theft crimes in the United States is growing. The process for a victim to clear her or his name and credit report can be time-consuming and expensive.

Think Critically

1. What are two credible resources you can use to find information on identity theft?
2. Prepare a 4- to 5-minute speech on identity theft. Include these points in the speech along with others you think are important:
   - An explanation of identity theft
   - Types of crimes related to identity theft
   - Statistics about identity theft, such as the number of crimes or people affected
   - Strategies for consumers to use to avoid identity theft

283

PART 4

SAVING AND INVESTING

OUTCOMES

After successfully completing this part, students should be able to:

* **List** reasons for savings and investing.
* **Explain** principles of saving and investing.
* **Describe** investment strategies.
* **Describe** investment options and how they relate to risk and return.
* **List** sources of investment information.
* **Explain** how to buy and sell securities.
* **Describe** the role of regulatory agencies in the investment industry.

IN PART 4, SAVING AND INVESTING, you will consider how saving and investing can help you achieve your goals. You will learn about saving and investing options and strategies. You will explore sources of data that can be helpful to investors. You will learn how to buy and sell securities. You will also learn about several agencies that protect and assist consumers and investors.

UNDERSTANDING SAVING AND INVESTING

© Getty Images/PhotoDisc

hapter 10 focuses on saving and investing. Some aspects of saving and investing overlap. However, there is a difference between saving and investing. Saving and investing can help you accomplish short-term and long-terms goals. You will want to consider the risk involved and the amount you can expect to earn when choosing investments. In this chapter, you will learn the difference between saving and investing. You will also explore some reasons for saving and investing and some strategies for getting the most from your investments.

ONLINE RESOURCES

Personal Financial Literacy
Web site:

Data File

Vocabulary Flashcards

Beat the Clock: Saving and Investing

Chapter 10 Supplemental Activity

Search terms:
- liquidity
- investment risk
- diversification
- dollar averaging
- bull market
- bear market

Reasons for Saving and Investing

OUTCOMES

- Explain the difference between saving and investing.
- Describe reasons for saving and investing.
- Describe the concept of financial security.
- Explain what is meant by retirement planning.

SAVING AND INVESTING

The purpose of saving is to accumulate money for future use. Saving money is important because it means you are planning for future needs and wants. When you are saving money, the emphasis is on safety. In Chapter 5, you learned about various methods for saving money. A savings account, a certificate of deposit, and a money market account are all good, safe ways to save. Because these types of accounts are insured by the FDIC, you can be assured that money you place in such an account is safe.

Investing money is another way to plan for future needs. The purpose of investing is to make your money grow. Investing is sometimes explained as using money to make more money. For example, you may use money to buy real estate such as a house. You might also buy **stocks**, which are shares of ownership in a corporation. Your hope is that the house and stocks will be worth more several years later when you sell them than when you bought them. If so, you will have more money when you sell the investments than when you bought them.

Money in a savings account or money market account that you plan to leave there for a long time can be considered a type of investment. However, the interest rate and the money earned in such an account are typically low compared to other types of investments. As mentioned earlier, safety is the primary advantage of a savings account. Other types of investments involve risk. The amount of money that can be made and the risk involved are issues of concern with investments.

With many investments, you do not know how much the money you invest will earn. You could even lose the money you invest. For example, when you buy stocks, you are buying a share of a corporation. The company may do well, and the value of the stocks may grow. However, the company could fail. In this case, you might lose the money you invested in stocks. When investors think the chances of making money are good, they accept the risk involved with investments.

The goals you want to accomplish with money you save may be short-term or long-term goals. Investments are often long-term and may be part of a plan to accomplish long-term goals. Some short-term and long-term reasons for saving and investing are discussed in the following sections.

SHORT-TERM NEEDS

Saving is a good way to have money to handle short-term needs or wants that are not part of your regular spending. For example, you may want to save money to pay for a trip or to purchase a home theater system. Savings can also be used to handle unexpected expenses, such as repairs to a roof that is damaged by a storm. Savings accounts are considered liquid assets. **Liquidity** is a measure of the ability to turn an asset into cash quickly.

Contingency Planning

Contingencies are emergencies or other unplanned or possible events. For example, suppose you are driving home from work and a tire blows out. You need money to pay for a new tire, towing, or other related expenses. You may not have enough cash on hand to pay these expenses. You need to get to money quickly without borrowing (using credit and paying interest charges).

Having enough savings available so that you can pay for emergencies is critical. An **emergency fund** is an amount of money you set aside for unplanned expenses. A fund of $500 is enough to cover many types of emergencies. You might keep this sum as the minimum in your checking account. In other words, you typically do not allow the account balance to fall below $500. However, you can spend that $500 in case of an emergency.

Vacations

Taking vacations is a healthy thing to do. Many people want a break from time to time—to get away from the usual stresses in life. A vacation also helps refresh tired minds and bodies so that people are ready to go back to school or work.

Vacations can be simple and inexpensive, such as going camping or hiking. Vacations can be elaborate and expensive, such as flying to Europe for a 2-week stay in a resort. Setting aside money for vacations allows you to plan for the kind of vacations you would like to take. One type of plan might involve taking short and inexpensive vacations for 2 or 3 years and then taking one expensive vacation every third or fourth year. As you earn more (and save more), you can plan more expensive vacations.

© Rubberball

Savings can be used to help pay for emergency expenses.

Meeting Goals

You may have short-term goals that saving money can help you accomplish. These goals may involve things you want to get done within the next few weeks or months. For example, you may wish to attend a wedding or go to a special event, such as a concert. You may want to buy a new car and need to save money for the down payment. To meet your goals, you may need to start setting aside money well ahead of the event.

LONG-TERM NEEDS

Both saving and investing can help meet long-term needs and wants. For example, parents may start investing money when a child is young to pay for the child's college education. Many people want to own a home. They may save money for a down payment and then buy a house as an investment. Everyone needs to think about retirement and how to pay for expenses when no longer working.

In Chapter 4, you learned about basic needs (such as food and shelter), other needs (such as education and transportation), and wants (such as a vacation trip). You also studied how to create a financial plan. Such a plan has personal goals that relate to your wants and needs. Your financial goals relate to the money or assets needed to achieve personal goals. The plan includes a timeline for each goal. Selecting saving and investment options can be an important part of creating a financial plan.

To think about your needs and goals, you could create a plan such as the one shown in Figure 10-1.1 on page 289. The plan should list short-term and long-term goals and set a timeline for meeting each goal. You should also think about how much money you will need and how to save or invest for each goal. The amount that an investment grows is called the return. You may need to choose investments with a high rate of return to meet your goals.

Education

College expenses can be met with a plan that includes loans, scholarships, spending savings or money from investments, and working. Many students work during the summers and save money to pay for some of their college expenses. Some students work part-time and go to school full-time. Others work full-time and go to school part-time. Working to help pay for college lowers the amount of money you may need to borrow. You could start saving now to have money for this need. Parents of young children can invest money that will grow while the children grow. Money from the investment can be used to pay for education when the children reach college age.

Buying a House

A house can be a good investment that grows in value over several years. Buying a house may require using savings. Savings may be used to buy a home or to make a down payment on a home. Many lenders require buyers to make a down payment of 5 percent or more of the purchase price when buying a house. For example, suppose you buy a house for $180,000. You may be required to have a down payment of $9,000 to get a loan for 95 percent of the purchase price. You may need to save money

288

Personal Goal	Financial Goal	Steps to Take	Timeline
Short-Term Goals			
Take a camping trip next summer	Own camping gear and have money for transportation and supplies	Save $50 per month	6 months
Attend a concert in a nearby city	Have money for a ticket, hotel room, food, and transportation	Save $75 per month	4 months
Long-Term Goals			
Travel in a motor home	Own a motor home and have money for gas and traveling expenses	Invest $200 per month at a high rate of return	10 years
Swim in my own pool	Have a swimming pool constructed at my home	Invest $125 per month at a high rate of return	6 years

for a few months or years to have the down payment amount. You may also need to save money to pay for closing costs on a home mortgage.

Providing for a Family

Many people plan to have children in the future. These people need to plan for the expenses involved in raising children. Housing, food, clothing, medical care, and child care are examples of expenses parents must meet for at least 18 years. According to a U.S. Department of Agriculture report, a parent in the United States can expect to spend about $130,000 or more to raise a child from birth through age 17.[1]

Having children will affect daily living expenses, vacations, and even how parents plan for retirement.

Many people make investments to provide for future needs of their families.

---

[1] *Expenditures on Children by Families, 2005*, U.S. Department of Agriculture, Center for Nutrition Policy and Promotion, Miscellaneous Publication No. 1528-2005, April 2006, p. 12.

For example, when children are young, parents need life insurance to take care of their children's needs if something happens to the parents. As children get older, plans shift to providing the children with money for education and helping them get started living on their own. When children are adults and leave home, many people move into a new phase of their lives. This often involves retirement or part-time work, moving to a smaller house, or moving to a different area. Investments made during a person's working years can help provide money for activities in later life.

Financial Security

Financial security is the ability to prepare for future needs and meet current expenses to live comfortably. For most people, financial security is built on saving and investing. It means having enough resources so that you will have enough to eat, proper clothing, a safe and comfortable place to live, medical care, and other items that you need. Government agencies and other organizations provide information about financial security online, as shown in Figure 10-1.2.

People desire to be financially secure throughout their lives. For many people, however, financial security must be built over time. When you first begin working and living on your own, you may need to spend most of your earnings to cover current expenses. As you save and invest, you start to build the resources that will provide for your future security.

Retirement Planning

Many people want to retire from working full-time and enjoy more leisure time. They may want to take more vacations and see new places. They also want to be able to live comfortably without worrying about how their bills will be paid. Some people want to retire as soon as they can afford to do so. Others enjoy their work or need the money earned and want to work as long as they can.

FIGURE 10-1.2

Information about building financial security is provided online.

Address   http://www.csrees.usda.gov/ProgView.cfm?prnum=5379   Go

CSREES   Cooperative State Research, Education, and Extension Service   Home   Contact Us   Site Map   Search

About Us   Emphasis Areas   Funding Opportunities   Business with CSREES   Newsroom

Financial Security

Economics & Commerce

Agricultural Markets and Trade
Farm Financial Management
Financial Security
Public Policy
Small & Home-based Business
Related
Communities at Risk
Environmental & Resource Economics

Overview | In Focus | Funding | Partners | Events | Results/Impacts | Resources | Contacts

Overview

Too many individuals and families are experiencing financial crisis because of inadequate savings, too much debt, and poor planning for potential major life events. On average, U.S. households carry about $8,000 in credit card debt, up two-thirds compared to a decade ago. More than half of Americans report living paycheck to paycheck. During the past decade, the rate of personal bankruptcy in the U.S. rose by 69 percent. Working through land-grant universities and other partners, CSREES targets programs for youth, financially vulnerable populations, and consumers making financial decisions through their lifetime. The overall goal is for people to acquire the knowledge, skills, and motivation to build financial security. Programs focus on behavioral change, starting

Source: U.S. Department of Agriculture, Cooperative State Research, Education, and Extension Service, Financial Security, http://www.csrees.usda.gov/ProgView.cfm?prnum=5379 (accessed July 18, 2006).

INVESTMENT EXAMPLES			
Amount Invested	Interest Rate	Investment Term	Maturity Value
$10,000 investment	6%	20 years	$ 32,071
$10,000 investment	6%	30 years	$ 57,435
$1,000 investment	8%	30 years	$ 10,063
$1,000 investment	8%	40 years	$ 21,725
$1,000 per year investment	5%	20 years	$ 33,066
$1,000 per year investment	5%	30 years	$ 66,439
$1,000 per year investment	5%	40 years	$120,800
$100 per month investment	7%	25 years	$ 81,007
$100 per month investment	7%	30 years	$ 121,997
$100 per month investment	7%	40 years	$262,481

FIGURE 10-1.3

The investment term and the interest rate have a big effect on the maturity value of an investment.

Retirement planning should begin the day you start working. You can begin thinking about retirement even earlier, as you choose a career. Think about what you would like to do and how you would like to live when you retire. Then think about the amount of monthly income you will need to support this lifestyle. Many people, especially the elderly, require long-term medical care at some time during their lives. Retirement plans should include how to pay for long-term care if it is needed.

You should begin saving and investing money for retirement at a young age. The sooner you begin investing, the longer your money will have to grow. Figure 10-1.3 shows comparisons of amounts invested at the same rate but for a different number of years.

Building Communications Skills

GOOD NEWS MESSAGES

A good news message is one that the reader will find favorable or be happy to receive. Good news messages are often written to inform people that their requests have been granted. Thus, the reader is looking for the answer and is expected to respond favorably. Often, the writer can use this opportunity to build goodwill with the reader. The reader will be feeling positive about the main message of the letter.

When writing a message that is good news, use a direct approach. The answer or main point of the message should be placed early in the message. Details should be presented in later paragraphs. For example, the opening of a good news letter might be, "Congratulations, Mr. Mendez. You have been selected to receive a $5,000 scholarship."

A good news message should be clear, leaving no doubt about the answer or point to be shared. The letter should be complete, giving all the details needed. The letter should also be concise. It should use enough words to sound friendly and courteous but not be too wordy.

291

10-1 REVIEW

10-1 Activity 1 Can You Recall?

Answer these questions to help you recall what you have read. If you cannot answer a question, read the related section again.

1. How is investing money different from saving money?
2. Why are savings accounts often safer than other investments?
3. List three short-term goals that could be reasons for saving.
4. What is an emergency fund, and why should you have one?
5. Why does meeting long-term goals often require saving and investing? Give two examples of long-term goals that can be met with money from investments.
6. What is financial security?
7. When should you begin retirement planning?

10-1 Activity 2 Goals for Saving and Investing

People have many purposes for saving and investing. These purposes can be defined in terms of goals, both short-term and long-term.

1. Create a table with four columns similar to the one shown in Figure 10-1.1. The column headings should be as follows:
   o **Personal Goals**
   o **Financial Goals**
   o **Steps to Take**
   o **Timeline**
2. List at least one short-term and two long-term personal goals in the table.
3. List a financial goal for each personal goal. Include steps to take and a timeline for each goal. Enter the total amount of money you think you will need to meet each goal.

292

Saving and Investing Principles

OUTCOMES

- Discuss the concept of risk versus return.
- List some types of risk that savers and investors may face.
- Describe the possible tax advantages of long-term saving and investing.

GROWTH OF PRINCIPAL

When money is set aside for savings, it should be growing. That is, the principal amount on which interest is computed should get larger over time. The principal grows when you deposit more money into the account. The principal can also grow through compounding interest. With compound interest, the interest amount is calculated for the first period. For example, the period might be 1 month or 1 year. The interest amount is added to the principal amount that was deposited in the account. This becomes the new, higher principal amount. Interest is calculated on the adjusted principal amount for the next period. This cycle continues, with the interest being added to the previous principal amount each time the interest is calculated. As the principal increases over time, the value of the investment grows. Figure 10-2.1 on page 294 shows interest compounded quarterly for 2 years.

RETURN ON INVESTMENT

When you put money into savings or an investment, you expect the value of the savings or investment to grow. The amount that the savings or investment grows is called the return. Return on investment (ROI) is a measurement of return given as a percentage. ROI tells how much you will receive, either in cash (such as interest on a savings account) or in increased value (such as with real estate). When you compare the ROI on several investment options, you can pick the one that has the highest return. Computing ROI is simple. To find the ROI, divide the amount you gained (either in interest or in increased value) by the amount you invested. The gain could also include other amounts you received, such as dividends. A dividend is money paid to stockholders when a corporation makes profits. Figure 10-2.2 on page 294 shows how ROI is calculated. When you compare the ROI for different investment choices, you can see which has the best return. Based on the return and the risk involved, you would choose an investment option.

FIGURE 10-2.1

COMPOUND
INTEREST EXAMPLE

COMPOUND INTEREST (Annual Interest Rate 6%)				
Period (Quarterly)	Principal	Rate	Interest	Adjusted Principal
1	$5,000.00	0.015	$75.00	$5,075.00
2	$5,075.00	0.015	$76.13	$5,151.13
3	$5,151.13	0.015	$77.27	$5,228.39
4	$5,228.39	0.015	$78.43	$5,306.82
5	$5,306.82	0.015	$79.60	$5,386.42
6	$5,386.42	0.015	$80.80	$5,467.22
7	$5,467.22	0.015	$82.01	$5,549.22
8	$5,549.22	0.015	$83.24	$5,632.46

FIGURE 10-2.2

RETURN ON
INVESTMENT
EXAMPLE

RETURN ON INVESTMENT			
Purchase Price	Selling Price	Gain	ROI
$500.00	$525.00	$25.00	5.00%

Selling Price – Purchase Price = Gain

Gain/Purchase Price = ROI

RISK AND RETURN

When selecting an investment, the buyer must weigh the risk involved against the possible return expected. The higher the risk you are willing to take, the greater your possible return may be. If you are not willing to take much risk, then you cannot expect high returns. Risk-free investments are guaranteed by the U.S. government. For example, savings accounts that are insured by the FDIC have no risk. As a result, the guaranteed rate of interest is low compared to rates for other investments. Other ways of saving and investing have more risk. As the risk rises, so does the possibility of a high return. The ideal investment would have all of these features:

○ The principal is safe (no risk).
○ The rate of return (earnings) is high.
○ The investment is liquid (you can get your money quickly without a penalty).
○ You can invest quickly and easily.
○ There are no costs of investing, and you can buy in with small amounts.
○ The investment is tax-free (both the earnings and the long-term gains) or tax-deferred.

Unfortunately, there are no investments that meet all of these criteria. So you must decide how much risk you are willing to take and what rates of return will meet your goals.

Investment Risk

Investment risk is the potential for change in the value of an investment. For example, when you buy stock in a company, you risk having the stock price fall. If the company goes out of business, the stock may become worthless. In this case, you may lose the money you invested.

The value of an investment can go up and down over time. Poor management or unexpected events may affect how well a company performs. For example, a company may discover that a product must be recalled because it is defective. Replacing the product or paying consumers for the recalled product may cost the company a lot of money. When this happens, the price of the company's stock may fall. Your investment may temporarily lose value. The price of the stock may go up again when the company announces the release of a new product. These changes in stock prices are to be expected.

Natural disasters may also affect the value of an investment. When a storm, earthquake, hurricane, or flood occurs, it creates damage. The event may destroy crops, buildings, businesses, and lives. A disaster can cause prices to rise or fall. If crops are destroyed, stock prices for companies in that industry may fall. Shortages caused by these events may lead to prices rising in some industries. Other industries benefit because work is created in rebuilding or repairing damage.

Natural disasters, such as a hurricane, can damage investment properties.

Few investments go up in value all of the time. With investment risk, you are looking for investment choices that, on the whole, go up more than they go down. The goal is to have your investments be worth more at the end of the year than they were at the beginning of the year.

Inflation Risk

When prices are rising rapidly in the economy, your investment may lose value. **Inflation risk** is the chance that the rate of inflation will be higher than the rate of return on an investment. When this occurs, your investment loses value. For example, assume you bought a bond. A **bond** is a debt instrument that is issued by a corporation or government. The issuer must pay the bondholder the principal (the original amount of the loan) plus interest when the bond matures. Suppose the bond has a fixed interest rate of 5 percent. If inflation is lower than 5 percent, your investment is holding its value. If inflation rises to 7 or 8 percent, however, your investment is losing value. Even though you may have more dollars, you will not be able to purchase as many goods or services with those dollars.

Industry Risk

Industry risk is the chance that factors that affect an industry as a whole will change the value of an investment. For example, suppose you invest in a company that is in the oil industry. If oil prices and profits are rising, then your investment is likely to gain in value. If alternate energy sources

295

are found, however, then investments in the oil industry could lose value. People might start buying other types of fuel, and the price of oil could drop. Industry risk occurs in all types of businesses.

Political Risk

Political risk is the chance that an event in politics (laws, policies, wars, or elections) will affect the value of an investment. For example, when a new President is elected in the United States, the stock market sometimes reacts positively, and stock prices go up. One political party may seem to be more pro-business than another. When candidates from this party are elected, stock prices may rise. The opposite may also be true.

Political events in this country, as well is in other countries, affect markets. Wars, terrorist activities, and radical shifts in governments can affect markets significantly. When the news is good, stock prices tend to rise. When the news is bad, prices tend to fall. Political events are out of your control. However, you must consider how political events will affect your investment choices. Some investments are more vulnerable than others.

© Digital Vision

Political events, such as elections, can affect the stock market.

296

Stock Risk

Stock in a company can go up or down in value. **Stock risk** is the chance that activities or events that affect a company will change the value of an investment. For example, the employees of a company might go on strike. When this happens, fewer products may be produced than planned. Sales and income may be lower than expected. This may cause the price of the company's stock to fall. During later periods, the company may do well, and stock prices may increase. Many companies do not perform well all of the time. Companies that show steady growth and strong overall performance over time are good investments.

TAX ADVANTAGES

When you set aside money for future retirement, such as in an IRA (individual retirement arrangement), the money may be tax-deferred. **Tax-deferred** means that there are no taxes on gains until the money is taken from the account. Also, you may not have to pay taxes on the amounts placed in the account until later. This tax advantage allows your investment to grow for years without being taxed. When you retire and take money from the account, you may be in a lower tax bracket. You are taxed only on the portion you take out of the account.

Some savings and investments are tax-free. For example, interest earned on Series EE and Series I U.S. savings bonds is tax-free in some instances if it is used for education. Information about the tax benefits of U.S. savings bonds is provided online, as shown in Figure 10-2.3. Interest earned on municipal bonds (bonds issued by local cities and counties) may be free from federal income tax. Tax-free choices protect your gains and earnings.

People with higher incomes may choose tax-deferred or tax-free investments because their tax rates are high. Suppose a person is in a

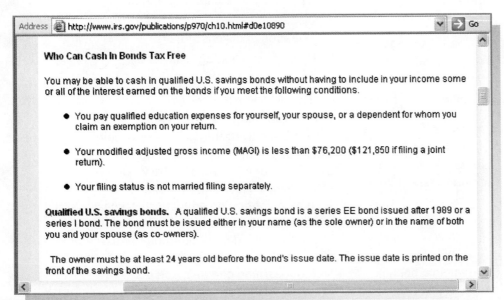

Address http://www.irs.gov/publications/p970/ch10.html#d0e10890   Go

Who Can Cash In Bonds Tax Free

You may be able to cash in qualified U.S. savings bonds without having to include in your income some or all of the interest earned on the bonds if you meet the following conditions.

- You pay qualified education expenses for yourself, your spouse, or a dependent for whom you claim an exemption on your return.

- Your modified adjusted gross income (MAGI) is less than $76,200 ($121,850 if filing a joint return).

- Your filing status is not married filing separately.

Qualified U.S. savings bonds. A qualified U.S. savings bond is a series EE bond issued after 1989 or a series I bond. The bond must be issued either in your name (as the sole owner) or in the name of both you and your spouse (as co-owners).

The owner must be at least 24 years old before the bond's issue date. The issue date is printed on the front of the savings bond.

Source: U.S. Department of the Treasury, Internal Revenue Service, *Publication 970 (2005), Tax Benefits for Education,* http://www.irs.gov/publications/p970/ch10.html#d0e10890 (accessed July 20, 2006).

FIGURE 10-2.3

Some U.S. savings bonds are good choices for saving to pay for education.

297

FIGURE 10-2.4

*A tax-free investment
may be the better
choice, even though
it pays a lower interest
rate.*

INVESTMENT COMPARISON

Taxable	Tax-Free
Corporate Bond at 7% Interest	Government Bond at 5% Interest
The investor pays federal tax at a rate of 35%. For the interest earned, 7% × 65% is the amount the investor keeps. The rest is paid in tax.	The investor keeps all the interest earned at 5%.
$0.07 \times 0.65 = 0.0455 = 4.55\%$	

35 percent tax bracket. That means each dollar earned is taxed at this rate. If \$1,000 is earned on an investment, \$350 is paid in tax. If, however, this person invests in a tax-free bond and earns \$1,000 in interest, there is no tax. Thus, interest rates on tax-free choices are often lower than market rates. However, the tax-free investment may be the better choice, as shown in Figure 10-2.4.

Success Skills

LIFELONG LEARNING

Lifelong learning means acquiring new skills and knowledge throughout your life. Information is growing more rapidly than our ability to keep pace. While you may not be able to keep pace with all there is to know, you can stay current in areas that are of interest to you.

One area in which lifelong learning is especially important is your career. In past decades, many people worked for the same company and even in the same job for their entire careers. That situation is no longer common. Today, many people are employed by several different companies and in several types of jobs during their working years. Continuing education is essential to be prepared for career changes.

Lifelong learning can also help you as you save and invest in an effort to build financial security. Being aware of changes in technology, science, medicine, political events, the environment, and business practices can help you make better investment decisions.

By practicing lifelong learning, you will:

- Be a more valuable employee.
- Be prepared for career changes.
- Be better prepared to make saving and investing decisions.
- Be more interesting to others.
- Know more about protecting yourself from all kinds of risk.

Lifelong learning involves reading about new and different things. It means being aware of events happening in your community, your country, and the world. It often involves learning new skills. You may take continuing education classes or college courses to learn skills. Training may be provided by your employer to teach new job skills. Whatever methods you use, lifelong learning can help you achieve financial success.

298

10-2 Activity 1   Can You Recall?

Answer these questions to help you recall what you have read.
If you cannot answer a question, read the related section again.

1. Explain how risk and return are related to each other.
2. Describe the ideal investment.
3. What is investment risk? What are some factors that can affect investment risk?
4. What is a bond?
5. What is inflation risk?
6. Name some events that might affect political risk.
7. How are tax-free earnings different from tax-deferred earnings?
8. Describe the possible tax advantages of long-term saving and investing.

10-2 Activity 2   Investment Criteria

The criteria for an ideal investment appear in the following list. For each situation below, tell which two criteria you think would be the most important for choosing a savings plan or an investment.

o   The principal is safe (no risk).
o   The rate of return is high.
o   The investment is liquid (you can get your money quickly without a penalty).
o   You can invest quickly and easily.
o   There are no costs of investing, and you can buy in with small amounts.
o   The investment is tax-free (both the earnings and the long-term gains) or tax-deferred.

1. Joshua plans to create an emergency fund to pay for unexpected expenses.
2. Maria wants to see her money grow over several years. She has a separate fund for emergencies that is in a liquid, no-risk account.
3. Chin wants to save money for retirement. He has a separate fund for emergencies that is in a liquid, no-risk account. He has other investments to help achieve other long-term goals.
4. Ellen wants to save money to pay for a college education for her daughter, who is now 3 years old.

299

Saving and Investing Strategies

OUTCOMES

- Explain how to use a systematic strategy for saving and investing.
- Explain the dollar-cost averaging strategy.
- Explain how a diversification strategy can lower risk.
- Explain the difference between a bull market and a bear market.
- Discuss buying and selling strategies in times of economic growth and decline.

SYSTEMATIC SAVING AND INVESTING

Systematic means regular, orderly, or done according to a plan. Systematic saving is a strategy that involves regularly setting aside cash that can be used to achieve goals. Once money is set aside in savings, ideally it should remain there until used to meet a planned goal. The amount should be the most you can comfortably afford to save each pay period. Some people find it convenient to have a set amount withheld each month from their paychecks. Others make a monthly payment to a savings plan, just like paying a bill. Some people find that they can set aside a portion of any raise they receive at work. That way, the amount is not money they depend on to meet current expenses.

Systematic investing is a strategy that involves a planned approach to making investments. For example, when you first start investing, you may wish to buy safe and liquid investments. In later years, you may want to take more risk so your principal can grow faster over time. When you get extra cash, such as a bonus, you might wish to buy a high-risk investment in the hope of getting high returns. Systematic saving and investing is important for building financial security in the long term.

Long-Term Focus

A saving and investing plan is designed for growth in the long run, not for short-term results. Investors may need to hold investments for 20 or more years to get the returns they want. In any given year, investments may actually lose money. Over time, however, gains exceed losses on sound investments. For example, suppose investments in the stock market have grown at an annual rate of more than 7 percent over any 20-year period of time. This does not mean that, in any given year, stocks earned 7 percent. In fact, in some years, the return may have been very low. In other years, the return may have been more than 20 percent. Investors must plan to hold investments for the long term to achieve substantial growth over time. As a young person, you should set investing and savings goals that focus on the future.

You can track prices of stocks and other investments using Internet sites. Stock prices are also shown in many newspapers. You might want to track a stock that interests you for several weeks to see how much the price changes. The chart in Figure 10-3.1 shows changes in the price of a stock over a period of 12 years.

Achieving financial goals requires training and discipline, just as preparing for a marathon does.

Dollar-Cost Averaging

One strategy for buying stocks or other investments is dollar-cost averaging. With **dollar-cost averaging**, a person invests the same amount of money on a regular basis, such as monthly. The amount is invested regardless of whether prices are high or low. Sometimes the investor pays more and gets fewer shares. Sometimes the price is low and more shares are purchased. Overall, the dollar cost per share may be less than the average price. Using this strategy, investors do not have to study the stock market and try to determine the best time to buy stocks.

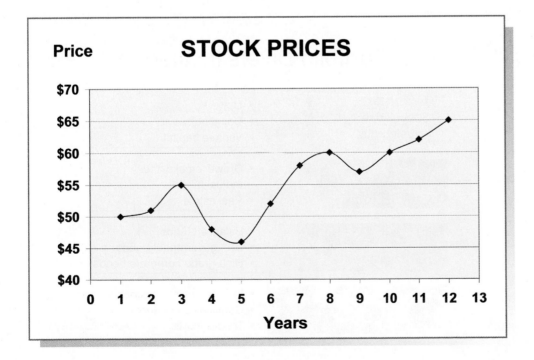

FIGURE 10-3.1

Stock prices may go up or down over the long term.

301

DIVERSIFICATION

Diversifying is a very important saving and investing principle. **Diversification** is holding a variety of investments for the purpose of reducing risk. When one type of investment goes down in value, there may be others that go up. Thus the losses of one area are offset by the gains in others. It is important for investors to choose more than one type of investment. This is to avoid "having all your eggs in one basket." If a company fails, the investor could lose everything if he or she has only that one investment.

All of a person's savings and investments make up that person's investment portfolio. An **investment portfolio** is a collection of assets, such as certificates of deposit, stocks, bonds, real estate, and other holdings. In order to lower risk over time, the portfolio should be diversified. A portfolio should have a strong foundation of safe investments. For example, insured savings accounts and certificates of deposit are safe investments. The portfolio should have some relatively safe, low-risk investments. These might include U.S. bonds and conservative mutual funds. A mutual fund is operated by a professional investment firm. The firm sells shares in the mutual fund and invests the money in a variety of stocks, bonds, and other investments. Mutual funds have specific objectives, such as growth (high earnings) or balance (good earnings with acceptable risk). Mutual funds allow investors to have diversified holdings within one investment.

A portfolio could include some higher-risk choices that have the potential for high returns. Growth stocks and real estate are examples. Some people also include speculative investments. These options have high earnings potential. However, they are also high-risk. For this reason, some people include only a few or no speculative investments in their portfolios.

Over time, the portfolio should gain in value at a rate greater than the rate of inflation. Each investor must decide how much of each type of investment to include. A sample portfolio is shown in Figure 10-3.2.

FIGURE 10-3.2

An investment portfolio may contain several types of investments.

Portfolio Diversification

Speculative Investments	• Options • Commodities • Venture capital
Growth Investments	• Growth stocks and mutual funds • Real estate
Conservative Investments	• Balanced funds • U.S. government bonds • High-grade corporate bonds
Foundation	• Insured savings accounts • Certificates of deposit • Treasury bills

302

Chapter 10 Understanding Saving and Investing

Investment choices will vary based on the person's age, income, family situation, goals, and attitude toward risk. You will learn more about various types of investments in Chapter 11.

UNDERSTANDING THE MARKET

Having a basic understanding of the market will help you make better investing decisions. The **market** refers to any place where investments are bought and sold. There are stock markets and bond markets. There are real estate markets and markets for precious metals such as gold and silver. For most things that an investor may want to buy or sell, a market exists. The term *market* is also used to refer to price levels or other market conditions. For example, the statement "The market was off today" may mean that prices in the stock market were low compared to prices on other recent days.

Bull Market

A **bull market** exists when stock prices are steadily increasing. A bull market may last a few months to a few years. During a bull market, price advances are often followed by profit-taking. Profit-taking occurs when people who own stocks that have increased in price sell those stocks. This selling activity may cause prices to drop for a while. The bull market does not end, however, because a few stocks drop in price. As long as the general trend is toward increasing stock prices, it is still considered a bull market.

When prices are rising, this may be a good time to sell certain stocks. Suppose a company in which you have stock has been performing poorly in recent months. This could be a sign that the company is poorly managed. It could mean that the demand for products that this company makes is falling. There could be some other problem that you do not know about. If stock prices in the market overall are rising, the price of this one stock may also go up. This could be a good time to sell a stock that you expect to do poorly in the future.

Bear Market

A **bear market** exists in the stock market when prices are steadily decreasing. Bear markets may last from a few months to a year or more. This is a good time to buy stocks that are sound investments because prices are lower. At times in a bear market, there is a lot of buying activity. This can cause a temporary rise in stock prices. The bear market does not end, however. As long as the general trend is toward declining stock prices, it is still considered a bear market.

303

Economic Conditions

Investors should consider economic conditions when forming an investment strategy. There will always be the rising and falling of the economy that causes prices to rise and fall. It is a normal part of the market and how it works.

MARKET TIMING

In investing, the old saying goes, "Buy low, and sell high." The question is, How do you know when prices have reached their lowest point (so you can buy)? How do you know when prices have reached their highest point (so you can sell)? The answer is simple. You do not know; you can only make an educated guess.

To be good at investing, you have to choose timing principles that you follow. For example, you may own a certain stock or another investment and check it every day or week to see what its price is. When you see a downward trend in price, it might be the time to sell. Some experts say, however, that when prices are falling, that is the time to buy stocks that you think are a sound investment. You can get more shares of stock for less money when you "buy low."

When prices for stocks that you own are rising, this may be the time to sell. If you have owned the stocks for a long time and they have gained in value, you can take some of the profits by "selling high."

When to buy and when to sell is up to each investor. Some people leave those decisions to the experts. They buy shares in a mutual fund rather than buying individual stocks or other investments. Experts at the investment firm decide when to buy and sell the individual investments that make up the fund.

When the economy is in a period of general growth, the market for many investments is growing. Economic growth is often defined as a period of time when people are working (low unemployment rate), profits are good, wages are rising, and people are optimistic. When a company's profits are rising, its stock prices often rise as well. When this happens with many companies, overall prices in the market rise. Investors who think that the market will continue in a growth trend may choose this time to buy stocks. They think the stocks will grow in value. Investors who think the growth trend is about to end may choose this time to sell stocks. They want to sell at the current high prices before the market begins a downward trend.

When the economy is in a period of general slowdown, the market for investments is declining. Prices may be falling. Economic decline can be a good time to buy stocks that you think are sound investments. You can buy while prices are low. This increases your chance of making profits when you sell at some future date. Some investors think it is important not to spend (or invest) everything during an economic growth period. Instead, they wait for a period of decline and buy then, taking advantage of lower prices.

304

Ethics

Economic conditions can change quickly in times of emergency. For example, when a natural disaster occurs, there are inevitable shortages. If a flood occurs, people may desperately need clean water to drink. They may need gasoline, food, and other necessities. Businesses that have these essential goods have two choices—they can keep their prices the same, or they can raise their prices. If they raise prices to what is considered an unfair amount, this is known as price gouging.

Some people think it is good business to raise prices when demand is high. They view this process as simply supply and demand forces at work. Others think that price gouging is unethical. They believe businesses are taking advantage of people who are unable to buy elsewhere or do without the product. Some states have laws against price gouging in times of declared civil emergencies.

What can you do to avoid being a victim of price gouging? The best strategy is to plan ahead. Prepare for emergencies by having essential items on hand. Keep a supply of clean drinking water and food packaged to prevent spoilage to feed your family for several days. Gather blankets, flashlights, a portable radio, and batteries ready for use. Have a corded phone on hand. A cordless phone may not work if electrical power is out. Buying essential items ahead of time will allow you to avoid paying higher prices during an emergency.

© Joe Skipper/Reuters/Landov

Buy essential items ahead of time to avoid paying high prices during an emergency.

305

10-3 Activity 1   Can You Recall?

Answer these questions to help you recall what you have read. If you cannot answer a question, read the related section again.

1. Explain how to save and invest using a systematic strategy.
2. Why is having a long-term saving and investment strategy important?
3. What is dollar-cost averaging? What is the advantage to using this investment strategy?
4. How does diversification lower investment risks?
5. What is an investment portfolio?
6. What types of investments should be the foundation of an investment portfolio?
7. What are some factors that will affect the types of investments a person may need in an investment portfolio?
8. How is a bull market different from a bear market?
9. When the economy is growing and stock prices are rising, why might an investor sell stocks?
10. When the economy is slowing down and stock prices are falling, why might an investor buy stocks?

10-3 Activity 2   Systematic Saving and Investing

 Allison is 24 years old. She works part-time while going to school. She is able to save $50.00 a month. She now has $600.00 in savings. She would like to buy some type of investment that will give her more return than the 1.5 percent she is able to earn on a savings account. Allison is able to save systematically. She can set aside this money for 10 years or more and can continue to set aside $50.00 per month.

1. How should Allison plan to invest (in terms of risk and liquidity) at this point in her life?
2. Open the *Excel* file *CH10 Future Value* from the data files.
3. Look at the example problem provided in the worksheet. This investor is making an initial investment of $500.00. An additional $100.00 per month will be invested for 30 years (360 payments). The interest rate is 7 percent. The value of the investment after 30 years will be $126,055.35.

306

4. Use the Calculator section of the worksheet to enter data for Allison's investment. Enter **0.08** for an 8 percent annual interest rate.

5. Allison wants to leave her investment in place for 10 years. Multiply 10 years times 12 months per year to find the total number of payments. Enter this number in the worksheet.

6. Enter **50.00** as the amount of the monthly payments.

7. The present value of the investment is $600.00, the initial amount she will invest. Enter the present value amount **600.00** in the worksheet.

8. The maturity value will be calculated automatically. What will be the value of Allison's investment after 10 years?

Marketing, Sales & Service

EXPLORING CAREERS IN MARKETING, SALES, AND SERVICE

Do you like to work with people? Are you good at persuading others to take action? If the answer is yes, a career in marketing, sales, and service might be right for you. Jobs in this career area are varied. Some jobs involve advertising and promoting products. Others involve buying, merchandising, or direct selling. Storing and shipping products and customer support provide many jobs in this area. E-marketing, or selling and promoting products on the Internet, is also part of this career area.

Jobs in marketing and sales are found in businesses and government. This job area also includes entrepreneurs such as small business owners. The need for jobs in marketing, sales, and service is expected to grow over the next few years. The outlook varies somewhat by job.

Skills Needed

Some of the skills and traits needed for a career in marketing, sales, and service include the following:

- Knowledge of products
- Communications skills
- Computer/technology skills
- Leadership skills
- Ability to work with others showing patience and tact
- Decision-making skills
- Problem-solving skills

Job Titles

Many jobs are available in marketing, sales, and service. Some job titles for this career area include the following:

- Customer service representative
- Graphic designer
- Information systems manager
- Marketing manager
- Market researcher
- Merchandise buyer
- Retail salesperson
- Sales manager
- Shipping/receiving clerk

Explore a Job

1. Choose a job in marketing, sales, and service to explore further. Select a job from the list above, or choose another job in this career area.
2. Access the *Occupational Outlook Handbook* online. A link to the site is provided on the Web site for this textbook.
3. Search for more information about the job you selected to answer these questions:
   - What is the nature of the work this job involves?
   - What is the job outlook for this job?
   - What training or qualifications are needed for this job?
   - What are the median annual earnings for this job?

Summary

- The purpose of saving is to accumulate money for future use with an emphasis on safety of the money. The purpose of investing is to use money to make more money. The emphasis is on growth with acceptable risk.

- Saving and investing begin with meeting short-term needs, such as emergencies, vacations, and current goals.

- Liquidity is the ability to turn an asset into cash quickly and without penalty.

- To meet long-term needs, such as building financial security, you must plan carefully for saving and investing.

- The principal amount of an investment can grow when you add more money to your investment. It can also grow through compounding interest.

- Return on investment (ROI) is a measurement of return given as a percentage. Looking at ROI allows you to compare investment choices.

- Risk and return are related: the more risk you are willing to accept, the higher the return you may be able to earn.

- All investors take risks such as investment risk, inflation risk, industry risk, stock risk, and political risk.

- Saving and investing can provide tax advantages when gains are tax-free or tax-deferred (taxed later).

- Systematic saving is a strategy that involves regularly setting aside cash that can be used to achieve goals according to a planned investment schedule.

- A saving and investing plan is designed for growth in the long run, not for short-term results.

- Using a dollar-cost averaging strategy, a person invests the same amount of money on a regular basis regardless of market conditions or prices.

- Diversification means owning a variety of investment choices to lower risks. A portfolio is a collection of these choices.

- The market refers to any place where investments are bought and sold.

- In a bull market, prices are steadily increasing over time. In a bear market, prices are steadily decreasing over time.

- Economic growth often leads to rising prices and increased buying. Economic decline often leads to falling prices and decreased buying. Both conditions can present good opportunities for investors.

- Price gouging is charging unreasonably high prices for essential goods, such as food and fuel, at certain times when demand is high, such as in times of emergency.

309

Key Terms

bear market	emergency fund	liquidity
bond	financial security	market
bull market	industry risk	political risk
contingencies	inflation risk	stock risk
diversification	investment	stocks
dollar-cost averaging	portfolio	tax-deferred
	investment risk	

ACTIVITY 1
Review Key Terms

Use the key terms from Chapter 10 to complete the following sentences:

1. Shares of ownership in a corporation are called _____.

2. A measure of the ability to turn an investment into cash quickly is called _____.

3. Unplanned events, such as emergencies, are called _____.

4. When taxes are not levied against gains until the money is taken from the account, the investment is said to be _____.

5. The chance that factors that affect an industry as a whole will change the value of an investment is called _____.

6. A(n) _____ is a collection of investments, such as stocks, bonds, and real estate.

7. Saving and investing the same amount of money each month regardless of market conditions is using the _____ strategy.

8. A(n) _____ is a debt instrument issued by a corporation or government that requires the issuer to pay the bondholder the loan principal plus interest at maturity.

9. When stock prices are steadily decreasing over time, this type of market is called a(n) _____.

10. The potential for change in the value of an investment is called _____.

11. Holding a variety of investments in order to reduce risk is called _____.

12. The chance that an event in politics will affect the value of an investment is called _____.

13. _____ is the ability to prepare for future needs and meet current expenses to live comfortably.

14. The chance that activities or events that affect a company will change the value of an investment in that company is called _____.

15. When stock prices are steadily increasing over time, this type of market is called a(n) _____.

16. An amount of money set aside to handle expenses related to unplanned events is called a(n) _____.

310

17. The chance that the rate of inflation will be higher than the rate of return on an investment is called _____.

18. Any place where investments or assets are bought and sold is called a(n) _____.

ACTIVITY 2
Math Minute

Round your answers to the nearest percent.

1. Jerry bought stock for $350.00. A year later, he sold it for $385.00. What is his return in dollars? What is his return on investment?

2. Brandy sold her collection of model cars for $600.00. She had purchased them for $520.00 a year earlier. What is her return in dollars? What is her return on investment?

3. Pablo bought 25 shares of a stock for $150.00 a share. He received dividends of $3.00 per share each year for 5 years. After 5 years, Pablo sold the stock for $155.00 a share. What is his return in dollars? What is his return on investment?

4. Keiko bought 46 shares of stock for $22.12 each. She sold the stock for $17.00 per share a year later. What is her return in dollars? What is her return on investment?

ACTIVITY 3
Investment Strategies

 TEAMWORK

Work with a classmate to complete this activity.

1. Read each of the following scenarios.

2. Describe the saving and investing strategy you would advise for each scenario. Give reasons why you selected this strategy.

Scenario A
Ben Fong has saved $1,000. Currently, the money is earning 0.5 percent interest in a checking account. Ben works part-time and goes to high school. He plans to start college in 4 or 5 years. Ben does not have any other savings or investments.

Scenario B
Bill and Barbara Wilson are a married couple. Both of them are working, and they pay taxes at a high rate (35 percent). They have saved $5,000 and wish to invest it for the future. They have other savings and retirement plans, including both low-risk and high-risk investments.

Scenario C
Gloria Vega just inherited $1,500 from her uncle. She is single, 25 years old, and living with her parents. Gloria works full-time while attending college part-time. She has some savings ($2,500) and no investments.

311

ACTIVITY 4
Portfolio Diversification

 An investment portfolio is a group of assets, such as certificates of deposit, stocks, and bonds. The portfolio should be diversified to lower risk. Investment choices will vary based on the person's age, income, family situation, goals, and attitude toward risk. They will also vary depending on the amount of money to be invested. In this activity, you will think about how to select types of investments for a diversified portfolio.

Assume that you are 28 years old. You have completed college and have a job that pays $40,000 a year. You have no debt. You have no dependents that you help support. You have savings of $30,000. You have decided to create a diversified investment portfolio.

Answer the following questions to help you think about how to structure your portfolio. Refer to Figure 10-3.2 on page 302 for examples of each part of a portfolio. However, you should select amounts for each category based on your own ideas about investing and how comfortable you are with taking risks.

1. What percentage of your savings will you place in the foundation portion of the portfolio? What will this amount be in dollars? What types of investments will be in this part of the portfolio?
2. What percentage of your savings will you place in the conservative investments portion of the portfolio? What will this amount be in dollars? What types of investments will be in this part of the portfolio?
3. What percentage of your savings will you place in the growth investments portion of the portfolio? What will this amount be in dollars? What types of investments will be in this part of the portfolio?
4. What percentage of your savings, if any, will you place in the speculative investments portion of the portfolio? What will this amount be in dollars?
5. What amount of money will you plan to invest each coming month or year to help build your portfolio?
6. What long-term goals will you keep in mind as you choose your investments?

ACTIVITY 5
Track Stock Prices

 academic.cengage.com/school/pfl

Tracking a stock's price for several weeks or months before buying the stock is a common investment strategy. If the stock price rises and falls often, you may be able to buy when the price is low. Stock prices are available online and in many newspapers. Typically, the user must enter or find a symbol (a series of letters) that represents the company. For example, the symbol for Wal-Mart Stores is WMT. If you do not know

Chapter 10   Understanding Saving and Investing

the symbol for a company, you can find it online. In the following sample symbol search screen, the user enters the name of the company; selects a type of investment, such as Stocks; and chooses a market. When the search is complete, the symbol appears.

Sample Symbol Search Screen

Name	Type	Market
Wal-Mart Stores	Stocks	U.S.

Symbol	
WMT	Search

Depending on the Internet site or newspaper, various information is provided about the stock. The opening price of the stock, the closing price (also called Last Trade), and any change in the stock price are usually shown, as in the following example:

Wal-Mart Stores, Inc. (WMT)	
Date	7-21-06
Close (Last Trade)	43.72
Change	⇩ 0.57
Previous Close	44.29
Open	44.51

1. Select a large corporation with which you are familiar.

2. Access the Internet and find a site that gives stock quotes. Links to several such sites can be found on the Web site for this textbook. You can find other sites by entering **stock quotes** in a search engine.

3. Search to find the market symbol for this company if you do not know it.

4. Find the Close (Last Trade) price for the stock for the current date. Record the date and the price.

5. Continue to find and record the Close (Last Trade) price of the stock every 1 to 3 days for the following 2 or 3 weeks as your teacher directs.

6. Create a line chart to show the changes in the stock price. Use Figure 10-3.1 on page 301 as an example for your chart. Use **Days** or **Weeks** instead of Years for your chart.

CHAPTER

11

SAVINGS AND Investing Options

© Blend Images

hapter 11 presents savings and investing options that have low, medium, or high risk. Some of these investment options are more liquid than others. Some can be purchased for a small amount of money. Others can be bought only with larger investments. No one investment is likely to meet all your needs. You will learn to consider risk, liquidity, and rate of return as you choose investments for various purposes.

Low-Risk Investment Options

OUTCOMES

- Discuss the importance of having liquid savings.
- Give examples of savings options that are liquid.
- Give examples of low-risk savings and investment options.
- Explain how corporate bonds are different from government bonds.
- Discuss how annuities can be used to provide for financial security.

SAVINGS

Saving is setting aside money to meet future needs. Having savings to handle short-term needs is especially important. When you have enough savings, you will not need to borrow money to handle unexpected expenses. Savings should be in a form that is liquid. This means that savings should be in cash or in a savings or investment option that can quickly be changed into cash.

A checking account or savings account in a bank that has no restrictions on withdrawals is an example of a safe, liquid savings option. Interest earned on the account may be very low. Low return is acceptable because the purpose of the account is to have funds available when needed. Keeping a certain minimum balance in a checking or savings account may have other advantages. For example, you may not have to pay bank service fees for the account.

Some investments cannot be quickly changed into cash. Others can be changed quickly but require payment of a penalty for doing so. These investments are **illiquid**. Investors choose these options because they typically pay higher returns than those that are liquid. Many investors seek to balance their investments. They want to have some options that give high returns. They want to have other savings or investments that are liquid and that can be changed to cash quickly when needed.

Savings Accounts

A savings account in a bank, credit union, or other insured financial institution is a good option to choose for meeting short-term needs. Savings accounts in banks are low-risk. They are insured by the FDIC up to the legal limit of $100,000 per depositor per bank. Savings accounts usually do not have withdrawal penalties. Some or all of the money can

Having enough cash to pay your bills is important.

be withdrawn at any time. Thus, savings accounts are liquid. However, the account may have some restrictions. For example, the depositor may be able to write only a limited number of checks per month on the account. A savings account typically pays a low interest rate. The rate is usually higher, though, than for a checking account.

Money Market Accounts

A money market account is another good option to choose for liquid savings. This type of account pays the market rate of interest on the money deposited. A money market account is liquid. You can withdraw some or all of the money at any time. Money market accounts may have some restrictions. For example, the number of checks you can write in a month may be limited. A minimum balance, such as $1,000 or $5,000, may be required to open a money market account.

Money market accounts are low-risk if they are insured. You can open an insured money market account at a bank or credit union. Because they are low-risk, these accounts pay a low rate of interest compared to some other investments. You can also open a money market account at a brokerage firm or other investment business. These accounts are not insured. They often pay a higher rate of interest than insured accounts. However, they carry a higher risk. When interest rates start rising in the economy, money market account rates will also rise. Thus, a money market account is a better cushion against inflation than a savings account.

Certificates of Deposit

A certificate of deposit, also called a CD, is a time deposit. This means that the money you deposit is set aside for a fixed amount of time at a set interest rate. A typical CD is not a liquid investment. You must pay a penalty if you withdraw the money before the stated time. CDs purchased at banks and credit unions are safe because they are insured by the FDIC. Thus, a CD is a low-risk investment, but it is not liquid.

Interest rates paid on CDs are typically higher than rates paid for savings accounts or money market accounts. The higher rate is paid because you agreed to leave the money for a stated period of time. You may get a higher rate by agreeing to leave the money on deposit for a longer time period. For example, the interest rate for a CD with a term of 6 months may be 2.75 percent. The interest rate for a CD with a term of 36 months may be 4.25 percent.

WITHDRAWAL PENALTIES

If you redeem a CD early, you will typically pay a penalty. Be sure to ask about the penalty if you buy a CD. Early withdrawal penalties are meant to discourage depositors from withdrawing the money before the stated time period. The penalty may be 6 months' interest or more. In such cases, you can lose part of your principal if you withdraw money early. Figure 11-1.1 on page 317 shows an example of the penalty terms for a CD.

316

FIGURE 11-1.1

**EARLY WITHDRAWAL
PENALTY ON A CD**

Certificate of Deposit
Amount Deposited: $5,000.00
Interest Rate: 5% yearly
Term: 5 years

Penalty for Early Withdrawal
If the money is withdrawn before 5 years, the penalty imposed will equal 365 days'
interest, whether earned or not.

Sample Scenario
The money is withdrawn after 180 days.

$5,000.00 × 0.05 × 180/365 = $ 123.29 Interest Earned
$5,000.00 × 0.05 × 365/365 = $250.00 Penalty
$5,000.00 Amount Deposited
  + 123.29 Interest Earned
$ 5,123.29
  − 250.00 Penalty
$ 4,873.29 Amount Received

SPECIAL FEATURES

CDs pay higher interest when money is set aside for a long period of time.
They also pay higher interest for large amounts. A jumbo CD is a CD for
a large sum of money, usually $100,000 or more, with a term of a year or
longer. CDs that pay higher rates of interest often have higher withdrawal
penalties. You can earn good interest on this type of CD if you are able
to leave your money on deposit for the full term.

INVESTMENTS

Investments vary in term, risk, rate of return, and relative liquidity. Options
that are low-risk typically pay a lower rate of return than those with
higher risk. Options that are long-term typically pay higher rates than
those that are short-term.

To be liquid, an investment must be easily converted to cash. There
should also be no significant loss of the amount invested. Whether or not
an investment is liquid depends on several factors. If there are investors
who are willing to buy when you wish to sell an investment, then the
investment can be turned into cash quickly. However, there is no guarantee that the selling price will be higher than the price you paid for the
investment. Thus, you could lose part of the amount invested. If there are
no investors who are willing to buy the investment when you want to sell
it, you will not be able to get cash quickly.

Some investments are considered very safe because they are insured.
Others that are not insured are also considered fairly safe. This is because
the company or government body issuing them is financially sound.

Savings Bonds

A bond is basically a loan that a buyer makes to a bond issuer. The bond
issuer may be a government or a corporation. A U.S. savings bond is
issued by the federal government. The bond is designed to be a long-term

317

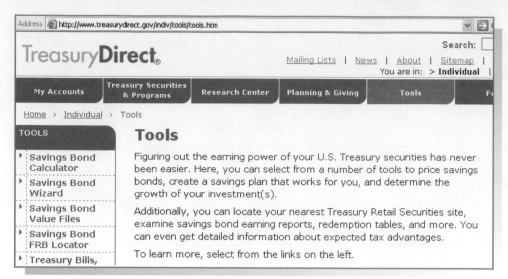

FIGURE 11-1.2

The TreasuryDirect Web site provides tools to help investors.

Source: TreasuryDirect, Tools, http://www.treasurydirect.gov/indiv/tools/tools.htm (accessed August 8, 2006).

investment. Some U.S. savings bonds are issued at a **discount**. That means you pay less than face value. For example, you can purchase a $100 (face value) Series EE paper savings bond for $50. As interest is earned on the bond, it will grow to be worth $100 (the maturity value). Thus, when you **redeem** or cash in the bond, you will receive $100.

Series EE Bonds pay a guaranteed rate if they are not redeemed early. When a savings bond reaches maturity, interest may continue to compound for several years. This type of bond is low-risk because it is guaranteed by the U.S. government. Because it is low-risk, however, the rate of return is lower than for some other investment options.

While you can get your money quickly (cash the bonds when you want), you will forfeit the interest you would have earned if you cash the bond early. Thus, a savings bond is not considered a liquid investment. Some savings bonds can be a good way to save for a child's education. Interest is not taxable until the bond is cashed. If the bond is used for education expenses (for you or your children), then the interest may not be subject to federal taxes when the bond is cashed.

U.S. savings bonds can be purchased through banks or at the TreasuryDirect Web site. This site also provides tools to help you create a savings plan using bonds. You can access the TreasuryDirect Web site, shown in Figure 11-1.2, using the link provided on the Web site for this textbook.

Corporate and Government Bonds

Bonds are issued by companies and governments. Some bonds are sold at face value. Others are sold at a discount or a premium. When you buy a bond at a discount, you pay less than face value for the bond. For example, if the face value of the bond is $5,000, you pay less than that. Bonds may be sold at a discount to increase the overall profit from the bond and make the bond more attractive to investors. Bonds sold at a premium sell for more than the face value. Some bonds are very attractive to investors, perhaps because they have a high coupon rate. These bonds may sell at a premium for more than the face value.

You may receive regular interest payments from a bond. Many bonds pay interest twice a year (semiannually). The annual rate of interest paid

318

FIGURE 11-1.3

RETURN ON A SHORT-TERM INVESTMENT

Corporate Bond

Face Value: $5,000.00

Discount Rate: 4%

Coupon Rate: 4% yearly (paid semiannually)

Term: 5 years with 2 years remaining until maturity

Purchase Price:

$5,000.00 × 0.04 = $200.00 Discount Amount

$5,000.00 − $200.00 = $4,800.00 Discounted Purchase Price

Semiannual Interest:

$5,000.00 × 0.04 = $200.00 Interest per Year ($100.00 each semiannual payment)

$200.00 × 2 years = $400.00 Total Interest Received

Return on Investment:

At the end of the second year, the bond is redeemed for $5,000.00.

$5,400.00 Total Amount Received

−4,800.00 Amount Invested

$ 600.00 Total Profit in Dollars

$600.00/$4,800.00 = 0.125 = 12.5% Total Return on Investment

on a bond is called the coupon rate. The rate is set at the time the bond is issued and typically does not change. When you redeem the bond, you exchange it for the face value. Bonds are redeemed when they have matured. Figure 11-1.3 illustrates how you can make money buying a corporate bond at a discount.

A callable bond has a clause that allows the issuer to repay the bond early (before the maturity date). The bond will be redeemed at a set amount. The amount is typically higher than the face value of the bond. However, the total amount of interest received will be less than if the bond was held until its maturity date. If interest rates have been falling, you may not be able to reinvest the money you receive from the bond at the same rate. Only investments at lower rates may be available. The amount you receive for the bond could also be less than the price for which you could sell the bond. Because of these risks, callable bonds typically pay a higher coupon rate than other similar bonds.

A zero coupon bond does not pay yearly interest. The bond is sold at a deep discount and grows in value over time. You receive the face value of the bond at maturity. For example, you might buy a zero coupon bond for $12,000. In 10 years, at the maturity date, you might redeem the bond for $19,000. This type of bond can be a good way to invest for a particular long-term need, such as paying for a child's education.

CORPORATE BONDS

Corporate bonds are issued by corporations to raise money. Bonds are a form of borrowing for the company. The money is used for various purposes, such as building new factories or buying equipment. Corporate bonds pay a fixed coupon rate. The interest is subject to income tax. Any amount you gain when you redeem the bond is also taxed. In Figure 11-1.3, you would pay taxes on the $400 interest earned. You would also pay taxes on the $200 gain you realized when you redeemed the bond.

319

Corporate bonds are typically offered for sale in multiples of $1,000 or $5,000. They have various terms to maturity. Corporate bonds with terms of up to 2 or 3 years are short-term bonds. Bonds with terms of from 2 or 3 to 10 years are medium-term bonds. Bonds with terms of more than 10 years are long-term bonds.

Some corporate bonds are considered low-risk investments; others are not. The risk depends on the issuing company's ability to make interest payments and repay the bond. Bond rating services study the financial health of bond issuers. They assign risk ratings to the bonds offered for sale. Investors can use these ratings to judge the risk of buying a bond. Standard & Poor's Corporation is an example of a company that provides ratings for bonds, as well as other services.

Investment-grade bonds have high ratings and are considered fairly low-risk. Speculative-grade bonds have lower ratings. These bonds are sometimes called junk bonds or high-yield bonds. They are not considered low-risk. However, they are attractive to some investors because they pay higher rates than investment-grade bonds.

GOVERNMENT BONDS

Government bonds are issued by the U.S. Treasury or by U.S. government agencies. These bonds are low-risk when held to maturity. You do not have to pay state and local taxes on the income from some government bonds. These bonds make a good tax shelter. A **tax shelter** is an investment that allows you to legally avoid or reduce income taxes.

Municipal bonds are issued by states, counties, cities, and towns. They are used to pay for projects such as roads or public buildings. You do not have to pay federal, state, or local taxes on the income from many municipal bonds. Municipal bonds are rated to help investors consider the risk involved. Many municipal bonds are considered low-risk. Although it is possible for a government unit to go bankrupt, it is not very likely. The tax shelter feature also makes these bonds attractive.

Municipal bonds are often issued to pay for projects such as public buildings.

Brokerage Accounts

You can open an account at an investment company. This account may pay interest like a savings account, or it may be a clearing account. A **clearing account** is an account used to buy and sell investments. Money is taken from the account to buy them. When they are sold, money is put back into the account. Brokerage accounts are not insured. However, they are considered low-risk when placed with a reputable investment company. The accounts work a lot like a checking account. The account is liquid. However, there may be restrictions such as a limit to the number of checks you can write in a month or year. Interest earnings are usually higher than for checking or savings accounts in banks, but the risk is higher as well.

Annuities

An **annuity** is a contract purchased from an insurance company. It guarantees a series of regular payments for a set time. To buy an annuity, you would pay a monthly payment into the account for a set number of years

320

(such as 20). You could also invest a lump sum. Then, at the end of the set number of years, the annuity would start paying you monthly payments. Many people who buy annuities use them as a source of retirement income. They are fairly safe, but only as safe as the company you invest your money with. Annuities are not insured. When you pay into an annuity, the interest that is growing is not taxed. Annuities are tax-deferred, which means the interest will be taxed when you receive the monthly payments.

Life Insurance Plans

When you buy a life insurance plan (other than term insurance), the policy gains in cash value. Life insurance provides a low rate of return on your money. However, it also provides death benefits. Many life insurance policies allow you to borrow money. If the loan is not repaid, the life insurance death benefit is reduced by the amount of the loan. This type of investment is illiquid. Some people think it is a good choice because it forces them to save while they also buy insurance. Like annuities, these investments are only as safe as the company from which you buy. The plans are not insured.

Building Communications Skills

BAD NEWS MESSAGES

A bad news message is one that the reader will not find favorable or will not be happy to receive. When writing a message that is bad news, use an indirect approach. With an indirect approach, the writer attempts to break the news gently and keep the reader's goodwill.

In the first paragraph, state or refer to the issue or decision to be made. Give facts or logical reasoning to support the denial or other unfavorable news. Your goal is to convince the reader that the decision is the right one even before the decision is stated. The bad news comes only after the reader is prepared to hear it.

In the second paragraph, state the denial or other bad news. Bad news can often be cushioned by talking about what can be done, rather than just stating what cannot be done. Make the explanation clear and logical. Give details as needed. Use a positive tone throughout the letter.

In the third paragraph, state action you want the reader to take, if that applies to the situation. Close the letter on a positive note. For example, thank the reader for his or her business, or mention a project you will work on together in the future. The message should make the reader should feel important and think that her or his concerns have been heard. Your goal is to have the reader accept the news and keep the reader's goodwill.

11-1 Activity 1   Can You Recall?

Answer these questions to help you recall what you have read. If you cannot answer a question, read the related section again.

1. Explain why having liquid savings is important.
2. Give three examples of options for liquid savings.
3. Why is a savings account considered a low-risk savings option?
4. How is a money market account different from a regular checking account?
5. Explain the purpose of early withdrawal penalties for CDs.
6. Why do some CDs pay higher interest rates than other CDs?
7. List several examples of low-risk savings and investing options.
8. When a bond sells at a discount, do you pay more or less than the face value of the bond? Why might a bond sell at a discount?
9. How are corporate bonds different from government bonds?
10. What is the purpose of a clearing account?
11. Explain how an annuity can help provide financial security during retirement.
12. How can an investment be considered low-risk if it is not insured?

11-1 Activity 2   Low-Risk Investing

Many people start investing with short-term and low-risk choices. They want the investments to be liquid so that they can get their money quickly if needed. In the two cases below, consider the risk and liquidity of savings and investing options. Give advice to each of the investors.

1. Antonio is working full-time. He started his first job 6 months ago. He pays his bills and has $300 a month remaining. Rather than spend this money, Antonio has decided to set it aside for the future. He has signed an annuity contract whereby he will pay $300 a month for the next 20 years. Then he will start receiving payments from the annuity, or he can leave the money there to gain more earnings until he retires. He has no savings account or other investments at this point. Has Antonio made a good investment choice? Are there other options that might be better for him to consider for his portfolio at this time?

2. Emiko is working part-time while she goes to college. Because she has a scholarship, she is able to save $50 per month. Emiko has decided to leave the $50 she saves each month in her checking account. While the account does not pay interest, she is able to avoid a monthly service fee of $8 because she has enough money to meet minimum deposit requirements. What do you think of Emiko's decision? Are there other good options that she might consider for saving or investing her money?

Medium-Risk Investment Options

- List the various kinds of retirement plans that can be opened by an individual.
- Describe retirement account options provided through employers.
- Discuss the importance of portability for retirement plans.
- Describe mutual fund investing and give advantages of investing in mutual funds.

RETIREMENT ACCOUNTS

Some savings and investments are held in retirement accounts that are not taxed until the money is withdrawn. These accounts are tax shelters. This allows the money in the account to grow faster because earnings are computed on the entire balance.

Retirement accounts are a good way to save for the future. Some types of accounts are insured and have very low risk. Other options are not insured and have higher risk and higher potential returns. You can choose the types of savings or investment options in some retirement accounts. For example, you could include CDs or stocks. If the plan is provided by an insured bank, a retirement account invested in CDs would be insured. Money invested in stocks and bonds is not insured even if the account is held in an insured bank. These accounts are not liquid but are long-term investments.

Individual Plans

You can open retirement accounts as an individual. This means you must also manage them, or make choices about how to save or invest the money. Many individual plans allow you to deposit money pretax. This lowers your taxes now, while you are working. If money is withdrawn before age 59½, it is taxed at regular rates. Withdrawals are also subject to a 10 percent penalty. There are exceptions, such as withdrawals for medical expenses or education. Also, there comes a time when the money must be taken out of the account. Currently, money must be withdrawn from some retirement accounts at age 70½, even if you are not retired.

IRA ACCOUNTS

An IRA (individual retirement arrangement) allows individuals to deposit money into an account during their working years. The money deposited may be tax-deductible. Taxes are paid on the money and interest earned when the money is withdrawn during retirement.

Money set aside for a traditional IRA can be deducted from gross income if you meet certain requirements. This lowers your income tax. IRAs are tax-deferred, which means you will not pay taxes on the money earned until it is withdrawn. IRA accounts can be set up at banks and other financial companies. You can choose the types of investments. If you choose a CD rather than stocks, you will take less risk, but you will also have lower returns. IRA accounts are managed by the investor. They are a good long-term plan for providing retirement income. Money must be taken from the accounts at age 70½, even if you are not retired.

You can open an IRA at banks and other financial institutions.

With a Roth IRA, you cannot make pretax contributions. In other words, you cannot deduct the amount you contribute from your gross income. However, if you meet certain requirements, the earnings on a Roth IRA are tax-free. Thus, when you retire, the money you withdraw will not be taxable. You can choose the types of investments for a Roth IRA. No minimum distribution rules apply. You do not have to withdraw money from a Roth IRA at age 70½.

A Spousal IRA is set up to benefit a spouse who does not work outside the home. To qualify, you must file a joint tax return. The amount that can be set aside is limited, based on your income. After 2008, the maximum IRA contribution per year is $5,000 ($4,000 until then).

SEP ACCOUNTS

The SEP (simplified employer plan) is similar to an IRA. It is for self-employed small business owners and their employees. SEPs work like IRAs, except that the amount of money that can be set aside is higher. SEP contributions are deducted from gross earnings. This money is not taxed until it is withdrawn. As with an IRA, the investor chooses how the money is invested.

Often called the SEP-IRA, the SEP is a simple plan for those who are fully or partly self-employed. There are no IRS filing or paperwork requirements. However, there is a limit as to how much can be set aside by small business owners.

KEOGH ACCOUNTS

A Keogh account is similar to a SEP, but it has more complex filing rules. It also has higher limits and is available to self-employed professionals and their employees. Up to $40,000 can be deposited each year. Doctors, lawyers, accountants, and others set up these plans to provide for retirement. Contributions are deducted from taxable income. The money is not taxed until it is withdrawn. Like other retirement accounts, a Keogh account is managed by the investor. It can include low-risk or high-risk investments.

325

Employer-Sponsored Plans

Many employers provide some type of retirement plan for their employees. Often it is part of the employee's benefits package. These plans are sometimes very good options for workers. You can set aside money pretax. In some cases, the money you set aside may be matched by money contributed by the employer. Although you will pay taxes when you withdraw the money, the plan is a good option for providing retirement income.

401(k) ACCOUNTS

A 401(k) plan is a tax-deferred plan for employees. The employee sets aside money each month with a pretax payroll deduction. There is a limit to the amount the employee can contribute. In 2006, the amount was $15,000. The amount can change each year. These accounts and their earnings are not taxed until the money is withdrawn. At retirement, they are taxed as ordinary income.

Employer contributions are optional. Sometimes companies match a certain percentage of employee deposits. The match may range from 25 to 100 percent. For example, suppose a company does a 30 percent match. For every dollar saved by the employee, 30 cents is added to that account by the company. Employers do a match in order to encourage employees to save for retirement. The 401(k) is also a part of benefits packages of many large companies. Employees can choose investments for their 401(k) fund, based on their willingness to take risk.

403(b) ACCOUNTS

A 403(b) account is a retirement plan for employees of nonprofit organizations or educational institutions. Teachers, school staff, nurses, doctors, professors, librarians, and ministers are examples of people who may qualify for a 403(b) plan. Some employers offer tax-sheltered annuities for their 403(b) retirement plans. Money is set aside by workers through payroll deduction. It is not matched by employers. The employee is allowed to choose investments for the money deposited. As in other retirement accounts, earnings and contributions are not taxed until the money is withdrawn.

PENSION PLANS

Some employers offer retirement accounts that are paid for entirely by the employer. These accounts are called defined benefit plans or simply pension plans. Pension plans provide payments to retired workers. Typically, employees must work for the company for a certain number of years to qualify. The payment amounts vary depending on the number of years worked, the worker's salary, and other factors.

Many employees have retirement accounts as part of their benefits package.

© Getty Images/PhotoDisc

Pension plans are offered by fewer companies now than in the past. Employees do not make choices about investments. When the employees receive payments (at retirement), they must pay tax on the money.

PORTABILITY

Many retirement accounts are portable. This means you can take the account with you when you leave a job. **Rollover** is the process of moving an investment balance to another qualified account. For example, you may be working for a company that has a 401(k) or a 403(b) retirement account. If you leave your job at the company, you can take the money you contributed with you. Once the account is vested, you can also take with you

Ethics

BREAKING COMMITMENTS

Some companies provide retirement pensions as part of their benefits package for employees. This benefit represents a commitment by the employer. Employees count on the pension plan to help provide money for their retirement. There is no problem as long as the company does well and pays in the required amount to fund the pension plan.

Many companies have stopped offering pension plans. Some companies that still provide the plans have not funded them at the level needed to pay the promised benefits. This means the plans may not have enough money to pay workers when they retire. Other companies have changed the rules that govern their pension plans; for example, to reduce benefits. The company might go bankrupt and be unable to provide the promised benefits. These actions often leave employees without some of their promised retirement benefits.

The Pension Benefit Guaranty Corporation (PBGC) is a federal corporation created by the Employee Retirement Income Security Act of 1974. Its mission is to protect retirement incomes of millions of American workers with defined benefit pension plans. When a pension plan fails, workers may receive some benefits from the PBGC. However, they may not get some benefits that they have been promised, such as health care benefits.

Although the company's actions may not be illegal, some people think it is unethical to deny retired workers the benefits they were promised. In discussing a new law to regulate pension plans, U.S. President George W. Bush said, "You should keep the promises you make to your workers. If you offer a private pension plan to your employees, you have a duty to set aside enough money now so your workers will get what they've been promised when they retire."[1] The Pension Protection Act of 2006, signed on August 17, 2006, sets new rules about how and when pension plans must be funded. The new law may help fix problems with existing pension plans. However, it also encourages employers and workers to use other types of retirement plans, such as 401(k)s.

Workers should not rely solely on a pension plan provided by an employer. There is also no guarantee that the government will continue to provide retirement benefits. Workers should save and invest to provide for their retirement income.

327

---

[1] The White House, "President Bush Signs H.R. 4, the Pension Protection Act of 2006," August 17, 2006, http://www.whitehouse.gov/news/releases/2006/08/20060817-1.html (accessed August 21, 2006).

money your employer contributed to the account. An account is **vested** when the employee has met certain requirements, such as time of employment. When you are vested, you have rights to the account. Vesting often occurs after 3 to 6 years of continuous employment. When you leave that job, you can roll over your 401(k) to an IRA account. You may also be able to roll over the account to an account provided by a new employer. Rollovers have a time limit and other rules.

INVESTMENTS WITH MEDIUM RISK

In order to earn a higher return, some people are willing to take some risk. Medium-risk investments will increase your return without raising the risk beyond reason. With many medium-risk choices, the investor can choose how much risk he or she is willing to take.

Mutual Funds

A **mutual fund** is operated by a professional investment firm. The firm sells shares in the mutual fund and invests the money in a variety of stocks, bonds, and other investments. Mutual funds are focused on a chosen investment strategy. Mutual fund companies manage many different types of mutual funds. If you invest with one of these companies, you can pick the type of investment strategy that appeals to you. If you choose a higher-risk fund, you might make more money. However, you could also lose money, including your principal. Mutual funds are often thought of as a good way to get started investing.

Mutual fund companies sell shares to many investors. These investors are pooling their money with that of other investors to reduce risk. The mutual fund company is in the business of buying and selling. Its advisors are watching companies and markets. When you invest your money with a mutual fund company, you are paying for the firm's expertise. This allows you to spend your time doing other things. It also lowers your risk because your investment is diversified.

Buying mutual funds is a form of **indirect investing**. With this indirect investment, you invest in the mutual fund company. The company makes the investment purchases and sales. You are investing indirectly in the choices of your mutual fund company. In other words, you own shares of the mutual fund company, not shares of stock in the companies in which it invests. When you choose a certain type of fund, the mutual fund company will select the combination of investments its analysts think is best to meet the fund's goals. Figure 11-2.1 on page 329 describes various types of mutual funds.

With mutual funds, the investor can also choose a combination of funds. This is called **asset allocation**. The investor could pick investments that have a variety of risks. An example of asset allocation is shown in Figure 11-2.2 on page 329.

Family Home

Most financial experts believe that buying your own home is the best investment you will ever make. They also agree that home ownership is not always liquid. You must be willing to wait to sell when the **market**

328

MUTUAL FUNDS

Fund Type	Description
Balanced funds	Invest in a diversified portfolio that includes some low-risk, some medium-risk, and some high-risk stocks. These funds strive for balance between growth and income. The objective is to reduce overall risk while maximizing return.
Bond funds	Invest primarily in bonds. If the bonds are tax-free, this advantage is passed along to investors.
Global funds	Invest in international companies, new industries in foreign countries, and companies in the world marketplace.
Growth funds	Invest in companies that will grow over the long run. Gains will be made when companies reach their potential. These are often considered high-risk investments in the short run.
Income funds	Invest in bonds and stocks that produce steady and reliable dividends. These dividends are passed along to investors.
Index funds	Invest in securities to match a market index with the goal of having returns similar to those of that index.
Money market funds	Invest in short-term securities that go up or down with current interest rates and the economy.
New venture funds	Invest in new and emerging businesses and industries. These are considered high-risk (but also high-return) choices.
Precious metal funds	Invest in companies that are associated with precious metals, such as gold, silver, and platinum.
Stock funds	Invest primarily in stocks. They could be categorized into types of stocks—blue-chip, technology, medical, etc.

FIGURE 11-2.1

Investors can choose from several types of mutual funds.

ASSET ALLOCATION

Percent of Holdings	Type of Fund	Reason for Choice
25%	Bond fund	For stability and to offset risk of other funds
25%	Growth fund	To invest in high-risk choices that could grow greatly over time
25%	Global fund	To benefit from world economic growth
25%	Money market fund	To provide liquidity and short-term gains

FIGURE 11-2.2

ASSET ALLOCATION WITHIN A MUTUAL FUND

329

is rising. Because the costs of buying are so high, it usually takes several years to make a profit. When you own your own home, you should take good care of it to protect your investment. Over the long run, home ownership is a fairly safe investment, with value that often grows faster than the rate of inflation.

Technology Corner

TRACKING INVESTMENTS IN A SPREADSHEET

People who buy investments should check the progress of their investments often. A good way to do this is to set up a spreadsheet that shows purchase price, monthly or yearly change in value, percentage change in value, and ending value. This allows you to track each investment over time. It also allows you to compare investments. Most importantly, it helps you to decide when it is time to change your investment strategy. If one type of investment is going steadily down in value over time, or not increasing as fast as others, it may be time to make a change.

Microsoft Excel has a feature that allows you to get updated stock quotes in a worksheet. If you want to see the prices of several stocks or mutual funds each day or week, this feature can save you time. Simply enter the recognized symbol for a stock in the worksheet. Click outside the cell, and then click the **Smart Tag** that appears. (Smart Tags must be turned on.) Choose **Insert refreshable stock price** from the menu, as shown in Figure 11-2.3. Select a location for the quote and related information to appear and click **OK**. You must be connected to the Internet to access stock quotes.

FIGURE 11-2.3

Excel provides a feature to insert refreshable stock quotes.

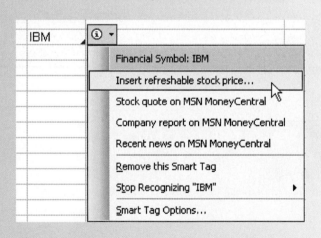

IBM

Financial Symbol: IBM

Insert refreshable stock price...

Stock quote on MSN MoneyCentral

Company report on MSN MoneyCentral

Recent news on MSN MoneyCentral

Remove this Smart Tag

Stop Recognizing "IBM"

Smart Tag Options...

330

11-2 Activity 1 Can You Recall?

Answer these questions to help you recall what you have read. If you cannot answer a question, read the related section again.

1. List three types of retirement accounts that can be opened by an individual.
2. How are traditional IRAs and Roth IRAs similar? How are they different?
3. What types of retirement accounts are available for people who are self-employed?
4. Describe three types of employer-sponsored retirement plans.
5. What is the advantage to having a tax-deferred investment account?
6. Why is having a retirement account that is portable important?
7. Explain why mutual funds are a form of indirect investing.
8. Give two advantages of buying mutual funds rather than individual stocks or bonds.
9. What is asset allocation?
10. Which type of mutual fund has a better potential for high returns: a bond fund or a stock fund? Which of these two funds has a higher risk?

11-2 Activity 2 Compare Returns on Mutual Funds

Investors who buy mutual funds have many funds to choose from. Some funds have the potential for high returns but also have high risk. Other funds have lower risk but also provide lower returns. In this activity, you will create a chart to compare returns for funds that have low, medium, and high risk. The three funds are described below.

Balanced Fund
This fund seeks current income, long-term growth of capital and income, and preservation of capital. This is a low-risk fund.

Index Fund
This fund seeks above-average returns by investing at least 80 percent of its assets in equity securities, which are primarily stocks. The fund's risk profile is similar to that of the Standard & Poor's 500 Index. This is a medium-risk fund.

331

Growth Fund

This fund seeks long-term gains by normally investing at least 80 percent of its assets in stocks of companies with above-average earnings growth. This is a high-risk fund.

Returns for each fund for a period of 8 years are shown in the following table:

Year	Balanced Fund	Growth Fund	Index Fund
1998	14.01%	6.53%	28.84%
1999	3.89%	58.17%	12.37%
2000	−1.83%	−13.52%	−7.75%
2001	−5.23%	−33.59%	−10.87%
2002	−18.91%	−24.88%	−22.85%
2003	18.21%	34.83%	23.67%
2004	6.78%	4.94%	8.78%
2005	6.84%	11.82%	7.60%

1. Open the *Excel* file *CH11 Funds Data* from the data files. This file contains the returns data for the three mutual funds as shown in the table.
2. Create a line chart or a column chart to compare the returns data for the three funds. Note that the returns for some years are negative numbers. (If you do not have *Excel* or other spreadsheet software, create a chart manually using graph paper.)
3. Key **RETURNS COMPARISON** for the chart title. Include a legend to identify the line or column for each fund.
4. Adjust the scale and format the chart as needed to make the data easy to understand.
5. Which fund had the highest return in any 1 year? Which fund had the lowest return in any 1 year?
6. Which fund had the smallest amount of change over the years?
7. Which two funds had similar returns?
8. Which fund would you choose if you were planning to invest in one of these funds? Why?

High-Risk Investment Options

OUTCOMES
- Describe several high-risk investment options.
- Compare common stock with preferred stock.
- Describe direct investing and the risk it involves.
- Discuss trading futures contracts for commodities.
- Explain why indirect investing options reduce risk.

STOCKS

When you buy stock in a corporation, you become a stockholder. A stockholder owns shares of the company. Stockholders make money in two ways. One way is by receiving dividends. The other way is by selling the stock at a price that is higher than the price paid for the stock. This increase in selling price is referred to as growth (in value). A stock that pays annual dividends is attractive to an investor who needs the income (such as at retirement). Buying stocks and holding them for growth is a long-term strategy. You are betting that the value of the stock will go up over time.

The number of shares a stockholder owns may increase due to stock splits. In a stock split, the number of shares a company has sold is divided into a larger number. For example, in a two-for-one split, each person who owned 100 shares of stock will now own 200 shares. If the stock price before the split was $100, the price will now be $50. However, the stock may increase in price over a few years back to $100 per share. An investor who bought 100 shares at $75 per share would have 200 shares to sell at $100 per share.

Stocks are considered risky because an individual company could fail regardless of how big it is or how long it has been in business. There are many risks faced by businesses, from inflation risk to political risk. Stocks can be sold at any time as long as there is a buyer willing to purchase the stocks. However, if the stock price is low, the investor may want to hold the stock until the price rises. Otherwise, the investor will lose money on the investment.

Common Stock

Many companies have two types of stock: common stock and preferred stock. Owners of **common stock** may share in the profits of the company through dividends. They have voting rights in decisions made by shareholders,

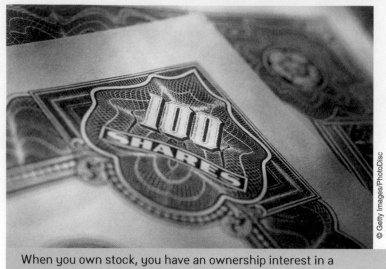

When you own stock, you have an ownership interest in a corporation.

such as who the company directors will be. They take a higher risk than owners of preferred stock. Common stock has no guaranteed dividends. If the company does well, the stockholder shares in the profit in the form of dividends. The directors of the corporation decide if a dividend payment is to be made. Stock dividends are taxable. There is no guarantee that the value of the stock will go up. Investors should review the selling prices of stocks they own often to see whether the prices are going up or down. If the price of a stock keeps going down over time, the investor may want to sell the stock and invest in another option.

Preferred Stock

In many companies, owners of **preferred stock** have a guaranteed dividend rate. This rate is paid before common stockholders get paid a dividend. Because there is less risk, preferred stock costs more than common stock. Preferred stockholders do not have voting rights. If the company goes bankrupt, they get paid before common stockholders.

Direct Investing

Buying investments directly from companies and holding them individually is known as **direct investing**. If you buy the stock of a company and hold that stock, you are taking a high risk. That is because you have a lot of money in one place. This plan does not spread risk. You can, however, lower your risk by buying many different types of stocks and other direct investment options. You can learn more about direct investing in stocks at the U.S. Securities and Exchange Commission Web site, as shown in Figure 11-3.1.

FIGURE 11-3.1

Investors can buy stocks directly from some companies.

Source: U.S. Securities and Exchange Commission, Direct Investment Plans: Buying Stock Directly from the Company, http://www.sec.gov/answers/drip.htm (accessed August 14, 2006).

Focus on . . .

Day traders are individuals who attempt to make money by buying and selling stocks and bonds. These investments are not held for long-term growth. They are held just long enough to make a profit. When the day trader sees a stock's price rising, the stock is sold for a quick profit. When the day trader sees prices dropping for stocks that are good values, the trader buys. As soon as prices come up again, the trader takes the profit by selling. If the price does not rise again, the trader takes a loss.

Day traders must be aware of general market conditions. They also must be familiar with companies, products, and industries in which they trade. By carefully watching the market and keeping track of trends, day traders can make considerable profits over time. Of course, they are bound to make mistakes at times. They might sell before the stock hits its peak price or select a stock that loses value. Because they trade so often, day traders must also consider trading fees and expenses when calculating actual profits.

BUSINESS VENTURES

You may decide to start a small business. You could also loan money to someone so that person can start a business. More than half of all small businesses fail each year, making this a very risky investment. If the business succeeds, however, it can be a profitable investment. A **business plan** is a document that outlines how a business plans to succeed. It includes the company mission, the financing needs, the marketing plan, the management plan, and the operating plans for the company. The plan attempts to show how the business will make a profit. Before you invest in a business venture, be sure to read and understand the business plan. You could make a lot of money, or you could lose your investment.

COLLECTIBLES

Collectibles are art objects, coins, decorative plates, books, baseball cards, or other items bought for their investment value. Some collectible items will go up in value over time. Others will not. The investor must decide which items she or he thinks will go up in value. Coins are a commonly collected item. When coins are rare, they gain in value. Buying collectibles is a very risky investment choice. When collecting, have a clear goal in mind. Decide whether you are collecting items as an investment or whether you are simply buying items that you like for your own enjoyment. If you are buying items as an investment, do market research to learn which items may increase in value. Also, do research to learn about the items so you can tell whether an item is authentic or a replica. Being able to prove that an item is authentic is especially important for art objects and sports memorabilia.

335

Rental property can be a profitable investment.

RENTAL PROPERTY

Individuals can buy real estate beyond a family home. If you buy a house and rent it to tenants, you will receive rent for income. Buying rental real estate has risks and responsibilities. The tenant (renter) takes possession of a valuable piece of property. The tenant must take reasonable care of it. You, the owner, are responsible for repairs and maintenance. This may mean fixing or replacing the roof, painting, and other upkeep. The property may increase in value over time. Thus, an investment in rental property can provide current income and long-term growth. Other forms of rental property besides a single-family home include duplexes, apartment complexes, and vacation property.

FUTURES CONTRACTS AND COMMODITIES

Futures contracts are another type of high-risk investment. A **futures contract** is an agreement to buy or sell a specific commodity or currency at a set price on a set date in the future. A **commodity** is a specific item of value that is bought and sold in a marketplace. It could be soybeans, silver, live cattle, coffee, or other items.

Buying and selling a futures contract does not transfer ownership. It spells out the terms under which the commodity or currency will be bought or sold at a later date. Futures contracts are often used by sellers and buyers as a way to hedge, or reduce the likelihood of losing money in the future. For example, suppose a company has agreed to buy fuel in the future at a set price. The company might also want to buy some

336

fuel futures contracts. If the price of the fuel rises, then the company may make enough money on the futures contracts to pay for the increased price of the fuel itself.

As you have probably guessed, investing in this category is very risky. You will have no control over what happens to prices for commodities. For example, the weather during the growing season may have a big effect on the price for products such as corn or orange juice. Investors who have an in-depth knowledge of how the market for a particular product fluctuates may be able to do well trading commodities. For example, suppose a farmer has grown corn for 20 years. This farmer has studied the conditions that affect corn prices, such as weather and the amount of corn already in storage from previous years. This farmer may have the knowledge needed to do well trading futures contracts for corn. However, the same farmer might know little about currency markets and might not do well trading currency. Investors in futures contracts should realize that you could make—or lose—a lot of money in a short time.

Success Skills

MANAGING STRESS

Stress is a state of mental or physical tension. Many types of changes in life can cause stress. The change can be good, like getting a new job, or bad, like being ill. Stress is not always harmful. Sometimes stress can cause a person to take actions or learn new ways to handle a situation that can be helpful. In other instances, stress can cause problems. Emotional upset, trouble sleeping or concentrating, and even disease can be caused by too much stress.

Everyone experiences stress in daily life. Because too much stress can be harmful, you need to learn to manage factors that cause stress and take steps that will help you cope with stress. Stress is unique to each person. What is relaxing to one person may be stressful to another. The key to stress management is finding things that will work for you. Follow these guidelines to help you control and cope with stress:

- Identify situations that cause negative stress in your life. Take whatever steps you reasonably can to avoid or change these situations.
- Seek counseling to help you deal with serious stressful events.
- Schedule work and other activities to allow time to complete them without rushing, if possible.
- Find activities that help you relax, such as a hobby, a sport, or volunteer work.
- Spend time with family or friends in relaxing settings. Remember the value of laughter to help relieve tension and put situations in perspective.
- Get enough rest and sleep, and eat a healthy diet. These steps will help you be more physically fit and better able to cope with stress.
- Exercise and stay active throughout life. Physical activity can also help you stay fit and be better able to cope with stress.

337

Source: U.S. Securities and Exchange Commission, Real Estate Investment Trusts, http://www.sec.gov/answers/reits.htm (accessed August 15, 2006).

REAL ESTATE INVESTMENT TRUSTS

REITs (real estate investment trusts) are also known as real estate stocks. A REIT is a corporation. It may own and operate income-producing property. An apartment building that rents to families and a factory building that rents to a business are examples of income-producing properties. A REIT may lend money to real estate developers. It may also invest in securities backed by real estate mortgages.

Buying shares in a REIT is a form of indirect investing, similar to buying shares in a mutual fund. When REITs make profits, the profits are distributed to shareholders. You own shares of stock in the REIT. You do not own the individual pieces of property purchased by the REIT. Your money is invested indirectly in the real estate market. Many REITS are publicly traded. You can buy shares of these REITs on the stock exchanges. Because of the nature of real estate, REITs outperform many other investment funds over the long run. You can learn more about REITs on the U.S. Securities and Exchange Commission Web site, as shown in Figure 11-3.2.

INVESTMENT CLUBS

An investment club is a group of people who pool their money together to buy and sell investments. The group may be small—just a few people who work together to buy something they could not afford as individuals. For example, three or four couples may jointly buy a vacation home and share the time using it. The group may also be hundreds of people who do not know each other. Investment clubs may buy stocks, bonds, or other investments. Clubs may take part in direct investing, as in buying stocks, or indirect investing, as in buying mutual funds. An investment club usually has stated goals and buys certain kinds of investments to reach those goals.

11-3 Activity 1 Can You Recall?

Answer these questions to help you recall what you have read.
If you cannot answer a question, read the related section again.

1. Describe two ways to make money from stocks.
2. Compare common stock with preferred stock.
3. Why are common stocks considered a risky direct investment? Why do common stockholders take more risk than preferred stockholders?
4. What is a business plan? Why is studying the business plan important when considering a business venture investment?
5. Why are collectibles considered high-risk investments?
6. What risks are associated with owning rental property?
7. What are two ways in which an investor can make money on rental property?
8 What is a futures contract? Give three examples of commodities.
9. How does a REIT work? Why is it safer than direct investment in real estate (owning rental property)?
10. What is an investment club?

11-3 Activity 2 High-Risk Investing

Suppose your investment portfolio is well balanced, with short-term investments, stocks, bonds, and mutual funds. You own your own home. Recently, you unexpectedly received a large sum of money. You want to take some risk and invest the money in hopes of making a high return.

1. Consider the investment options listed below. Select the option you would buy.
2. Give an advantage and a disadvantage of your choice. Give reasons you chose that option.
   o Buy rental real estate.
   o Pool your money with others in an investment club.
   o Invest in a small business venture.
   o Buy futures contracts for a commodity.
   o Buy a large number of shares in one corporation.
   o Buy a painting by a well-known, popular artist.

339

EXPLORING CAREERS IN HOSPITALITY AND TOURISM

Do you love to cook? Are you good at dealing with the public? Would you enjoy planning events such as meetings and parties? Do you want to own a bed-and-breakfast inn someday? If the answer to any of these questions is yes, a career in hospitality and tourism might be right for you. This career area includes a wide variety of jobs. Hotel managers and workers, theme park and resort workers, travel agents, tour guides, chefs, and other restaurant workers are all part of this career area.

Jobs in hospitality and tourism are found in government and in businesses. This job area also includes entrepreneurs. Many caterers, inn owners, and event planners handle the daily work and management of their own companies. The need for jobs in this area is expected to grow in the next few years. The outlook varies somewhat by job.

Skills Needed

Some of the skills and traits needed for a career in hospitality and tourism include the following:

- Management skills
- Communications skills
- Ability to work well with others
- Math skills
- Computer skills
- Decision-making skills
- Problem-solving skills
- Leadership skills

Job Titles

Many jobs are available in hospitality and tourism. Some job titles for this career area include the following:

- Executive chef
- Flight attendant
- Hotel desk clerk
- Hotel manager
- Meeting planner
- Restaurant owner or manager
- Theme park manager or worker
- Travel agent
- Zookeeper

Explore a Job

1. Choose a job in hospitality and tourism to explore further. Select a job from the list above, or choose another job in this career area.

2. Access the *Occupational Outlook Handbook* online. A link to the site is provided on the Web site for this textbook.

3. Search for more information about the job you selected to answer these questions:
    - What is the nature of the work this job involves?
    - What is the job outlook for this job?
    - What training or qualifications are needed for this job?
    - What are the median annual earnings for this job?

Review

Summary

- Investors should consider risk, return, and liquidity when making savings and investing choices.
- Savings accounts are low-risk and liquid, but the return is low.
- A money market account is a good option to choose for liquid savings.
- A certificate of deposit is a low-risk investment, but it is not liquid. Withdrawal penalties may apply if you withdraw money from a CD before the set time period.
- A U.S. savings bond is designed to be a long-term investment. Bonds can be purchased through banks or at the TreasuryDirect Web site.
- Bonds are issued by companies and governments. Government bonds and investment-grade corporate bonds are considered low-risk.
- Annuities are low-risk, illiquid investments. Some people purchase them to provide retirement income.
- Individual retirement plans include IRAs, SEPs, and Keoghs. Some of these plans are tax shelters because they lower tax liability.
- Employer-sponsored retirement accounts include 401(k), 403(b), and employer-provided pension plans. These are often part of an employee's benefit package.
- When you are vested, you can take your retirement account with you when you leave a job. A rollover is the process of moving an investment balance to another qualified account such as an IRA account.
- Mutual funds are a form of indirect investment with medium risk. You choose the types of funds to increase or reduce risk through asset allocation.
- Buying a home has risks but can provide good returns when home values rise faster than inflation.
- Buying individual stocks is a high-risk investment choice. Common stock is more risky than preferred stock.
- Business ventures, collectibles, and rental property have high risk, but they also have the potential for high returns.
- Futures contracts for commodities are considered speculative, or at the highest level of risk.
- Buying shares in a REIT is a form of indirect investing, similar to buying shares in a mutual fund. When REITs make profits, the profits are distributed to shareholders.
- An investment club is a group of people who pool their money together to buy and sell investments.

341

Key Terms

annuity	common stock	mutual fund
asset allocation	direct investing	preferred stock
business plan	discount	redeem
clearing account	futures contract	rollover
collectibles	illiquid	tax shelter
commodity	indirect investing	vested

ACTIVITY 1
Review Key Terms

Use the key terms from Chapter 11 to complete the following sentences:

1. Buying stock in a mutual fund or REIT is a type of _____.

2. _____ is the process of moving a retirement account balance to another qualified retirement account.

3. A(n) _____ is a contract purchased from an insurance company that guarantees a series of regular payments for a set time.

4. Shares of _____ may pay a guaranteed dividend to shareholders.

5. A(n) _____ is a document that outlines how a business plans to succeed.

6. When an employee is _____, he or she has legal rights to a retirement account.

7. Buying stocks or bonds directly from companies and holding them individually is known as _____.

8. A(n) _____ is an item of value that is bought and sold in a market, such as corn or silver.

9. Items bought for their investment value, such as art objects or coins, are called _____.

10. Choosing a combination of stocks, bonds, mutual funds, or other investments to limit risk and increase returns is known as _____.

11. When an investment cannot be turned into cash quickly without a penalty, it is said to be _____.

12. A(n) _____ is used to deposit money from stock sales and to pay for stocks when they are purchased.

13. An investment that allows investors to legally avoid income taxes is called a(n) _____.

14. The difference between a bond's selling price and its face or maturity value is the _____.

15. A(n) _____ is an agreement to buy or sell a specific commodity or currency at a set price on a set date in the future.

16. Shares of stock that represent ownership interest and give stockholders voting rights in the company are called _____.

342

17. When you cash in a bond at maturity, you _____ the bond.

18. An investment fund that consists of stocks, bonds, and other investments focused on a strategy, such as balance or growth, is called a(n) _____.

ACTIVITY 2
Math Minute

1. You have a CD for $1,000. The interest rate is 5 percent annually, and the term is 5 years. The CD has an early withdrawal penalty. If the money is withdrawn before 36 months, no interest is paid, and a penalty of 6 months' interest is levied. If you withdraw the money after 12 months, what penalty will you pay? How much money will you get?

2. You have a CD for $1,000. The interest rate is 5 percent annually, and the term is 5 years. The CD has an early withdrawal penalty. If the money is withdrawn before 36 months, interest is paid for the time the money is in the account, but a 6-month interest penalty is deducted. If you withdraw the money after 12 months, what penalty will you pay? How much money will you get?

3. You purchased a house for $125,000. You spent $15,000 for repairs and redecorating, property taxes, and other expenses. You sold the house 1 year later for $160,000. How much profit did you make on the house? What is your return on investment?

4. You purchased 100 shares of stock at $125 per share. One year later, the price of the stock has risen to $150 per share. What is the percentage increase in the stock price?

5. You own 75 shares of stock in a corporation. The company issues a three-for-one stock split. How many shares do you now own?

ACTIVITY 3
Risk and Liquidity

TEAMWORK
Critical Thinking

Work with a classmate to complete this activity.

1. Open the *Word* file *CH11 Grid* from the data files. This file contains the grid shown on the following page.

2. Complete the grid of investments based on risk, return, and liquidity. In each square of the grid, write one or more investments that fit the criteria. For example, in the first square, write the name of a savings or investing option that is liquid and has low risk. Write **None** in a square if no investment meets both the criteria.

3. Pick one type of investment from each column (one that has low risk, one with medium risk, and one with high risk) that you would consider having in your portfolio. Give an advantage and a disadvantage of each one.

343

	Low Risk	Medium Risk	High Risk
Liquid			
Low Return			
Medium Return			
High Return			

ACTIVITY 4
Research Mutual Funds

 academic.cengage.com/school/pfl

Indirect investing is a good way to have a diversified portfolio and to reduce risk. Mutual funds offer expert management and are available for various investment strategies, such as growth or a balance of good return with reasonable risk. In this activity, you will research one mutual fund on the Internet.

1. Access the Internet. Use a search engine to find sites that tell about mutual funds. Use the term **mutual fund list** for the search. You could also include other words in the search box, such as **bonds**, **growth**, or **stocks**, to find a particular type of mutual fund.

2. Review two or three Web sites that tell about mutual funds. Choose one fund. For that fund, record this information:
   ○ Fund name
   ○ Fund trading symbol
   ○ Strategy of the fund (such as balance or growth)
   ○ Holdings (list of investments the fund contains)
   ○ Performance in recent years (percent of return each year)

3. Find the selling price of a share in the mutual fund. You may have to visit a different Web site that provides market quotes to find the price. The price will likely be labeled NAV (for net asset value). The NAV is the price of one share in the fund at the close of trading on a particular day.

4. What do you think is the risk level of this mutual fund—low, medium, or high?

344

ACTIVITY 5
Rental Property Return on Investment

Buying real estate to rent is an option that has higher risk than some other investments. However, the returns can be good. Assume you have purchased a single-family home that you intend to rent. The house will rent for $750 per month. You will have the following expenses:

- Monthly mortgage $390
- Monthly insurance $60
- Taxes every 6 months $340
- Repairs (yearly estimate) $500
- Monthly lawn care or snow removal $100

1. Calculate the total yearly expenses you will have for the rental property.

2. Calculate the total rent you will receive in a year. Assume the house is rented for the full 12 months per year.

3. What is your return on investment for the property?

4. Some of your expenses have increased, as shown below. Calculate the total yearly expenses you will have for the rental property after the cost increases.
   - Monthly insurance $70
   - Taxes every 6 months $380
   - Yearly lawn care or snow removal $1,400

5. What is the new return on investment for the property?

6. What might you do to increase your return on investment?

345

BUYING AND SELLING INVESTMENTS

© Digital Vision

Chapter 12 covers the basics of buying and selling investments. You will learn about doing research before you invest to help you make better choices. Much information about investing is available. Some information is free; some is very costly. You will also learn about many regulatory agencies. They are designed to protect you, the investor, when you buy and sell securities.

ONLINE RESOURCES

Personal Financial Literacy Web site:

> **Data Files**
>
> **Vocabulary Flashcards**
>
> **Beat the Clock: Buying and Selling Investments**
>
> **Chapter 12 Supplemental Activity**

Search terms:
- auction market
- discount broker
- over-the-counter market
- market order
- stock split
- stockbroker

12-1

Researching Investments

OUTCOMES

- Describe the types of financial information found in magazines, newspapers, and newsletters.
- Describe the type of data found in company reports.
- Explain how to find investing information on the Internet.
- List figures that can be used to compare the performance or value of companies.
- Explain how investment professionals help investors.

SOURCES OF INFORMATION

Some people hire a stockbroker or financial planner to help them choose investments. Other people do research and make choices on their own. Either way, investors need a basic knowledge of financial markets. Keeping informed about current market conditions helps investors make better choices.

Magazines

Business magazines, such as *BusinessWeek, Fortune*, and *Forbes*, contain information that can be helpful to investors. In these magazines, you can read business articles and get experts' opinions on various topics related to investing and the economy. For example, suppose the experts say that the economy is growing. As a result, you can expect interest rates to rise. Knowing this, you may want to avoid buying a CD or bond with a low, fixed rate. Reading business magazines can help you understand the economy and the markets. This, in turn, will help you choose the right investments at the right times.

You can also find good information in news magazines such as *Time, Newsweek*, and *U.S. News & World Report*. Read these magazines to study world events that affect the economy and investments. The magazines also have regular features that include financial advice.

Several magazines give information about saving, investing, and personal finance. Examples include *Money, Consumer Reports*, and *SmartMoney*. You can read articles in these magazines about people who have been successful. The articles can help you can learn from their mistakes and profit from their successes.

Newspapers

One of the best sources for current information is the financial sections of newspapers. You will find articles about business triumphs and failures. You can read about new products and services. You will also see articles about the latest business scandals and frauds. Price quotes for securities are provided in many newspapers. The word *securities* refers to stocks, bonds, mutual funds, and other investments. The information you learn can help you make better investment choices.

The *Wall Street Journal* and *Barron's* are two national newspapers that report financial news and other events that affect markets. They provide market price quotes and articles about national and world events. These articles discuss market data and predict how it will affect the stock market. For example, when the Fed raises interest rates, different parts of the market are affected in different ways. (The credit industry will benefit, and stock prices will rise.) These newspapers are geared to the business world, but consumers can benefit from reading them as well.

Staying informed about the economy can help you make better investment choices.

© Digital Vision

Investor Newsletters

Many financial advisors prepare free newsletters for their clients. The newsletters contain data about economic events and trends. The advisors may also make comments about certain stocks, bonds, or mutual funds. They may recommend that investors buy or sell securities. This data can help investors decide how to manage their portfolios.

Investors can subscribe to newsletters that give financial advice. Examples of these newsletters are *Standard & Poor's Stock Reports*, *Moody's Investor Service*, and *Value Line Investment Survey*. The newsletters may discuss how to reduce risk, changing market conditions, stocks to watch, and other information related to investing. Subscriptions to newsletters may cost from $50 to $1,000 per year.

Company Reports

All companies that sell stock to the public must publish yearly annual reports. An **annual report** is a company's report to shareholders about the financial position of the company. It also tells about profits or losses and plans for the future. These reports are free, and many are available online as well as in print. A page from an annual report is shown in Figure 12-1.1 on page 349. This page gives information about the company stock and dividends. Annual reports include information that investors can use to compare one company to another. You can see how each company is doing over time. If you are considering investing in a company, learn as much as you can about the company.

The Internet

Investors can find information about companies, products, and market trends on the Internet. One of the best ways to find information is to

THE THOMSON CORPORATION
2005 ANNUAL REPORT

Corporate Information

Corporate Headquarters

Metro Center One Station Place
Stamford, Connecticut 06902
United States

tel 203.539.8000

generalinfo@thomson.com

Stock Exchange Listings

Common shares (symbol: TOC):

- Toronto Stock Exchange (TSX)
- New York Stock Exchange (NYSE)

Series I I preference shares
 (symbol: TOC.PR.B):

- Toronto Stock Exchange (TSX)

Capital Stock

Shares outstanding as of December 31, 2005:

- Common: 648,948,992
- Series I I preference: 6,000,000

Controlling shareholder:
Kenneth R. Thomson
(approximately 69% of common
shares)

2005 Financial Calendar

Year end: December 31
Quarterly results: announced on April 27
(Q1), July 27 (Q2) and October 26 (Q3).

Common Share Dividends

At the discretion of the directors. Paid on
March 15/June 15/September 15/December
15 or on the first business day thereafter.
Declared in U.S. dollars but can be paid in
Canadian dollars or U.K. pounds sterling at the
holder's option (see also note 15, page 86).

Further information is available from the
registrar.

Dividend Reinvestment Plan

Eligible common shareholders may elect to
have cash dividends reinvested in common
shares. Further information is available from
the registrar.

Employees

As of December 31, 2005, we had
approximately 40,500 employees.

Annual and Special Meeting of Shareholders

Wednesday, May 3, 2006, 12:00 p.m. at
Roy Thomson Hall
60 Simcoe Street
Toronto, Ontario, Canada

Transfer Agent and Registrar

Computershare Trust Company of Canada 100
University Avenue, 9th Floor

Toronto, Ontario M5J 2Y1
Canada

tel 1.800.564.6253 (United States, Canada) tel
514.982.7555 (outside North America)
www.computershare.com

Auditors

PricewaterhouseCoopers LLP Suite 3000, Box 82

Royal Trust Tower

Toronto-Dominion Centre Toronto, Ontario
M5K 1G8 Canada

Further Information

Please visit www.thomson.com for corporate
and management news and more detailed
information on individual Thomson businesses,
products and services.

349

Source: Thomson Corporation, Annual and Quarterly Reports, http://www.thomson.com/corp/investor_relations/ir_annquarterly_reports.jsp (accessed August 22, 2006).

INTERNET SITES	
Site Name	**Information Provided**
Bloomberg.com	News articles; market data for stocks, bonds, currency, mutual funds, commodities, and other securities; investment tools; online tutorials for investing; and other features
CNNMoney.com	Current financial news and information to help investors make better decisions
Kiplinger	Tools to help beginners get started. Investors can use this site to track investments in both stocks and mutual funds.
Morningstar®	Articles related to investments, stocks in the news, research reports, newsletters, a feature to track and analyze a portfolio, and other tools
Reuters®	Business and investing articles, stock quotes, bond and currency news, and a feature to track investments

use a search engine. Google, Yahoo!, AltaVista®, and other search engines allow users to search for data on almost any topic. Users can find out about companies, stocks, bonds, mutual funds, brokerage firms, and banks. Many businesses provide company data on their Web sites. You can find a company Web site by entering its name in a search engine. Figure 12-1.2 lists some Internet sites that investors might find helpful. Links to the sites are provided on the Web site for this textbook. Some sites allow investors to set up a free account and monitor investments.

Using Research Data

A great deal of information about investing is available in print and online. Investors need to know about the economy and current market trends. They also need to learn about specific companies or funds in which they may want to invest. News articles are a good source of information on the economy and markets. Annual reports and online profiles are good sources of data about specific companies or mutual funds.

Web sites such as Yahoo! Finance allow the user to enter a company symbol to find data about the company. The current stock price for the company is given. News articles related to the company or industry may also appear. A history of stock prices, stock splits, and dividend data is available. Key numbers and financial statements are provided. Much of the same data can be found in company annual reports. Data is also available for mutual funds. All this data can help investors evaluate the company or mutual fund.

With so much data available, investors may feel overwhelmed. They may not understand all the data or know how to compare companies or funds. Figure 12-1.3 on page 351 describes a few key figures that investors can use to compare companies. Investors who plan to choose stocks or mutual funds on their own may want to take classes or read books to learn more about investing. Many investors seek advice from experts when deciding how to invest.

COMPARISON FIGURES	
Figure	**Description**
Current stock price	This price is the amount investors are willing to pay for a share of ownership in the company.
Number of employees	Increases or decreases in the number of employees can reflect growth or downsizing.
Market cap (capitalization)	The total value of a company in the stock market (total shares outstanding times price per share). This figure, along with revenue, indicates the size of a company.
Revenue	The amount of money received from business activities. This may be mostly from sales of products and/or services to customers.
Net income or profit	The amount of money earned after deducting all the business's expenses. To investors, this number is more important than revenue.
Profit margin	Profit shown as a percentage. It is the net income divided by revenue for the same period.
P/E ratio	The price earnings ratio compares the selling price of a company's common stock to the annual profits per share. Fast-growing or low-risk companies may have higher P/E ratios than slow-growing or low-risk companies. This ratio is an important measure of a stock's value.
Current ratio	A measure of a company's ability to pay its current debts from current assets. It indicates a company's liquidity and financial strength. The current ratio is calculated by dividing the total current assets by the total current liabilities.

ADVICE FROM PROFESSIONALS

Choosing which stock, bond, mutual fund, or other investment to buy is an important decision. Many investors seek advice from experts in the investing field. A fee is typically charged for investment advice or for making a sale or purchase for an investor.

A **stockbroker** is a person who buys and sells securities on behalf of others. Stockbrokers may also provide advice on which products to buy. The broker will make commissions on the items the investor buys.

A financial planner is an advisor who helps people make investment decisions to meet stated goals. Typically, investors are asked to give data about assets owned and income earned. They also list their goals, such as saving for retirement or paying for a child's college education. The planner considers this information and suggests options that will help meet the investor's goals. Some financial planners also sell securities, such as stocks and bonds. They may make a commission on products they sell.

351

Investors may go to some banks and credit unions for financial advice. Employees at these companies are licensed to sell securities that are endorsed by the company. They make a commission on products they sell. Some banks offer their own brand of securities. Rather than investing directly, investors can choose the bank's investment account. This is similar to owning shares of a mutual fund.

Choose advisors that you can trust to help you make the right choices. Be sure that they have proper licenses, bonds, and certifications. Ask how long they have been working for the bank or investment company. Also ask if they are members of the NASD (National Association of Securities Dealers). The NASD Web site provides a Broker Check feature. This feature allows you to learn about the background and license status of firms and brokers. Many state governments also provide similar data. Ask how your confidential and personal data will be protected by the broker or company. Deal only with advisors and companies that you think are properly licensed and qualified and have your interests in mind.

Building Communications Skills

PERSUASIVE MESSAGES

The goal of a persuasive message is to convince the reader to take (or not take) some action. For example, you may want the reader to buy a product or donate money to a charity.

It is tempting to write a very long message to persuade someone to do as you think they should. However, long messages are often discarded without being read. People may not read a long and detailed message unless they have asked for it. Thus, the message must be concise as well as clear and convincing.

You must gain the reader's attention and give solid reasons for the person to take action. The reader may have an opinion or bias that you must overcome. Your arguments must be logical and appealing. In the first paragraph, give one good reason why the reader should keep reading. In the middle paragraph(s), explain your position and give evidence to support it. In the final paragraph, give the reader a reason to take action or accept your position. Use a positive tone throughout the message.

12-1 Activity 1   Can You Recall?

Answer these questions to help you recall what you have read.
If you cannot answer a question, read the related section again.

1. Describe the types of financial information found in print items such as magazines, newspapers, and newsletters.
2. List three magazines that give information and advice about spending and investing.
3. List two newspapers that provide information helpful to investors.
4. Explain why an investor might be willing to pay for a subscription to an investor newsletter.
5. Describe the type of information available in a company annual report.
6. Give two examples of Internet search engines you could use to find information about companies or investments.
7. Explain ways you can find investing information on the Internet.
8. List several figures that can be used to compare the performance or value of companies.
9. How do investment professionals, such as stockbrokers or financial planners, help investors?
10. What steps can you take to be sure a stockbroker is qualified to give investing advice or make purchases for an investor?

12-1 Activity 2   Research Companies

 academic.cengage.com/school/pfl

1. Choose three large corporations to research. Choose companies from the list below or others approved by your teacher.

Company	Trading Symbol	Company	Trading Symbol
Allstate Corp.	ALL	Johnson & Johnson	JNJ
Boeing Co.	BA	Kroger Co.	KR
Chevron Corp.	CVX	Mattel Inc.	MAT
Dow Chemical	DOW	Merrill Lynch	MER
Humana Inc.	HUM	Tyson Foods	TSN

353

2. Access the Internet. Use a search engine to find the Web site for each company you chose, or find data about the company on sites such as Yahoo! Finance. A link to this site is provided on the Web site for this textbook. For each company, find the following information:
   - Industry sector or primary business
   - Current stock price
   - Revenue for last year
   - Net income for last year
   - Profit margin for last year
   - P/E ratio for last year
   - Current ratio for last year

3. Create a table that compares the three companies. Use the table that follows as an example. Enter the data you found in columns 2, 3, and 4.

Company name			
Industry or primary business			
Current stock price			
Revenue			
Net income			
Profit margin			
P/E ratio			
Current ratio			

4. Which company had the highest revenue?
5. Which company had the highest net income?
6. Which company had the highest P/E ratio?
7. Did each company have a current ratio of 1 or above? If not, which ones did not?
8. Have you heard or read any current news reports about this company or its industry? If so, what were the main points of the reports?
9. Would you consider one or more of these companies a good investment? Why or why not?

Buying and Selling Securities

OUTCOMES

- Explain the difference between the primary market and the secondary market for securities.
- Compare buying stock on a securities exchange to buying in the over-the-counter market.
- Describe the steps in a buy transaction on a stock exchange.
- List advantages of direct investing.
- Compare a full-service stockbroker to a discount broker and an online broker.
- Discuss types of stock market orders.
- Explain the purpose of market timing strategies.

TRADING SECURITIES

Securities are stocks, bonds, and other financial investments. When securities are bought or sold, they are said to be traded. Investors can trade directly or use the services of a broker. Investors can trust a professional to manage the investments, or they can be involved in all the decisions.

Primary Market

The **primary market** is one in which new issues of securities are sold. Proceeds of sales go to the issuer of the securities sold. New security issues (stocks and bonds) are issued through investment banks. An investment bank is a company that helps corporations raise money by selling stocks and bonds. A fee is charged for this service. The process takes many months to complete. New security offers are often in the form of initial public offerings. An **initial public offering** (IPO) is a company's first sale of its stock to the public. IPOs are often made by small or young companies seeking to expand their business. They can do this with the money raised by selling stock. In 1999, in one of the largest IPOs in Wall Street history, UPS (United Parcel Service) raised $5.27 billion in its IPO.[1]

---

[1] UPS, "UPS Launches Class A-1 Tender Offer," February 4, 2000, http://www.pressroom.ups.com/pressreleases/archives/archive/0,1363,3544,00.html (accessed August 28, 2006).

UPS raised more than $5 billon in its IPO.

Secondary Market

The **secondary market** is one in which securities are bought from current investors. A buyer is trading with someone who already owns the stock. After stock is sold in the primary market, it can be resold many times in the secondary market. Many securities are listed on securities exchanges. Some can also be found in the over-the counter market.

SECURITIES EXCHANGES

A **securities exchange** is a place where brokers buy and sell securities for their clients. Securities listed on the exchange have been accepted for trading at that exchange. The New York Stock Exchange (NYSE) is one of the largest security exchanges in the world. It lists more than 3,000 stocks. The exchange has 1,366 stockbroker members. These members can buy and sell securities. The American Stock Exchange (AMEX) and various regional stock exchanges are smaller. They have less strict requirements for companies to be listed than does the NYSE. Securities exchanges are auction markets. An **auction market** is one in which a stock is sold to the highest bidder. Both buyers and sellers compete with others for the best price. The steps in a transaction to buy stock are shown in Figure 12-2.1 on page 357.

THE OVER-THE-COUNTER MARKET

The **over-the-counter market** is a network of dealers who buy and sell stocks and other securities. These stocks are not listed with a securities exchange. Stocks issued by several thousand companies are traded this way. NASDAQ is an electronic marketplace for over-the-counter stocks. This computerized system allows investors to buy and sell stocks through their brokers. More than 5,000 stocks are listed on NASDAQ. When stock is traded, offers to buy are matched with offers to sell.

356

STEPS IN A STOCK BUY TRANSACTION

The following are steps an investor would take to buy stock traded on the New York Stock Exchange:

1. The investor calls or e-mails the broker and asks him or her to buy shares of stock.
2. The broker relays the order electronically to a representative at the stock exchange.
3. A clerk for the broker at the exchange receives the message and gives it to a floor broker.
4. The floor broker goes to the trading post at which this stock is traded.
5. The floor broker negotiates a buy from the floor broker of the stock being sold.
6. After the trade is made, the floor broker relays a message to the clerk and to the consolidated ticker tape.
7. The sale appears on the ticker tape.
8. A confirmation is sent to the investor's broker.
9. The broker notifies the investor that the transaction is complete.
10. The investor's account reflects money exchanged for stock at the price and quantity agreed upon.

DIRECT INVESTING

Many companies have direct investing plans. Direct investing allows you to buy stock directly from a corporation. You do not use a brokerage company. Direct investing allows you to reinvest dividends as well. With this option, cash dividends are used to buy more shares of stock. People who do direct investing can use a spreadsheet to keep track of their investments, as shown in Figure 12-2.2 on page 358.

Direct investing can be risky. When you buy stock in only one company, you have not diversified. However, you could use direct investing to buy stocks in several companies. Buying U.S. government savings bonds is also a form of direct investing. This type of investment is low-risk.

Direct investing offers many advantages. One advantage is avoiding taxes. When cash dividends are converted to new shares of stock, they are not taxed. Investors can acquire many shares this way. Interest on U.S. savings bonds is not taxable until the bond is cashed. If the bond is used for education expenses, then the interest may not be subject to federal taxes when cashed.

With direct investing, there are no brokerage fees to pay. This advantage makes direct investing attractive to some investors. Another advantage is that you know which securities you have at all times. When you buy direct, you make the decisions about the items to buy and sell and the timing of the transactions.

Sometimes corporations issue a stock dividend instead of a cash dividend. A **stock dividend** is a dividend paid in the form of new shares of stock instead of cash. Stockholders have more shares of stock for future growth. A **stock split** occurs when a company issues more stock to current stockholders in some proportion. For example a two-for-one split means that for every share you own, you get an additional share of stock. Stock dividends and stock splits involve no brokerage fees or costs to investors, and they are not taxable income.

357

FIGURE 12-2.2

People who do direct investing should keep track of the performance of their investments.

	A	B	C	D	E	F	G
1				STOCK RECORD			
2							
3	Stock A						
4	Purchase Date	No. of Shares	Price Paid per Share	Sold Date	No. of Shares	Price Received per Share	ROI
5	12/2/20--	500	$55.25				
6	3/30/20--	100	$58.45	12/28/20--	100	$68.00	21.9%
7							
8							
9	Date	Closing Price		Average Price Paid		$55.78	
10	1/3/20--	$55.00					
11	2/1/20--	$57.25					
12	3/1/20--	$58.95					
13	4/1/20--	$52.50					
14	5/1/20--	$53.78					
15	6/1/20--	$57.50					
16	7/1/20--	$59.32					
17	8/1/20--	$59.25					
18	9/1/20--	$60.35					
19	10/1/20--	$65.50					
20	11/1/20--	$70.65					
21	12/1/20--	$68.50					
22							
23	Average Price	$59.88					
24	Highest Price	$70.65					
25	Lowest Price	$52.50					
26							
27							

At some companies, employees can buy stock in the company. Some companies give shares of stock to employees as part of a benefits package. There are no brokerage fees or other costs for the employee in these transactions.

BROKER SERVICES

When you use the services of a stock agent or broker, you pay this person to buy or sell securities on your behalf. From some brokers, you also get advice about what and when to buy and sell. Although these services cost money, they can help you invest wisely.

Full-Service Brokers

If you buy securities through a full-service stockbroker, you will receive advice about what to buy. A stockbroker is a licensed professional who buys and sells securities for her or his clients. Stocks, bonds, mutual funds, and commodity futures contracts are examples of securities traded through stockbrokers. The broker will consider your investment goals. He or she will try to help you achieve those goals through your investment choices. You will be charged a commission or fee for the services provided. You will receive regular reports of activity and account balances.

The stockbroker will consider the information you provide. You should clearly state your financial goals. Be honest about your tolerance for risk. Be realistic in what you expect for returns on the money you invest. This information, along with her or his knowledge about the market and securities, will be used to select stocks or other investments for you. The broker will recommend securities to buy and sell and the timing of those trades. Merrill Lynch and A.G. Edwards are examples of full-service brokerage firms.

Ethics

CHURNING

Brokers earn fees for buying and selling securities for clients. Some may charge as much as $75 for a single trade. The more trades they make, the more money they earn. When a broker is constantly buying and selling stocks, the client may or may not be making profits. Trading securities primarily to make money from sales commissions is called churning.

Churning is illegal under rules of the Securities and Exchange Commission (SEC). However, it can be hard to prove. Brokers are not liable for losses when they buy and sell for their clients. Investors sign a waiver that states brokers are not responsible for losses in stock trades.

Securities trading should be done with the intent to benefit clients. Trading for the purpose of generating fees for the broker is unethical. How will you know if this is happening? It may be hard for the average investor to know that he or she is being taken advantage of. If you think you have been a victim of churning, you can report the problem to the SEC using an online form. Visit the SEC Web site, shown in Figure 12-2.3, to learn more.

FIGURE 12-2.3

Churning can be reported online at the SEC Web site.

Address http://www.sec.gov/answers/churning.htm   Go

Home | Previous Page

U.S. Securities and Exchange Commission

Churning

Churning refers to excessive buying and selling in your account by your broker. For churning to occur, your broker must exercise control over the investment decisions in your account, either through a formal written discretionary agreement or otherwise, and must engage in excessive trading in light of the financial resources and character of the account for the purpose of generating commissions.

The major securities industry self-regulatory organizations have rules prohibiting churning. You'll find the NASD's churning rule – Rule 2310-2(b)(2) – in the "NASD Manual." To request a copy of the New York Stock Exchange's churning rule – Rule 408(c) – please call the NYSE at (212) 656-2744.

If you believe your broker has churned your account or engaged in another sales practice abuse, please send us your complaint using our online complaint form.

Source: U.S. Securities and Exchange Commission, Churning, http://www.sec.gov/answers/churning.htm (accessed August 28, 2006).

359

Discount Brokers

A **discount broker** works for a firm that buys or sells securities on behalf of investors. The term *discount broker* is also used to refer to the brokerage firm. The fees or commissions charged by a discount broker are much lower than those charged by a full-service broker. The firm may charge a flat fee for its services of buying and selling. An amount such as $12.95 per transaction is a typical fee. Discount brokers offer limited services. They do not give advice or help manage assets. However, some firms do offer free research reports. A discount broker has the same qualifications as a full-service broker. Fidelity Investments is an example of a discount brokerage company.

Online Brokers

Many brokerage firms offer their services online. Online brokers charge low fees. They also give the least amount of service. They do not provide investment advice or manage assets. Some firms do offer free research reports. You must make your own decisions about buying and selling. Once you decide, you set up an account with an online broker. Different types of accounts are available. Investors can make single trades. Some sites also offer automatic investment plans that help users invest on a regular basis. Sharebuilder and TD Ameritrade are examples of online brokerage services.

Commissions and Fees

Stockbrokers make money when stocks are bought and sold for clients. Some brokerage firms have minimum commissions of $25 to $60. Additional fees may be charged based on the number of shares and on the value of the stock being traded. On the trading floor of a stock exchange, stocks are traded in round lots or odd lots. A **round lot** is 100 shares or multiples of 100 shares of stock. An **odd lot** is fewer than 100 shares. When you buy less than a round lot, there is an additional fee.

Discount brokers usually charge a flat fee, such as $8.95 per transaction. However, for odd lots or small amounts, they often have higher fees. For example, when the trade amount is less than $1,000, the transaction fee may be higher.

STOCK TRANSACTIONS

Once you have decided to buy or sell a stock, there are four types of transactions, called orders, that you can request.

- A **market order** is a request to buy (or sell) a stock at the current market value. In an auction market, the broker will try to get you the best price as soon as possible. There is no guarantee of what you will pay or receive. The stock will be auctioned to the highest bidder, and you may or may not buy or sell the stock at the price you hoped to get.
- A **limit order** is a request to buy (or sell) a stock at a specific price. When you are buying, a limit order ensures that you will not pay more than a set dollar amount. When you are selling, the order

360

There is a healthy competition between full-service brokers and other types of brokers. A smaller fee for services is one reason people choose discount or online brokers. There are other factors to consider as well. One factor is the amount of information available and how much it costs. If you have to pay extra to get the information you need to make good choices, then discount brokers may not save you money in the long run.

Another factor to think about is the amount of help you will need to make wise investment choices. If you do not have the time or expertise to study the market, you may find that your choices are not very profitable. You may be better off paying higher fees for sound investment advice from a full-service broker.

Investors should also look at how easy it is to buy and sell. Investors must compare services in terms of the type of trading they want to do. For example, do you want to trade online or by phone? Where is the nearest office? How often do investors receive statements? What is the charge for services such as research? What are all the fees that will be charged for having an account? Are there minimum deposits? Consider all these factors carefully to help decide which type of broker is right for you.

ensures that you will not get less than a specific dollar amount if the stock is sold.

○ A **stop order** is a request to sell at the next available time after the price reaches a certain amount. This type of order protects an investor from a sudden drop in price.

○ A **discretionary order** is an order to buy (or sell) a stock that lets the broker get the best possible price. The broker also determines the best time to buy. This type of order may involve a range of shares, such as buying odd numbers of shares if they are available. Discretionary orders give the broker the power to use her or his experience and judgment to make good decisions.

MARKET TIMING

A market timing plan is a strategy used to increase profits and reduce costs. There are several timing plans you can use, regardless of the type of securities you buy and sell.

Selling short is selling stock that has been "borrowed" from a brokerage firm and must be replaced at a later date. You are hoping to make a sell agreement today for more money than you will have to pay for the stock at a later time. This is a lawful thing to do (if the brokerage firm allows it), but it is highly risky. You are hoping that prices will drop. If prices for the stock do not drop, you will lose money.

361

Buying on margin is a transaction in which you borrow part of the money to buy stock. The cash you use to pay for the rest of the purchase is called the margin. The margin amount is set by the Fed. This is a form of leverage, or borrowing money to make a profit on a stock transaction. You may make less than if you paid for the stock yourself. However, you can buy more stocks with less money and thus possibly make more profits.

In some cases, the value of the stock purchased may drop by an amount equal to the margin. When that happens, the investor may be given a margin call. The investor must immediately provide more money or sell the stock in order not to default on the loan. Buying on margin is a risky strategy. Figure 12.2-4 illustrates buying on margin.

Buy and hold is a long-term plan in which investors make money in three ways. First, they will receive dividends over the years. Second, the price of the stock will go up (giving them long-term capital gains). Third, the stock may split. When a stock splits, they gain additional shares of stock. They do not have to pay commissions on the stock gained, and there is no tax to be paid on the added shares.

Regardless of your investment plan, you will find market timing important. You want to sell at prices that are higher than the amount you pay for investments. Understanding the economy and its signals can help you do this. You will not always earn profits, but with careful timing, you may be able to gain more than you lose.

FIGURE 12-2.4

Buying on margin involves borrowing part of the money to buy stocks.

BUYING ON MARGIN EXAMPLE

1. Marijen invests $5,000 and borrows $5,000 from a brokerage firm. She buys 500 shares at $20 per share ($10,000 purchase price). She uses the stock certificates as security for the loan (as required by the Fed) at 5% annual interest.

2. Six months later, the stock has increased in value to $30 per share. Marijen sells the stock for $15,000 (500 × $30 = $15,000). She pays commissions and fees of $150.

3. From her net proceeds of $14,850, Marijen repays the $5,000 loan plus $125 interest ($14,850 − $5,125 = $9,725). When she subtracts the $5,000 she originally invested, Marijen has made $4,725 net profit.

Note: There is no guarantee that the stock price will rise. If the stock price drops, Marijen has to pay interest on the loan and wait to sell the stock. If she sells when the price has dropped, she will lose money (principal).

A *blog* (a shortened form of *Weblog*) is an online place where you can find short articles or comments on a particular subject area. Blogs usually include text messages. However, some blogs contain photos, videos, or sound. Blogs may read like a journal, and they are often shown with the most recent entry first. A blog may be posted by one individual. Some blogs are posted by companies or organizations. Several people may write the postings in a blog. Access to many blogs is free. Some blogs charge a fee for access.

Many blogs that deal with investing are available. Fidelity Investments' Amazon blog is one example. It contains articles related to many areas of investing. Retirement pensions, the market for gold, and increasing your investment knowledge are examples of the topics covered.

Seeking Alpha™ is a network of blogs with articles posted by people such as portfolio managers, research analysts, and financial advisors.

Investors may find the articles and comments posted on blogs helpful when making investment decisions. They should be careful, however, about accepting the information posted on all blogs. Some blogs give comments on the investing strategy and ideas of one person. This person may or may not be qualified to give investing advice. Consider the source of the posting when deciding on its value. Is the article written by a person trained to give investing advice? Are sources listed so facts can be checked? Does the advice make sense when you think about other articles you have read? Answering these questions can help you tell the value of a blog posting.

363

12-2 Activity 1 Can You Recall?

Answer these questions to help you recall what you have read. If you cannot answer a question, read the related section again.

1. What is the difference between the primary market and the secondary market for securities?
2. What is an IPO? What is its purpose?
3. How does buying stock on a securities exchange differ from buying in the over-the-counter market?
4. List the steps in a buy transaction on a stock exchange.
5. List three advantages of direct investing.
6. What services do investors receive from a full-service broker?
7. What is an advantage of using a discount broker or an online broker rather than a full-service broker? What is a disadvantage?
8. What is a round lot in a stock order? What is an odd lot in a stock order?
9. Describe four types of stock market orders.
10. Explain the purpose of a market timing plan, and list three market timing plans.

12-2 Activity 2 Track Stock Performance

When investors use a full-service broker to buy stocks, they receive regular reports about the stocks. Investors who use direct investing or a discount broker should track their stocks regularly. In this activity, you will record stock purchases and related data in an *Excel* spreadsheet.

1. Open the *Excel* file *CH12 Stocks* from the data files. This file contains information about a stock purchased earlier. (A real stock name has not been used in this activity as it would be when you track stock you actually own.)
2. You purchased Stock A on December 2 last year. You have recorded the closing price for the stock at the beginning of the month for 6 months. Record the following closing prices in the worksheet:

Date	Closing Price
7/1/20--	$ 71.86
8/1/20--	$80.92
9/1/20--	$83.91
10/1/20--	$85.45
11/1/20--	$88.50
12/1/20--	$85.00

3. Enter a formula in cell B24 to find the average price of the stock for the prices recorded.

4. Enter a formula in cell B25 to find the highest price of the stock for the prices recorded.

5. Enter a formula in cell B26 to find the lowest price of the stock for the prices recorded.

6. On March 30 of the current year, you bought another 100 shares of Stock A at $69.00 per share. Record this data in the worksheet. (You can use the real current year instead of 20--.)

7. On December 28, you sold 100 shares of the stock at $86.00 per share. Enter this data in the worksheet.

8. Enter a formula in cell F9 to find the average price per share for the stocks you purchased. (Multiply the price by the number of shares for each purchase. Add the two amounts. Divide by the total number of shares purchased.)

9. Enter a formula in cell G6 to find the return on investment for the 100 shares you sold. You use a discount broker with very low fees, so you will not include the trade fees in the ROI calculation. Use the average price per share for the stocks you purchased in the ROI formula. (Reminder: ROI = total amount received − total amount paid/ total amount paid)

10. Create a line chart to show the closing price for Stock A for each of the 12 prices recorded. Use **STOCK A PRICES** for the chart title. Do not include a legend. Save the chart on a separate sheet in the workbook. Format the scale and other features for an attractive chart.

11. When could you have sold to receive a higher price than you received for the 100 shares you sold?

12. When would have been the best time (lowest price) to buy more of this stock between May 1 and September 1?

Regulatory Agencies

OUTCOMES

- Describe independent agencies that regulate and supervise the securities industry.
- Describe government agencies that regulate and supervise the financial industry.
- Explain the purpose of the Sarbanes-Oxley Act.

INDEPENDENT AGENCIES

Banks, brokerage companies, and other financial businesses are limited and controlled by a number of agencies. These agencies make or enforce rules and regulations. They act to protect consumers in many ways.

Federal Deposit Insurance Corporation

The Federal Deposit Insurance Corporation (FDIC) is an independent agency created by Congress in 1933. Its purpose is to promote public confidence in the banking system. It also supervises banks and other financial institutions to maintain a stable and sound banking system. The FDIC monitors advising, investment accounts, and practices at banks. These activities assure consumers that lawful and ethical practices are being used.

The FDIC insures deposits in banks and other financial institutions, such as savings and loan companies. Checking accounts, savings accounts, and other deposits, up to $100,000 per depositor per bank, are covered. Generally, separate coverage is provided for retirement accounts. This means that accounts such as an IRA held in an insured bank may be covered for up to $250,000. The FDIC provides an Electronic Deposit Insurance Calculator for consumer use. This calculator, described in Figure 12-3.1 on page 367, allows you to find the insurance coverage of your accounts at each FDIC-insured bank.

The FDIC also provides other consumer resources. At the FDIC Web site, you can find information about many topics related to investing. Other topics of interest to consumers are also discussed. For example, your right to financial privacy and how to avoid being a victim of identify theft are discussed.

National Credit Union Administration

The National Credit Union Administration (NCUA) is a federal agency that charters and supervises federal credit unions. It also supervises state-chartered credit unions across the country. The NCUA insures savings

FDIC

Calculator

Electronic Deposit Insurance Estimator (EDIE) > Calculator

Using the Calculator

Enter information about all your Personal Accounts and/or Business Accounts for a single FDIC-Insured Institution in the sections below. To obtain accurate results, your entries must reflect the information contained in the deposit account records of your institution. If you need further description on the purpose of this page, click on **Page Help** at the bottom of the page.

Please enter your FDIC-Insured Institution's name: [   ]

Personal Accounts (including Sole Proprietorships)

After you have entered the name of your financial institution above, enter your Account Name and Balance in the boxes below. Then answer the question whether the account is a Living Trust, In-Trust-For or Payable-on-Death account by selecting yes or no. Next answer the question whether this is an IRA/Keogh account by selecting yes or no.

Source: Federal Deposit Insurance Corporation, Electronic Deposit Insurance Estimator (EDIE), http://www2.fdic.gov/edie/ (accessed August 30, 2006).

FIGURE 12-3.1

The FDIC provides a calculator to help depositors find their insurance coverage for accounts.

deposits in federal credit unions and other member credit unions. Most share accounts in federally insured credit unions are insured for up to $100,000. Retirement account insurance protection is separate from coverage on other credit union accounts. Retirement accounts, such as an IRA, at insured credit unions are covered for up to $250,000.

The NCUA provides resources for its credit union members. It also provides resources for consumers, including workshops and financial advising. The NCUA Share Insurance Estimator is available on the NCUA Web site. It is an educational resource that gives a detailed explanation of insurance coverage.

National Association of Securities Dealers

The National Association of Securities Dealers (NASD) is a private, nonprofit organization. It is responsible for self-regulation of the securities industry. The NASD monitors trading on the NASDAQ stock market and other selected markets. Almost all securities firms that do business with the U.S. public are members of the NASD. It registers member firms and has rules to govern their behavior. It also checks to see that firms follow the rules. Firms breaking the rules may be charged high fines.

Protecting investors is a primary goal of the NASD. The NASD looks at advertising related to securities. Its goal is to see that ads are accurate and do not mislead the public. The NASD also licenses stockbrokers. Investors can find information about licensed brokers on the NASD Web site. The NASD provides materials in print and on its Web site to educate the public about investing. Its Investor Alerts give current news about investment scams and problems.

© Digital Vision

NASD sponsors continuing education programs for stockbrokers.

367

Pension Benefit Guaranty Corporation

The Pension Benefit Guaranty Corporation (PBGC) is a federal corporation. Its mission is to protect retirement incomes of workers with defined benefit pension plans. These plans are designed to pay a monthly benefit to retired workers. The amount is commonly based on the person's former salary and years spent on the job.

The PBGC collects insurance payments from companies that offer pension plans to their workers. It also earns money from investments. When a covered pension plan ends or fails for some reason, the PBGC pays some benefits to the retired workers. However, retirees may not get some benefits promised by the company. For example, health care benefits may not be covered. The maximum benefit is set by law. It depends, in part, on the year in which your plan ended. Your age at the date you begin receiving benefits is also a factor. Monthly maximum benefits tables are provided on the PBGC Web site. A link to the PBGC Web site is provided on the Web site for this textbook.

The PBGC Web site provides news releases related to pension plans, as shown in Figure 12-3.2 on page 369. It also offers helpful information about topics such as the following:

- How to learn if your pension plan is insured by PBGC
- How a pension plan may end
- Benefits likely to be provided to workers in the plan
- Survivor benefits
- How to start collecting pension benefits

Success Skills

LEADERSHIP

Leadership is often defined as the ability to influence others. Leaders are those who accept responsibility and take the lead. They are often known by their roles, such as coach, manager, or mentor. Every leader has a unique leadership style. This style reflects the leader's actions and ways of communicating to motivate people and achieve goals.

Creating plans and motivating others to get work done are important tasks for a leader. Leaders are able to inspire others. A leader does not do all the work but is able to achieve goals by managing a team. A good leader builds strategic alliances—friendships with the right people who help get things done.

Leaders often have to deal with people in difficult situations and overcome obstacles to achieving goals. Leaders face many challenges, but they do not give up. They learn and grow. They earn the respect of others, who willingly follow.

Developing leadership skills can help you be successful at school and at work. At school, you can use leadership skills in clubs, sports, and other teams. At work, leadership skills can be important even if you are not in a management position. You may need to lead a committee, work group, or project team. Success at work contributes to job security and promotions. These, in turn, can help you build financial security.

368

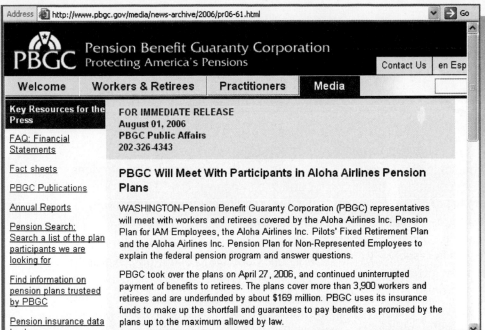

FIGURE 12-3.2

The PBGC uses insurance funds to pay pension benefits.

Source: Pension Benefit Guaranty Corporation, "PBGC Will Meet With Participants in Aloha Airlines Pension Plans," August 1, 2006, http://www.pbgc.gov/media/news-archive/2006/pr06-61.html (accessed September 1, 2006).

GOVERNMENT AGENCIES

The U.S. government has agencies that seek to protect consumers. One role of these agencies is **oversight**. Through oversight, or supervision, they help protect investors from unlawful actions. States also have agencies that help protect investors.

Securities and Exchange Commission

The Securities and Exchange Commission (SEC) is the primary overseer and regulator of the U.S. securities markets. It oversees securities exchanges, brokers and dealers, investment advisors, and mutual funds. The SEC works with other federal and state agencies and with private organizations.

The SEC tries to maintain fair and orderly markets and foster business growth. It also enforces securities laws. Typical law violations include insider trading, accounting fraud, and giving false information about companies or securities.

A primary goal of the SEC is to protect investors. The SEC requires public companies to give meaningful and accurate data to the public. This data includes financial reports. Having the data helps investors make informed decisions.

Department of the Treasury

The U.S. Department of the Treasury is the primary federal agency responsible for the economic security of the United States. It has a wide range of duties related to financial issues. It seeks to help citizens by fostering an economy with growth and job opportunities.

369

12-3   Regulatory Agencies

The Sarbanes-Oxley Act of 2002 (SOX) was passed in July 2002. The act is also known as the Public Company Accounting Reform and Investor Protection Act of 2002. This law created new and stronger standards for U.S. public companies and for accounting firms. The law was created in response to scandals in large companies. These scandals involved fraud or misconduct by company officers. They resulted in losses for investors and company employees.

SOX requires improved financial reporting, audits, and accounting services for public companies. The SEC has adopted rules that require companies to comply with the law.

The law established a new agency, the Public Company Accounting Oversight Board. The agency's purpose is to oversee and regulate accounting firms in their roles as auditors of public companies.

Information about many saving and investing topics is available online at the Department's Web site. The Department of the Treasury is a member agency of the U.S. Financial Literacy and Education Commission. The commission provides a Web site called MyMoney.gov. The site allows consumers to order a free *My Money* tool kit. The site also provides

FIGURE 12-3.3

The MyMoney.gov Web site offers valuable information for consumers.

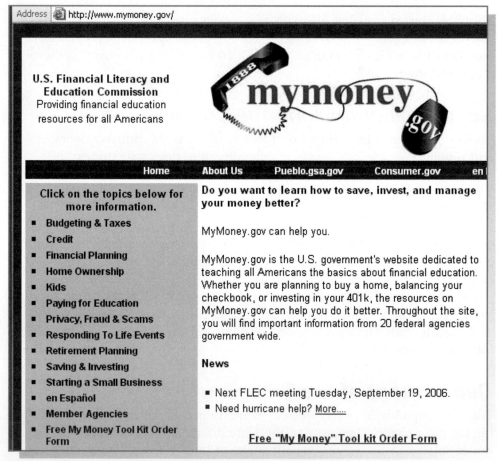

Source: MyMoney.gov, http://www.mymoney.gov/ (accessed September 2, 2006).

370

consumers with information about topics such as saving and investing, privacy, retirement planning, and starting a business. A link to the Web site is provided on the Web site for this textbook.

Internal Revenue Service

The Internal Revenue Service (IRS) is a bureau of the U.S. Department of the Treasury. Its role is to help taxpayers understand and meet their tax responsibilities. It also seeks to ensure that those who owe taxes pay them.

In Chapter 2, you learned about paying taxes and completing simple IRS tax forms. When you own, buy, or sell securities, you may need to report this activity as part of your tax return. Figure 12-3.4 shows a portion of Form 1040A. This form has several lines on which taxpayers report interest, dividends, and capital gains.

Form 1040EZ is the simplest tax form to complete. Form 1040A allows more options for income and deductions to be entered. Some sections require the filer to attach additional forms, often called schedules. For example, Form 1099-INT shows interest income earned during the year. This form is sent to individuals by the bank that pays the interest. Taxable interest must be reported on your tax return. If a taxpayer sells stocks or bonds during the tax year, that activity must be reported on Schedule D of Form 1040.

Taxpayers should read the tax form instructions carefully to be sure all investing activity is properly reported. Taxpayers who have many investments and several transactions during the year may want to hire a trained tax preparer to complete the forms.

The Federal Reserve

The Federal Reserve System is the central bank of the United States. Its purpose is to provide the nation with a safe and flexible financial system. Its activities are in four general areas as follows:

- Conducting monetary policy
- Providing financial services to the U.S. government, financial institutions, and the public
- Supervising and regulating banking
- Keeping the country's financial systems and markets stable

The Federal Reserve is covered in more detail in Chapter 5, Banking Procedures.

FIGURE 12-3.4

Data related to investments must be reported on tax forms.

Income		
Attach Form(s) W-2 here. Also attach Form(s) 1099-R if tax was withheld.	**7** Wages, salaries, tips, etc. Attach Form(s) W-2.	**7**
	8a **Taxable** interest. Attach Schedule 1 if required.	**8a**
	b **Tax-exempt** interest. **Do not** include on line 8a. **8b**	
	9a Ordinary dividends. Attach Schedule 1 if required.	**9a**
	b Qualified dividends (see page 25). **9b**	
	10 Capital gain distributions (see page 25).	**10**
If you did not get a W-2, see page 24.	**11a** IRA distributions. **11a**	**11b** Taxable amount (see page 25). **11b**
Enclose, but do not attach, any payment.	**12a** Pensions and annuities. **12a**	**12b** Taxable amount (see page 26). **12b**
	13 Unemployment compensation and Alaska Permanent Fund dividends.	**13**
	14a Social security benefits. **14a**	**14b** Taxable amount (see page 28). **14b**
	15 Add lines 7 through 14b (far right column). This is your **total income.** ▶	**15**

Source: Internal Revenue Service, 2005 Form 1040A, http://www.irs.gov/pub/irs-pdf/f1040a.pdf (accessed September 2, 2006).

12-3 Activity 1   Can You Recall?

Answer these questions to help you recall what you have read. If you cannot answer a question, read the related section again.

1. What is purpose of the FDIC? How does it benefit consumers?
2. What is the NCUA? What does it do?
3. What is the NASD? What does it do?
4. What organization is responsible for protecting the retirement incomes of workers with defined benefit pension plans?
5. What is meant by government oversight of the securities industry?
6. What does the SEC do to protect investors?
7. What prompted passage of the Sarbanes-Oxley Act of 2002? How does this law help protect consumers and investors?
8. What is the primary federal agency responsible for the economic security of the United States? How does it help citizens?
9. What organization provides the MyMoney.gov Web site? What types of information are available on the site?
10. How does the IRS help consumers? What tax form is used to report details of stock trades?

12-3 Activity 2   Tax Reporting for Investments

 Investors who sell stocks and bonds (except for retirement investment accounts) will need to fill out tax Form 1040. They will also need to complete Schedule D to find the amount of capital gain or loss on sales. If you buy and sell stocks using a broker, the broker should supply the information needed to prepare Schedule D.

1. Open the PDF file *CH12 Schedule D* from the data files. Print the form. This form is Schedule D, which is used to report investment activity for Form 1040.
2. Write your name and Social Security number on the first line of the form. If you do not have a Social Security number or want to keep your number private, use 000-22-1111 as the number.
3. You had the investment activity shown in the following table. Part I of the form is used to report the sale of assets held for 1 year or less. The *Sales Price* is the amount you received less any trading fees. The *Cost or Other Basis* is the amount you paid for the stock plus

trading fees. Enter the data in Part I, line 1, of the form. (If you were actually completing a tax return, you would use real stock names instead of Stock A, Stock B, etc.)

Description of Property	Date Acquired	Date Sold	Sales Price	Cost or Other Basis
Stock A, 100 shares	4/1/2005	9/30/2005	$ 1,050.00	$ 900.00
Stock B, 300 shares	3/20/2005	11/3/2005	$3,000.00	$2,500.00

4. Calculate the amount of gain or loss for each stock. Enter the amount in Part I, column F, of the form.

5. Total the short-term sales price amounts. Enter the amount on line 3.

6. Leave lines 4, 5, and 6 blank. Find the total of Part I, column F, and enter the amount on line 7, column F.

7. Part II of the form is used to report activity for assets held more than 1 year. Enter the following data in Part II on line 8:

Description of Property	Date Acquired	Date Sold	Sales Price	Cost or Other Basis
Stock C, 200 shares	5/15/2002	8/30/2005	$3,000.00	$2,400.00
Stock D, 100 shares	6/20/2004	7/31/2005	$ 900.00	$ 1,000.00

8. Find the total of the sales prices in column D. Enter this amount on line 10.

9. Calculate the amount of gain or loss for each stock. Enter the amount in Part II, column F. Enter an amount that is a loss in parentheses.

10. Leave lines 11, 12, 13, and 14 blank. Calculate the total amount of gain or loss from the amounts in Part II, column F. Enter this amount on line 15.

11. Total the amounts from lines 7 and 15. Enter the amount on line 16.

12. On line 17, check the *Yes* box. Leave lines 18 and 19 blank.

13. On line 20, check the *Yes* box.

14. Leave lines 21 and 22 blank. You have now completed Schedule D. Information from this form would be used to complete Form 1040.

EXPLORING CAREERS IN AGRICULTURE, FOOD, AND NATURAL RESOURCES

Do you like to work outdoors? Are you good at making plants grow? Is caring for animals something you like to do? If the answer is yes, a career in agriculture, food, and natural resources might be right for you. Jobs in this area are varied. You might choose to be a farm or ranch worker, growing crops or caring for livestock. You might choose to be a farm owner or manager, directing the work of others. You might also work in one of the many areas related to processing or marketing food or natural resources.

Jobs in this career area are found in government and businesses. The need for jobs in the agriculture, food, and natural resources career area is expected to grow. Job outlook varies by job.

Skills Needed

Some of the skills and traits needed for a career in agriculture, food, and natural resources include the following:

- Math and science skills
- Communications skills
- Computer/technology skills
- Management skills
- Decision-making skills
- Problem-solving skills

Job Titles

Many jobs are available in the agriculture, food, and natural resources field. Some job titles for this career area include the following:

- Botanist
- Farm supply store manager
- Farmer or rancher
- Forest worker or logger
- Greenhouse manager
- Mining engineer or technician
- Produce buyer
- Veterinarian
- Water quality manager

Explore a Job

1. Choose a job in the agriculture, food, and natural resources field to explore further. Select a job from the list above, or choose another job in this career area.
2. Access the *Occupational Outlook Handbook* online. A link to the site is provided on the Web site for this textbook.
3. Search for more information about the job you selected to answer these questions:
   - What is the nature of the work this job involves?
   - What is the job outlook for this job?
   - What training or qualifications are needed for this job?
   - What are the median annual earnings for this job?

Summary

- Investors should do thorough research before buying stocks, bonds, or other investments.
- Investors can find helpful information in magazines, newspapers, and newsletters related to investing.
- Corporate annual reports are free, and many are available online. They provide information about the company that can be helpful to investors.
- Investors can find information about companies, products, and market trends on the Internet.
- Investors can use key figures, such as revenue, net income, and P/E ratios, to compare companies.
- Professionals, such as stockbrokers, financial planners, and investment advisors, can help investors choose securities to buy or sell.
- When buying stocks in the primary market, investors buy directly from the issuer. When buying stocks in the secondary market, investors buy from another investor who owns the stock.
- Securities exchanges are auction markets, where stocks are sold to the highest bidder.
- The over-the-counter market is a network of dealers who sell stocks not listed on an exchange.
- Direct investing is buying stock directly from a corporation or bonds directly from the issuer. Direct investing allows investors to avoid transaction fees.
- Both full-service and discount brokers buy and sell securities for clients. Full-service brokers also provide investing advice and other services. Many brokers offer their services online through Web sites.
- Brokers charge fees or commissions for their services.
- Different types of stock market orders can be placed when trading on a securities exchange. Market orders and limit orders are two examples.
- Market timing strategies can be used to help investors decrease losses and increase profits.
- Many independent and governmental agencies regulate and control the investing industry. They seek to protect consumers by providing stable markets and fair trading practices.
- The Sarbanes-Oxley Act of 2002 helps protect consumers with new and stronger standards for U.S. public companies and for accounting firms.

375

Key Terms

annual report
auction market
blog
buy and hold
buying on margin
discount broker
discretionary order
initial public offering

limit order
market order
odd lot
oversight
over-the-counter
    market
primary market
round lot

secondary market
securities exchange
selling short
stock dividend
stock split
stockbroker
stop order

ACTIVITY 1
Review Key Terms

Use the key terms from Chapter 12 to complete the following sentences:

1. A licensed person who buys or sells stock for clients at fees much lower than a full-service broker charges is called a(n) _____.

2. When you buy a(n) _____, you are buying 100 shares or multiples of 100 shares of stock.

3. When a company issues shares of stock to shareholders instead of a cash dividend, this is called a(n) _____.

4. A(n) _____ is a request to buy stock at the current market price.

5. A company's report to stockholders, called a(n) _____, tells about the financial position of the company.

6. A network of dealers who buy and sell stocks (not as part of a securities exchange) is the _____.

7. Selling stock that has been borrowed and must be replaced later is called _____.

8. _____ is a long-term timing plan whereby you hold stock for many years.

9. A(n) _____ is a request to sell stock when the price reaches a certain amount.

10. An order to sell stock that allows the broker to get the best possible deal is a(n) _____.

11. Buying shares of stock from current owners of the stock takes place in the _____.

12. Buying shares of stock directly from the issuer of the stock takes place in the _____.

13. _____ is the process of buying stock with a partial loan and repaying the loan when the stock is sold.

14. A(n) _____ takes place when a company issues more stock to shareholders in proportion to the stock they already own.

15. A market in which stock is sold to the highest bidder is a(n) _____.

376

16. A company's first sale of its stock to the public is called a(n) _____.

17. Supervision of the markets by government, called _____, is for the purpose of protecting investors from unlawful actions.

18. A(n) _____ is a licensed person who buys and sells securities for investors.

19. An online place where you can find short articles or comments on a particular subject area is called a(n) _____.

20. A(n) _____ is a request to buy or sell stock at a set price.

21. Fewer than 100 shares of stock is known as a(n) _____.

22. A(n) _____ is a place where brokers buy and sell stock for their clients.

ACTIVITY 2
Math Minute

1. You plan to buy 100 shares of stock for $45.00 per share. If you use a full-service broker, the fee will be a 2 percent commission on the purchase price. Investment advice is included at no extra cost. What will be the amount of the commission you must pay? If you use a discount broker, you will pay a fee of $9.95 for this round lot purchase. No investment advice is provided. You have already paid $100.00 for an investing newsletter to help you decide which stock to buy. Which broker would you use and why?

2. You plan to buy 35 shares of stock for $22.18 per share. If you use a full-service broker, you must pay a 2 percent commission on the purchase price. You must also pay $10.00 for an odd-lot sale and $15.00 because this is a small purchase. What is the total amount you must pay? If you use a discount broker, you will pay a fee of $34.95 for this odd lot purchase. You have already paid $100.00 for an investing newsletter to help you decide which stock to buy. Which broker would you use and why?

ACTIVITY 3
Research a Company

  academic.cengage.com/school/pfl

Before buying stock in a company, investors should learn about the company, its history, and its outlook for the future. Work with a classmate to research a company that interests you.

377

2. Do research to learn all you can about the company. Look for information in magazine and newspaper articles and on the Internet. If possible, get a copy of the company's annual report. Keep a record of the source information for all the articles you read, whether in print or online.

3. Write a report or give an oral report to present what you have learned about the company. Include several of the following points and others that you think would help an investor decide whether to buy stock in the company.
   - Company name and trading symbol
   - Industry that the company is a part of
   - Major products or services the company sells
   - Location of the company headquarters
   - Number of employees
   - Brief history of the company
   - Plans for expansion or new product areas
   - Other topics in the news related to the company
   - Current stock price
   - Range of stock prices over the last year
   - Revenue for last year
   - Income for last year
   - P/E ratio and current ratio
   - Dividends paid
   - Stock splits
   - Risk level for the company stock

ACTIVITY 4
Stocks and Strategy

Critical Thinking

Before buying a stock, you must select an investing strategy. For example, you may plan to buy medium-risk growth stocks and hold them for several years. You might decide to buy income stocks that pay high dividends. Your choices will reflect your needs and what you think about the economy and the future of certain companies. They will also reflect the risks you are willing to take.

1. Open the *Word* file *CH12 Stock Descriptions* from the data files. Read the descriptions of various types of stocks found in this file.

2. Miquel is making his first stock purchase. He has some other investments, mostly safe and liquid ones. Which type of stock do you think Miquel should buy? Why do you recommend this choice?

3. Hanae is seeking more risk and larger returns for 20 years from now. Which type of stock do you think she should buy? Why do you recommend this choice?

4. Larry is retired. Which type of stock do you think he should buy? Why do you recommend this choice?

5. Linda has inherited a large amount of money. She wants to invest it and is willing to take moderate risk. Which type of stock do you think she should buy? Why do you recommend this choice?

378

BUSINESS ETHICS EVENT

The FBLA Business Ethics event allows students to respond to ethical situations. Students work in a team of two or three members. A situation is given that presents ethical questions. Students must prepare a presentation to respond to the situation.

Evaluation

Students who take part in this event are judged on their ability to:

- Define clearly the ethical issue(s) involved in the situation.
- State clearly the team's position about the ethical issue(s).
- Present an effective ethical solution to the issue.
- Organize thoughts and solutions clearly.
- Show self-confidence and poise while presenting.
- Involve all team members in the presentation.

Sample Scenario

Mario applied for a job as an accounting clerk in a local company. On his resume and application, Mario overstated his qualifications for the job. He stated that he had worked in a similar job for 5 years. Mario had worked for his previous employer for 5 years. However, he worked for only 2 years as an accounting clerk. For 3 years, he worked as a cashier. Mario has a Bachelor's of Business Administration degree. His major area of study was economics. The job ad requested that the applicant have a degree in accounting. Mario stated that his college major was accounting. Mario was hired for the job.

Think Critically

1. What might be some negative outcomes for the employer that result from Mario's overstating his qualifications?
2. How might Mario's actions affect other applicants for the job?
3. What may happen if the employer discovers that Mario was not truthful on his resume and application?

379

GLOSSARY

A

adjustable rate mortgage A loan agreement in which the interest rate, payment amount, and length of the loan can change over time

adjusted balance method A method of computing finance charges in which interest is calculated after charges and payments for the current period have been applied

advertising A method of informing consumers and promoting and selling products

amortization Repaying a debt by making regular payments of principal and interest over a period of time

annual report A company's report to stockholders about the financial position of the company

annuity A contract purchased from an insurance company that guarantees a series of regular payments for a set time

asset allocation Choosing a combination of stocks, bonds, mutual funds, or other investments to limit risk and increase returns

assets Money and items of value that you own

auction market A market in which stocks or other securities are sold to the highest bidder

automatic deposit Money electronically added to a checking or savings account; no currency or paper checks are involved

automatic payments Payments that are made by transferring money electronically from a checking account to another account every billing period

automatic withdrawal Money deducted from an account and electronically transferred to another party

automobile insurance Protection for the owner of an automobile for collision and other damage to cars and occupants

average daily balance method A method of computing finance charges in which interest is calculated using the average outstanding daily balance for the billing cycle

B

balloon payment A large loan payment that is much higher than the other payments and that must be paid at a set time, often as the last loan payment

bankruptcy A legal procedure to relieve a person who cannot pay debts of those debts or to create a payment plan for paying some of the debts

bear market A period of time when stock market prices are steadily decreasing

beneficiary The person to whom the face value of a life insurance policy is paid

benefits Forms of pay for a job other than salary or wages, such as vacation and holidays

blog An online place where you can find short articles or comments on a particular subject area

bond A debt instrument issued by a corporation or government that requires the issuer to pay the bondholder the loan principal plus interest at maturity

bounced check A check that is returned by the bank for non-sufficient funds (NSF); also called a bad check

budget A spending and saving plan based on expected income and expenses

bull market A period of time when stock market prices are steadily increasing

business plan A document that outlines how a business plans to succeed

buy and hold A long-term plan of holding stock for several years to receive dividends and make capital gains

buying on margin Buying stock with borrowed money and repaying the loan when the stock is sold or when the loan is called

C

cafeteria plan A benefit package that allows employees to select the options they want from a number of choices

cashier's check A check issued by the bank against bank funds

certificate of deposit A deposit of money set aside for a fixed amount of time at a fixed interest rate

certified check A personal check for which payment is guaranteed by the bank on which it is drawn

Chapter 7 Liquidation A type of bankruptcy, also known as straight bankruptcy, in which the debtor gives up property and has debts discharged

Chapter 13 Wage Earner Plan A type of bankruptcy in which the debtor repays part or all of the unsecured debt over a set time period; then remaining debts are discharged

check A written order to a bank to pay the stated amount to the person or business named on the check from a certain account

checkbook register A record in which transactions of a checking account (checks, other withdrawals, deposits, and fees) are kept

checking account A demand deposit that allows the account holder easy access to the money and allows checks to be written on the account

clearing account An account used to hold money for buying and selling securities

closing costs Expenses the borrower must pay in order to get a loan, such as appraisal fees, credit report fees, recording costs, and inspection fees

collateral Property that can be used as security for a loan, such as land, a house, or a car

collectibles Items bought for their investment value, such as art objects, coins, decorative plates, books, and baseball cards

commission A set fee or a percentage of a sale paid to a salesperson instead of or in addition to salary or wages

commodity An item of value that is bought and sold in a marketplace, such as soybeans, silver, or coffee

common stock Shares of stock in a corporation that represent ownership and entitle the owner to voting rights

compound interest Interest that is earned on both principal and interest previously earned on savings

contingencies Unplanned or possible events, such as emergencies

co-pay The amount a patient pays each time for using a medical service

cosigner A person who agrees to repay a loan if the borrower does not repay it

cost-plus pricing Setting a price based on the cost to produce or acquire and deliver a product plus a markup for profit margin

cost-push inflation A situation in which producers raise prices to reflect higher costs of creating products

credit The ability to borrow money with the agreement to pay it back later. The repayment usually includes interest.

credit card fraud A crime in which someone intentionally uses another person's credit account to steal money or goods

credit report A document that gives a person's credit history and current status with regard to credit and income

criteria Standards or rules by which something can be judged

D

debit card A bank card that allows the account holder to make purchases and to withdraw cash from an account at an ATM

debt consolidation The process of getting one loan to pay all other existing debts

deductible The amount you must pay before insurance starts to pay

deflation The lowering of overall price levels

delinquency The failure to do what your duty or the law requires, such as making loan payments; an overdue debt

demand The willingness and ability of consumers to buy products and services

demand-pull inflation A situation in which prices increase because consumers want to buy more goods and services than producers supply

deposit Money added to a checking, savings, or other financial account

direct investing Buying investments directly from companies and holding them individually

disability insurance Income protection coverage to replace a portion of normal earnings when the insured is unable to work due to an injury or illness that is not job-related

discharge A court order that pardons the debtor from paying some debts

discount The difference between a bond's selling price and its face or maturity value

discount broker A licensed person who buys or sells stock for clients at fees much lower than those a full-service broker charges

discount rate The rate banks are charged to borrow money from the Federal Reserve

discretionary income The amount of money a person has to spend after needs are met

discretionary order An order to buy or sell a stock at the best price according to the broker's judgment

disinflation A situation in which prices are rising, but at a slow rate

disposable income The money a person has available to spend or save after taxes have been paid

diversification Holding a variety of investments in order to reduce risk

dividend Money paid to stockholders of a corporation

documentation Records that can be used to support a claim

dollar-cost averaging Saving or investing the same amount on a regular basis, such as monthly, regardless of market conditions

E

economist A person who studies the economy and tries to predict what will happen, using current and projected data

economizing A consumer spending pattern of saving as much as possible and spending only when necessary

economy All the activities related to making and distributing goods and services in an area

emergency fund Money set aside to handle expenses related to unplanned events

endorsement A signature or instructions written on the back of a check authorizing a bank to cash or deposit the check

entrepreneur Business owner; person who takes the risks of owning a business

Equal Credit Opportunity Act A federal law that makes discrimination illegal when granting or denying credit

equity loan A loan in which the equity in a home is used as security for the loan

ethics A system of moral values that people consider acceptable

excise tax Tax on the sale of certain goods such as tobacco or on activities such as highway use by heavy trucks

exemption Property that a debtor is allowed to keep in a bankruptcy proceeding

F

face value The stated sum of a life insurance policy, payable at the death of the insured

Fair Credit Billing Act A federal law governing how credit disputes are to be handled

Fair Credit Reporting Act A federal law giving consumers the right to know what is in their credit file and the right to challenge information in that file

Fair Debt Collection Practices Act A federal law that forbids the use of abusive practices when collecting debts

federal funds rate The rate at which banks can borrow money from the excess reserves of other banks

financial aid Money received from an outside source to help pay for education and training

financial goals Methods used to pay for personal goals

financial plan An overall plan that contains personal goals you want to accomplish, a timeline for reaching those goals, and methods you will use to finance them

financial planner A person who provides financial advice to individuals

financial resources Money or other items of value that people can use to acquire goods and services

financial security The ability to prepare for future needs and meet current expenses to live comfortably

fixed expenses Expenses that do not change each month, such as rent, insurance, and car payments

fixed rate An interest rate on credit that remains the same each month

foreclosure A legal process a creditor can use to force the sale of mortgaged property to repay the mortgage when a borrower does not make mortgage payments

futures contract An agreement to buy or sell a specific commodity or currency at a set price on a set date in the future

G

garnishment A proceeding in which a creditor may legally take possession of money or goods held by a third party in payment of a borrower's debt

goal   A plan that is based on values or desired outcomes

grace period   The amount of time you have before a credit card company starts charging you interest on your new purchases

group life insurance   Life insurance available through an employer or an organization, covering a group of people and offering lower premiums than for individual policies

H

hard skills   The ability to perform technical tasks or complete procedures

health insurance   A plan for sharing the risk of medical costs from injury and illness

homeowner's policy   Property insurance to protect the owner from risk of loss in the home

hyperinflation   Rapidly rising, out-of-control prices increasing at rates of 50 percent or higher

I

identity theft   The act of using someone's personal information without his or her permission to commit fraud or other crimes

illiquid   Not able to be turned into cash quickly and without a penalty

impulse buying   Making a purchase without thinking about it ahead of time

indirect investing   Buying shares in a company, such as a mutual fund company, that buys and holds stocks or other securities

industry risk   The chance that factors that affect an industry as a whole will change the value of an investment

inflation   An increase in the general level of prices for goods and services

inflation risk   The chance that the rate of inflation will be higher than the rate of return on an investment

initial public offering   The stock offering in which a company first sells stock to the public

installment credit   A credit account for a set amount (no new charges can be added). Payments are made and the balance is paid off in a set period of time.

installment loan   A type of debt in which you borrow money for a period of time with an agreed-upon interest rate and repayment plan

interest   Money paid for the use of money, as in the cost of a loan

Internet   A worldwide network of computers that can share information

investment portfolio   A collection of assets (investments), such as stocks, bonds, real estate, and other holdings

investment risk   The potential for change in the value of an investment; also called portfolio risk

J

job description   A document that gives details about the tasks, duties, skills, education, and experience required for a job

job market   The wide variety of jobs and careers that exist at one point in time

job scout or agent   A computer program that searches the Internet to find job listings that meet certain criteria and returns those listings to the user

job skills   Specific tasks or procedures a person can do to complete a job

job title   A name given to a particular job

L

liability   Any debt you owe that must be repaid

life insurance   A plan that pays money to a beneficiary when the insured person dies. Some plans also build cash value.

limit order   A request to buy or sell a stock at a set price

line of credit   A preapproved amount that can be borrowed

liquidity   A measure of the ability to turn an asset into cash quickly

loss   Some type of physical injury, damage to property, or absence of property or other assets

M

market   Any place where investments or assets are bought and sold

market-based pricing   Setting a price based on existing prices for similar products already in the marketplace

market order   A request to buy or sell a stock at the current market value

minimum wage   The lowest pay rate allowed by law for each hour of work

monetary policy   Actions taken by the Federal Reserve to influence money and credit conditions in the economy in an effort to affect employment levels and prices

money market account   A savings option that pays the current market rate of interest on the money deposited and may have restrictions on withdrawals

money order   A type of prepaid check that directs payment of a sum of cash to a payee

mortgage   A loan that is used to secure financing for the purchase of a house or other real estate

mutual fund   An investment fund that consists of stocks, bonds, and other investments focused on a strategy, such as balance or growth

N

net worth   The amount of your assets (what you own) minus your liabilities (what you owe)

O

odd lot   A designation given to fewer than 100 shares of stock that are bought or sold together

online banking   A service that allows you to make payments and manage your bank account using the bank's Web site

opportunity cost   A benefit or an item you give up when you choose to buy another benefit or item

optimizing   A consumer spending pattern of spreading money to cover as many needs as possible or to get the highest value for the money spent

oversight   Supervision, as in the government overseeing the investment industry to protect investors from unlawful actions

over-the-counter market   A network of dealers who buy and sell stocks that are not listed on an exchange

over-the-limit fee   A fee creditors charge to customers who charge more than their credit limit

overtime pay   Pay for hours worked beyond the set regular number for a job

P

paid holidays   Days a worker is paid for working but does not actually work, such as Christmas and Thanksgiving

penalty   A fee charged for violating an agreement, such as a credit agreement

permanent life insurance A plan that provides money to a beneficiary at the death of the insured and builds cash value

personal goals Things a person wants to achieve, such as taking a trip

personal leave Days a worker is paid for working even though he or she is absent for personal reasons

personal loans Loans that are based on personal creditworthiness and do not require collateral

phishing An e-mail scam designed to get individuals to give out personal information such as bank account numbers

political risk The chance that an event in politics (laws, policies, wars, or elections) will affect the value of an investment

portable insurance Insurance you can convert to an individual policy when you leave employment at a company

postdated check A check written with a date that will occur in the future

preferred stock Shares of stock in a corporation that may pay guaranteed dividends

premium The price you pay for insurance

prepayment penalty A fee charged for paying off a loan before the agreed-upon time

previous balance method A method of computing finance charges in which interest is calculated on the previous balance, before charges and payments made in the current period are applied

primary market A market in which new issues of securities are sold to investors by the issuer

prime rate The interest rate that banks charge to their most creditworthy business customers, such as corporations

principal An amount of money that is set aside (saved or invested) on which interest is paid

probability The likelihood of some risk actually resulting in a loss

productivity A measure of the efficiency with which goods and services are made

profit The amount left after all costs are deducted from the income of a business

R

real-cost inflation A situation in which prices increase because the cost of getting resources or the cost of resources themselves becomes more expensive

rebate A refund of part of the purchase price of an item

recourse A remedy or action taken to seek aid, such as for the correction of an error

redeem To turn in something, such as a bond, and receive cash in exchange

reflation A situation in which prices are high, drop, and then rise to their previous high level

renter's insurance A plan that protects renters from the risk of losing personal property as well as from liability for injuries to others

repossession The process of taking an asset used for collateral, such as a car, and selling it to pay for a debt

revolving credit An account that the account holder can charge to as often as desired, up to a certain dollar limit. The account holder makes payments, usually each month. The entire debt or part of the debt can be paid each month.

risk The chance of injury, damage, or economic loss

rollover The nontaxable transfer of funds from one qualified retirement plan to another

round lot A designation given to 100 shares of stock or multiples of 100 shares that are bought or sold together

Rule of 72 A math formula that calculates how long it will take for money earning a set rate of interest to double

S

sales finance company A type of lender that makes a loan for the purchase of consumer goods, such as cars or household appliances

savings account A demand deposit that has some restrictions as to how quickly or easily you can get your money

scam A fake offer, sale, or other gimmick designed to cheat consumers

scholarship A gift of money or other aid (free tuition or books) made to a student to help pay for education

secondary market A market in which securities are bought from other investors

secured loan A debt agreement in which the borrower pledges property of value, called collateral, as security for the loan repayment

securities exchange A place where brokers buy and sell securities listed on the exchange for their clients

self-insure To set aside money to be used in the event of injury or loss of assets

selling short Selling stock that has been borrowed and must be replaced at a later date

service credit The ability to receive services and pay for them later

sick leave Days a worker is paid for working but did not work due to illness

soft skills Nontechnical skills such as leadership or the ability to communicate clearly

spending limit The maximum amount you are willing to spend for an item

stockbroker A licensed person who buys and sells securities on behalf of others

stock dividend Shares of stock issued by a company to its stockholders instead of a cash dividend

stock risk The chance that activities or events that affect a company will change the value of an investment

stocks Shares of ownership in a corporation

stock split Issuing more stock in a company to shareholders in proportion to the stock they already own

stop order A request to sell a stock when the price reaches a certain amount

stop payment A bank service that directs the bank not to honor a check you wrote or lost

stop-loss provision A feature of a health care plan that provides 100 percent coverage after a certain amount is paid toward medical expenses

store accounts Credit offered through individual stores, companies, or other merchants

student loan A debt that is used to finance education costs

subsidized student loan A loan used to pay for education on which interest is not charged until after the student graduates from the educational program

supply The quantity of goods and services that producers are willing and able to provide

T

target audience A specific group of people for whom advertising or other messages are created

tax A required payment for the support of a government, such as income tax or sales tax

tax-deferred Free from tax for a period of time; for example, until the earnings are taken from an investment account

tax shelter An investment that allows you to legally avoid or reduce income taxes

term life insurance Insurance that is in effect for a stated period of time and provides a death benefit only; pure insurance

time value of money A concept that says money received in the future is worth less than money received today because of inflation

tip Money, often a percentage of the total bill, or a gift given to a person for performing a service and often based on the quality of service provided

trade-off The choice to give up a particular benefit or item to get another that you think is more desirable

transfer payments Money or benefits received from the government without working for them at the time they are received

Truth-in-Lending Act A federal law requiring that consumers be fully informed about the true cost of credit; also known as the Consumer Protection Act of 1968

tuition The charge for instruction at a school

U

umbrella policy Coverage for catastrophic expenses in addition to your car and home insurance

unearned income Money received from sources other than working in a job

U.S. savings bond A discount savings bond issued by the U.S. government

V

value A principle that reflects the worth you place on an idea or action

value-based pricing Setting a price based on how much the seller thinks the consumer is willing to pay

variable expenses Expenses that can go up and down each month

variable rate An interest rate that changes at the discretion of the credit card company or lender

variances Differences between planned income or expenses and actual income or expenses

vested Having ownership rights, as for a pension or retirement plan

W

wants Things people desire to buy that are beyond basic or other needs

wire transfer The process of sending money electronically rather than using paper checks

index

385

388